eating
out in
pubs

The 2014 edition of our guide contains details of over 570 pubs. As ever, the crucial factor for selection in the guide is the quality of the food served, and though the style of cooking and the menus may vary from one pub to the next, our independent inspectors ensure that each and every pub listed reaches the required standards.

Cooking in British pubs continues to reach new heights, and there is an enormous amount of choice now available to diners. Some pubs proudly take the organic route with the support of small local suppliers, while others focus more on regional specialities and long-established local recipes. Some serve creative, contemporary cooking with more of an international flavour, but equally, there are plenty offering traditional British favourites too.

If you're having trouble choosing where to go, the descriptive texts give an insight into the individual character of each pub, highlighting what we found to be most memorable and charming, and the accompanying pictures reveal a little bit more of their personality.

Some of these pubs serve their food by the fireplace in the bar; others may have a more formal dining room, but whatever their style, they all have one thing in common: carefully prepared, flavoursome food made from fresh, quality ingredients.

Readers of the Michelin Eating Out in Pubs guide write thousands of letters and emails to us every year, praising or criticising current entries or recommending new entries. Please keep these coming and help us to make the next edition even better.

MICHELIN
A better way forward

S0-BBJ-440

contents

Midlands

East of
England

London

East

How to use this Guide

How to find a pub

There are 3 ways to search for a pub in this guide:
- use the regional maps that precede each section of the guide
- use the alphabetical list of pubs at the end of the guide or
- use the alphabetical list of place names also at the end of the guide

Town / Village name

One of our favourite selections

Country or region and county names

Coloured tab

England
- East Midlands
- East of England
- London
- North East
- North West
- South East
- South West
- West Midlands
- Yorkshire & The Humber

Scotland

Wales

Ireland
- Northern Ireland
- Republic of Ireland

Bruntingthorpe

England • East Midlands • Leicestershire

The Joiners

7

Church Walk, Bruntingthorpe, LE17 5QH
Tel.: (0116)2478258
Website: www.thejoinersarms.co.uk

VISA

 Greene King IPA and Sharp's Doom Bar

You can't help but feel that the locals had a part to play in the naming of this pub, which started life in the naming of this and has since been renamed The Joiners. Set in a small rural village, this neat, whitewashed building dates back to the 17C and boasts characterful wood floors and low beams. Run by an enthusiastic husband and wife team, it's more of a dining pub than a place for a casual drink; although the group of regulars crowded round the pine-fitted bar would probably tell you otherwise. Menus display a mix of refined pub classics and more brasserie-style dishes, all cooked and presented in a straightforward yet effective manner. There's a good value set lunch and a wide selection of wines by the glass; Thursday is 'fish night'.

Closing times
Closed Sunday dinner and Monday
booking essential

Prices
Meals: £ 12 (lunch) and a la carte £ 23/35

Typical Dishes
Crispy pork salad, hoisin & wonton wafers
Hake with chorizo, new potato hash & lemon oil
Pear tarte Tatin, honey & ginger ice cream

Between Leicester and Husbands Bosworth off A 5199

32

Name, address, telephone, and website of the establishment

15
Entry number

Each pub or inn has its own entry number.

This number appears on the regional map at the start of each section to show the location of the establishment.

Pubs with bedrooms

For easy reference, those pubs that offer accommodation are highlighted In blue on the maps

Symbols

🍴 Meals served in the garden or on the terrace

🍷 A particularly interesting wine list

🐕 No dogs allowed

VISA Visa accepted

AE American Express accepted

D Diners Club accepted

MC MasterCard accepted

✂ credit cards not accepted

N New establishment in the guide

Long Whatton

N Royal Oak

The Green, Long Whatton, LE12 5BD
Tel.: (01509)843694
Website: www.theroyaloaklongwhatton.co.uk
🍴 🐕 **VISA** MC

🍺 St Austell Tribute and Sharp's Doom Bar

England • East Midlands • Leicestershire

This pub may no longer boast the majestic oak tree it was once named after but it does now have a delightful apple tree in its spacious grounds, where, from June to August, a large marquee plays host to summer weddings. Set at the heart of a sleepy village, it's owned by two brothers, who have totally modernised the place, creating a spacious yet cosy bar and a more intimate dining room. Menus offer plenty of choice, from sandwiches and soup through to sharing platters, old pub favourites and appealing main courses, with many dishes displaying a quirky touch – such as the deconstructed Scotch egg with homemade piccalilli or home-cured salmon with beetroot horseradish slaw. Well-equipped, up-to-date bedrooms are located in an adjacent block.

Closing times
Open daily
Prices
Meals: £ 12 and a la carte
£ 20/36
🛏 **7 rooms:** £ 85/99

Typical Dishes
Salmon & chive fishcake
Rabbit, pigeon & pork trio
Chilled rhubarb & custard crumble

🚗 4 mi northwest by A 6 and B 6324. In the centre of the village. Parking.

(33)

Closing times, prices, rooms

Approximate range of prices for a three-course meal, plus information on booking and annual closures.

Some inns offering accommodation may close mid-afternoon and only allow guests to check in during evening hours. If in doubt, phone ahead.

Room prices range from the lowest-priced single to the most expensive double or twin.

Breakfast is usually included in the price.

Prices are given in £ sterling, except for the Republic of Ireland where €uro are quoted.

How to get there

Directions and driving distances from nearby towns, an indication of parking facilities and any other information that might help you get your bearings. Nearest Underground / train station indicated for London entries.

The blackboard

An example of a typical starter, main course and dessert, chosen by the chef.

Whilst there's no guarantee that these dishes will be available, they should provide you with an idea of the style of the cuisine.

The *Pub* of the *year*

The Greyhound on the Test

31 High Street Stockbridge
Hampshire SO20 6EY

Tel: 01264 810833
website : *www.thegreyhoundonthetest.co.uk*

see page 304 for more details

Throughout the year, our team of full-time inspectors have been travelling across Great Britain and Ireland, selecting the best establishments to add to the tenth edition of the MICHELIN Eating Out In Pubs guide.

Each year we choose one pub to be crowned our 'Pub of the Year': a pub with a warm welcome, friendly service, plenty of atmosphere and, most importantly, a pub which serves great food.

The Location

The pretty town of Stockbridge is found in the heart of the rolling Test Valley. It lies between Andover and Romsey, and was once part of the old drovers' route from Wales; the wide, sweeping layout of the High Street allowed sheep and cattle to be easily driven through town.

This is a town best-known for its fishing: the River Test flows under the High Street and the oldest fishing club in England, the Houghton Club, was founded here in 1882. Many chalk streams flow in and around the town, and running alongside the river is the Test Way footpath, which follows the disused Sprat and Winkle railway line.

The Pub

Among the many independent specialist shops, you'll find the Greyhound on the Test, a well-run, tastefully styled pub behind an unusual mustard-coloured façade. The experienced owner, Lucy Townsend, knows a thing or two when it comes to running a successful pub. She keeps a keen eye on the day to day running of the place and her cheerful nature rubs off on the young serving team, who are equally welcoming and attentive, and clearly take pride in what they do.

At over 600 years old and with a Grade II listing, it's a place with plenty of character. Taller visitors will have to duck to avoid the low timbers in the bar, and the wood burning stoves are a welcoming feature. Since Lucy took over, it's been refurbished, and it's elegant décor gives it an almost French bistro feel. If that's not enough, the garden, too, is a fabulous spot – and with over a mile of River Test fishing rights, it's a fly fisherman's dream.

The Food

The chef, Alan Haughie, is classically trained and this shows through his choice of flavour combinations, but his cooking is also refined and the presentation is definitely modern. Dishes have a pleasing depth of flavour thanks to his judicious use of first class produce – every ingredient on the plate plays a role – and there's no unnecessary over-adornment.

They open for breakfast with the likes of smoked haddock or the Greenfield Farm Full English, then for lunch and dinner they offer a selection of robust British classics. There are starters such as braised cod cheeks; a comforting 'on toast' section; main dishes like steak with chateaubriand sauce; and interesting sides such as sweet potato gratin – not forgetting a hearty special of the day, which might be local rabbit cassoulet or oxtail and oyster pudding. The good value set lunch keeps the regulars happy, game and seafood are a feature, and if you've been out on the river, the chef will happily cook your catch.

The Bedrooms

Situated on the first floor, the bedrooms have also been smartly refurbished. Each has been individually designed by Lucy herself – in a chic, modern country style – and features floral fabrics and a fresh, understated colour scheme. They all come with magazines and cafetière coffee, most have king-sized beds and two have river views. An array of snacks, soft drinks and spirits are available from the honesty bar.

Inspectors' favourites

A ll the pubs in this guide have been selected for the quality of their cooking. However, we feel that several of them deserve additional consideration as they boast at least one extra quality which makes them particularly special.

It may be the delightful setting, the charm and character of the pub, the general atmosphere, the pleasant service, the overall value for money or the exceptional cooking.

To distinguish these pubs, we point them out with our "Inspectors' favourites" Bibendum stamp.

We are sure you will enjoy these pubs as much as we have.

11

Beer
in the U.K.
and Ireland

It's easy to think of beer as just bitter or lager. But that doesn't tell half the story. Between the two there's a whole range of styles and tastes, including pale ales, beers flavoured with spices, fruits and herbs, and wheat beers. It's all down to the skill of the brewer who'll juggle art, craft and a modicum of science to create the perfect pint.

Grist and wort may sound like medieval hangover cures, but they're actually crucial to the brewing process. Malted barley is crushed into grist, a coarse powder which is mashed with hot water in a large vessel called a mash tun. Depending on what sort of recipe's required, the brewer will add different cereals at this stage, such as darker malt for stout. The malt's natural sugars dissolve and the result is wort: a sweet brown liquid, which is boiled with hops in large coppers. Then comes the most important process of all: fermentation, when the hopped wort is cooled and run into fermentation vessels. The final addition is yeast, which converts the natural sugars into alcohol, carbon dioxide and a host of subtle flavours.

Finally, a beer has to be conditioned before it leaves the brewery, and in the case of cask conditioned real ales, the beer goes directly into the cask, barrel or bottle. The yeast is still active in there, fermenting the beer for a second time, often in a pub cellar. All the time there's a delicate process going on as the beer is vulnerable to attack from micro-biological organisms. But as long as the publican cares about his beer, you should get a tasty, full-flavoured pint.

Beer's as natural a product as you can get. This is what's in your pint:

Barley
It's the main ingredient in beer and rich in starch. Malted before brewing to begin the release of sugars.

Hops
Contain resins and essential oils, and used at varying times to give beer its distinctive flavour. Early on they add bitterness, later on they provide a spicy or citrus zest.

Yeast
Converts the sugars from the barley into alcohol and carbon dioxide during fermentation. It produces compounds that affect the flavour of the beer.

Water
Burton and Tadcaster have excellent local water, and that's why they became great ale brewing centres. Meanwhile, the water of London and Dublin is just right for the production of stouts and porters.

Real quality

The modern taste for real ale took off over thirty years ago when it looked like the lager industry was in the process of killing off traditional "warm ale". There are several styles, but the most popular in England and Wales is bitter, which boasts a seemingly inexhaustible variety of appearance, scent and flavour. You can have your bitter gold or copper of colour, hoppy or malty of aroma, dry or sweet of flavour (sweet flavoured bitter? This is where the term "bitter" is at its loosest). Sometimes it has a creamy head; sometimes no head at all. Typically, go to a Yorkshire pub for the former, a London pub for the latter.

Mild developed its popularity in Wales and the north west of England in Victorian times. Often dark, it's a weaker alternative to bitter, with a sweetish taste based on its hop characteristics.
In Scotland, the near equivalent of bitter is heavy, and the most popular draught ales are known as 80 shilling (export) or 70 shilling (special). And, yes, they have a heavy quality to them, though 60 shilling ale – or Light – is akin to English mild.
Full-bodied and rich, stouts (and their rarer porter relatives) are almost a meal in themselves. They're famously black in colour with hints of chocolate and caramel, but it's the highly roasted yeast flavour that leaves the strong after taste.

YOU ALREADY KNOW THE MICHELIN GUIDE,
NOW FIND OUT ABOUT THE MICHELIN GROUP

MICHELIN
A better way forward

The Michelin Adventure

It all started with rubber balls! This was the product made by a small company based in Clermont-Ferrand that André and Edouard Michelin inherited, back in 1880. The brothers quickly saw the potential for a new means of transport and their first success was the invention of detachable pneumatic tyres for bicycles. However, the automobile was to provide the greatest scope for their creative talents.

Throughout the 20th century, Michelin never ceased developing and creating ever more reliable and high-performance tyres, not only for vehicles ranging from trucks to racing cars but also for underground transit systems and aeroplanes.

From early on, Michelin provided its customers with tools and services to facilitate mobility and make travelling a more pleasurable and more frequent experience. As early as 1900, the Michelin Guide supplied motorists with a host of useful information related to vehicle maintenance, accommodation and restaurants, and was to become a benchmark for good food. At the same time, the Travel Information Bureau offered travellers personalised tips and itineraries.

The publication of the first Michelin road map, in 1910, was an instant hit! In 1926, the first regional tourist guide to France was published, devoted to the principal sites of Brittany, and before long each region of France had its own Green Guide. The collection was later extended to more far-flung destinations, including New York in 1968 and Iceland in 2012.

In the 21st century, with the growth of digital technology, the challenge for Michelin maps, guides and digital services is to continue to develop alongside the company's tyre activities. Now, as before, Michelin is committed to improving the mobility of travellers.

MICHELIN TODAY

- 69 production sites in 18 countries
- 113,400 employees from all cultures and on every continent
- 6,000 people employed in the Michelin Technology Centre
- A commercial presence in more than 170 countries

Moving
for a world

Moving forward means developing tyres with better road grip and shorter braking distances, whatever the state of the road.

CORRECT TYRE PRESSURE

RIGHT PRESSURE

- Safety
- Longevity
- Optimum fuel consumption

-0,5 bar

- Durability reduced by 20% (- 8,000 km)

-1 bar

- Risk of blowouts
- Increased fuel consumption
- Longer braking distances on wet surfaces

forward together
where mobility is safer

It also involves helping motorists take care of their safety and their tyres. To do so, Michelin organises "Fill Up With Air" campaigns all over the world to remind us that correct tyre pressure is vital.

WEAR

DETECTING TYRE WEAR

MICHELIN tyres are equipped with tread wear indicators, which are small blocks of rubber molded into the base of the main grooves at a height of 1.6 mm. When tread depth is the same level as indicators, the tyres are worn and need replacing.

Tyres are the only point of contact between vehicle and the road, a worn tyre can be dangerous on wet surfaces.

NEW TYRE

WORN TYRE
(1,6 mm tread)

The photo shows the actual contact zone on wet surfaces.

Moving forward
means sustainable mobility

By 2050, Michelin aims to cut the quantity of raw materials used in its tyre manufacturing process by half and 99.8% of the company's tyres are produced in ISO 14001 certified factories. The design of MICHELIN tyres has already saved billions of litres of fuel and, by extension, millions of tonnes of CO_2.

Similarly, Michelin prints its maps and guides on paper produced from sustainably managed forests and is diversifying its publishing media by offering digital solutions to make travelling easier, more fuel efficient and more enjoyable!

The group's whole-hearted commitment to eco-design on a daily basis is demonstrated by ISO 14001 certification.

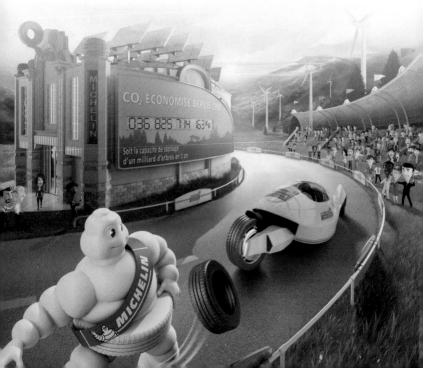

Chat with Bibendum

Go to www.michelin.com/corporate/EN/home

Find out more about Michelin's history and the latest news about the company's products and services.

QUIZ

Michelin develops tyres for all types of vehicles. See if you can match the right tyre with the right vehicle…

A vision of England sweeps across a range of historic buildings, monuments and rolling landscapes. This image, taking in wild natural borders extending from the rugged splendour of Cornwall's cliffs to pounding Northumbrian shores, seeks parity with a newer picture of Albion: redefined cities and towns whose industrial past is being reshaped by a shiny, steel-and-glass, interactive reality. The country's geographical bones and bumps are a reassuring constant: the windswept moors of the south west and the craggy peaks of the Pennines, the summery orchards of the Kentish Weald, the "flat earth" constancy of East Anglian skies and the mirrored calm of Cumbria's lakes. The pubs of England have made good use of the land's natural bounty over the past decade; streamlined establishments have stripped out the soggy carpets and soggier menus and replaced them with crisp décor and fresh, inventive cooking. England's multi-ethnic culture has borne fruit in the kitchens of your local…

An area that combines the grace of a bygone age with the speed of the 21C. To the east (Chatsworth House, Haddon Hall and Burghley House) is where Pride and Prejudice came to life, while Silverstone to the south hosts the Grand Prix. Market towns are dotted all around: Spalding's cultivation of tulips rivals that of Holland, Oakham boasts its stunning Castle and Great Hall, and the legendary "Boston Stump" oversees the bustle of a 450 year-old market. The brooding beauty of the Peak District makes it the second most visited National Park in the world. Izaak Walton popularised the river Dove's trout-filled waters in "The Compleat Angler" and its surrounding hills are a rambler's dream, as are the wildlife habitats of the National Forest and the wind-swept acres of the pancake-flat fens. Above it all looms Lincoln Cathedral's ancient spire, while in the pubs, local ale – typically brewed in Bakewell, Dovedale or Rutland – slips down a treat alongside the ubiquitous Melton Mowbray pie.

Beeley

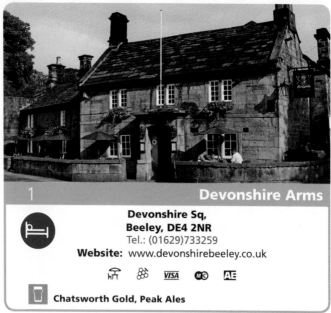

1   Devonshire Arms

**Devonshire Sq,
Beeley, DE4 2NR**
Tel.: (01629)733259
Website: www.devonshirebeeley.co.uk

Chatsworth Gold, Peak Ales

Part of the estate, this inn is just minutes from Chatsworth House, in a small hamlet also owned by the Duke and Duchess of Devonshire. There are two clear parts to the place: a homely bar with exposed stone, oak beams and open fires, and a modern extension with a glass-fronted wine cave and village views. If you're making a flying visit, have afternoon tea; if you've got longer, choose something from the classical main menu or try one of the daily changing game dishes from the blackboard – either cooked to order or hot off the rotisserie. Produce comes from the surrounding villages, as well as from green-fingered locals who swap their wares for beer tokens. Bedrooms in the main inn are cosy; those next door are larger and brighter.

Closing times
Open daily
Prices
Meals: a la carte £ 27/39
14 rooms: £ 109/239

Typical Dishes
Black pudding &
buttered trout
Sea bream with brown
shrimps
Passion fruit brûlée

 5 mi southeast of Bakewell by A 6 and B 6012. Parking.

2 Samuel Fox Country Inn

**Stretfield Rd,
Bradwell, S33 9JT**
Tel.: (01433)621562
Website: www.samuelfox.co.uk

Bradfield Ales

Closing times
Closed 3-17 January

Prices
Meals: £ 20 (early dinner)
and a la carte £ 22/34

4 rooms: £ 85/130

The dramatic, hilly landscape of the Hope Valley is likely to be the first thing that catches your eye, and the curious pub sign depicting a fox sitting beneath an umbrella, the next! It makes sense, however, when you discover that Samuel Fox, a famed local businessman, was one of the inventors of the steel-ribbed umbrella. The attractive light-stone building dates back over 200 years and conceals a cosy bar with a wood-burning stove and a pleasant restaurant. At lunch, choose from specials such as homemade terrine with chutney and brioche, and at dinner, slow-cooked local pork belly with chorizo – a nod to the chef's stint in Andalucia; on Friday nights, try the popular 'secret supper' small plates. Bedrooms are homely and well-kept.

Typical Dishes
English asparagus with deep-fried egg
Braised shoulder of lamb with 'hotch potch'
White chocolate cheesecake

 12 mi northwest of Baslow by A 623 and B 6049. Parking.

Eckington

3   **Devonshire Arms**

**Lightwood Ln,
Middle Handley, Eckington, S21 5RN**
Tel.: (01246)434800
Website: www.devonshirearmsmiddlehandley.com

Bradfield Farmers Blonde, Barlow Brewery Ales, Kelham Island Ales and Welbeck Abbey Ales

Be sure to admire the views as you make your way over to the South Yorkshire and Derbyshire border, where you'll find this smartly updated inn. In summer, fight for a spot on the small terrace; otherwise, choose from one of several modern rooms – including the private dining area, 'Tom's Kitchen', which is perfect for a special occasion. Fresh, seasonal ingredients are at the core of the menu, with the likes of thick gammon and double fried eggs or steak and ale suet pie with triple-cooked chips – and you may well struggle to make it through to dessert! They like to keep things local and their suppliers are acknowledged on a blackboard above the fire, with eggs coming from just down the road and much of the meat, from the butcher's opposite.

Closing times
Closed Monday except bank holiday lunch and dinner Sunday

Prices
Meals: a la carte £ 20/39

Typical Dishes
Potted trout
Gressingham duck with carrot & star anise purée
Coconut panna cotta

 2 mi southeast of Eckington by B 5056 and Lightwood Rd. Parking.

4   **Inn at Troway**

Snowdon Ln,
Troway, Eckington, S21 5RU
Tel.: (01246)290751
Website: www.relaxeatanddrink.co.uk

🖼 *VISA* 🅼🅲

🍺 **Thornbridge Ales**

England • East Midlands • Derbyshire

This early Victorian pub is set in a picturesque location and offers delightful views out over the rolling countryside; make the most of these by grabbing a seat either on the terrace or in the airy rear dining room. This is an area popular with walkers and the food is satisfyingly hearty; perfect for refuelling after a brisk morning hike. Among the earthy options available on the wide-ranging menu might be steak and Thornbridge ale pot pie, homemade fishcake and chips or honey and rosemary glazed shank of lamb. 'Beat the clock' dishes are served between 5pm and 7pm, with customers paying the equivalent of the time they arrive, so arrive at 5 for a £5 dish. There's a fine selection of regional ales and staff bend over backwards to help.

Closing times
Open daily
booking advisable
Prices
Meals: a la carte £ 18/33

Typical Dishes
Prawn cocktail
Fish & chips
Sticky toffee pudding

 *7.5 mi southeast of Sheffield by A 61 and B 6056 (Eckington Rd). Parking.*

Elmton

5

Elm Tree

**Elmton,
S80 4LS**
Tel.: (01909)721261
Website: www.elmtreeelmton.co.uk

Black Sheep Bitter and Golden Sheep, Kelham Island Easy Rider, Adnams Broadside and Green King IPA

This 18C stone building takes its name from an elm tree which used to stand on the village green. It was once a wheelwright's by day and a pub by night, and the fact that it's now wholly a pub evidently pleases the loyal band of locals sitting at the brightly lit bar. Head left for a seat by the wood-burning stove or through to the rear for a more intimate experience – or in summer, out into the one acre garden. The menu reads like a roll call of pub classics, with the likes of liver and bacon, gammon steak with Ted's egg and chips, homemade Derbyshire steak burger, and specials that could include mushroom and wild garlic ravioli. Dishes are good value and presented in a modern manner, and all ingredients are sourced from within 10 miles.

Closing times
Closed Tuesday

Prices
Meals: £ 11
(weekday lunch)
and a la carte £ 18/38

Typical Dishes
Pigeon with truffle oil
31-day aged sirloin steak
White chocolate crème brûlée

4 mi northeast of Bolsover by A 632 signed off B 6417. In centre of village. Parking.

30

6

Chequers Inn

**Hope Valley,
Froggatt, S32 3ZJ**
Tel.: (01433)630231
Website: www.chequers-froggatt.com

**Peak Ales Bakewell Best, Buxton Brewery Kinder
Downfall and Bradfield Brewery Farmers Blonde**

This 16C inn is built right into the stone boulders of Froggatt Edge and even has a direct path from its garden up to the peak. As traditional inside as out, it's a comfortingly no-nonsense sort of place, boasting an open fire, gleaming brass, a large bar and a quieter, cosier room across the hall. The majority of diners are walkers, but the jolly team welcome one and all as if they were locals. Cooking is unfussy, wholesome and tasty, featuring classical dishes that always include fish and chips, bangers and mash, and a pie. More imaginative specials such as roast partridge or seared scallops and black pudding appear on the blackboard – and often a local Bakewell pudding too. Bedrooms are simple and comfy; No.1, to the rear, is the quietest.

Closing times
Closed 25 December
Prices
Meals: a la carte £ 22/31
6 rooms: £ 85/115

Typical Dishes
Crispy pheasant leg
with bacon
Braised pork belly with
red onion sauce
Cointreau panna cotta
with lemon sorbet

3 mi north of Baslow on A 625. Situated on the edge of the village. Parking.

Shirley

7   N **Saracen's Head**

Church Ln,
Shirley, DE6 3AS
Tel.: (01335)360330
Website: www.saracens-head-shirley.co.uk

Greene King IPA and St Edmunds, Moorland Old Speckled Hen, Timothy Taylor Landlord

Set opposite a striking church, in a remote, picturesque village, the Saracen's Head may not seem like the kind of place where you need to book, but arrive without a reservation and you could be disappointed. Pass the chefs hard at work in the kitchen and you'll arrive in a bright, open bar with rustic furnishings, which leads through to a high-ceilinged dining room with exposed beams and an open-fired room filled with local art. The large, frequently changing menu is chalked up on a blackboard over the fireplace and lists good old favourites such as prawn cocktail, pressed ham hock or crisp roast duck with orange syrup; consider your options carefully, as with portions this large, it's unlikely you'll make it through all three courses!

Closing times
Open daily
booking essential
Prices
Meals: a la carte £ 20/40

Typical Dishes
Crab & avocado mayonnaise
Roast duck with orange & ginger compote
Brandy snap with raspberries

 Between Ashbourne and Bralisford off A 52. Parking.

Three Horseshoes Inn

44-46 Main St,
Breedon on the Hill, DE73 8AN
Tel.: (01332)695129
Website: www.thehorseshoes.com

🏠 *VISA* ⓜⓒ

🍺 **Marston's Pedigree and Shardlow Narrowboat**

This large, whitewashed building may not look much like a pub but open the door and you can rest assured you're in the right place. It's more of a dining pub than your typical village local but it's still characterful – full of books, artefacts and paintings. Numerous interlinking rooms allow you to create a different experience every time you come: choose an antique table beside the exposed brick fireplace, an intimate corner in one of the smaller rooms, or in summer, a pleasant alfresco spot. A friendly, efficient team point out the blackboards that are scattered about the place, displaying classical, seasonal dishes which prove robust and flavoursome. If 3 courses is too much, don't worry – you can buy something from the shop to take home.

Closing times
Closed 25-26 December,
1 January and Sunday
dinner

Prices
Meals: a la carte £ 20/40

Typical Dishes
Chicken liver parfait with tomato chutney

Rib-eye steak with walnut butter

Chocolate whisky trifle

🚗 *Signposted off A 42 between Castle Donington and Ashby-de-la-Zouch. Parking.*

Bruntingthorpe

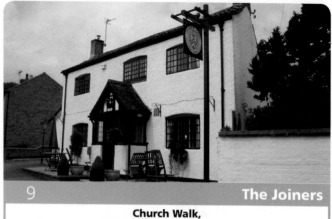

9 **The Joiners**

**Church Walk,
Bruntingthorpe, LE17 5QH**
Tel.: (0116)2478258
Website: www.thejoinersarms.co.uk

Greene King IPA and Sharp's Doom Bar

You can't help but feel that the locals had a part to play in the naming of this pub, which started life as the Joiners Arms and has since been renamed The Joiners. Set in a small rural village, this neat, whitewashed building dates back to the 17C and boasts characterful wood floors and low beams. Run by an enthusiastic husband and wife team, it's more of a dining pub than a place for a casual drink; although the group of regulars crowded round the pine-fitted bar would probably tell you otherwise. Menus display a mix of refined pub classics and more brasserie-style dishes, all cooked and presented in a straightforward yet effective manner. There's a good value set lunch and a wide selection of wines by the glass; Thursday is 'fish night'.

Closing times
Closed Sunday dinner and Monday
booking essential
Prices
Meals: £ 15 (lunch) and a la carte £ 24/34

Typical Dishes
Chicken liver parfait with chutney
Medallions of beef with sauce Diane
Liquorice & blackcurrant panna cotta

 Between Leicester and Husbands Bosworth off A 5199. Parking.

10   **Royal Oak**

**The Green,
Long Whatton, LE12 5BD**
Tel.: (01509)843694
Website: www.theroyaloaklongwhatton.co.uk

 **St Austell Tribute, Sharp's Doom Bar and Blue Monkey 99
Red Baboons**

This pub may no longer boast the majestic oak tree it was once named after but its spacious grounds still remain a draw; where, from June to August, a large marquee plays host to summer weddings. Set at the heart of a sleepy village, it's owned by two brothers who have totally modernised the place, creating a spacious yet cosy bar and a more intimate dining room. Menus offer plenty of choice, from sandwiches and soup through to sharing platters, old pub favourites and appealing main courses, with many dishes displaying a quirky touch – such as the deconstructed scotch egg with homemade piccalilli or the home-cured salmon with beetroot horseradish slaw. The well-equipped, up-to-date bedrooms are in an adjacent block; one has a whirlpool bath.

Closing times
Open daily
Prices
Meals: £ 13 and a la carte
£ 19/40

🛏 **7 rooms:** £ 79/95

Typical Dishes
Cullen skink arancini
Beef fillet with wild mushroom & roasted garlic
Iced lemon meringue parfait

🚗 *4 mi northwest of Loughborough by A 6 and B 5324.
In the centre of the village. Parking.*

Stathern

11   **Red Lion Inn**

**2 Red Lion St,
Stathern, LE14 4HS**
Tel.: (01949)860868
Website: www.theredlioninn.co.uk

  VISA **MC**

Grainstore Brewery Ales, Fuller's London Pride,
Oldershaw Heavenly Blonde and Brewster's Ales

Set in the village centre, this spacious creamwashed pub with its rustic bar and characterful dining rooms is very much part of the community. Whilst it maintains a healthy drinking trade, it's the food here that's the main attraction. The latest produce from the kitchen garden informs the menu and the à la carte has a map of suppliers' locations on the back – and it's reassuring that they don't stray too far from the doorstep; you'll find sausages from the village butcher, game from the Belvoir Estate and cheese from the nearby dairies. Cooking is straightforward and unfussy, resulting in a pleasing mix of refined pub classics with the odd local or global twist, and dishes with more of a restaurant style. Service is friendly and attentive.

Closing times
Closed Sunday dinner and Monday
booking essential

Prices
Meals: £ 18 (weekdays) and a la carte £ 21/39

Typical Dishes
Oxtail & whitebait with turnip remoulade
Lemon sole with wild garlic & parsley velouté
Panfruttone & butter pudding

 8 mi north of Melton Mowbray by A 607. Parking.

12   **Berkeley Arms**

59 Main St,
Wymondham, LE14 2AG
Tel.: (01572)787587
Website: www.theberkeleyarms.co.uk

Marston's Pedigree, Greene King IPA, Grainstore Brewery Cooking and Belvoir Brewery Star Bitter

This attractive village pub dates back to the 16C and is currently under the control of an enthusiastic local couple, who have plenty of experience in the hospitality industry. As you enter, a roaring fire greets you; turn left for the low-beamed bar with its tiled floor and pine tables or right for a slightly more formal dining room. The relaxed, personable service is overseen by charming owner Louise, while her husband, Neil, is hard at work behind the scenes, preparing an appealing seasonal menu of locally sourced produce. Dishes are gutsy and satisfying – there's a daily changing selection of bar snacks and a balanced à la carte of slightly more adventurous, modern offerings, such as braised pig cheek or sea bass with fennel and chorizo.

Closing times
Closed first 2 weeks January, 10 days summer, Sunday dinner and Monday

Prices
Meals: £ 19 (weekdays)/22 and a la carte £ 21/40

Typical Dishes
Grilled pigeon with pickled vegetables
Rack of lamb with ratatouille
Chocolate fondant with banana ice cream

7 mi east of Melton Mowbray off B 676. In centre of village. Parking.

England • East Midlands • Leicestershire

Belchford

13

Blue Bell Inn

1 Main Rd,
Belchford, LN9 6LQ
Tel.: (01507)533602
Website: www.bluebellbelchford.co.uk

🍺 *VISA* Ⓜ️ Ⓓ

🍺 **Batemans XB, Timothy Taylor Landlord**

Set in a tiny village at the heart of the Lincolnshire Wolds, this welcoming whitewashed pub is a popular stop-off point for ramblers navigating the Viking Way. It was originally named after the bluebell flower but a previous landlord was unhappy with the moniker, so he split the word in two and hung a big blue fibreglass bell outside. You enter into a traditional bar with a copper counter and comfy sofas, which in turn leads through to a bright red dining room – a popular spot come evening time. Menus cover all bases, offering honest, home-cooked dishes which are big on flavour; maybe devilled whitebait or potted shrimps, followed by corned beef hash, twice-baked cheddar soufflé or whole locally smoked trout. Comforting nursery puddings follow.

Closing times
Closed 6-21 January
Prices
Meals: a la carte £ 15/32

Typical Dishes
Pork terrine with tomato chutney
Beer-battered haddock & chips
Sticky toffee pudding

 *4 mi north of Horncastle by A 153 and right hand turn east. Parking.*

14 **Wheatsheaf Inn**

Main St,
Dry Doddington, NG23 5HU
Tel.: (01400)281458
Website: www.wheatsheaf-pub.co.uk

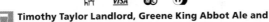

Timothy Taylor Landlord, Greene King Abbot Ale and
Batemans XB

Set next to a characterful 17C church and overlooking a pretty village green, this smartly kept pub positively beckons you through the door. Once inside, you'll discover a cosy bar with a wood burning stove, settles scattered with cushions, and plenty of wood panelling, as well as a laid-back restaurant with upholstered chairs and painted stone walls; while to the rear, a small courtyard makes the perfect suntrap. The light bites lunch menu keeps things simple, offering unfussy dishes that keep the locals happy, such as beef, ale and mushroom pie, while the à la carte presents some more ambitious offerings like braised blade of beef – supplemented by daily blackboard specials in the evening. The local steaks and twice-baked chips are a hit.

Closing times
Closed Monday except
bank holidays

Prices
Meals: a la carte £ 19/37

Typical Dishes
Breaded cod cheeks &
Yorkshire chorizo
Roast duck breast,
confit leg & fondant
potatoes
Lemon tart with
raspberry sorbet

11 mi northwest of Grantham by B 1174 and A 1. Parking.

Fulbeck

15 **Hare & Hounds**

**The Green,
Fulbeck, NG32 3JJ**
Tel.: (01400)273322
Website: www.hareandhoundsfulbeck.com

🍴 _VISA_ Ⓜ©

Marston's Pedigree and EPA

Built in 1680 as a house, the Hare & Hounds has not long been a pub but ever since the current owners (who also have the Brownlow Arms at Hough-on-the-Hill) took over and spent some money on the place, it has been enthusiastically adopted by the locals. The owners' ethos of 'simple pub classics done well' goes down a storm – the menus are refreshingly concise and local produce is to the fore. There's a soup, pie and pasta of the day and steaks from the chargrill are the choice of many. Service is cheerful and the pub is charmingly decorated; you can eat wherever you like – in the bar or in either of the dining rooms. There are smart, comfortable bedrooms in the old stables and the pub also hosts popular jazz evenings.

Closing times
Closed 25 December and Sunday dinner
Prices
Meals: a la carte £ 22/34
8 rooms: £ 55/75

Typical Dishes
Thai-spiced crab cakes
Assiette of pork with creamed potatoes
Pear tarte Tatin

7.5 mi northwest of Sleaford signed off A 17. In the village centre. Parking.

16 Wig & Mitre

**30-32 Steep Hill,
Lincoln, LN2 1LU**
Tel.: (01522)535190
Website: www.wigandmitre.com

VISA MC AE ◇

 Young's London Gold, Batemans XB and Black Sheep Ales

Nestled among period shops on a steep hill, this well-established, part-14C pub is something of a Lincoln institution; standing midway between the castle, used as a court – hence the 'Wig' – and the cathedral – hence the 'Mitre'. There's a cosy bar downstairs, and two period dining rooms and a light, airy beamed restaurant above. The menu changes quarterly, displaying largely classical dishes with the odd Mediterranean or Asian influence. There's a blackboard of daily specials, a good value weekday set selection and, for those who enjoy a hearty homemade breakfast, they open at 9am. With wine books and maps dotted about the place and over 20 wines by the glass, it comes as no surprise to find that they own the next door wine shop too.

Closing times
Open daily
Prices
Meals: £ 14/20
and a la carte £ 20/34

Typical Dishes
Scallops with sweet & sour peppers

Chicken breast wrapped in pancetta

Steamed butterscotch pudding

Close to the Cathedral. Lincoln Castle car parks adjacent.

Market Rasen

17 **Advocate Arms**

**2 Queen St,
Market Rasen, LN8 3EH**
Tel.: (01673)842364
Website: www.advocatearms.couk

 **Adnams Southwold Bitter, Greene King IPA and
Theakston Best Bitter**

This building started life in the early 19C as the Gordon Arms Hotel and is located just a few steps away from the main market square. Apart from the original revolving door, there's not much of its past to be seen nowadays as, courtesy of a top-to-toe refit, it's now smart and modern, with large etched glass walls dividing the place into a large bar and two dining areas. It's open from early in the morning to late at night, so you can pop in and start your day with a bacon sandwich or break up your shopping with afternoon tea. Lunch sticks to good old pub classics, while at dinner, mature local steaks are a speciality. Puddings are satisfyingly traditional and tasty regional cheeses are a feature. Bedrooms are spacious and well-equipped.

Closing times
Open daily
Prices
Meals: a la carte £ 21/37
10 rooms: £ 50/100

Typical Dishes
Twice-baked Lincolnshire Poacher soufflé
Rack of lamb with rosemary & garlic
Triple chocolate millefeuille

 In town centre, opposite the main market square. Parking.

18 | **Bustard Inn**

**44 Main St,
South Rauceby, NG34 8QG**
Tel.: (01529)488250
Website: www.thebustardinn.co.uk

 VISA **MC** **AE**

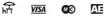 **Batemans Yella Belly Gold, Cheeky Bustard and guest ales**

From the outside it resembles a schoolhouse, but The Bustard Inn is hardly bookish. Its flag-floored bar is simple and uncluttered while the spacious, beamed restaurant, with its cream-tiled floor and exposed brick, has a touch of the Mediterranean about it. There's a great value set lunch menu available Tues-Sat (also offered at dinner Tues-Thurs), while the more ambitious à la carte shows the chef's talents off to the full. Dishes might include fillet of Lincolnshire beef, pan-fried sea trout or homemade venison sausages, and satisfying desserts like sticky toffee pudding. Wine isn't overlooked, with reasonable mark-ups and a fine selection of clarets – or you can slay your thirst with a pint of specially brewed 'Cheeky Bustard' beer.

Closing times
Closed 1 January, Sunday dinner and Monday except bank holidays

Prices
Meals: £ 17
(weekday lunch)
and a la carte £ 22/48

Typical Dishes
Pan-fried scallops with chorizo
Fillet of beef with potato & bacon cake
Mississippi mud pie with coffee ice cream

4 mi west of Sleaford by A 17 and minor road south. Parking.

England • East Midlands • Lincolnshire

Stamford

19

Bull & Swan

**St Martins,
Stamford, PE9 2LJ**
Tel.: (01780)766412
Website: www.thebullandswan.co.uk

🌂 **VISA** **MC** **AE** **◑**

Nene Valley Ales, Grainstore Brewery Ten Fifty and Adnams Southwold Bitter

This stone-built pub started life as a medieval hall house, before being converted into a travellers inn during the late 1600s. It changed name several times until settling on the Bull & Swan in 1739, when it was taken over by Walter Robinson, a former coachman to the Earl of Exeter, and it remains the only public house south of the river. There's a characterful beamed bar with a lively atmosphere and a slightly more formal dining room. The wide-ranging menu offers something to suit all tastes, from sharing slates to classics such as Lincoln Red rib-eye steak or haslet with free range fried eggs and bacon; on Sundays try the roasting pot for four with all the trimmings. Stylish, individually designed bedrooms boast Egyptian cotton sheets.

Closing times
Open daily
Prices
Meals: a la carte £ 25/47
🛏 **7 rooms:** £ 80/425

Typical Dishes
Potted Cromer crab
Aged rib-eye with chips
Dark chocolate fondant

🚗 *0.5 mi south of the town centre on B 1081. Parking on London Rd.*

20   **Red Lion**

**Main St,
East Haddon, NN6 8BU**
Tel.: (01604)770223
Website: www.redlioneasthaddon.co.uk

VISA   MC   AE   D

Courage Directors and Young's Bitter

This thatched honey-stone inn is located right in the heart of the attractive village of East Haddon, and boasts a terrace to the front, along with pretty gardens to the rear. It was originally a farmhouse but has been sympathetically extended, resulting in a pleasing mix of wood panelling, exposed bricks and beams, and wood and slate flooring. Although there are always plenty of local drinkers, it's the food that's the main focus here: menus offer upgraded pub classics, such as a mutton cottage pie or a venison and duck burger, and for those who like a hands-on approach, they offer cookery classes in the adjacent barn. Service is enthusiastic and attentive, and bedrooms are warm and welcoming – one even has a roll-top bath in the room.

Closing times
Closed Sunday dinner
Prices
Meals: a la carte £ 21/29
🛏 **7 rooms:** £ 80/110

Typical Dishes
Scotch egg with caper & parsley mayonnaise
Ox cheek with smoked bacon cabbage & mashed potato
Treacle tart with marmalade ice cream

 8.5 mi northwest of Northampton off A 428. Parking.

England • East Midlands • Northamptonshire

Easton-on-the-Hill

21

Exeter Arms

**21 Stamford Rd,
Easton-on-the-Hill, PE9 3NS**
Tel.: (01780)756321
Website: www.theexeterarms.net

[VISA] [MC]

Black Sheep Ale and Castle Rock Harvest Pale

This 18C inn has been sympathetically yet stylishly restored by its owner, a local sheep farmer with a passion for good food. The interior has a unique charm and is adorned with copper pans, enamel signs, old hop sacks and hop bines, as well as an antique mangle and a clothes horse. The bar is kept exclusively for drinkers – for dining there's a snug candlelit restaurant and a stylish Lloyd Loom furnished conservatory which opens out onto the terrace. An array of menus offer everything from retro sandwiches and tasty pizzas to 'home comforts' and the chef's signature dishes (classics given a modern twist); in winter you'll find venison, partridge and pheasant from the local shoots. Stylish, well-appointed bedrooms have smart, modern bathrooms.

Closing times
Closed Sunday dinner
Prices
Meals: a la carte £ 22/40
6 rooms: £ 70/110

Typical Dishes
Homemade British charcuterie

Confit duck leg & duck hash brown

Sticky toffee pudding with ginger & honey ice cream

 2.5 mi southwest of Stamford on A 43. Parking.

22   Falcon Inn

**Fotheringhay,
PE8 5HZ**
Tel.: (01832)226254
Website: www.thefalcon-inn.co.uk

🚫 **VISA** **MC** **◑**

🍺 **Fuller's London Pride, Greene King IPA and Digfield Fool's Nook**

In the pretty village of Fotheringhay – the birthplace of Richard III and the deathplace of Mary Queen of Scots – under the shadow of a large church, sits the attractive, ivy-clad Falcon Inn. It boasts a neat garden and a small paved terrace, a pleasant private dining annexe and a beamed bar with an unusual display of 15C bell clappers. You'll find the regulars playing darts and drinking real ales in the small tap bar, and the diners in the conservatory restaurant with its wicker chairs, formally laid tables and garden outlook. Good-sized menus include unusual combinations and some interesting modern takes on traditional dishes; you might find purple sprouting broccoli in your stilton soup or red pepper and dandelion dressing on your crab.

Closing times
Open daily
Prices
Meals: £ 14 (weekdays)
and a la carte £ 26/37

Typical Dishes
Scallops with cauliflower purée & black pudding
Fennel & coriander braised pork belly
Vanilla panna cotta

🚗 *3.5 mi north of Oundle by A 427 off A 605. In the centre of the village. Parking.*

England ● East Midlands ● Northamptonshire

Titchmarsh

23 Wheatsheaf

**1 North St,
Titchmarsh, NN14 3DH**
Tel.: (01832)732203
Website: www.thewheatsheafattitchmarsh.co.uk

Sharp's Doom Bar, Fuller's London Pride, Greene King IPA

Sitting in the middle of the delightful village of Titchmarsh is this charming honey-stone inn, which dates from 1640. It's run by a husband and wife team who have successfully given it a modern makeover whilst also keeping the pub's inherent character. Decorated with striking wildlife photographs, the main bar has a lovely warm and welcoming feel, helped along by a wood-burning stove; of the two more formal dining rooms, the Garden Room is the most popular. The seasons are sufficiently reflected in the menu and all of the breads and ice creams are homemade. Local Aylesbury duck is often a highlight, as are dishes like braised feather blade of beef. Puddings have more of a continental feel and could feature panna cotta or crème brûlée.

Closing times
Closed Sunday dinner

Prices
Meals: £ 18
(weekday lunch)
and a la carte £ 17/37

Typical Dishes
Chicken, leek & tarragon terrine

Pork tenderloin in a herb crumb

Crème caramel with oranges

2 mi northeast of Thrapston by A 605. In the centre of the village. Parking.

24

**Main St,
Caunton, NG23 6AB**
Tel.: (01636)636793
Website: www.wigandmitre.com

🛏 *VISA* ⓜ ⒶⒺ ⓞ

🍺 **Marston's Pedigree, Batemans GHA and Black Sheep Best Bitter**

With tan coloured bricks and a wrought iron pergola, this doesn't look much like your typical village pub; step inside, however, and locals supping cask ales will soon reassure you. When the weather's right, make for the large front terrace hung with colourful flower baskets. When it's not so good, head for the bar, with its scrubbed pine furniture and daily papers, or the traditional restaurant with its polished period tables and wheel-back chairs. Seasonally changing menus offer detailed, classically based cooking with Mediterranean influences. Daily specials include plenty of fish and there's also a good value 3 course menu. If breakfast is your thing, they open at 9am Mon-Sat with the likes of smoked salmon, scrambled eggs and champagne.

Closing times
Open daily
Prices
Meals: £ 14/17
and a la carte £ 21/35

●
Typical Dishes
Twice-baked soufflé
Locally sourced steak
Dark chocolate
marquise

England ● East Midlands ● Nottinghamshire

🚗 *7 mi northwest of Newark by A 616, 6 mi past the sugar beet factory. Parking.*

49

Colston Bassett

25   The Martins Arms

**School Ln,
Colston Bassett, NG12 3FD**
Tel.: (01949)81361
Website: www.themartinsarms.co.uk

 VISA MC

Castle Rock Harvest Pale, Greene King IPA, Marston's
Pedigree and Timothy Taylor Landlord

Blazing log fires cast a welcoming glow in the cosy bar of this creeper-clad pub; full of feminine touches like fresh flowers, comfy cushions, tea lights and gleaming copperware. Originally a farmhouse on the Martin family estate, it contains several articles salvaged from the original manor house, including the carved Jacobean fireplace and the old library shelves – now used to hold drinks in the bar. Said bar is the place for an impromptu lunch, while the period furnished dining rooms, adorned with hunting pictures, are more suited to a formal dinner – but do book in advance. The monthly changing menu has a meaty, masculine base with a mix of classical and more modern dishes; portions are hearty and there's plenty of game in season.

Closing times
Closed dinner 25 December and 1 January
Prices
Meals: a la carte £ 27/47

Typical Dishes
Martins Arms black pudding scotch egg

Poached smoked haddock

Buttercream carrot cake

 East of Cotgrave off A 46. Parking.

26 **Reindeer Inn**

**Main St,
Hoveringham, NG14 7JR**
Tel.: (01159)663629
Website: www.thereindeerinn.com

VISA MC AE

 Black Sheep Best Bitter and Castle Rock Harvest Pale

It would win no prizes in a beauty contest and its interior is infinitely more shabby than it is chic, but this hub-of-the-village pub serves such tasty, good value food that you simply won't care. In winter everyone appreciates the blazing log fire and the cosy, relaxed atmosphere, while in summer, the cricket pitch behind the pub becomes the focal point, with drinks delivered through a hatch when a game is in full swing. Reasonably priced menus offer an eclectic mix; alongside recognisable dishes like rib of beef and pan-fried calves liver, you will also find more unusual offerings like pork cheeks braised in cider or vegetable tagine. Themed evenings like fish and lobster night go down a storm – and they even provide a takeaway service.

Closing times
Closed Tuesday lunch, Sunday dinner and Monday
booking essential at lunch

Prices
Meals: £ 11/23
and a la carte £ 24/38

Typical Dishes
Smoked haddock scotch egg

Rib of beef with roast garlic aioli

Stem ginger bread & butter pudding

 5 mi south of Southwell by A 612. Parking.

Clipsham

27   Olive Branch & Beech House

**Main St,
Clipsham, LE15 7SH**
Tel.: (01780)410355
Website: www.theolivebranchpub.com

Olive Ale, Timothy Taylor Landlord, Brewsters Pale Ale and Freedom Four

If it's the bucolic character of a proper country inn you're after, then the Olive Branch is a good bet, with its charmingly understated bar and dining rooms. It has the heart and soul of a real community pub and you'll find local farmers here enjoying a pint, as visitors locate their table thanks to the little blackboards that bear their name. There's a delightful garden, a friendly, informative serving team and a chef who gives regular cookery demonstrations in the old barn. Classic dishes might include ham hock terrine, roast chump of lamb or sausage and mash; the provenance of ingredients is listed on the menu, pasta dishes feature heavily and there's plenty of game in season. Stylish bedrooms include a host of extras.

Closing times
Open daily
booking essential
Prices
Meals: £ 20/25
and a la carte £ 25/42

6 rooms: £ 98/195

Typical Dishes
Barbary duck salad
Roast chump of lamb with chorizo potatoes
Croissant bread & butter pudding

 9.5 mi northwest of Stamford by B 1081 off A 1. Parking.

28 **Wheatsheaf Inn**

1 Stretton Rd,
Greetham, LE15 7NP
Tel.: (01572)812325
Website: www.wheatsheaf-greetham.co.uk

 Brewsters Ales, Oldershaw Ales, Great Oakley Ales and Oakham Ales

If you're on your way to Rutland Water, it's well worth diverting via this little village for a visit to the Wheatsheaf – but be careful not to overshoot the parking space as you pull in or you'll end up in the stream. The first thing you notice as you walk through the door is the aroma of freshly baked bread, which sits tantalisingly on the bar and often contains onion on Sundays. The owners may have experience in London but they've wisely kept this as a family-friendly country pub complete with a pool table and a dartboard. Where they do use their experience is in the kitchen: robust, modern British cooking comes with hints of the Med, and cleverly uses cheaper cuts to keep the prices down. Sunday lunch is a steal and desserts are a must.

Closing times
Closed first 2 weeks January, Monday except bank holidays and Sunday dinner

Prices
Meals: a la carte £ 20/33

Typical Dishes
Deep-fried chorizo fritters
Sea bass with asparagus & chive butter
Sticky ginger pudding

 Just off the A1 on the B 668 to Cottesmore and Oakham. Parking.

England • East Midlands • Rutland

Hambleton

29 Finch's Arms

**Oakham Rd,
Hambleton, LE15 8TL**
Tel.: (01572)756575
Website: www.finchsarms.co.uk

ʰⁿ̅ *VISA* **MC** **AE**

🍺 **Grainstore Rutland Bitter and Castle Rock Harvest Pale**

Cross the threshold of this quaint stone inn and you're transported to a different world, where'll you find a quaint bar, a small anteroom with huge flowers stencilled on the walls, two very stylish dining rooms with vast windows overlooking Rutland Water, and a delightful terrace which shares the view. Assured, seasonal dishes use local lamb, beef and game, and range from appealing sharing boards on the 'bar and terrace' menu through to partridge breast with Lincolnshire Poacher salad or loin of lamb with buttered cabbage on the good value set and à la carte menus. Desserts are satisfyingly old school, featuring the likes of rice pudding with homemade plum jam, and afternoon tea is also an option. Ultra-modern bedrooms complete the picture.

Closing times
Open daily
Prices
Meals: £ 16/19
and a la carte £ 22/40

🛏 **10 rooms:** £ 80/130

Typical Dishes
Black pudding with cauliflower purée

Local venison with celeriac purée & juniper sauce

Apple & blackberry crumble

 3 mi east of Oakham by A 606. Parking.

30   **Marquess of Exeter**

52 Main St,
Lyddington, LE15 9LT
Tel.: (01572)822477
Website: www.marquessexeter.co.uk

Marston's Pedigree and Brakspear Bitter

This attractive 16C thatched pub is located in a pleasant village in the heart of the Rutland countryside. Locals gather in the cosy, flag-floored bar, beside inglenook fireplaces and under characterful exposed beams; while further on through, there's a relaxed, rustic dining room with chunky scrubbed tables, old leather chairs and a range. The daily menu offers tasty, classical combinations that let good quality ingredients stand out; they even grow their own vegetables and keep chickens and pigs at the bottom of the garden. There's an appealing 'Lunch for Less' menu and specials written up on gilt mirrors, while the sharing plates – maybe rib of beef or shoulder of lamb – are firm favourites too. Comfy bedrooms are found across the car park.

Closing times
Closed 25 December

Prices
Meals: £ 14 (lunch)
and a la carte £ 25/32

17 rooms: £ 80/125

Typical Dishes
Pork, chorizo & black pudding terrine
Pan-fried calves' liver with sage & onion dressing
Coffee and hazelnut parfait

Just south of Uppingham, signposted off A 6003, in the middle of the village. Parking.

Lyddington

31

Old White Hart

**51 Main St,
Lyddington, LE15 9LR**
Tel.: (01572)821703
Website: www.oldwhitehart.co.uk

VISA MC

Great Oakley Wot's Occurring, Greene King IPA, Nene Valley DXB

This pub offers all you'd expect from a traditional 17C coaching inn – and a lot more besides. It's got the chocolate box village setting, the open fires, the comfy corners and the seasonally changing menu of hearty, classic dishes; but it also has a cosy, relaxing ambience, charming service led by the lovely owner, a 10-piste petanque pitch (plus a petanque team), and stylish, individually decorated bedrooms with excellent bathrooms and homely extras. It will come as no surprise to hear that they're usually busy, but there's plenty of space for everyone, whether that be in one of the two beamed bars, in the split-level restaurant, out at a picnic table in the neat garden or on the smart, canopy-covered front terrace.

Closing times
Closed 25 December and Sunday dinner in winter

Prices
Meals: a la carte £ 22/37

10 rooms: £ 65/100

Typical Dishes
Thermidor of smoked salmon & crayfish
Saddle of venison and ox cheek
Amaretti biscuit & truffle slice

Just south of Uppingham signposted off A 6003; opposite the village green. Parking.

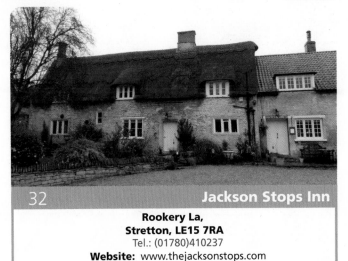

32 Jackson Stops Inn

Rookery La,
Stretton, LE15 7RA
Tel.: (01780)410237
Website: www.thejacksonstops.com

🛏 *VISA* 💳

🍺 **Grainstore Ten Fifty and Cooking**

This lovely stone and thatch pub started life as The White Horse but was later jokingly renamed by the locals when the 'Jackson-Stops' estate agent sign stood outside for so long. Inside it's divided into several areas, each with its own unique feel, including a small open-fired bar, a cosy barn and a two-roomed restaurant. Dishes are largely rooted in tradition but a few display some interesting touches, so you might find a starter like chicken liver pâté with redcurrant and Earl Grey consommé, followed by a main course of beef and venison casserole with stilton and herb dumplings, or confit duck leg with parsnip mash and pancetta cassoulet. Cooking is pleasingly price-conscious and features locally reared meats and produce smoked nearby.

Closing times
Closed Monday except bank holidays and Sunday dinner

Prices
Meals: £ 14 (lunch) and a la carte £ 28/41

Typical Dishes
Timbale of prawns with trout & lobster

Lamb trio with redcurrant & merlot jus

Brown sugar pavlova

8 mi northwest of Stamford by B 1081 off A 1. Parking.

Wide lowland landscapes and huge skies, timber-framed houses, a frowning North Sea canvas: these are the abiding images of England's east. This region has its roots embedded in the earth and its taste buds whetted by local seafood. Some of the most renowned ales are brewed in Norfolk and Suffolk. East Anglia sees crumbling cliffs, superb mudflats and saltmarshes or enchanting medieval wool towns such as Lavenham. Areas of Outstanding Natural Beauty abound, in the Chilterns of Bedfordshire and Hertfordshire, and in Dedham Vale, life-long inspiration of Constable. Religious buildings are everywhere, from Ely Cathedral, "the Ship of the Fens", to the fine structure of Long Melford church. The ghosts of great men haunt Cambridge: Newton, Darwin, Pepys and Byron studied here, doubtless deep in thought as they tramped the wide-open spaces of Midsummer Common or Parker's Piece. Look out for Cromer crab, samphire, grilled herring, Suffolk pork casserole and the hearty Bedfordshire Clanger.

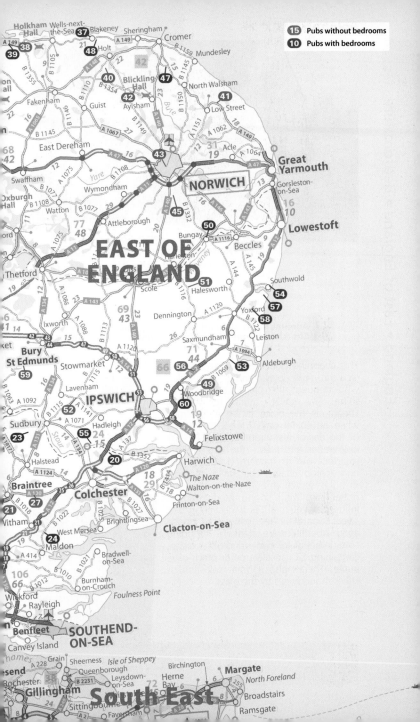

Bolnhurst

1 | Plough at Bolnhurst

**Kimbolton Rd,
Bolnhurst, MK44 2EX**
Tel.: (01234)376274
Website: www.bolnhurst.com

**Adnams Southwold Bitter, Hopping Mad Hoppiness,
Churchend Goat's Milk and Buntingford Highwayman IPA**

This charming pub has 15C origins and is a hit with locals and visitors alike, who frequent the place come rain or shine. The garden, with its trickling stream, is the place to be in summer, while on colder days there's the choice of the bar or restaurant; both with cosy low beams and fires – the latter a little smarter, with its modern wallpaper and upholstered chairs. The same seasonal menu is served throughout, with many dishes displaying strong Mediterranean influences; you might find roast chorizo or sweet Spanish pickles, followed by 28-day aged Aberdeenshire steaks – including côte de boeuf for two – and other dishes containing Sicilian olive oil or black olive purée. There's also a great selection of cheeses and wines by the glass.

Closing times
Closed 2 weeks January, Sunday dinner and Monday

Prices
Meals: £ 16 (weekday lunch)/25 and a la carte £ 29/49

Typical Dishes
Loch Duart salmon with horseradish soufflé
Slow-cooked lamb noisette with butternut squash
Rum baba with Chantilly cream

 On B 660, 7 mi north of Bedford. Parking.

2 **Hare & Hounds**

The Village,
Old Warden, SG18 9HQ
Tel.: (01767)627225
Website: www.hareandhoundsoldwarden.co.uk

 Young's Bitter, Wells Eagle IPA and Courage Directors

With its ornate feature bargeboards and attractive manicured shrubs, this pub could easily appear on the front of any chocolate box. A charming building set in an idyllic village, it boasts four cosy rooms with brightly burning fires, bucket chairs and squashy banquettes, as well as a friendly team. If you're looking to eat, there's the choice of blackboard bar 'snacks' – although you could hardly call them so, as you might find fish and chips or pie of the day – or a monthly changing à la carte that offers robust, flavoursome dishes such as sea bass, pheasant or venison. Bread and pasta are made on the premises; meat is from local farms; fish is from sustainable stocks; and they have an allotment planted with various herbs, salad and berries.

Closing times
Closed 26 December,
1 January, Sunday dinner and Monday except bank holidays

Prices
Meals: a la carte £ 24/36

Typical Dishes
Tempura king prawns with chilli, soy & lime
Pan-fried mackerel with wild garlic pesto
Caramelised apple tart

3.5 mi west of Biggleswade by A 6001 off B 658. Parking here and at village hall.

Shefford

3   Black Horse

**Ireland,
Shefford, SG17 5QL**
Tel.: (01462)811398
Website: www.blackhorseireland.com

VISA   MC   AE

Fuller's London Pride, Freedom Four and Freedom Stout

Don't be deceived by the picture perfect exterior; if you're looking for a quaint country inn, you're in the wrong place. It may look traditional from the outside, but inside it's as stylish and modern as you can get. Contemporary light fittings are set amongst marble-style flooring and a granite-topped counter, and there's a walled courtyard complete with mirrors and fairy lights. The friendly staff serve an equally eclectic mix of generously portioned dishes. Lunch could include anything from 'pie of the day' to a smoked salmon scotch egg, while dinner might offer potted beef cheeks followed by suprême of arctic char or four bone rack of lamb on summer vegetable tagine. Accessed via a meandering garden path, the bedrooms are comfy and cosy.

Closing times
Closed 25-26 December, 1 January and Sunday dinner

Prices
Meals: a la carte £ 23/34

🛏 **2 rooms:** £ 55

Typical Dishes
Carpaccio of beef
Fillet of haddock & chips
Rhubarb crème brûlée

 1.5 mi northwest of Shefford by B 658 and Ireland rd. Parking.

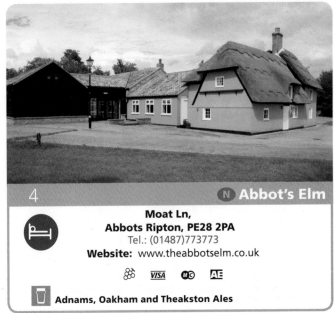

4 **Abbot's Elm**

**Moat Ln,
Abbots Ripton, PE28 2PA**
Tel.: (01487)773773
Website: www.theabbotselm.co.uk

VISA **M©** **AE**

Adnams, Oakham and Theakston Ales

It's hard to believe this attractive thatched inn is actually a reconstruction of its 17C predecessor; part destroyed by fire in 2010, now only the elegant brick fireplace remains from its former days. Inside it's surprisingly modern, with an open-plan layout and a vaulted, oak-beamed roof. The bar offers light bites, hot plates such as smoked haddock with bubble and squeak, and a 'menu du jour'; while later in the week there's also an à la carte and a tasting menu served in the formal dining room, where you'll find appealing dishes such as honey-roast duck breast. Cooking is hearty and flavoursome and the passionately compiled wine list offers most choices by the glass or carafe. Cosy bedrooms come with free wi-fi and fluffy bathrobes.

Closing times
Open daily

Prices
Meals: £ 14/24
and a la carte £ 19/42

3 rooms: £ 55/85

Typical Dishes
Fricassee of lamb's kidneys
Sea bream, crab & pea risotto
Sticky toffee pudding

Just over 6 mi north of Huntingdon by B1514, A141 and B1090. Parking.

Bourn

5

Willow Tree

29 High St,
Bourn, CB23 2SQ
Tel.: (01954)719775
Website: www.thewillowtreebourn.com

🛖 🐾 *VISA* ⓜ©

Woodeforde's Wherry, Milton Brewery Pegasus and Justinian

It may be named after a majestic British tree – the likes of which you'll find blowing elegantly in the wind as you enter the car park – but this pub is far from your usual affair. The life-sized cow model in the garden is the first clue as to the quirky nature of the place, followed inside by the feeling of being inside a 'House and Home' magazine, courtesy of chandeliers, gilt mirrors and Louis XV style furniture dotted about the place. Menus offer everything from old pub classics to more ambitious dishes such as scotch duck egg, rabbit terrine or venison haunch Rossini, and they offer a 'Summer Deckchair' menu and afternoon tea from May-September. These are accompanied by an appealing wine list, with most selections available by the glass.

Closing times
Open daily
Prices
Meals: a la carte £ 13/46

Typical Dishes
Goat's cheesecake with beetroot crisps

Lamb rump with braised cabbage & bacon

Chocolate délice with milk ice cream

🚗 *3 mi south of Cambourne by A 1198 off B1046. In the centre of the village. Parking.*

6   **Eltisley**

2 The Green, Eltisley, PE19 6TG
Tel.: (01480)880308
Website: www.theeltisley.co.uk

 Wells Eagle IPA and guest ales

You might imagine that this chic, stylish gastro-pub is a strictly dining affair, but the contemporary bar is equally as welcoming to drinkers as diners; the latter can sit and watch their meal being prepared from the windows in the snug. For a more formal occasion head through to the restaurant, where grey walls meet wood and tile flooring, and bold designs are offset by swanky chandeliers. Large parties should ask for the 'Wurlitzer', a stylish high-backed semi-circular banquette, while for summer dining the terrace is ideal. Cooking is simple, unfussy and relies on quality local ingredients: meat is from nearby farms and vegetables, from their allotment. Everything from the bread and pasta to the desserts and ice cream is homemade.

Closing times
Closed Monday in winter and Sunday dinner

Prices
Meals: a la carte £ 22/40

Typical Dishes
Chicken & ham terrine with piccalilli
Eltisley beef burger with gherkin mayo
Crème brûlée

Between St Neots and Cambridge, signposted off A 428. Parking.

67

Elton

7

Crown Inn

**8 Duck St,
Elton, PE8 6RQ**
Tel.: (01832)280232
Website: www.thecrowninn.org

VISA **MC** *AE*

Tydd Steam Golden Crown Ale

With its 17C honey-stone walls, charming thatched roof and lovely location in a delightful country parish, the Crown Inn really is a good old English pub. Sup a cask ale or two beside the characterful inglenook fireplace in the bar, then head through to the cosy dining room, the large decagonal conservatory or out onto the spacious decked terrace. The same seasonally changing menu is served throughout, featuring old British favourites such as steak and ale pie, homemade cider and apple sausages or lamb with bubble and squeak. Bedrooms are smart, modern and individually designed – some have four-posters, sleigh beds or roll-top baths – and if you fancy treating yourself in the morning, you can order a hamper and enjoy breakfast in your PJs.

Closing times
Open daily

Prices
Meals: £ 21/30
and a la carte £ 25/38

8 rooms: £ 65/120

Typical Dishes

Steamed mussels with cider, garlic, cream & bacon

Root vegetable cottage pie, potato & goat's cheese crust

Glazed lemon tart

Midway between Oundle and Peterborough signposted off A 605. Parking.

8

Blue Bell

**10 High St,
Glinton, PE6 7LS**
Tel.: (01733)252285
Website: www.thebluebellglinton.co.uk

 Greene King IPA, Abbot and Old Speckled Hen

The pretty village of Glinton is home to the Blue Bell and also to its experienced owners who, after some spending time away, have returned home. A pretty flower display greets you at the front and there's a pleasant terrace round the back; while inside there are plenty of nooks and crannies in which to hide yourself away. In true pub style, there's plenty of space beneath the old 18C beams for the local drinkers, and the atmosphere is suitably warm and welcoming. Lunch offers pub favourites, generously filled sandwiches and tempting salads in a choice of sizes, while dinner steps things up a gear with some more modern dishes like maple-glazed duck breast with confit leg croquette… and be sure to save room for one of their tasty desserts.

Closing times
Closed Sunday dinner and Monday
Prices
Meals: a la carte £ 20/31

Typical Dishes
Scallops & black pudding
Pork belly, pear purée & crackling
Strawberry & vanilla cheesecake

🚗 *5 mi north of Peterborough off A15 in centre of village. Parking.*

England • East of England • Cambridgeshire

9

The Cock

**47 High St,
Hemingford Grey, PE28 9BJ**
Tel.: (01480)463609
Website: www.cambscuisine.com

🖻 *VISA* 🆖 AE

🍺 **Great Oakley Wot's Occurring, Nethergate IPA and
Oldershaw Newton's Drop**

As you approach this 17C country pub you'll come across two doors: one marked 'Pub', leading to a split-level bar and the other marked 'Restaurant', leading to a spacious dining room. Run by an experienced team, it has a homely feel, with warm fabrics, comfy seating and attractively papered walls. In winter, the best spot is beside the fire, while in summer, it's by the French windows. Cooking rests firmly on the tried-and-tested side of things, with classic pub staples such as lamb shank and belly pork, good value set lunches and an extensive list of daily changing fish specials. A tempting sausage board offers an appealing mix of homemade sausages from their 75+ recipes, along with different sauces and several varieties of mashed potato.

Closing times
Open daily
booking essential

Prices
Meals: £ 17 (weekday lunch) and a la carte
£ 22/35

Typical Dishes
Duck parcel, sweet soy
& ginger dressing
Duck breast with
creamed Savoy
cabbage
Vanilla & anise poached
pear with sorbets

🚗 *The village is 5 mi east of Huntingdon signposted off A 14.
Parking.*

10 **Crown and Punchbowl**

**High St,
Horningsea, CB25 9JG**
Tel.: (01223)860643
Website: www.thecrownandpunchbowl.com

VISA MC AE ◑

Shepherd Neame Master Brew

England • East of England • Cambridgeshire

The clue that this is more of a dining than a drinking establishment lies in the fact that there's no real bar; however, the Crown and Punchbowl still delivers on pubby character thanks to its beams, open fires and chunky wood tables. When it comes to dining, there's plenty of choice, with a seasonally changing à la carte, daily specials and a popular 'sausage board'. The kitchen does traditional – such as a delicious blade of beef or sticky toffee pudding – as well as modern, with dishes like fish terrine and horseradish sorbet or deconstructed millionaire's shortbread. The seared scallops are a permanent feature and there's a sophisticated element to all of the cooking. Relax on the pleasant terrace then head for one of the simple bedrooms.

Closing times
Closed 26 December-
1 January, dinner Sunday
and bank holiday Monday
Prices
Meals: a la carte £ 25/42
5 rooms: £ 75/100

Typical Dishes
Confit duck with
coriander rösti

Pan-seared fillet of
sea bream, saffron &
lemon risotto

Yorkshire rhubarb
délice

Just off the A 14, northeast of Cambridge. Parking.

England • East of England • Cambridgeshire

11
Pheasant

**Village Loop Rd,
Keyston, PE28 0RE**
Tel.: (01832)710241
Website: www.thepheasant-keyston.co.uk

 **Nene Valley NVB, Adnams Broadside and Southwold
Bitter**

Recently returned to its former owners, this picture postcard pub is quite simply delightful. Hidden away in a sleepy hamlet, it has a lovely countryside feel, with exposed beams and hunting scenes galore; John Bull wallpaper features and, in the dining room, bread is carved under the watchful eye of a stuffed albino pheasant. The wide-ranging seasonal menu has something for everyone, from nibbles like salted almonds or crispy squid through to tasty dishes like venison terrine or sea trout with shrimp butter. There's a classic section for the more traditional diner and an incredible value set menu too. An excellent selection of wines comes courtesy of the owner, who is a Master of Wine, and staff are warm, gracious and attentive.

Closing times
Closed 2-15 January,
Sunday dinner and Monday
booking essential
Prices
Meals: £ 15/30
and a la carte £ 21/41

Typical Dishes
Gnocchi with thyme &
parmesan
Saddle of rabbit with
borlotti beans
Tarte Tatin with
cinnamon ice cream

 Signposted off junction 15 of A 14. Parking.

12

Hole in the Wall

**2 High St,
Little Wilbraham, CB21 5JY**
Tel.: (01223)812282
Website: www.holeinthewallcambridge.com

 Woodeforde's Wherry, Brandon Saxon Gold and Black Bar Daylight Moment

Local workers used to leave their empty tankards in a hole in this charming 16C pub's wall; these would then be filled, ready for them to pick up on their way home. The hole may have long since been closed up, but you can still sup a pint in the pub's cosy, beamed bar. Better still, enjoy a meal prepared with zeal by the young chefs; one of whom was a past MasterChef finalist. The regularly changing, seasonal menu offers starters like sardines on toast or lamb koftas, with main courses such as Blythburgh pork chop or Barbury duck breast and heartwarming, classical desserts like rice pudding or marmalade and almond cake. Lunch is a steal; homemade bread is baked twice a day, and they are partial to a bit of meat curing and smoking too.

Closing times
Closed 2 weeks January, 1 week September-October, Sunday dinner and Monday
booking advisable

Prices
Meals: £ 14 (lunch) and a la carte £ 23/33

Typical Dishes
Pea soup with Jersey Royal tortellini

Barbary duck, pickled cucumber & spiced caramel

Doughnuts with lemon meringue

Just off the A 14 east of Cambridge, the Wilbrahams are signposted off A 1303. Parking.

Madingley

13 **Three Horseshoes**

High St,
Madingley, CB23 8AB
Tel.: (01954)210221
Website: www.threehorseshoesmadingley.com

Adnams Southwold Bitter and Everards Tiger

Set in a pretty village, famous for its stunning hall, this appealing pub with its whitewashed walls and attractive thatched roof fits right in. To the front, scrubbed wooden tables are set beside a small bar and a welcoming fireplace; to the rear, a more formal conservatory with Lloyd Loom chairs looks out over the garden. The interesting bar menu offers modern dishes such as truffled mac and cheese, slow-cooked egg with onion soubise or hanger steak with kimchi purée; the daily changing à la carte follows suit, featuring the likes of smoked eel with green tea and wasabi cotta or haunch of venison with cime di rapa and morcilla crumb. The bar is a lively place, so if you're looking for a romantic table for two, make for the conservatory.

Closing times
Open daily
booking advisable
Prices
Meals: a la carte £ 20/46

Typical Dishes
Slow-cooked egg with king brown mushroom

Roast canon & shoulder of lamb

Violet ice cream with frozen chocolate

 West of Cambridge signposted off A 1303. Parking.

14 **Beehive**

**62 Albert Pl,
Peterborough, PE1 1DD**
Tel.: (01733)310600
Website: www.beehivepub.co.uk

Fuller's London Pride, Willbur Wood D.N.A. and Castor Ales

Just off the city centre ring road might not be your first choice of location for a pub but it's close at hand for shoppers and has stood here long enough to have built up a steady group of regulars. Owners James and Sharon have lived in the area all their lives and, remembering the pub in its heyday, jumped at the chance to get the place up and running again when it was closed and put on the market. It now has a smart, modern interior with stripped floorboards, a zinc-topped bar and a mix of high stools, armchairs and banquettes. When it comes to the food, it's well-presented, flavoursome and satisfying; the house pâté with chutney is a must, followed by a classic like slow-cooked shoulder of lamb or a pub favourite such as toad in the hole.

Closing times
Closed 1 January and
Sunday dinner
Prices
Meals: a la carte £ 19/33

Typical Dishes
Crispy fried crab cake
Fillet of pork
Wellington with
buttered greens
Chocolate fondant
with pistachio
ice cream

In the centre of the city just off Bourges Boulevard. Pay and display parking across the road.

Stilton

15   Village Bar (at Bell Inn)

**Great North Rd,
Stilton, PE7 3RA**
Tel.: (01733)241066
Website: www.thebellstilton.co.uk

Old Speckled Hen, Greene King IPA, Oakham Ales and
Digfield Ales Fool's Nook

It's hard to believe that this sleepy market town is just minutes off the A1, or that this 17C inn – famous as the birthplace of stilton cheese – is set on what was once the most popular coaching route from York to London. Look closely, however, and you can still see the distances to the major cities inscribed on what was the original archway from the road to the stables. Step inside and you have the choice of a characterful bar or more modern bistro setting. Classically based menus offer plenty of choice and stilton appears in many of the dishes, so you might find stilton and walnut pâté followed by Grasmere Farm pork and stilton sausages, and then a 'Stilton Sampler' cheeseboard. Cosy, traditional bedrooms can be found in the adjoining inn.

Closing times
Closed 25 December
Prices
Meals: a la carte £ 21/37

Typical Dishes
Chicken liver parfait
British rib-eye steak
Sticky toffee pudding

In the centre of the village. Parking.

16 · Anchor Inn

**Sutton Gault,
CB6 2BD**
Tel.: (01353)778537
Website: www.anchor-inn-restaurant.co.uk

Humpty Dumpty Little Sharpie and Nethergate Growler

It may seem like a strange name for a pub that's nowhere near the coast – but it does have some watery connections. Built in 1650, this building was originally used to house the workers who created the Hundred Foot Wash in order to alleviate flooding in the fens. If you fancy a river view, head for the wood-panelled rooms to the front of the bar, where you'll discover a pleasant outlook and a tempting menu, which might include smoked eel, pork loin in Parma ham, tea-infused duck or the house speciality of grilled dates wrapped in bacon. There are always some fish specials chalked on the board, while others occasionally use produce from the nearby Denham Estate. Neat, pine furnished bedrooms include two suites; one boasts river views.

Closing times
Open daily

Prices
Meals: £ 14 (weekday lunch)/18 and a la carte £ 23/40

🛏 **4 rooms:** £ 60/155

Typical Dishes
Pigeon breast with crispy bacon & beetroot jelly

Pork loin and belly with black pudding

Dark chocolate fondant with orange parfait

Off B 1381; from Sutton village follow signs to Sutton Gault; pub is beside the New Bedford River. Parking.

Thriplow

17

 Green Man

**2 Lower St,
Thriplow, SG8 7RJ**
Tel.: (01763)208855
Website: www.greenmanthriplow.com

⛱ *VISA* ⓂⒸ

🍺 **Woodfordes Wherry, Blackbar Daylight Moment and Brandon Rusty Bucket & Saxon Gold**

When the previous owner of this 19C village pub retired, she was reluctant to sell it to one of the large breweries, so 153 of the local residents pulled together and bought the place before putting it out to tender. The couple who won the bid have plenty of experience when it comes to running a successful pub and have made some changes; you'll find squashy leather sofas by an open fire and a simple dining room decorated with fresh flowers – along with a lovely suntrap of a garden in which to bask. The menu is fairly concise and largely British but there are always a few influences from further afield; you might find lamb koftas or Skagen – a Scandinavian take on a classic prawn cocktail. They also brew their own beers via the local brewery.

Closing times
Closed Sunday dinner and Monday
Prices
Meals: a la carte £ 20/34

Typical Dishes
Ham hock & smoked chicken terrine
Duck with potato rösti & pickled cucumber
Tarte Tatin

 4 mi west of Duxford off A505 in centre of village. Parking

18 **White Hart**

Main St,
Ufford, PE9 3BH
Tel.: (01780)740250
Website: www.whitehartufford.co.uk

 VISA **MC** **AE**

 Adnams Southwold Bitter, St Austell Tribute, Castle Rock Harvest Pale

England • East of England • Cambridgeshire

This delightful 17C inn stands at the centre of the charming village of Ufford. Outside, there's a super sun-trap of a terrace and garden, while inside, there's a cosy bar housing an interesting collection of railway signs, farm implements and chamber pots – as well as a pleasant beamed restaurant with exposed stone walls and a lovely little conservatory. The menu offers a broad range of dishes, from simple sandwiches to starters of beetroot cured salmon or seared scallops with wild mushroom cream, followed by Thai-style fish casserole or creamy rabbit pie; and much of the meat comes from their farm. Sweet, country bedrooms each have their own florally inspired style; one boasts a four-poster and the two twin rooms outside allow dogs to stay.

Closing times
Open daily
Prices
Meals: a la carte £ 23/41
6 rooms: £ 70/100

Typical Dishes
Scallops with pancetta & wild mushrooms
Fillet of pork and Camembert Wellington
Sticky toffee pudding with caramel sauce

Ufford is signposted off B 660 northwest of Peterborough. Parking.

Clavering

19 **Cricketers**

**Clavering,
CB11 4QT**
Tel.: (01799)550442
Website: www.thecricketers.co.uk

VISA MC AE

Adnams Ales

This deceptively spacious pub sits opposite the cricket pitch in a sleepy village and is popular with locals and visitors alike – with plenty of cosy, welcoming bedrooms for the latter. The blackboard menu above the fire in the bar informs you of the dishes of the day; head to the dining room with its exposed beams, horse harnesses and polished brass for a more 'restauranty' feel. The menu offers Italian dishes with the occasional global influence: expect tasty homemade pasta and wood-fired specialities alongside Thai-style mussels or chicken Kiev stuffed with wild mushroom and truffle butter. Bread is baked daily and produce is sourced as locally as possible; the owners' son, Jamie Oliver, provides fruit, veg and herbs from his organic garden.

Closing times
Closed 25-26 December
booking essential
Prices
Meals: a la carte £ 20/37
20 rooms: £ 68/135

Typical Dishes
Home-cured gravadlax
Trio of spring lamb
Salted caramel &
chocolate tart

On the main road through the village close to the cricket pitch. Parking.

20 **Sun Inn**

**High St,
Dedham, CO7 6DF**
Tel.: (01206)323351
Website: www.thesuninndedham.com

 **Adnams Broadside and Crouch Vale Brewers Gold,
Fat Cat and West Berkshire Side Pocket for a Toad**

Despite its bright, modern exterior, this is a pub that's rooted in history. It's located in the heart of a picturesque village, opposite a delightful church, and dates back to the 15C. The interior is just the right side of shabby, with a large panelled area and a beautiful wooden bar stocked with real ales and topped with homemade sausage rolls. There's also a relaxed, art-filled dining room. Cooking has an Italian slant: the weekly set menu offers two simple choices, along with wines; while the main menu features hearty, rustic dishes in two sizes – including a large selection of antipasti, followed by the likes of bollito misto, braised cuttlefish with squid ink or lemon sole with radicchio. Bedrooms are snug; two have a Scandic feel.

Closing times
Closed 25-26 December

Prices
Meals: £ 16 (weekdays)
and a la carte £ 21/35

7 rooms: £ 85/150

Typical Dishes

Asparagus & quail's egg with pecorino

Veal chop with borlotti beans & Swiss chard

Panna cotta with rhubarb & Grappa

 In the centre of the village. Parking.

Fuller Street

21 Square & Compasses

**Fuller Street,
CM3 2BB**
Tel.: (01245)361477
Website: www.thesquareandcompasses.co.uk

🍺 *VISA* **M©**

Dark Star Hophead and Maldon Farmer's Nelson's Blood

This pub is hidden deep in the Essex countryside, down a labyrinth of lanes, so you might just need that compass after all. A charming little pub with low beams, wood burning stoves and cosy character aplenty, this is a place that offers genuine hospitality from its hands-on owners and a friendly team. It has a small locals bar with gravity fed casks and a dining room displaying numerous certificates and menus from the owners' pasts on its exposed brick walls. Unfussy menus offer the usual pub classics like home-cooked gammon or Stokers Ale pie, while the daily changing blackboards might list terrines of locally shot game or pan-fried fish caught nearby. Unashamedly traditional puddings feature the likes of spotted dick or rhubarb crumble.

Closing times
Closed Sunday dinner
booking essential
Prices
Meals: a la carte £ 20/32

Typical Dishes
Breast of pigeon with black pudding
Wing of skate, lemon, caper & parsley butter
Sticky toffee pudding

 Between Braintree and Chelmsford off the A 131. Parking.

22 **Queens Head**

**Queen St,
Fyfield, CM5 0RY**
Tel.: (01277)899231
Website: www.thequeensheadfyfield.co.uk

Adnams Southwold & Broadside

Don't make the mistake of trying to go in the front door – you have to enter to the side or rear of this characterful 16C pub. It's located in the heart of the village and has a pretty garden which leads down to the banks of the river. The interior is just as inviting though, with its original beams, inglenook fireplaces and galleried upper level. The extensive menu changes every two months and is supplemented by blackboard specials. Dishes take on more of a restaurant than a pub style, offering the likes of English asparagus with a crispy quail's egg, prosciutto and hollandaise, followed by soy-glazed salmon with spiced crab linguine and shellfish consommé. They hold regular Garrett sessions (folk, roots and acoustic dinner concerts).

Closing times
Closed 1-7 January,
Sunday dinner and Monday
Prices
Meals: £ 19 (lunch)
and a la carte £ 25/39

Typical Dishes
Scallops with cauliflower purée
Chicken suprême with seasonal vegetables
Chocolate torte, salted caramel

3 mi north east of Chipping Ongar on B 184 in centre of village. Parking.

Gestingthorpe

23  **Pheasant**

**Gestingthorpe,
CO9 3AU**
Tel.: (01787)465010
Website: www.thepheasant.net

VISA **MC**

**Adnams Southwold Bitter, Mauldons Pleasant Pheasant
and regular guest beers**

Set on the edge of a pretty little village, this 16C pub is every bit a true country inn. Run by a former landscape gardener and his wife, it centres around sustainability, with a one acre garden over the road where they grow vegetables and keep chickens and bees. The hub of the pub is a very inviting low-beamed bar and the locals come in their droves for biweekly 'Thirsty Thursday'. The cooking keeps things simple, offering heartwarming dishes in traditional combinations; maybe a prawn cocktail, followed by belly pork or local venison, finished off with an apple crumble. To keep the regulars happy, they also serve takeaway fish & chips. Modern bedrooms are across the car park and feature good quality bedding and views over rolling fields.

Closing times
Closed first 2 weeks January
Prices
Meals: £ 15 (lunch)
and a la carte £ 22/36
5 rooms: £ 80/165

Typical Dishes
*Pigeon breast,
beetroot & walnut
salad*

*Belly pork
with caramelised cider
gravy*

*Vanilla panna cotta
with strawberries*

 Between Sudbury and Castle Hedingham off B1058. Parking.

24   The Bull

**2 Maldon Rd,
Great Totham, CM9 8NH**
Tel.: (01621)893385
Website: www.thebullatgreattotham.co.uk

Adnams Southwold Bitter & Greene King IPA

This attractive roadside pub dates back to the 1500s and boasts a beautifully landscaped rear garden and terrace, as well as distant views of West Mersea from the picnic tables in front. There are lots of different rooms inside, including a beamed bar and a snug frequented by the locals; it's been modernised but it still retains the pubby character you'd expect of a building its age. Seasonal dishes look to Europe for their inspiration, so you might find crayfish Niçoise salad or linguine; there are also some great British classics like Barnsley pork chop or beer-battered haddock with triple-cooked chips, and a good value lunch menu too. Individually decorated, contemporary bedrooms are located in a cottage and named after local villages.

Closing times
Open daily.
Prices
Meals: £ 16
(weekday lunch)
and a la carte £ 23/39

🛏 **4 rooms:** £ 75/85

Typical Dishes
Devon crab
Gloucester Old Spot
pork belly with lemon
& capers
Rhubarb parfait

 Between Tiptree and Maldon on B 1022. Parking.

Hatfield Broad Oak

25

Duke's Head

**High St,
Hatfield Broad Oak, CM22 7HH**
Tel.: (01279)718598
Website: www.thedukeshead.co.uk

VISA **MC** **AE**

**Greene King IPA, Sharp's Doom Bar and Timothy Taylor
Landlord**

Run by an enthusiastic couple who help support nearby sports clubs and host plenty of community events, this spacious 17C pub is the very definition of a proper village local. It features a large terrace and a pleasant garden with a children's tree house, and behind its smart modern façade, has a bright, relaxed feel. When it comes to the food, dishes are tasty, well-crafted and of a good size; you might find omelette Arnold Bennett or bubble and squeak, followed by chicken Kiev, king prawn spaghetti or pumpkin and chestnut gnocchi. These can be eaten in a laid-back, pine-furnished room or in the more formal, pre-laid dining room. If you're just after some nibbles, the bar, with its open fire and low level seating, is always a good bet.

Closing times
Closed 25-26 December
Prices
Meals: a la carte £ 21/35

Typical Dishes
Mushroom & spinach stack with red onion marmalade

Roast cod with scampi Provençale sauce

Rhubarb & praline parfait

 In the centre of the village. Parking.

26 | **Bell Inn**

**High Rd,
Horndon on the Hill, SS17 8LD**
Tel.: (01375)642463
Website: www.bell-inn.co.uk

 Greene King IPA and Crouch Vale Ales

If you're wondering about the hot cross buns, the story goes that past landlord Jack Turnell took over the pub on Good Friday, whereupon he nailed a bun to one of the beams; since then, a bun has been added every year – the cement version marking the wartime rationing. The Bell has been run by the same family for the last 70 years, although dates back nearly 12 times that. Drinkers will find themselves at home in the wood-panelled bar, while diners can choose from a beamed area or more formal restaurant. Cooking uses quality produce to create classically based dishes with a modern touch; maybe apple tart with a glass of malted milkshake. Bedrooms are styled after famous Victorian mistresses; those in Hill House display thoughtful extras.

Closing times
Closed 25-26 December and bank holidays

Prices
Meals: a la carte £ 19/40

27 rooms: £ 50/120

Typical Dishes
Mackerel fish-cake with creamed horseradish

Herb-roasted lamb chump with crushed peas

Lemon and thyme crème brûlée

 In the centre of the village. Parking.

Pattiswick

England • East of England • Essex

27   Compasses at Pattiswick

**Compasses Rd,
Pattiswick, CM77 8BG**
Tel.: (01376)561322
Website: www.thegreatpubcompany.co.uk

 VISA

Bishop Nick's Hersey, Adnams Southwold, Red Fox
Compasses Gold and Woodeforde's Wherry

This remote pub started life as two estate workers' cottages, and its name comes from its far-reaching, 360° countryside views. Large gardens with plenty of seating make the most of this panorama, while the mini playground ensures any kids in your party will be kept happy. Inside, it's smart and spacious, with open fires, chatty local staff and a warm, relaxing feel. Lunch sees the likes of sandwiches, a ploughman's or a Melton Mowbray pork pie with piccalilli, while the wide-ranging à la carte keeps things traditional with potted shrimps, ox cheek or a hearty roast mutton shepherd's pie. Food is laudably local, with game from the surrounding estate. Nursery puddings might include warm treacle tart or a fruit crumble with custard.

Closing times
Open daily
Prices
Meals: a la carte £ 19/33

Typical Dishes
Moules marinière

Honey-glazed
canon of lamb with
dauphinoise potatoes

Treacle tart with
clotted cream

 Between Braintree and Coggeshall signposted off A 120.
Parking.

28   **Waggoners**

**Brickwall Close,
Ayot Green, AL6 9AA**
Tel.: (01707)324241
Website: www.thewaggoners.co.uk

VISA **MC** **AE** **①**

**Sharp's Doom Bar, Greene King IPA and Abbot Ale,
Adnams Broadside and Fuller's London Pride**

Set on the edge of the Brocket Hall Estate, this 17C pub was once a popular stop-off point for stagecoaches and a favourite haunt of the estate workers. It has plenty of charm, with a delightfully simple open-fired bar providing a pleasant spot for weary walkers, locals and their dogs, and a very formal linen-laid dining room adding a more serious tone. The bar menu provides a list of unfussy snacks, while the à la carte presents much more ambitious offerings, with prices to match. Both the owner and chef are French, so dishes might include sautéed frogs legs or foie gras ballotine, followed by duck leg confit or veal roulade with caramelised onion tart. Daily specials are often presented on gueridon trolleys and usually feature a fish dish.

Closing times
Open daily
booking advisable
Prices
Meals: £ 17/25
and a la carte £ 25/39

Typical Dishes
Foie gras & chicken liver parfait
Sea bass with honey noodles
Peanut butter parfait

2.5 mi south of Welwyn off B 197. Parking.

29

Golden Fleece

**20 Green End,
Braughing, SG11 2PG**
Tel.: (01920)823555
Website: www.goldenfleecebraughing.co.uk

**Adnams Southwold Bitter, Buntingford Royston Red,
Nethergate Augustinian, Courage Directors and Wadsworth 6X**

This part-16C property was left to go to rack and ruin for ten long years so, when it finally found a buyer, it was in need of some real TLC. Who better to take on the challenge, than a couple who grew up in the village: one of whom had their first job – aged 13 – at this very pub? It's not hard to see why they – and their many regulars – are so fond of it, with its spacious garden, pretty terrace overlooking the village and period features like a vast inglenook fireplace. Food is tasty and comforting, with popular dishes including Millionaire's bun (fillet steak in a bread roll), suet pudding and the Golden Fleece smokey. Old-school puddings might include a warming blackberry sponge with custard. Gluten and dairy free options are available.

Closing times
Closed 25-26 December and Sunday dinner

Prices
Meals: a la carte £ 21/33

Typical Dishes
Potted ham hock with
piccalilli
Confit of beef in a
Savoy cabbage parcel
Mango & chilli upside-
down pudding

 In the middle of the village, on B 1368. Parking.

30 **Tilbury**

**Watton Rd,
Datchworth, SG3 6TB**
Tel.: (01438)815550
Website: www.thetilbury.co.uk

VISA MC AE

Brakspear Bitter and Oxford Gold

This lovingly restored pub is part-owned by TV chef Paul Bloxham and can be found down a series of winding roads in a pretty little village. It's very much a dining pub and the three characterful rooms are packed full come the weekend; in summer, try for a spot on the terrace with its pizza oven and grill menu – otherwise, head for the snug, the 'Red Room' or the main dining room. Menus follow the seasons and seafood plays a big part – you can even order your lobster in advance. Pub classics such as calves' liver and mash and dry-aged steaks sit alongside the likes of Wobbly Bottom goat's cheese gallette or scotch quails' egg remoulade salad. The cheeseboard is priced by the slice, so you can choose as few or as many cheeses as you like.

Closing times
Closed Sunday dinner
Prices
Meals: £ 14 (lunch)
and a la carte £ 18/42

Typical Dishes
Cod cheeks
with coriander
couscous
Pot-roast chicken
with asparagus & wild
garlic
Warm chocolate
marshmallow brownie

4 mi southeast of Stevenage signposted off A 602. Parking.

Flaunden

31

Bricklayers Arms

Hogpits Bottom,
Flaunden, HP3 0PH
Tel.: (01442)833322
Website: www.bricklayersarms.com

🍺 Tring Side Pocket, Sharp's Doom Bar, Vale VPA, St Austell
Tribute and Marlow Rebellion IPA

This pub is tucked away by itself on the outer reaches of a small hamlet, so you'll need a good navigator when trying to find it. Part-built in 1722, it was originally two cottages, before becoming a butcher's, a blacksmith's and later, an alehouse. Inside it's rather smart, with polished tables and fresh flowers everywhere; the areas to the side of the bar being more formally laid than those in front. This isn't the place for a quick snack (a glance at the menu will show there are none), but somewhere serving good old-fashioned, French-inspired dishes. Sunday lunch is a real family affair and if you've only time for a fleeting visit, have a hearty pudding on the terrace. The wine list is a labour of love, featuring boutique Australian wines.

Closing times
Closed 25 December

Prices
Meals: £ 15 (weekdays)
and a la carte £ 22/44

Typical Dishes
Crab with home-
smoked salmon

Breast of guinea fowl
with pheasant sausage

Chocolate fondant,
pistachio ice cream

 5 mi northeast of Amersham signposted off the A 404.
Parking.

32 **Alford Arms**

**Frithsden,
HP1 3DD**
Tel.: (01442)864480
Website: www.alfordarmsfrithsden.co.uk

 🚬 *VISA* Ⓜ️Ⓒ 🅰️🅴

🍺 **Marlow Smuggler, Tring Side Pocket for a Toad and Sharp's Doom Bar**

Set among the network of paths that run across the Chilterns, this attractive Victorian pub is a popular destination for hikers – and when you're trying to squeeze your car into a tight space on the narrow country lane, arriving by foot may suddenly seem the better option. The pleasant garden flanks the peaceful village green – where you might spot the odd Morris dancer or two – and the warm bar welcomes four-legged friends as equally as their owners. The traditional menu has a strong British stamp and follows the seasons closely, so you're likely to find salads and fish in summer and comforting meat or game dishes in winter; these might include belly pork with sticky parsnips, a lamb and rabbit shepherd's pie or a tempting blackboard special.

Closing times
Closed 25-26 December
Prices
Meals: a la carte £ 21/37

Typical Dishes
Crispy tarragon & mustard lamb's breast
Asparagus pearl barley risotto
Caramelised brioche pain perdu

🚗 4.5 mi northwest of Hemel Hempstead signposted off A 4146. Parking.

33 | **Radcliffe Arms**

**31 Walsworth Rd,
Hitchin, SG4 9ST**
Tel.: (01462)456111
Website: www.radcliffearms.com

Buntingford Ales, Redemption Trinity and Nethergate Old Growler

Named after a renowned local family, the Radcliffe Arms enjoys its position as a true neighbourhood pub. It might have been modernised but this is still a friendly, relaxed place for the town's drinkers to gather, supping on gravity fed real ales or debating which of the 13 varieties of gin or 28 wines by the glass are best. The central bar is surrounded by a mix of wooden tables and chairs, and there's a small conservatory to the rear. Tasty cooking includes a few pub classics but it's more about well-presented, restaurant-style dishes here; you might find beetroot risotto, daube of beef or the locals' favourite, tiger prawns with chilli sauce. If you fancy it, you can even visit both before and after work, as they open at 8am for breakfast.

Closing times
Open daily

Prices
Meals: £ 12
(weekday lunch)
and a la carte £ 23/36

Typical Dishes
Carpaccio of venison
Slow-cooked blade of beef
Apple tart & caramel sauce

A short walk from the high street in the direction of the station. Limited parking.

34   Fox and Hounds

**2 High St,
Hunsdon, SG12 8NH**
Tel.: (01279)843999
Website: www.foxandhounds-hunsdon.co.uk

 Adnams Southwold Bitter, Broadside, Saffron Blonde and Tring Brewery Ales

London to Hertfordshire isn't the biggest of moves but swapping the hustle and bustle of crowded streets for the peace and quiet of the countryside is a move that childhood sweethearts James and Bianca – now husband and wife – believe was well worth making. If the weather's good, sit in the garden or on the terrace; if not, find a spot in the pleasant bar or dining room. Menus are concise, offering tasty, unfussy dishes that display a clear understanding of flavours. There are a few pub classics alongside more restaurant-style dishes such as salt and pepper squid or scallops with herb butter, and there's a popular seafood bar outside in the summer too. All of the pastas are homemade, they smoke their own fish and desserts are not to be missed.

Closing times
Closed 26 December,
Sunday dinner and Monday

Prices
Meals: £ 14 (weekdays)
and a la carte £ 23/36

Typical Dishes
Black pudding & fried
duck egg
Lemon sole & brown
shrimp butter
Buttermilk panna
cotta & rhubarb

Between Hertford and Harlow signposted off A 414, in the village centre. Parking.

35 **Sun at Northaw**

**1 Judges Hill,
Northaw, EN6 4NL**
Tel.: (01707)655507
Website: www.thesunatnorthaw.co.uk

**Buntingford Golden Plover, Adnams Broadside,
Nethergate Old Growler and Grain Harvest Moon**

This restored, part-16C pub sits by the village green. Deceptively spacious, it's contemporary in style, with a traditional edge. Cooking is original, so expect a wide range of dishes like crispy pigs' ears, spiced lamb pie, red gurnard or maybe even sea urchin. There's a strong regional slant here too: ingredients are sourced from the East of England, there are local ales and ciders behind the bar – as well as some English bottles on the wine list – and the toilet walls are even papered with Ordnance Survey maps of the area. Look out for wooden crates of veg scattered about the place and expect to see a chef coming to grab an onion or two. Service is friendly and the pub's affectionate dog, Smudge, may well wander over to welcome you too.

Closing times
Closed Sunday dinner and Monday except bank holidays when closed Tuesday

Prices
Meals: £ 13 (weekday lunch)/33 and a la carte £ 24/42

Typical Dishes
Grilled Suffolk razor clams
Braised Longhorn ox cheek
Quince & cobnut crumble

 Beside village green on main road through the village. Parking.

36   **Fox**

Willian,
SG6 2AE
Tel.: (01462)480233
Website: www.foxatwillian.co.uk

**Brancaster Best and The Wreck, Woodeforde's Wherry
and Adnams Southwold Bitter**

Set right in the heart of the village, opposite the green, is this smart, bright pub, which is proving extremely popular. Drinkers and diners vie for tables in the modern bar but there's also a contemporary, slightly colonial-style dining room and a sheltered terrace to choose from. Light wood floors and matching furniture feature throughout and the keener eye will notice a host of subtle references to Norfolk – home to the owner's other pubs. Dishes are modern with some Asian influences and there's a good choice of game in season; they also take their seafood seriously here, with the likes of herb-crusted Cromer crab and pan-fried golden ray on the menu. For those who just can't decide, 'The Fox Slate' for two provides the perfect solution.

Closing times
Open daily
Prices
Meals: a la carte £ 20/36

Typical Dishes
Crab with pear & cauliflower purée
Priors Hall pork sausage roll & belly
Rhubarb & custard doughnuts

3 mi northeast of Hitchin by A 505 and side road. Parking.

97

Blakeney

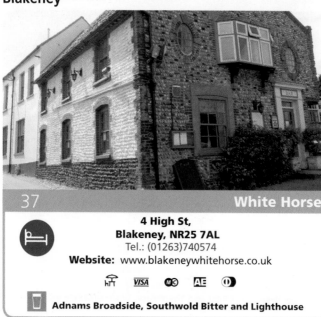

White Horse

4 High St,
Blakeney, NR25 7AL
Tel.: (01263)740574
Website: www.blakeneywhitehorse.co.uk

🛏 📶 **VISA** 🅜🅒 **AE** Ⓓ

🍺 **Adnams Broadside, Southwold Bitter and Lighthouse**

Maybe you've spent the afternoon bird-spotting along the beautiful north Norfolk coastline, or boating out to Blakeney Point to see the seals basking on the sandbanks. The invigorating sea air will no doubt have stoked your appetite, so head for something hearty to eat at this brick and flint former coaching inn. The same menu is served in all areas and changes according to what's freshly available and in season. Dishes might include British beef and oyster suet pudding or oven-roasted chicken breast, with tapas boards and seafood platters to share and desserts like iced rice pudding parfait with hot raspberry jam. Contemporary bedrooms come in various shapes and sizes; some are decorated in the bright blues and yellows of the seaside.

Closing times
Closed 25 December
booking advisable
Prices
Meals: a la carte £ 24/35
🛏 **9 rooms:** £ 80/170

Typical Dishes
Wiveton asparagus
with poached egg
Pork tenderloin with
paprika mash
White chocolate
parfait

🚗 *Just off the quay. Parking.*

Good Pub Food

Local Seafood

Stone Baked Pizza
eat in or take away

Brancaster Brewery Ales
from our own micro brewery

Children, muddy boots
and dogs welcome

38   **Jolly Sailors**

**Brancaster Staithe,
PE31 8BJ**
Tel.: (01485)210314
Website: www.jollysailorsbrancaster.co.uk

⛱   *VISA*   ⓜⓒ

**Brancaster Best and The Wreck, Grain Brewery Redwood
and Oak, Wolf Brewery Lupus**

'Eat, Drink and Be Jolly' is their motto and it's easy to do all three at this cosy, unaffected pub with its yesteryear charm; even the kids are sure to be kept happy with a play area, an ice cream hut and a special menu just for them. The pub is at least 250 years old and retains some rustic character in the form of tiled floors, wooden beams and wood-burning stoves. Cooking is straightforward and traditional, with blackboards listing everything from homemade scotch eggs or local crab to fish and chips or stone-baked pizza cooked to order in their own pizza oven. They don't take bookings in season, so make sure you get here early; nab one of the picnic benches in the garden and enjoy a pint of home-brewed Brancaster Best while you wait.

Closing times
Open daily

Prices
Meals: a la carte £ 19/25

Typical Dishes
Half a pint of smoked prawns
'Jolly' burger with chips
Sticky toffee pudding & vanilla ice cream

🚗 *Just off the quay. Parking.*

Brancaster Staithe

39

White Horse

**Brancaster Staithe,
PE31 8BY**
Tel.: (01485)210262
Website: www.whitehorsebrancaster.co.uk

hñ   *VISA*   **MC**

Brancaster Best and Oyster Catcher, Woodeforde's
Wherry and Adnams Ghost Ship

There's no denying that when sitting on the rear terrace or in the spacious conservatory, the views over the Brancaster Marshes and Scolt Head Island really make this pub. If you can't get a seat in either, panic not, as there's still the bar or the landscaped front terrace complete with its pleasant southerly aspect and patio heaters. On the all-day bar menu you'll find old favourites, a selection of tapas-style dishes and a few more ambitious offerings; while on the seasonally changing à la carte and daily specials, there'll be dishes such as dressed Cromer crab, confit Norfolk pork belly or marinated slow-cooked veal breast. Bedrooms have a crisp New England style; go for one of the Garden Rooms, as each comes with a private terrace.

Closing times
Open daily
booking essential
Prices
Meals: a la carte £ 24/33
🛏 **15 rooms:** £ 60/170

Typical Dishes
Seafood terrine
Local rolled rabbit
Banoffee pie

 On A 149 Hunstanton to Wells Rd. Parking.

40 **Hunny Bell**

**The Green,
Hunworth, NR24 2AA**
Tel.: (01263)712300
Website: www.thehoneybell.co.uk

 VISA MC AE

Woodforde's Wherry, Adnams Southwold Bitter and Wolf Lavender Honey

Part of the Animal Inns groups, this pub is the younger sister of the Wildebeest in Stoke Holy Cross – but it has a much more down-to-earth style. Inside it retains its stylish country interior which blends 18C features like wooden beams, exposed brickwork and flag floors with bold modern feature walls, leather sofas and a smart conservatory dining room. An appealing menu of pub classics means dishes like fish and chips or sausage and mash but we're not talking bog standard pub grub here; these are carefully crafted from local, seasonal produce – and even the bar snacks are homemade. Regular special events draw in plenty of regulars, as does the pleasant garden and the picnic benches on the patio; but make sure you book as they do get busy.

Closing times
Open daily
Prices
Meals: £ 19 and a la carte
£ 19/35

Typical Dishes
Norfolk dapple soufflé

Pork belly with apple & vanilla purée

Orange & cardamom crème brûlée

On the green. Parking.

Ingham

41

Ingham Swan

**Sea Palling Rd,
Ingham, NR12 9AB**
Tel.: (01692)581099
Website: www.theinghamswan.co.uk

 Woodforde's Ales

This attractive thatched pub, dating from the 14C and sitting in the shadow of a fine 11C church, lies in a small hamlet known for its delightful cricket field – all in all, a charming scene of English pastoral splendour. The cosy beamed interior is equally characterful and while this is clearly more of a dining pub, drinkers are still welcome. The one area which does break with tradition is the cooking, which is far from straightforward but clearly skilled; dishes are made up of many ingredients, albeit in classic combinations, and presentation adopts a contemporary style; even the fillet of beef is elevated to something a lot more interesting. Wine dinners and cookery classes are popular events. Bedrooms are too modest for us to recommend.

Closing times
Closed 25-26 December, Sunday dinner and Monday in winter
booking essential at dinner

Prices
Meals: £ 14 (weekday lunch)/28 and a la carte £ 26/47

Typical Dishes
Cromer crab
Salt marsh lamb, broad beans & girolles
Grand Marnier & milk chocolate mousse

 In the centre of the village. Parking.

42 **Walpole Arms**

**The Common,
Itteringham, NR11 7AR**
Tel.: (01263)587258
Website: www.thewalpolearms.co.uk

 **Woodforde's Wherry and Adnams Bitter, Broadside and
Ghost Ship**

This pretty 18C inn with carefully manicured gardens is set in a sleepy little village not far from Oulton, where the owners' family have been farming since the 1930s. The interior is surprisingly modern, yet nicely in keeping with the building's age: the beamed bar with its wood-burning stove provides a warm welcome and leads through to a more formal room with mock-bookshelf wallpaper. The menu champions local, seasonal ingredients, featuring produce from their farm and from just down the road. The chargrilled steaks, sea bass and herring roes are all surefire hits; you'll also find some influences from further afield, with the likes of taleggio and summer herb arancini or seeded halloumi with spiced couscous. Service is bright and bubbly.

Closing times
Closed 25 December
Prices
Meals: a la carte £ 18/38

Typical Dishes
Smoked salmon with
caper berries
Sea bass fillet
with baby leeks &
mash
Treacle tart with
vanilla ice cream

 In the centre of the village. Parking.

Norwich

43 Reindeer

**10 Dereham Rd,
Norwich, NR2 4AY**
Tel.: (01603)612995
Website: www.thereindeerpub.co.uk

**Thornbridge Jaipur, Elgood's Cambridge Bitter and
Oakham Inferno**

Despite being located on a busy main street just west of the ring road, the Reindeer's young owners seem to have found a niche for themselves and they have been steadily building up a keen local following. Inside, the pub has a good old rustic feel and, satisfyingly, plenty of space is kept aside for drinkers, who have 10 real ales and 12 keg beers, lagers and ciders to choose from. Cooking is straightforward and proudly British, employing lesser-used cuts in many of the dishes; bar snacks might include potted rabbit and duck hearts or beef dripping on toast, while the main menu features plenty of dishes for sharing. The old brewing room is now a venue for private groups and makes the perfect place for a celebration. Service is friendly.

Closing times
Closed 25-26 December and Monday

Prices
Meals: £ 23 and a la carte £ 20/33

Typical Dishes
Suffolk chorizo & clams

Lamb's heart, sage, bacon & celeriac

Ginger parkin with rhubarb jelly

 On A 1074 west of the city centre. Parking.

104

44 **Rose and Crown**

**Old Church Rd,
Snettisham, PE31 7LX**
Tel.: (01485)541382
Website: www.roseandcrownsnettisham.co.uk

 Adnams Southwold Bitter, Fuller's London Pride and Woodeforde's Wherry

Its warren of rooms and passageways, uneven floors and low beamed ceilings place the Rose and Crown squarely into the quintessentially English bracket of inns; and the bright dining rooms, the paved terrace and the impressive pirate ship for children in the garden add some 21C zing to the pub's 14C roots. Cooking is gutsy by nature and makes good use of local produce, with neatly presented dishes such as peppered tuna carpaccio or pan-roast salmon alongside trusty classics like sausage and mash or steak and chips. Service is efficient, they are well used to being busy and a good crowd of locals from the village can often be found enjoying a tipple at the bar. Bedrooms are quite a contrast to the rustic pub, being light and modern in style.

Closing times
Open daily
Prices
Meals: a la carte £ 19/35

16 rooms: £ 70/110

Typical Dishes
Sardines with cucumber
Plaice with Jersey Royals & sorrel butter
Gooseberry tart with elderflower sorbet

 In the middle of the village. Parking.

England • East of England • Norfolk

45

Wildebeest

**82-86 Norwich Rd,
Stoke Holy Cross, NR14 8QJ**
Tel.: (01508)492497
Website: www.animalinns.co.uk

Adnams Southwold Bitter and Marstons Burton Bitter

If you can't afford a safari, then a trip to the Wildebeest might be your next best bet, as it's unusually decked out in the style of an African savannah, with yellow walls, wooden wild animals and thick tree trunk tables. The young serving team are dressed in smart black dresses and act more as hostesses than waitresses, and the array of menus offer something a little bit different too. Cooking focuses mainly on modern British dishes but there are also some European influences to be found, with the likes of stone bass with parmentier potatoes, samphire, tomato fondue and salsa verde. Wednesday is steak night, when they offer various cuts from their own herd of cattle; the fore-rib presented on a wooden board is their signature dish.

Closing times
Open daily
booking essential

Prices
Meals: £ 15 (weekday lunch)/22 and a la carte £ 26/46

Typical Dishes
Hand-dived scallops with cauliflower

Canon of lamb with crayfish & mango salsa

Vanilla custard with poached rhubarb

 Just off the A 140, 5.5 mi south of Norwich. Parking.

England • East of England • Norfolk

46 — **Orange Tree**

**High St,
Thornham, PE36 6LY**
Tel.: (01485)512213
Website: www.theorangetreethornham.co.uk

Woodforde's Wherry, Adnams Southwold Bitter, Crouch Vale Brewers Gold

You're guaranteed a warm welcome at this popular 17C inn, as is your pooch, who can sit with you in the relaxed, open-fired bar while gnawing on a 'Scooby Snack'. If you fancy a more intimate affair, leave your four-legged friend at home and head for the contemporary restaurant, where wine racks temptingly adorn the walls. A vast array of menus offer everything from pub classics to restaurant-style dishes, via a list of vegetarian choices and daily specials. Flavours are vibrant and well-defined, and many dishes have an international feel, often arriving on boards or slates – you might find Brancaster crab spaghetti or garlic butter roast calves' liver. The desserts are a real highlight, and compact modern bedrooms complete the picture.

Closing times
Open daily
Prices
Meals: a la carte £ 25/42

🛏 **6 rooms:** £ 65/110

Typical Dishes
Wood pigeon breast & Jerusalem artichoke

Cod fillet with crab & lemon mash

Rhubarb tart, parfait & crumble

🚗 *4.5 mi northeast of Hunstanton on A 149. Parking.*

Thorpe Market

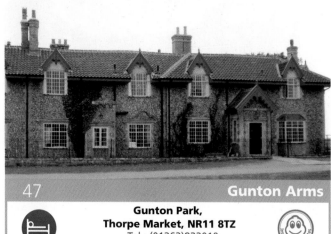

47   **Gunton Arms**

**Gunton Park,
Thorpe Market, NR11 8TZ**
Tel.: (01263)832010
Website: www.theguntonarms.co.uk

VISA   **MC**   **AE**

Adnams Broadside, Woodeforde's Wherry and Yetman's Red

Much of the 1,000 acre Gunton Estate has been lovingly restored over the last few decades, including the early 18C deer park, several ruined buildings and this charming pub. It has a super terrace for summer BBQs and an appealing mix of period furnishings and provocative modern art. Nibble on a venison sausage roll or Blythburgh pork crackling in the flag-floored bar – over a game of pool or darts – or head for a gnarled wood table beside the fireplace in the Elk Room. Here you can choose something cooked on the fire – such as an Aberdeen Angus steak – or from a selection of unfussy, fiercely seasonal British dishes like Barnsley lamb chop or mixed grill of Gunton fallow deer. Well-equipped bedrooms have a stylish, country house feel.

Closing times
Closed 25 December
booking advisable
Prices
Meals: a la carte £ 18/43
8 rooms: £ 85/165

Typical Dishes
Lamb's sweetbreads with wild garlic creamed spelt
Mixed grill of fallow deer with redcurrant jelly
Norfolk treacle and St Georges whisky tart

5.5 mi south of Cromer on A 149 a mile from Thorpe Market. Parking on edge of the estate.

48

Wiveton Bell

**Blakeney Rd,
Wiveton, NR25 7TL**
Tel.: (01263)740101
Website: www.wivetonbell.com

VISA **MC** **AE**

Woodeforde's Wherry, Yetman's Blue, North Norfolk Moongazer

With its lightly painted façade bearing a stylised scribble of its name, this place has all the hallmarks of a 'modernised' pub. Thankfully, this modernisation has been undertaken with style and care, so you'll find an attractive interior with beams, stripped floors, wood-burning stoves and a corner just for drinkers; as well as an airy restaurant and conservatory, a beautiful landscaped rear terrace and picnic benches out the front. The seasonal menu offers all the usual pub classics, carefully crafted from quality ingredients – many of which are locally sourced. You'll find bedrooms stylish and cosy; breakfast is continental but this could come as something of a relief considering the size of the portions served in the pub!

Closing times
Open daily
booking essential
Prices
Meals: a la carte £ 24/35

4 rooms: £ 80/140

Typical Dishes
Smoked trout & dill pâté

Belly pork with smoked bacon & calvados

Chocolate cake & mousse

Signposted off the A 149 just south of Blakeney. Parking.

Bromeswell

49 **British Larder**

**Orford Rd,
Bromeswell, IP12 2PU**
Tel.: (01394)460310
Website: www.britishlardersuffolk.co.uk

 Adnams Bitter and Broadside, Woodforde's Wherry

Once down-at-heel, this 17C pub has been updated in its look and transformed into a beacon for Suffolk produce, courtesy of its owners who have a passion for all things local. They even encourage their customers to donate produce to the pub – a blackboard behind the bar will list what 'glut' is required and any produce brought in is weighed and an agreed price is credited against the customer's next meal. The kitchen handles these ingredients deftly and will sometimes use modern techniques such as water-baths. Deli sharing boards feature at lunch, while dinner is more structured. The pub itself is smart and contemporary but still has an appealingly rustic edge. The enthusiastic owners also hold regular wine events and cookery classes.

Closing times
Closed Sunday dinner and Monday January-March

Prices
Meals: £ 18 (weekday lunch) and a la carte £ 24/67

Typical Dishes
Chicken & rabbit terrine
Truffled guinea fowl with braised hispi cabbage
Bitter chocolate crémeux

 2.5 mi northeast of Woodbridge on the A 1152. Parking.

50

Castle Inn

**35 Earsham St,
Bungay, NR35 1AF**
Tel.: (01986)892283
Website: www.thecastleinn.net

Earl Soham Victoria Bitter, Cliff Quay Sea Dog and Calvor's Premium

This sky-blue pub's open-plan interior includes dining areas and an intimate rear bar – the perfect spot for a coffee or a flick through a magazine. Cooking is fresh, simple and seasonal, and while lunch might see burger and chips or creamy risotto verde alongside doorstop sandwiches, the evening menu might include slow-cooked salt marsh lamb shoulder or pheasant breast wrapped in Parma ham. The Innkeeper's Platter is a perennial favourite and showcases local produce, including a great pickle made by the 'Rockin' Grannies'; keep an eye out for the cake stands too, with their homemade cakes and cookies. Themed evenings include 'pie and wine' night and 'film and food' night – complete with popcorn. Bedrooms are homely, warm and comfortable.

Closing times
Closed 25 December and Monday in winter

Prices
Meals: £ 16 (lunch) and a la carte £ 19/34

4 rooms: £ 65/95

Typical Dishes
Beetroot & whisky cured salmon gravadlax
Sichuan & marmalade pork belly
Deconstructed millionaire's shortbread

In the centre of town. Parking.

Fressingfield

51

Fox & Goose Inn

**Church Rd,
Fressingfield, IP21 5PB**
Tel.: (01379)586247
Website: www.foxandgoose.net

VISA **MC**

Adnams Best Bitter

This attractive 16C pub stands opposite the village green, and was built – and is still owned by – the 14C church next door. Inside it delivers all you would expect of a pub its age: wooden beams, tiled floors and open fireplaces, while for those who enjoy a more alfresco experience, there's a pleasant terrace overlooking the duck pond on the green. Choose an East Anglian ale from the casks behind the bar to sup alongside a good old classic pub dish or opt for a more restaurant-style offering from the specials list. If you fancy an altogether more sophisticated experience, however, head upstairs to the comfy lounge and linen-clad dining room, where dishes are modern with touches of originality and you'll find many more ingredients on the plate.

Closing times
Closed 2 weeks early January, 25-30 December and Monday
booking advisable
Prices
Meals: £ 20/45

Typical Dishes
Butternut squash with parmesan Royal
Sea bass with black truffle dumplings & spiced apple
Rhubarb with iced white chocolate parfait

By the village green. Parking.

52

Swan

**The Street,
Monks Eleigh, IP7 7AU**
Tel.: (01449)741391
Website: www.monkseleigh.com

VISA

Adnams Ales and various guest ales

The Swan's owners may originally hail from the north, but they have fully embraced their adopted home of East Anglia, and the wealth of produce the area offers provides ample inspiration for the frequently changing, seasonal menu of generous, flavourful dishes. Depending on the ingredients fresh in, these might include smoked haddock fish pie with creamy mash or lamb tagine with apricots, almonds and couscous, and – thanks to Nigel's background – they often include a smattering of Italian influences. Everything is made on-site; from the bread and terrines to the classic British puddings and ice creams. The thatched pub's beamed interior is fresh and bright, and the bubbly Carol serves locals and newcomers alike with warmth and efficiency.

Closing times
Closed 2 weeks July-August, Christmas, Sunday dinner and Monday

Prices
Meals: £ 14 (weekdays) and a la carte £ 23/35

Typical Dishes
Seared smoked salmon with guacamole
Pan-fried guinea fowl with wild mushrooms
Panna cotta with red fruits

 3.5 mi southeast of Lavenham on A 1141. Parking.

Snape

53   Crown Inn

**Bridge Rd,
Snape, IP17 1SL**
Tel.: (01728)688324
Website: www.snape-crown.co.uk

VISA *MC*

Adnams Ales

These days any pub worth its salt is serving produce sourced from the local area, but there aren't many who can claim to provide most of the meat for their menus – as well as the majority of the fruit and veg. The affable young owners of this characterful 15C former smugglers' inn raise pigs, goats, lambs, calves, ducks, turkeys, chickens and quails in the fields at the back. They'll even show you around if you ask nicely – although it's probably best to wait until you've eaten your calves' liver before taking a tour. It's easy to find a dish which appeals on the regularly changing menu; perhaps home-reared pork terrine, braised faggots or a cured meat platter. Staying the night? Rustic bedrooms have beamed ceilings and sloping floors.

Closing times
Open daily
Prices
Meals: a la carte £ 19/37
2 rooms: £ 70/90

Typical Dishes
Pork terrine with homemade chutney

Rib-eye with flat mushrooms & confit tomato

Carrot cake with goat's milk ice cream

 On B 1069, just north of Snape Maltings. Parking.

54

Crown

**90 High St,
Southwold, IP18 6DP**
Tel.: (01502)722275
Website: www.adnams.co.uk

☒ *VISA* ⓂⒸ

Adnams Ales

This 17C former coaching inn sits on the high street of a charming town, near to the brewery and only a hop, skip and a jump away from the sea. Its relaxed, traditionally styled bar and dining room are often buzzing with diners and the small, oak-panelled, nautically themed locals bar is a great place for a leisurely pint or two of Adnams of an afternoon. The same modern, seasonal menu is served throughout: choose from fresh, full-flavoured dishes like Dingley Dell ham hock terrine, Deben mussels with Broadside bacon and fries or Emmerdale Farm Red Poll beef short rib with garlic mash. Individual bedrooms have a contemporary, New England style and offer extras like robes and shortbread: those towards the rear are the quietest; 11 is the best.

Closing times
Open daily
Prices
Meals: a la carte £ 28/54
15 rooms: £ 135/255

Typical Dishes
Asparagus & pheasant egg
Roast rump of lamb with parsley root purée
Praline finger

🚗 *In the town centre. Parking.*

Stoke-by-Nayland

55 Crown

**Stoke-by-Nayland,
CO6 4SE**
Tel.: (01206)262001
Website: www.crowninn.net

VISA **MC** **AE** **D**

Adnams Southwold Bitter, Woodeforde's Wherry, Crouch Vale Brewers Gold and guest ales

If you find the newspapers on the bar too depressing, the wine list here is a great read: a well-priced, top quality selection with over 25 wines available by the glass – bottles are displayed in a glass-fronted room and can also be bought to take home. Globally influenced menus feature the latest produce from local farms and estates, while blackboards list seafood specials sourced from the east coast. Dishes might include game terrine, king prawn linguine or a locally reared rump steak – and each dish handily has a suggested wine match. Set in a great spot overlooking the Box and Stour river valleys, this smart pub also offers spacious, stylish bedrooms. All have king or super king sized beds, while some feature French windows and terraces.

Closing times
Closed 25-26 December
Prices
Meals: a la carte £ 18/34
🛏 **11 rooms:** £ 95/225

Typical Dishes
Pan-fried boneless quail

Lamb cutlets with wilted spinach & chorizo

Triple chocolate mousse

 8 mi north of Colchester by A 134. In the centre of the village. Parking.

56 **Ufford Crown**

**High St,
Ufford, IP13 6EL**
Tel.: (01394)461030
Website: www.theuffordcrown.com

 Adnams Southwold Bitter, Earl Soham Brandeston Gold, Cliff Quay Full Steam Ahead

Close to a nursery of the same name, you'll find this freshly painted former coaching inn, offering a warm welcome to one and all. A few steps lead down to a small walled terrace and the choice of two doors – one opening into the restaurant and the other, into the bar, which consists of a series of narrow rooms. It's run by enthusiastic husband and wife team, Max and Polly, and the head chef is Polly's brother, Will. Menus change daily, with dishes ranging from a crispy pork belly sandwich, lamb shank shepherd's pie or homemade beef and paprika sausages to potted crab, chargrilled duck hearts or rib of Ketley beef for 4 to share. Portions are generous and service is keen; finish with a tasty Valrhona brownie or a maple and pecan tart.

Closing times
Closed Tuesday
Prices
Meals: a la carte £ 20/34

Typical Dishes
Duck hearts with hoisin dressing
Braised beef with green peppercorn sauce
Chargrilled pineapple with rum & raisin ice cream

3 mi northwest of Woodbridge on B 1348.

Walberswick

57 **Anchor**

**Main St,
Walberswick, IP18 6UA**
Tel.: (01502)722112
Website: www.anchoratwalberswick.com

VISA **M©**

Adnams Broadside and Spindrift

Unusually for a pub, The Anchor is housed in an Arts and Crafts building. It's a welcoming, relaxing place, run by an enthusiastic, friendly team; there's a pleasant terrace and a path leading directly from the garden to the beach. But enough about the pub, for it's all about the food, wine and beer here. Owners Sophie and Mark are passionate about sourcing local, seasonal produce – with some ingredients even coming from their own allotment. Dishes are prepared with real care and global flavours punctuate the menu, so alongside British classics like fish and chips, you'll find Asian dressings, Indian spicing, tapas platters and risottos. Stay in one of the comfy chalet bedrooms and breakfast like a king on smoked haddock and jugged kippers.

Closing times
Closed 25 December
Prices
Meals: a la carte £ 26/33
10 rooms: £ 110/150

Typical Dishes
Pan-fried scallops
Mussel & saffron linguine
Lemon meringue roulade

In the centre of the village. Parking.

58 — Westleton Crown

**The Street,
Westleton, IP17 3AD**
Tel.: (01728)648777
Website: www.westletoncrown.co.uk

 VISA *MC* *AE*

Adnams Southwold Bitter

This good-looking, 17C former coaching inn, set in a pretty little village, delivers exactly what you'd expect and a little bit more. The bar welcomes you with its beams and open fires but, venture a little further in, and you'll find an attractive and surprisingly modern conservatory, as well as an appealing terrace and garden. The same seasonally pertinent menu is offered throughout, so you can eat your trio of Blythburgh pork or saddle of venison wherever you choose. If you're counting the pennies, come at lunchtime, when you'll find a second menu offering the likes of sausage and mash or Suffolk lamb stew. Those staying overnight will find that the bedrooms come in a crisp, uncluttered style and have particularly luxurious bathrooms.

Closing times
Open daily
Prices
Meals: a la carte £ 24/37
🛏 **34 rooms:** £ 90/215

Typical Dishes
Pan-fried quail with braised lentils

Breast of Gressingham duck with rösti potato

Chilled chocolate and salted caramel tart

🚗 *3 mi east of Yoxford signed off A 12. In the centre of the village. Parking.*

119

Whepstead

59   **White Horse**

Rede Rd,
Whepstead, IP29 4SS
Tel.: (01284)735760
Website: www.whitehorsewhepstead.co.uk

   VISA

 Adnams Ales

Everyone assembles in the attractive bar to look at the large wall menu, where each dish is displayed on a separate blackboard; this is the hub of this cheerfully run, 17C village pub, owned by a couple who established their reputation at The Beehive in nearby Horringer. There are three further areas to choose from: to the left, a beamed and characterful room which fills up quickly; to the right the brighter Gallery, so named as it shows local artists' work; and, at the back, a room for larger parties which leads out to the spacious garden and terrace. The kitchen's strength lies in the more conventional dishes like liver and bacon, grilled kippers and the pub's own homemade sausages; with treacle tart a favourite for dessert.

Closing times
Closed 1 week January, 25-26 December and Sunday dinner

Prices
Meals: a la carte £ 22/30

Typical Dishes
Jellied ham hock terrine with piccalilli

Seafood stew with tomato herb broth

Bread & butter pudding

Well signposted off the A 143, 4.5 mi south of Bury St Edmunds. Parking.

60

Crown

**Thoroughfare,
Woodbridge, IP12 1AD**
Tel.: (01394)384242
Website: www.thecrownatwoodbridge.co.uk

Adnams and Meantime ales

With its farmers' markets and a main street full of restaurants and cafés, the delightful riverside town of Woodbridge is up there with the best of them when it comes to foodie credentials; and all the more so since the arrival of the Crown. After a top-to-toe 21C makeover, this colourfully painted pub retains little evidence of its 17C roots; a glass-roofed, granite-floored bar sits at its centre, with four smart dining areas set around it. Bedrooms are stylish, with good facilities and service is polite, friendly and copes well when busy. The seasonal menu lists mainly modern classics; perhaps roast local partridge or Suffolk honey ham, with plenty of shellfish, including Deben oysters and mussels from the new beds.

Closing times
Open daily
Prices
Meals: £ 24 and a la carte £ 24/40
10 rooms: £ 90/180

Typical Dishes
Grilled Deben oysters with chorizo
Cider-braised rabbit
Plum rice pudding

At town centre crossroads. Parking.

Twenty-first century London may truly be called the definitive world city. Time zones radiate from Greenwich, and global finances zap round the Square Mile, while a vast smorgasbord of restaurants is the equal of anywhere on the planet. A stunning diversity of population now calls the capital its home, mixing and matching its time between the urban sprawl and enviable acres of green open space. From Roman settlement to banking centre to capital of a 19C empire, London's pulse has rarely missed a beat. Along the way, expansion has gobbled up surrounding villages, a piecemeal cocktail with its ingredients stirred to create the likes of Kensington and Chelsea, Highgate and Hampstead, Twickenham and Richmond. Apart from the great range of restaurants, London boasts over three and a half thousand pubs, many of which now see accomplished, creative cooking as an integral part of their existence and appeal. And you can find them sprinkled right the way across from zones one to five…

England • London

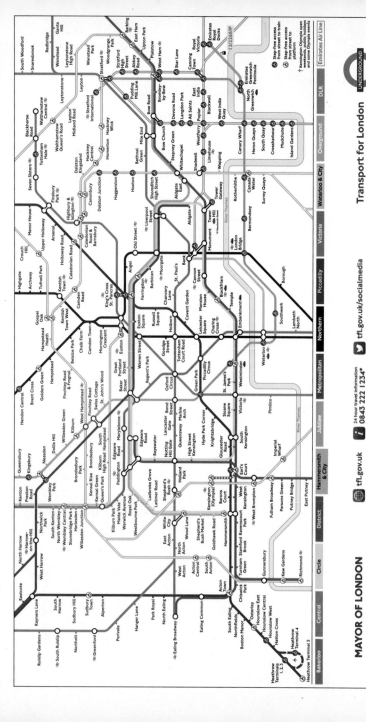

1 Paradise by way of Kensal Green

**19 Kilburn Ln,
Kensal Green, W10 4AE**
Tel.: (020)89690098
Website: www.theparadise.co.uk

 Wells Bombardier

Their slogan is 'they love to party at Paradise' and, frankly, who can blame them? This is so much more than just a pub, it's a veritable fun palace – upstairs plays host to everything from comedy nights to film clubs and you can even 'host your own roast' with friends in a private room. If you're coming in to eat then grab a squashy sofa in the Reading Room off the bar and share some of the terrific snacks; or sit in the dining room where the cooking is showy but satisfyingly robust. Whether it's potted meats, terrines, chateaubriand or poached turbot, it's clear that this is a very capable kitchen. The atmosphere throughout is great and helped along in no small way by a clued-up team who know their food.

Closing times
dinner only and lunch Saturday and Sunday

Prices
Meals: a la carte £ 26/31

Typical Dishes
Bury black pudding with potato purée

Skate wing with spinach, cockles & mussels

Blood orange 'Jaffa cake'

 ⊖ *Kensal Green. On-street parking.*

Brent

England • London

2

Salusbury

**50-52 Salusbury Rd,
Queen's Park, NW6 6NN**
Tel.: (020)73283286
Website: www.thesalusbury.co.uk

 VISA **MC**

 Greene King Abbot Ale

When your local pub is owned by someone with a passion for Italian food and reggae then you know it's going to be somewhere a little different. The central bar is the demarcation point: the louche turn left for loud music and a dimly lit bar; the hungry head for the incongruously demure looking dining room on the right. There's an impressive degree of authenticity to the Italian cooking; try one of the tasty salads like black radish with pomegranate and pecorino then go for their classic pappardelle with duck ragu. There are more fish dishes on the menu these days but what hasn't changed is portion size – you'll never reach dessert. If, however, you think you may be hungry again one day then call in at their well-stocked foodstore next door.

Closing times
Closed 25 December
booking essential

Prices
Meals: £ 25/40
and a la carte £ 19/35

Typical Dishes
Foie gras & chicken liver terrine
Sea bass baked in salt crust
Sticky toffee pudding

 ⊖ *Queen's Park. On-street parking.*

3   **Bull & Last**

**168 Highgate Rd,
Dartmouth Park, NW5 1QS**
Tel.: (020)72673641
Website: www.thebullandlast.co.uk

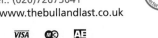

 Redemption Big Chief, London Fields Hackney Hopster and Bull & Last Journeyman

Dartmouth Park locals know a good thing when they see it and The Bull and Last, always full of character and life, is most certainly a good thing. If you haven't booked, it's still worth trying your luck as they keep the odd table back – mind you, with enticing bar snacks like pig's trotter wontons and soft shell crab tempura, you may simply find happiness at the bar ordering some of these to go with your pint. The cooking is gloriously robust and generous and the menu mainly British with some pasta dishes thrown in. The kitchen knows its way around an animal too – the charcuterie boards are very popular. Puds are traditional; cheese is in good order and the homemade ice creams are good. And where else can you get marrowbone for your dog?

Closing times
Closed 24-25 December
booking essential
Prices
Meals: a la carte £ 22/44

Typical Dishes
Chicken livers with chestnuts
Daube of beef with polenta & broccoli
Sticky toffee pudding

 Tufnell Park. On-street parking.

Camden

4 **Lady Ottoline**

11a Northington St, Bloomsbury, WC1N 2JF
Tel.: (020)78310008
Website: www.theladyottoline.com

Sambrook's Wandle Ale, Sharp's Doom Bar and Dark Star Hophead

Apart from some repair work on the cornicing and the tiled floor, this substantial red-brick Victorian pub is largely unchanged from when it was called The Kings Arms. The menus in the packed and slightly chaotic ground floor bar and the Queen Anne style upstairs dining room are not hugely different: cold winter nights see dishes like braised pig cheeks with lentils or venison haunch with squash purée. The kitchen takes more care with its cooking than one expects and dishes deliver on flavour. There's also a large selection of wine by the glass. This is the second pub for this husband and wife team and a sister to Princess of Shoreditch. It is named after the society hostess who was a friend to the Bloomsbury set.

Closing times
Closed 24 December-
2 January and bank holidays
Prices
Meals: a la carte £ 22/38

Typical Dishes
Sautéed chicken livers
Hake & Morecambe Bay shrimps
Warm chocolate & walnut cake

 ⊖ *Chancery Lane. On-street parking.*

5 · **Wells**

**30 Well Walk,
Hampstead, NW3 1BX**
Tel.: (020)77943785
Website: www.thewellshampstead.co.uk

 VISA **MC** **AE**

Adnams Broadside and Black Sheep

The Wells is named after Chalybeate Well which, in 1698, was given to the poor of Hampstead – it's about 30 yards away, next to that BMW. Equidistant between Heath and High Street, this handsome pub is split in two: downstairs is the busier, more relaxed part of the operation, while upstairs you'll find a formally dressed dining room. Apart from a couple of extra grilled dishes downstairs, the two areas share a menu, which is cleverly balanced to satisfy all appetites from spirited dog walker to leisurely shopper. Salads or seared scallops can be followed by sea bass, assorted pasta or duck confit; puds are good and they do a decent crumble. Add a commendable range of ales and wines and you have a pub for all seasons.

Closing times
Open daily
Prices
Meals: a la carte £ 22/40

Typical Dishes
Tomato, watermelon, feta & pumpkin seed salad

Plaice with caper, lemon & parsley butter

Apple & rhubarb crumble

Hampstead. Parking in Well Rd.

Camden

6 **York & Albany**

**127-129 Parkway,
Camden Town, NW1 7PS**
Tel.: (020)73883344
Website: www.gordonramsay.com/yorkandalbany

Meantime Ales

These days things are more egalitarian down at the York & Albany, a handsome 1820s John Nash coaching inn rescued by Gordon Ramsay after lying virtually derelict for years. Gone is the separation of bar and restaurant dining – you are now offered the same menu wherever you want to sit, whether that's in the bar, the back restaurant or downstairs next to the open kitchen. The menu has also been made a little more inclusive and now includes wood-fired pizzas and pasta dishes alongside more adventurous choices like lamb shoulder with braised celery and duck with hispi cabbage. It works well because the kitchen treats a burger with the same respect as they do a rib-eye steak, although service can still wobble at times. The bedrooms have character.

Closing times
Open daily
booking essential
Prices
Meals: £ 22 (weekday lunch) and a la carte £ 28/50

10 rooms: £ 205/387

Typical Dishes
Asparagus with crispy duck & morels
Fillet of sea bass with razor clams
Hazelnut & tonka bean cheesecake

 Camden Town. On-street parking.

England • London

7

Jugged Hare

**42 Chiswell St,
City of London, EC1Y 4SA**
Tel.: (020)76140134
Website: www.thejuggedhare.com

VISA MC AE ◑

 **Sambrook's Jugged Hare Pale Ale**

The famous 18C recipe created by Hannah Glasse, the UK's first domestic goddess, provided the inspiration for the renaming of this Grade II listed pub, previously known as The King's Head. It's an apt name because committed vegetarians may feel ill at ease – and not just because of the collection of glass cabinets in the bar which showcase the art of taxidermy. The atmospheric and appealingly noisy dining room, which has a large open kitchen running down one side, specialises in stout British dishes, with Denham Estate venison, Yorkshire guinea fowl and Cumbrian Longhorn steaks from the rotisserie and the grill being the highlights. If the main course doesn't fill you, puddings like treacle tart or bread and butter pudding will.

Closing times
Open daily
booking advisable
Prices
Meals: £ 27/48
and a la carte £ 26/61

Typical Dishes
Lamb's liver & kidneys
Mutton with creamed cabbage & bacon
Baked egg custard

⊖ Barbican. Limited on-street parking.

8
Duke of Sussex

**75 South Par,
Acton Green, W4 5LF**
Tel.: (020)87428801
Website: www.realpubs.co.uk

**Sharp's Ales, Twickenham Fine Ale and Triple fff
Hallelujah**

Perhaps it's part of the plan but the Duke of Sussex seems like a typical London pub, even from the front bar, but step through into the dining room and you'll be in what was once a variety theatre from the time when this was a classic gin palace, complete with proscenium arch, glass ceiling and chandeliers. If that wasn't unusual enough, you could then find yourself eating cured meats or fabada, as the menu has a strong Spanish influence. Traditionalists can still get their steak pies and treacle tart but it's worth being more adventurous and trying the sardines, the paella and the crema Catalana. This is a fun, enthusiastically run and bustling pub and the kitchen's enthusiasm is palpable. On Mondays it's BYO; Sunday is quiz night.

Closing times
Open daily
Prices
Meals: a la carte £ 18/33

Typical Dishes
Razor clams with spring onions
Hake with romesco sauce
Chocolate caramel tart

 Chiswick Park. Parking on adjacent street.

9 **The Grove**

**The Green,
Ealing, W5 5QX**
Tel.: (020)85672439
Website: www.thegrovew5.co.uk

VISA *MC* *AE*

Sambrook's Wandle Ale, Greene King St Edmunds and Truman's Runner

It's hard to avoid this beast of a place in central Ealing but then, why would you? It may be brewery owned and have undergone a typical London gastropub makeover, but it'll hit the spot – whether you're out with friends or after a candle-lit dinner. There's a huge front terrace dominated by drinkers but inside it's spilt into half-bar, half-restaurant; you can eat anywhere but the restaurant at the back is the quieter choice. The menus change monthly – lunch is pretty standard issue, but at dinner the skilful kitchen celebrates its classical roots. The easy-to-eat dishes add a distinctive French accent to the largely British ingredients; desserts are mostly crowd-pleasing classics and are equally satisfying.

Closing times
Open daily
Prices
Meals: £ 23/33

Typical Dishes
Asparagus & pea risotto
Pan-fried sea bream with sauce vierge
Vanilla parfait, strawberries & shortbread

⊖ Ealing Broadway. Free on-street parking after 7.30pm.

10

Empress

**130 Lauriston Rd,
Victoria Park, Hackney, E9 7LH**
Tel.: (020)85335123
Website: www.empresse9.co.uk

 **Camden Brewery Ales, Sambrook's Wandle and East
London Brewery Foundation**

The name of this 1850s pub was changed from the Empress of India as some customers arrived expecting chicken tikka – information which will dishearten history teachers everywhere. Queen Victoria has been demoted to the Empress of E9 but then everything is about being 'local' these days and that includes this re-launched pub. Sourdough comes from the baker down the road and their butcher and fishmonger are within walking distance; the menu is pleasingly seasonal and the cooking is several notches above usual pub fare. Dishes like risotto made with pearl barley and feta, or lamb's liver with lentils demonstrate that this is a kitchen with confidence and ability. Prices are kept in check and Sunday lunch is a very languid affair.

Closing times
Closed 25 December and Monday lunch except bank holidays

Prices
Meals: £ 10 (weekdays) and a la carte £ 23/28

Typical Dishes
Snails, bone marrow & wild garlic

Pork belly, spelt, hazelnuts & sage

Brown sugar panna cotta

England • London

11   Prince Arthur

**95 Forest Rd,
Hackney, E8 3BH**
Tel.: (020)72499996
Website: www.theprincearthurlondonfields.com

 Adnams and Sambrook's Ales

Those who judge by first impressions will probably walk on by as this slightly scruffy corner pub would struggle to entice anyone on looks alone. To be honest, the inside isn't much keener on the eye, apart from the stuffed animals and the postcard collection, but then this isn't about appearances, more about good food and convivial company. Sit anywhere in the U-shaped room and the amiable staff will be quick to come over. The menu reads appealingly: smoked salmon, terrines, fish and chips, sausage and mash – but the cooking is done with unexpected care and more than a little skill; fish from Billingsgate is handled particularly deftly. Just thinking about the deep-fried jam or cherry sandwich for dessert will be enough to seal an artery.

Closing times
Closed 25 December
dinner only and lunch Saturday-Sunday
Prices
Meals: a la carte £ 25/39

Typical Dishes
Cashel Blue & artichoke salad
Bream with sautéed gnocchi
Elderflower panna cotta

 Bethnal Green. On-street parking.

12   **Princess of Shoreditch**

**76-78 Paul St,
Shoreditch, EC2A 4NE**
Tel.: (020)77299270
Website: www.theprincessofshoreditch.com

**Sambrook's Pumphouse Pale Ale, East London Brewing
Co Foundation Bitter and Truman's Runner**

Apparently there has been a pub on this corner site since 1742 but it is doubtful many of the previous incarnations were as busy or as pleasant as the Princess is today. The owners have always been very hands-on and their welcoming attitude has rubbed off on their friendly staff; the pub comes with an appealing buzz and, to cap it all off, the prices are more than fair. It's set over two floors and the same menu is served throughout – although you can book upstairs. The menu changes daily, and sometimes between services; the food appears quite simple but the best dishes are those that come with a satisfying rustic edge, whether that's the buttery goose rillettes, the chicken pie with terrific mash or the tender pulled pork.

Closing times
Closed 24-27 December
booking essential
Prices
Meals: a la carte £ 23/30

Typical Dishes
Loch Duart smoked
salmon & marinated
beets
Pork belly & black
pudding croquettes
Sticky toffee pudding

 ⊖ *Old Street. On-street parking meters.*

13   **Anglesea Arms**

35 Wingate Rd, Hammersmith, W6 0UR
Tel.: (020)87491291
Website: www.anglesea-arms.com

 Otter Ales, Timothy Taylor Golden Best and Harveys Sussex Best Bitter

While the menu here changes daily and is largely governed by what its suppliers bring, some aspects remain constant: there's always pig's head terrine, prawns, a tart and a seasonal salad. Fish and game are handled well and dishes are pleasingly robust – try the delicious Orb of Joy: braised onion which comes with roast partridge. The treacle tart has a cult following but the ice creams and sorbets are delicious too. The pub has a cluttered, very lived-in look and gets properly crowded but has a refreshing honesty, with staff providing thoughtful advice. Look for its windows etched with the inviting words 'Pies and Hams' and 'Stout and Oysters'. Above the door is 'Mon Mam Cymru', Mother of Wales, as the Isle of Anglesey is known.

Closing times
Closed 25-26 December
bookings not accepted
Prices
Meals: a la carte £ 24/40

Typical Dishes
Asparagus with duck egg & summer truffle

Megrim sole with Jersey Royals

Chocolate & ale cake

⊖ Ravenscourt Park. On-street parking.

England • London

14 **Crabtree**

**4 Rainville Rd,
Hammersmith, W6 9HA**
Tel.: (020)73853929
Website: www.thecrabtreeW6.co.uk

 Guest ales

On a sunny day few things in life beat being by the river in a London pub and The Crabtree certainly makes the most of its location. Its beer garden, with its barbeque-style menu, can seat over 80, while the dining room boasts its own terrace overlooking the river – and if you haven't yet booked for lunch on Boat Race day then you're probably already too late. A variety of ploys are used to fill the equally large interior of this Victorian beauty, from BYO Mondays to quiz nights on Tuesdays. For lunch the selection varies from ciabatta sarnies to shepherd's pie; the evening menu is more adventurous. The kitchen does things properly – parfaits and terrines are highlights and fish is perfectly timed – but vegetarians are also looked after.

Closing times
Open daily
Prices
Meals: a la carte £ 24/35

Typical Dishes
Foie gras & chicken liver parfait
West Devon lamb rump
Summer berries with lemon syllabub

15 — Dartmouth Castle

**26 Glenthorne Rd,
Hammersmith, W6 0LS**
Tel.: (020)87483614
Website: www.thedartmouthcastle.co.uk

 Timothy Taylor Landlord and Sharp's Doom Bar

Plenty of locals pop into this Victorian pub just for a drink so you may find one of them has nabbed your table. It's worth biding your time though, as it's better than decamping to the upstairs room as the atmosphere up there isn't a patch on the bustling ground floor with its worn-in look and etched mirrors. Simply hand over your credit card and order at the bar to enjoy dishes from the well-priced and quite lengthy Mediterranean-influenced menu which is the same lunch and dinner. The antipasti platter for two is a winner and pasta dishes appear to come in two sizes – big or even bigger. The blackboard wine list is also a cut above your average pub list and uses the reliable Italian orientated merchant Liberty.

Closing times
Closed 23 December-
2 January and Saturday
lunch

Prices
Meals: a la carte £ 20/33

Typical Dishes
Cod & potato fritters
Grilled lamb skewer
with harissa
Apple & rhubarb
crumble

Hammersmith. On-street parking.

Hammersmith and Fulham

16 **Hampshire Hog**

**227 King St,
Hammersmith, W6 9JT**
Tel.: (020)87483391
Website: www.thehampshirehog.com

 Caledonian Ales

For many years the owners ran The Engineer, a much loved pub in Primrose Hill, before their lease ran out. They subsequently moved west, took over what was the Ruby Grand, did it up and gave it back its original name. The Hampshire Hog is a big old place and calls itself a 'pub and pantry' – the pantry is open for breakfast, tea and cakes and doubles as a private party room; the bright bar serves cocktails and snacks like scotch quail eggs and pork boards; and the large dining room focuses on freshness and seasonality. So, in spring, that means asparagus or broad bean risotto; a choice of daily salads and popular main courses like marinated leg of lamb. Like The Engineer, The 'Hog' comes with a terrific terrace and garden.

Closing times
Closed 24-25 December and Sunday dinner

Prices
Meals: £ 15/18 and a la carte £ 23/42

Typical Dishes
Terrine of salmon with smoked mackerel
Casserole of cod with mussels & clams
Orange & star anise crème brûlée

 Ravenscourt Park. On-street parking.

17   **Harwood Arms**

**Walham Grove,
Fulham, SW6 1QP**
Tel.: (020)73861847
Website: www.harwoodarms.com

 Sambrook's Wandle and Bath Gem

As this unremarkable looking Victorian pub is owned by the experienced triumvirate of Brett Graham of The Ledbury, Mike Robinson of The Pot Kiln and Edwin Vaux of the eponymous brewery, there was always a chance something special was going to happen inside. The menu and the environment chime perfectly together because the kitchen, which is undoubtedly a very skilled one, never forgets this is a pub and not a restaurant. The cooking is thoughtfully considered and carefully crafted but there's nothing too prissy or pretty – this is all about great British flavours. If there's game on the menu – perhaps slow-cooked shoulder for two or a perfectly judged T-bone of fallow deer – then grab it as Mike is a keen shot and Berkshire is his larder.

Closing times
Closed 24-27 December, 1 January and Monday lunch
booking essential

Prices
Meals: £ 20 (weekday lunch) and a la carte £ 35/43

Typical Dishes
Crisp pheasant eggs & ham hock

Wood pigeon with Yorkshire rhubarb

Bramley apple & cinnamon ice cream

 Fulham Broadway. On-street parking with restrictions.

18

Havelock Tavern

**57 Masbro Rd,
Brook Grn, Hammersmith, W14 0LS**
Tel.: (020)76035374
Website: www.havelocktavern.com

**Sambrook's Wandle Ale, Greene King Old Speckled Hen
and Sharp's Doom Bar**

The word 'gastropub' was first coined in the early '90s to describe pubs that offered great food while remaining true to their roots – and was never about pubs masquerading as restaurants. The warm and friendly Havelock Tavern was at the vanguard of this movement and little about its lived-in look has changed here over the years, which is probably why it's as busy as ever. Put your name down for a table at the bar, order a drink and then place your order from the blackboard menu which changes with each service and reflects the seasons. The food is comforting and prices fair while the freshness is underlined by the fact that dishes often run out; there could be a grilled mackerel or goujons of coley alongside a tagine or roast pork belly.

Closing times
Closed 25-26 December
Prices
Meals: a la carte £ 19/29

Typical Dishes
Red mullet with ginger
lime dressing
Bavette steak with
garlic & tarragon
butter
Polenta cake & lemon
sorbet

 Kensington Olympia. On-street pay & display parking.

19

Malt House

**17 Vanston Pl,
Fulham, SW6 1AY**
Tel.: (020)70846888
Website: www.malthousefulham.co.uk

Brakspear Bitter, Oxford Gold and Marston's Pedigree

Following the success of the Fox and Grapes in Wimbledon, Claude Bosi (of Hibiscus restaurant) and his brother Cedric chose this solidly built 18th century inn, around the corner from Stamford Bridge, as their second pub venture. Inside feels all very pristine and well-ordered: perhaps the bottles of sauce on the tables are there primarily to remind everyone that this really is still a pub. The menu is an appealing read, especially at lunch when the dishes are slightly more straightforward. The kitchen is clearly a very skilled and technically advanced one and dishes are visually appealing and easy to eat, although sometimes you wish there was a little less refinement and a tad more earthiness. There are six elegant bedrooms upstairs.

Closing times
Closed 25 December

Prices
Meals: £ 20 (weekday lunch) and a la carte £ 26/54

6 rooms: £ 125/140

Typical Dishes
Salad of feta, red onion & Jersey Royals
40-day aged Angus burger
Dark chocolate délice

England • London

20 Princess Victoria

**217 Uxbridge Rd,
Shepherd's Bush, W12 9DH**
Tel.: (020)87495886
Website: www.princessvictoria.co.uk

Timothy Taylor Landlord, Sambrook's Junction Ale and Sharp's Doombar

London has a wealth of fine Victorian gin palaces but few are as grand as The Princess Victoria. From the friezes to the etched glass, the portraits to the parquet floor, the last restoration created a terrific pub. Mind you, that's not all that impresses: there's a superb, wide-ranging wine list, with carafes and glasses providing flexibility; enticing bar snacks ranging from quail eggs to salt cod croquettes; a great menu that could include roasted skate wing or homemade pork and herb sausages; and, most importantly, cooking that's executed with no little skill. Those with proclivities for all things porcine will find much to savour – charcuterie is a passion here and the board may well include pig's cheeks and rillettes.

Closing times
Closed 24-28 December

Prices
Meals: a la carte £ 23/36

Typical Dishes
Herring roes on sourdough toast

Hake with anchovy & rosemary butter

Pineapple tarte Tatin

England • London

21   **Sands End**

135-137 Stephendale Rd, Fulham, SW6 2PR
Tel.: (020)77317823
Website: www.thesandsend.co.uk

 VISA **MC** **AE**

Sharp's Doom Bar, Black Sheep Bitter and Oxfordshire Ales Marshmellow

Sands End is probably not the best known part of London, or indeed Fulham, but no doubt its residents prefer it that way so they can keep their eponymous pub to themselves. It's a cosy, warm and welcoming one, with a central bar offering some nifty homemade snacks, but try resisting because the main menu – which changes every few days – is pretty appealing itself. There's a distinct British bias which amounts to more than merely name-checking the birthplace of the ingredients. Winter dishes like braised lamb neck or roast partridge with Savoy cabbage are particularly pleasing and West Mersea oysters a good way of starting things off. There's a well-chosen and equally equitably priced wine list that sticks mostly to the Old World.

Closing times
Closed 25 December
booking advisable

Prices
Meals: £ 14
(weekday lunch)
and a la carte £ 24/40

Typical Dishes
Smoked eel & potato pancakes
Corn–fed chicken and braised lentils
Valrhona chocolate bar

Fulham Broadway. On-street parking.

Haringey

22   Clissold Arms

**105 Fortis Green,
Fortis Green, N2 9HR**
Tel.: (020)84444224
Website: www.clissoldarms.co.uk

   VISA

Timothy Taylor Landlord, St Austell Tribute and Sambrook's Wandle Ale

Such is the growing reputation of The Clissold Arms that it may soon be better known for the quality of its cooking than its more long-standing claim to fame – that of having hosted The Kinks' first gig. Come at lunch and the menu and atmosphere make you feel you're in a proper pub, where you can expect classics like fishcakes or steak sandwiches. At dinner it all looks more like a restaurant, with loftier prices and slightly more ambitious, but still carefully prepared, dishes. The place is a lot bigger than you expect and, while staff could do with a little more guidance, it's often busy with locals grateful to have somewhere other than chain restaurants in their neighbourhood. The decked terrace has recently been extended.

Closing times
Open daily
Prices
Meals: £ 21 (weekdays)/30 and a la carte £ 20/45

Typical Dishes
Stuffed figs & goat's cheese

Lamb rump with seasonal vegetables

Dark chocolate brownie

 ⊖ East Finchley. Limited parking.

23 **Albion**

**10 Thornhill Rd,
Islington, N1 1HW**
Tel.: (020)76077450
Website: www.the-albion.co.uk

Caledonian Ales, Deuchers Ales and Ringwood Best Bitter

This Georgian jewel couldn't be better named and it's not just the wisteria-covered façade or the comfortingly worn-in look with its sofas and log fire that bring a patriotic tear to the eye. The menu also has a distinctive British feel with grills and rare breeds taking centre stage; Dexter, Belted Galloway and Longhorn beef all feature, along with Tamworth pork and Romney Salt Marsh lamb. For Sunday lunch expect a whole host of roast meats, and if you have 9 friends and the ability to plan ahead then consider pre-ordering the whole suckling pig. You can eat or drink anywhere – the bar has slightly more buzz than the restaurant. In summer everyone moves out into the walled garden at the back and barbeques become a regular feature.

Closing times
Closed 1 January
Prices
Meals: a la carte £ 22/38

Typical Dishes
Wood pigeon & braised chicory
Sussex rump with dauphinoise potatoes
Bramley apple crumble

Highbury & Islington. Free on-street parking after 6.30pm.

Islington

24

Barnsbury

**209-211 Liverpool Rd,
Islington, N1 1LX**
Tel.: (020)76075519
Website: www.thebarnsbury.co.uk

 Dark Star Hophead and guest ales

Apart from a tiresome tendency to change hands every now and again, the Barnsbury still manages to remain a reliable and welcoming local pub. The emphasis here may be more on the bar – beer drinking is given due deference and a blackboard lists the guest beers – but that doesn't stop the pub turning out gutsy and satisfying food for its many regulars. The menu is fairly concise, which allows the kitchen to fully master their repertoire, so there's a reassuring consistency and confidence to the preparation of dishes like pig's cheeks with mustard mash, salmon fishcakes with dill, and apple and rhubarb crumble. Sit at the front in among the drinkers – this is a livelier spot than the small dining area at the back.

Closing times
Closed lunch Monday-Wednesday
Prices
Meals: a la carte £ 13/22

Typical Dishes
Crispy Cajun squid
Sausage & mash with red wine gravy
Apple pie & custard

 Highbury & Islington. On-street parking.

England • London

25 **Drapers Arms**

**44 Barnsbury St,
Islington, N1 1ER**
Tel.: (020)76190348
Website: www.thedrapersarms.com

 Sambrook's Wandle Ale, Harveys Sussex Best Bitter and Dark Star Hophead

Celebrating British cuisine means more than just putting a few old favourites on the menu; it's about making great use of indigenous ingredients and introducing them to a wider audience. At The Drapers Arms those unfamiliar with our own bounteous larder can see humble produce like lamb's tongues, smoked eels, blade steak and rabbit used to create dishes that are satisfying, gutsy and affordable. Locals, or those who find themselves in Islington at midday for whatever reason, can take advantage of their steal of a lunch menu. Just ignore the fact that the staff can be a little too cool for school and simply enjoy the good food, unpretentious atmosphere and shabby chic interior of this busy Georgian pub, with its handsome façade.

Closing times
Open daily
bookings advisable at dinner
Prices
Meals: a la carte £ 22/34

Typical Dishes
Duck heart kebab
Steak & oyster pie
Buttermilk pudding

 Highbury & Islington. On-street parking.

Islington

26

House

63-69 Canonbury Rd, Canonbury, N1 2DG
Tel.: (020)77047410
Website: www.thehouse.islington.com

Sharp's Doom Bar and Greene King IPA

A couple of tables on the pavement does not a terrace make – if you want to see the Real McCoy then come to The House with its umbrellas, marble-topped tables, hedges and heaters. Inside it's pretty nice too, with one side given over to the drinkers, the other laid out in a bistro-style. An intimate atmosphere married with a laid back, friendly vibe adds to the appeal. Pubs classics and more contemporary creations jostle for supremacy but are done equally well; their spelt pizzas are proving very popular – aimed at children but largely hijacked by adults. Breakfast and brunch are offered at weekends but the pub also hosts wedding receptions for those who've got hitched at the Town Hall down the road, so check first.

Closing times
Closed Monday except bank holidays

Prices
Meals: £ 30 (weekdays)/38 and a la carte £ 23/35

Typical Dishes
Bayonne ham with celeriac remoulade

Rump steak with Lyonnaise potatoes

Classic raspberry `Mess`

 ⊖ Highbury & Islington. Free on-street parking after 6.30pm.

27 **John Salt**

**131 Upper St,
Islington, N1 1QP**
Tel.: (020)77048955
Website: www.john-salt.com

 No real ales offered

It's loud, slightly chaotic, ersatz industrial and all about barbecue – John Salt is so determinedly 'on trend' it'll make anyone over 30 feel ancient. Presumably named after the photorealist artist, it comes from the people who created The Fellow and The Owl & the Pussycat so they know what they're doing when it comes to lively bars. The menu gets full marks for originality; the cooking is all about smoke and coals, and influences stretch beyond the US to include Malaysia and Korea. There are some surprisingly delicate touches in amongst the charring and smoking, and some unexpected ingredient pairings. Whatever your age, ask for the mezzanine level otherwise you'll be fighting for elbow space with the drinkers and loungers by the bar.

Closing times
Closed 25-26 December and Monday lunch
booking essential
Prices
Meals: a la carte £ 20/29

Typical Dishes
Tempura oysters, beef fat mayo
Green chilli poussin
Banana dog

 Angel. Free on-street parking after 6.30pm.

England • London

28

Peasant

**240 St John St,
Finsbury, EC1V 4PH**
Tel.: (020)73367726
Website: www.thepeasant.co.uk

VISA **MC** **AE**

 Crouch Vale Brewers Gold, Two Cocks Roundhead and Meantime Brewery Pale Ale

From the outside it may be starting to look its age, but this senior member of the gastropub movement still pulls in plenty of punters. Come evening, you have two choices: stay in the bar and compete for a spare table with the city boys having a post-work pint, or book a table in the sanctuary of the sedate upstairs dining room with its circus-themed prints and posters. Downstairs comes with an easy, eat-on-the-hoof type of menu: squid tempura and sharing boards such a cheese or meze stand out and are ideal accompaniments to a pint. In the restaurant dishes such as sea bream with capers and brown shrimps, and honey-roast duck with celeriac purée, come with a greater degree of sophistication but still deliver on flavour.

Closing times
Closed 25 December-1 January and bank holidays except Good Friday

booking essential

Prices
Meals: £ 24 and a la carte £ 22/28

Typical Dishes
Pan-fried gnocchi & gorgonzola
Fillet of sea bass & broad beans
Rhubarb & orange custard tart

 ⊖ *Farringdon. On-street parking meters nearby; also free parking after 6.30pm and on Saturday after 1.30pm.*

154

 Pig and Butcher

**80 Liverpool Rd,
Islington, N1 0QD**
Tel.: (020)72268304
Website: www.thepigandbutcher.co.uk

🍴 *VISA* **MC** **AE**

🍺 **Sambrook's Wandle Ale, London Fields Brewery IPA and Bath Ales Gem**

Formerly The Islington Tap, this corner pub dates from the mid-19C when cattle drovers taking their livestock to Smithfield Market would stop for a swift one. Now sympathetically restored, it enjoys the same ownership as Lady Ottoline and Princess of Shoreditch. The busy bar offers an impressive number of bottled beers, while the dining room is secreted behind shelves of bric-a-brac. There's a strong British element to the daily menu and that's not just because they use words like 'Beeton' and 'Mrs'. Meat comes straight from the farm and is butchered and smoked in-house; fish comes from day boats off the south coast. Roasts take centre stage on Sundays; 'just like your mother's' they claim, which presumably means something different to us all.

Closing times
Closed 25-27 December and Monday-Wednesday lunch
booking advisable
Prices
Meals: a la carte £ 25/42

Typical Dishes
Black pudding & coddled egg

Venison & salt-baked beets

Jersey curd cake & raspberry sorbet

🚗 ⊖ *Angel. Free on-street parking after 6.30pm.*

30 **St John's Tavern**

**91 Junction Rd,
Archway, N19 5QU**
Tel.: (020)72721587
Website: www.stjohnstavern.com

Greene King Abbot Ale, Fuller's London Pride and Adnams Lighthouse

Having undergone an English Heritage restoration in recent years, St John's Tavern now stands as a beacon of hope on the stubbornly unchanging thoroughfare that is Junction Road. It doesn't disappoint inside either: the laid-back front bar does an appealing line in snacks like salt cod croquettes and mutton pasties, and there are few more warming spots in North London on a cold night than the large, boldly decorated rear dining room. The chefs list the provenance of their ingredients on a board next to the open kitchen, with Devon and Dorset seemingly the favoured counties. The daily menu is largely hardy and British but with nods to the Med; heartening terrines are a highlight, as is the delicious sourdough which is baked in-house.

Closing times
Closed 25-26 December and 1 January
dinner only and lunch Friday-Sunday
booking advisable
Prices
Meals: a la carte £ 21/34

Typical Dishes
Snails with bacon & wild garlic pesto
Pork chop with squash & beetroot
Brown butter & gingernut cheesecake

⊖ Archway. Pay & display parking; free after 6.30pm.

England • London

31   **Well**

**180 St John St,
Finsbury, EC1V 4JY**
Tel.: (020)72519363
Website: www.downthewell.com

 Sambrook's Jugged Hare Pale Ale

One of the smallest pubs in the Martin Brothers' portfolio is also one of the easiest to find, thanks to its wide expanse of blue canopy. This well-supported neighbourhood pub comes with the sort of food that is reassuringly familiar yet still done well, and service that instills confidence in the customer – just be sure to eat on the ground floor, rather than in the less welcoming basement. Whether it's asparagus soup or veal Holstein, dishes are cooked with care and deliver on flavour. A side dish between two is needed – the macaroni cheese is worth ordering even if it doesn't necessarily match up to what you're eating – and who isn't reassured by the presence of a crumble on a menu?

Closing times
Closed 25-26 December
Prices
Meals: a la carte £ 23/37

Typical Dishes
King scallops, garlic & parsley butter
Cornish fish stew
Rhubarb & ginger crumble

32   **Admiral Codrington**

**17 Mossop St,
Chelsea, SW3 2LY**
Tel.: (020)75810005
Website: www.theadmiralcodrington.com

Fuller's London Pride

If you're going to make one of your pubs the flagship of your bourgeoning organisation then it makes sense to choose the one that has 'Admiral' in its title. Cirrus Inns now run 'The Cod' and managed to touch it all up without tampering with it too much. Lunch means some fresh fish or a club sandwich in either the front bar or the rather smart restaurant with its retractable roof; in the evening the bar sticks to just serving drinks. Start with the terrific snacks, like pork crackling with apple sauce, then head for the more familiar, tried-and-tested dishes from the monthly-changing menu. Beef is big here and is aged in-house; the burgers have become popular, with new combinations communicated by Twitter.

Closing times
Closed 24-25 December
Prices
Meals: a la carte £ 21/66

Typical Dishes
Mussels & clams with white wine, cream & garlic
Admiral Cod's burger
Sticky toffee pudding

England • London

33 **Builders Arms**

13 Britten St,
Chelsea, SW3 3TY
Tel.: (020)73499040
Website: www.geronimo-inns.co.uk

VISA **M©** **AE**

 Wells Bombardier, Sharp's Doom Bar and Young's Ales

The Builders Arms is very much like a packed village local – the only difference being that, in this instance, the village is Chelsea and the villagers are all young and prosperous. The inside delivers on the promise of the smart exterior but don't expect it to be quiet as drinkers are welcomed just as much as diners. In fact, bookings are only taken for larger parties but just tell the staff that you're here to eat and they'll sort you out. The cooking reveals the effort that has gone into the sourcing of some decent ingredients; the rib of beef for two is a perennial favourite. Dishes are robust and satisfying and are not without some flair in presentation. Wine is also taken seriously and their list has been thoughtfully put together.

Closing times
Open daily
bookings not accepted
Prices
Meals: a la carte £ 20/40

Typical Dishes
Smoked duck breast &
poached pear
Pork belly with seared
foie gras
Chocolate brownie

 ⊖ South Kensington. On-street parking.

34

Cadogan Arms

**298 King's Rd,
Chelsea, SW3 5UG**
Tel.: (020)73526500
Website: www.thecadoganarmschelsea.com

VISA **MC** **AE**

Adnams Bitter and Sambrook's Jugged Hare Pale Ale

Look no further if you like pubs to feel the way they used to. Instead of turning this Victorian corner pub into a gastropub cliché, the Martin brothers – who also own the trendy Botanist at the smart end of the King's Road – respected its heritage and kept it a 'proper' pub, albeit one with decent food. Stuffed animals, antlers on the wall, original tiling and oak panelling give it a warm, unaffected feel. The best things on the menu are those that are filling, blokey and meaty, whether that's mutton with haggis, faggots or large steaks for two – and there's no let up with puds like treacle tart. In the billiard room upstairs you'll find three American 8-ball pool tables available to hire by the hour; snacks can be had up there too.

Closing times
Closed 25-26 December
bookings advisable at dinner
Prices
Meals: a la carte £ 20/40

Typical Dishes
Squid salad, garlic & lime
Braised rabbit leg & sautéed baby gem
Rhubarb & stem ginger crumble

 ⊖ South Kensington. On-street parking.

England • London

35

Chelsea Ram

**32 Burnaby St,
Chelsea, SW10 0PL**
Tel.: (020)73514008
Website: www.geronimo-inns.co.uk/thechelsearam

VISA MC AE

Sambrook's Junction Ale, Sharp's Doom Bar and Young's Bitter

The Chelsea Ram stands out from the crowd because it's got heart and soul – this is a pub that just feels right as soon as you walk in. It has always been a proper local and comes with a palpable sense of community, but not to the extent that interlopers are given the evil eye by the regulars at the bar. Thursday is steak night and Friday, fish night; you can come for brunch at weekends and can even join the Geronimo Club for regular cheese and wine tastings. Dining tables wind themselves around the bar, with quieter ones nestling at the back under a glass roof. Blackboard specials supplement the menu of sturdy pub classics and seasonal dishes. Alternatively, you can stand at the bar for a pint and a little pork pie.

Closing times
Closed 25 December

Prices
Meals: a la carte £ 21/35

Typical Dishes
Potted ham hock
Chargrilled swordfish
with an olive salad
Chocolate marquise

England • London

36   Lots Road Pub & Dining Room

**114 Lots Rd,
Chelsea, SW10 0RJ**
Tel.: (020)73526645
Website: www.lotsroadpub.com

VISA **MC** **AE**

Sharp's Doom Bar and Sambrook's Wandle Ale

At lunch expect to be joined by those from the nearby Design Centre; at dinner the place is colonised by good-looking locals and at weekends it's full of folk who've been busy buying antiques. The pub may be looking a little worn around the edges but when a kitchen occupies half the bar you just know they take their food seriously. The menu may be short and at first glance rather safe but they use good produce and cook it with care and respect. Blackboards offer 'season's eatings' and there's a daily recipe too. Look out too for the weekly 'wicked wines' selection where you can pick up a bargain. Steak is still a speciality and it's worth coming on Sunday for a roast and a Bloody Mary. They also have a great customer loyalty scheme.

Closing times
Open daily
Prices
Meals: a la carte £ 20/33

Typical Dishes
Pan-fried scallops
Rib-eye steak & chips
Lemon tart

 ⊖ *Fulham Broadway. On-street parking.*

37

Phoenix

**23 Smith St,
Chelsea, SW3 4EE**
Tel.: (020)77309182
Website: www.geronimo-inns.co.uk/thepheonix

Sharp's Doom Bar, Camden Brewery Pale Ale and Purity Ales

The same menu is served throughout and, while the bar has plenty of seating and a civilised feel, head to the warm and comfortable dining room at the back if you want a more structured meal or you're impressing a date. Blackboard specials supplement the menu which keeps things traditional: fish on a Friday, a pasta of the day and the likes of fishcakes or sausage and mash with red onion jam. For lunch, you'll find some favourites for late-risers, like eggs Benedict and, in winter, expect the heartening sight of crumbles or plum pudding. Wines are organised by their character, with nearly 30 varieties offered by the glass. The side dishes can bump up the final bill but The Phoenix remains a friendly and conscientiously run Chelsea local.

Closing times
Closed 25 December

Prices
Meals: a la carte £ 21/38

Typical Dishes
Artichoke vinaigrette
Rib-eye steak & roast bone marrow
Earl Grey chocolate fondant

 ⊖ *Sloane Square. On-street parking meters.*

38

Pig's Ear

**35 Old Church St,
Chelsea, SW3 5BS**
Tel.: (020)73522908
Website: www.thepigsear.info

VISA   MC   AE   ◑

🍺 **Sambrook's Junction Ale, St Austell Pale Ale and Camden Brewery Pale Ale**

This Chelsea pub may not look much like a foodie spot from the outside, or indeed from the inside, but it does have a refreshing honesty to it. Lunch is in the rough-and-ready ground floor bar, decorated with everything from 'Tintin' pictures to covers of 'Sounds' newspaper. There's a decent choice of 5-6 main courses and a wine list on a blackboard. With its wood panelling and dressed tables, the upstairs dining room provides quite a contrast, but the atmosphere is still far from starchy. Here the menu displays a little more ambition but cooking remains similarly earthy and the wine list has plenty of bottles under £30. The kitchen knows its way around an animal: slow-cooked dishes such as pork cheeks are done particularly well.

Closing times
Open daily
Prices
Meals: a la carte £ 21/50

Typical Dishes
Scallop ceviche with avocado
Pot-roast chicken & petits pois à la française
Dark chocolate torte

39   **Portobello House**

**225 Ladbroke Grove,
North Kensington, W10 6HQ**
Tel.: (020)31810920
Website: www.portobellohouse.com

⌂ *VISA* **MC** **AE** **①**

🍺 **Brakspear Portobello Ale**

Whether this is a pub, bistro or hotel – or even all three – may be up for discussion but what is indisputable is that Portobello House is a great addition to this end of Ladbroke Grove. It was formerly the Earl Percy and once hosted The Clash (as, seemingly, did every boozer in these parts) but has been given a complete makeover and now has 12 smart and contemporary bedrooms. Downstairs, the bar takes up most of the space and, in a reflection of the changing local demographic, offers beers and cocktails. There are plenty of sofas to relax on; grab the one by the open fire. The menu is a combination of British stoutness and Italian flair and the cooking is bold yet comforting; it is also decently priced, especially at weekday lunches.

Closing times
Open daily

Prices
Meals: £ 15
(weekday lunch)
and a la carte £ 19/32

🛏 **12 rooms:** £ 99/250

Typical Dishes
Avocado & quails egg
Onglet steak with potato cake
Vanilla panna cotta & rhubarb

🚗 ⊖ Ladbroke Grove. Free on-street parking after 6.30 pm.

165

England • London

40   **Fellow**

**24 York Way,
St Pancras, N1 9AA**
Tel.: (020)78334395
Website: www.thefellow.co.uk

VISA MC AE

Sharp's Doom Bar and St Austell Tribute

It was just a matter of time before a few decent pubs opened around the rapidly developing area of King's Cross. The Fellow is one of the busiest, attracting a youthful and local clientele; it also manages to give the impression it's been here for years. Eating happens on the dark and atmospheric ground floor, with drinkers heading upstairs to the even more boisterous cocktail bar. The menu is quite a sophisticated little number but the kitchen is up to the task. Start with ham hock terrine or potted crab, followed by roast rump of lamb or grilled haddock with champ. Desserts such as apple tart display a lightness of touch. The serving team are a bright, capable bunch. There is an outdoor terrace but you'll be surrounded by smokers.

Closing times
Open daily
Prices
Meals: a la carte £ 19/34

Typical Dishes
Crispy goat's cheese with beetroot & pine nuts
Duck breast with pak choi & spiced honey dressing
Apricot & basil panna cotta

 ⊖ *King's Cross St Pancras. Limited on-street parking.*

41 Canton Arms

**177 South Lambeth Rd,
Stockwell, SW8 1XP**
Tel.: (020)75828710
Website: www.cantonarms.com

 **Skinner's Betty Stogs, Timothy Taylor Golden Best and
Red Squirrel English IPA**

Its appreciative audience prove that the demand for fresh, honest, seasonal food is not just limited to smart squares in Chelsea or Islington. The oval-shaped bar dominates the room, with the front half busy with drinkers and the back laid up for diners, although it's all very relaxed and you can eat where you want. The kitchen's experience in places like the Anchor & Hope and Great Queen Street is obvious on their menu which features rustic, earthy British food, of the sort that suits this environment so well. Lunch could be a kipper or tripe and chips; even a reinvented toasted sandwich. Dinner sees a short, no-nonsense menu offering perhaps braised venison or grilled haddock, with daily specials like steak and kidney pie for two.

Closing times
Closed Christmas-New Year, Monday lunch, Sunday dinner and bank holidays
bookings not accepted

Prices
Meals: a la carte £ 19/31

Typical Dishes
Rabbit livers & snails on toast
Smoked Old Spot pork chop
Rum baba

Stockwell. Free parking in the evening.

Lambeth

42 Palmerston

**91 Lordship Ln,
East Dulwich, SE22 8EP**
Tel.: (020)86931629
Website: www.thepalmerston.net

 Sharp's Doom Bar, Harveys Sussex Best Bitter, Timothy Taylor Landlord, Skinner's Betty Stogs

The Palmerston has long realised that success for any pub lies in being at the heart of the local community. Since it's makeover a few years ago, this Victorian pub has been popular with families – just look at all those highchairs – and local artists, work decorates the walls. It has a comfortable, lived-in feel, along with a snug, wood-panelled rear dining room with an original and quite beautiful mosaic floor. The menu is as reassuring as the service and the cooking has a satisfying, gutsy edge. There's plenty of choice, from chowders and soups to well-judged fish but it's the meat dishes that stand out, like the mature steaks or lamb chops – and if they have grouse on the menu, then forsake all others and get in quick.

Closing times
Open daily

Prices
Meals: £ 14 (weekday lunch) and a la carte £ 27/64

Typical Dishes
Pan-fried squid with ink risotto

Duck breast with petits pois à la française

Fig tart & buttermilk ice cream

 East Dulwich (Rail). Free on-street parking in the evening.

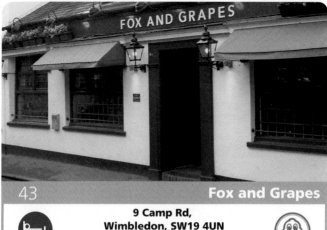

43   **Fox and Grapes**

**9 Camp Rd,
Wimbledon, SW19 4UN**
Tel.: (020)86191300
Website: www.foxandgrapeswimbledon.co.uk

VISA   **Ⓜ︎Ⓒ**

Sharp's Doom Bar and Black Sheep Best Bitter

Claude Bosi first made his mark in Ludlow where, along with his Hibiscus restaurant, he also had a pub. When he moved to London the plan was to open a pub again once his restaurant was established and this he duly did in 2011. Cedric, his brother, runs the show and one look at the menu confirms their credentials as honorary Brits: this is proper pub food. Their prawn cocktail is hugely popular, as is the Cumberland sausage with mash, the ale battered hake and Angus sirloin. Scotch egg is made with wild boar, and junket makes an appearance, which makes you forgive their sneaking in the odd Gallic touch like snails and some of the over-formality. Thankfully, the pub's bigger than it looks as it's very popular. It also has three cosy bedrooms.

Closing times
Closed 25 December
booking advisable
Prices
Meals: a la carte £ 25/36
3 rooms: £ 125

Typical Dishes
Crispy ox tongue &
salsa verde
Label Anglais chicken
Kiev
Sticky toffee pudding

🚗 ⊖ Wimbledon. On-street parking.

England • London

44 **Brown Dog**

28 Cross St,
Barnes, SW13 0AP
Tel.: (020)83922200
Website: www.thebrowndog.co.uk

Twickenham Grandstand, Sambrook's Wandle Ale and
Hackney Brewery Best Bitter

You really can't teach an old dog new tricks – because The Brown Dog remains a terrific neighbourhood pub and the locals clearly love it just the way it is. Mind you, this pretty Victorian pub is so well hidden in the maze of residential streets that it's a wonder any new customers ever find it anyway. The look fuses the traditional with the modern and service is bubbly and enthusiastic. Jugs of iced water arrive without prompting and the cleverly concise menu changes regularly. A lightly spiced crab salad or pint of prawns could be followed by a succulent rump of lamb, while puddings like sticky toffee date pudding or gooseberry cheesecake are also commendably priced.

Closing times
Closed 25 December
Prices
Meals: a la carte £ 23/36

Typical Dishes

Tiger prawns, parsley,
garlic & chilli

Bavette steak with red
wine & shallot jus

Hot chocolate brownie
sundae

45

King's Head

123 High St,
Teddington, TW11 8HG
Tel.: (020)31662900
Website: www.whitebrasserie.com

Fuller's London Pride, Sharp's Doom Bar and St Austell Tribute

Britain has its pubs and France its brasseries; The King's Head does its bit for the entente cordiale by combining both. Raymond Blanc's team has given this Victorian pub a tidy makeover and, although there might not be much character left, they have created a suitably warm environment. The brasserie at the back is run by a pleasant, enthusiastic team and the menus offer all comers plenty of choice. Classic brasserie dishes such as Toulouse sausages and beef stroganoff come with a satisfyingly rustic edge, while the dual-nationality element is maintained through the inclusion of a ploughman's board alongside the charcuterie. Steaks from the charcoal grill are popular and families are lured in by the decent kiddies menu.

Closing times
Closed 25 December

Prices
Meals: £ 14/17
and a la carte £ 18/34

Typical Dishes
Snails with garlic & herb butter

Beef stroganoff with pilaf rice

Waffles with caramelised apples

Richmond upon Thames

46

Victoria

**10 West Temple Sheen,
East Sheen, SW14 7RT**
Tel.: (020)88764238
Website: www.thevictoria.net

VISA MC

Fuller's London Pride and Timothy Taylor Landlord

Many pubs claim to be genuine locals – The Victoria is the real deal: it sponsors local clubs and the chef is patron of the local food festival; he also holds cookery workshops at the school next door. This is a beautifully decorated pub, with a restored bar with a wood burning stove and plenty of nooks and crannies; a few steps down and you're in the more formal conservatory overlooking the terrace. The cooking is modern British with the odd international note. Warm homemade bread could be followed by scotch egg with roast beetroot, cod with a white bean stew and, to finish, blood oranges with rhubarb sorbet. Produce is local where possible: veg is from Surrey and honey from Richmond. Service is engaging and there are bedrooms available.

Closing times
Open daily

Prices
Meals: £ 13 (weekdays)
and a la carte £ 23/40

7 rooms: £ 120/140

Typical Dishes
Pork & chicken liver pâté
Bream with fennel & pepper gratin
Spiced sugar millefeuille

England • London

47   **Anchor & Hope**

**36 The Cut,
Southwark, SE1 8LP**
Tel.: (020)79289898

 Young's Bitter, Wells Bombardier and guest ales

The Anchor & Hope is still running at full steam and its popularity shows no sign of abating. It's not hard to see why: combine a menu that changes with each service and is a paragon of seasonality, with cooking that is gutsy, bold and wholesome, and you end up with immeasurably rewarding dishes like suckling kid chops with wild garlic, succulent roast pigeon with lentils or buttermilk pudding with poached rhubarb. The place has a contagiously congenial feel and the staff all pull in the same direction; you may spot a waiter trimming veg or a chef delivering dishes. The no-reservation policy remains, so either get here early or be prepared to wait – although you can now book for Sunday lunch, when everyone sits down at 2pm for a veritable feast.

Closing times
Closed Christmas-New Year, Sunday dinner, Monday lunch and bank holidays
bookings not accepted

Prices
Meals: a la carte £ 26/37

Typical Dishes
Warm snail & bacon salad

Roast wood pigeon with semolina gnocchi

Raspberry Queen of puddings

 Southwark. On-street parking meters.

48 **Crooked Well**

**16 Grove Ln,
Camberwell, SE5 8SY**
Tel.: (020)72527798
Website: www.thecrookedwell.com

 Sharp's Doom Bar

Three friends scoured the south of England before finding this old boozer in Camberwell. They've done it up very cleverly because it manages to look both new and lived-in at the same time and also feels like a proper 'local'. There's a strong emphasis on beers, great cocktails and an interesting wine list with plenty available by the glass and pichet, but the pub's growing reputation is mostly down to its food. The kitchen mixes things up by offering stout, traditional classics like rabbit and bacon pie alongside more playful dishes such as a deconstructed peach Melba. There are lots of things 'on toast' at lunchtime, while dishes like scotch egg with Heinz tomato soup are designed to evoke memories of childhood.

Closing times
Closed Monday lunch
Prices
Meals: a la carte £ 20/34

Typical Dishes
Pigeon breast & lentils
Guinea fowl with Jerusalem artichokes
Rhubarb custard panna cotta

 ⊖ *Denmark Hill (Rail). Free on-street parking after 6.30pm.*

49

Garrison

99-101 Bermondsey St, Bermondsey, SE1 3XB
Tel.: (020)70899355
Website: www.thegarrison.co.uk

 Adnams Ales

You'd be hard pressed to find a more charming pub than The Garrison. With its appealing vintage look, warm atmosphere and delightful staff, it's the perfect antidote to those hard-edged boozers that we've all accidentally found ourselves in at some point. Open from 8am for smoothies and breakfast, it gets busier as the day goes on – and don't bother coming for dinner if you haven't booked. Booth numbers 4 and 5, opposite the open kitchen, are the most popular while number 2 at the back is the cosiest. Daily specials on the blackboard supplement the nicely balanced menu and the cooking is perky and bright, with a subtle Mediterranean slant. Salads are done well and there's a daily steak, while puds are of a more traditional bent.

Closing times
Closed 25-26 December
booking essential at dinner
Prices
Meals: a la carte £ 23/37

Typical Dishes
Sautéed mushrooms on toasted brioche

Lamb steak with redcurrant & mint sauce

Gingerbread with ginger ice cream

 London Bridge. On-street parking.

50

Gun

**27 Coldharbour,
Canary Wharf, E14 9NS**
Tel.: (020)75155222
Website: www.thegundocklands.com

 VISA MC AE

 Sambrook's Junction Ale, Jugged Hare Pale Ale and Adnams Southwold Bitter

The 18C Gun may have had a 21C makeover but that doesn't mean it has forgotten its roots: its association with Admiral Lord Nelson, links to smugglers and ties to the river are all celebrated in its oil paintings and collection of assorted weaponry. The dining room and the style of service are both fairly smart and ceremonial, yet The Gun is a pub where this level of formality seems appropriate. Dockers have now been replaced by bankers, the majority of whom rarely venture beyond the 35-day aged steak. This is a shame as the menu cleverly combines relatively ambitious dishes such as game or John Dory with more traditional local specialities like eel and oysters. Even the dessert menu offers a mix, from soufflés to stewed plums.

Closing times
Closed 25-26 December
Prices
Meals: a la carte £ 25/50

Typical Dishes
Roast breast of wood pigeon
Fillet of Cornish John Dory
Vanilla mousse & elderflower jelly

 ⊖ *Blackwall (DLR). On-street parking.*

England • London

51

Morgan Arms

**43 Morgan St,
Bow, E3 5AA**
Tel.: (020)89806389
Website: www.capitalpubcompany.com/The-Morgan-Arms

ⵔ   *VISA*   Ⓜ◎   AE

🍺 **London Fields Hackney Hopster, Adnams Explorer and
Sambrook's Wandle Ale**

This former boozer's clever makeover respects its heritage while simultaneously bringing it up to date. The bar's always busy while the dining area is more subdued. You'll find the kitchen keeps its influences mostly within Europe but also understands just what sort of food works well in a pub. The daily changing menu usually features pasta in some form and staples like whitebait - which come devilled in this instance - assorted tarts and the perennial favourite, fishcakes accompanied by a poached egg. What's more, prices are kept at realistic levels which make this pub appealing to those who live nearby and who like a little spontaneity in their lives. Look out for the occasional themed evening and charity auction.

Closing times
Closed 25 December

Prices
Meals: a la carte £ 21/32

Typical Dishes
Salt & pepper squid
Braised lamb shoulder
with soft polenta
Mascarpone panna
cotta

🚗 ⊖ *Bow Road. Parking meters in Tredegar Square
until 6.30pm, after 6.30pm parking outside.*

Tower Hamlets

52

Narrow

**44 Narrow St,
Limehouse, E14 8DP**
Tel.: (020)75927950
Website: www.gordonramsay.com

Fullers, Meantime and Adnams Ales

There can't be many London pubs with better views than The Narrow and Gordon Ramsay's group have made the most of the Thames-side location by wrapping a conservatory around this Grade II listed former dockmaster's house. The place has a real buzz, thanks largely to the many regulars at the bar, the occasional live music and the large number of diners which include plenty of tourists. The menu gives them an opportunity to discover our more traditional dishes such as scotch egg, cottage pie, toad in the hole and the ubiquitous fish and chips. Dishes on the whole hit the mark although the kitchen can be a little heavy-handed at times. Look out for the good value set menu, available at all times except after 7pm on Fridays and Saturdays.

Closing times
Closed 25 December
booking essential
Prices
Meals: £ 22 and a la carte
£ 26/50

Typical Dishes
Cured salmon with heritage beetroot
Rack of lamb with pan haggerty
Banana sticky toffee pudding

 Limehouse (DLR). Parking.

53 **Prince of Wales**

138 Upper Richmond Rd, Putney, SW15 2SP

Tel.: (020)87881552

Website: www.princeofwalesputney.co.uk

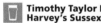 **Timothy Taylor Landlord, Sambrook's Wandle Ale and Harvey's Sussex Best**

Idiosyncratic decoration and good food make this substantial Victorian pub stand out. Its deep green walls are lined with tankards and its ceiling is covered in playing cards; head further in and you'll find the dining room in the old billiard room. Here lights are fashioned from antlers and its walls are decorated with vintage farming photos and a little taxidermy; mind you, it's so dimly lit you'll be pushed see anything. The kitchen is out to impress and its daily changing menu reads well, ranging from rabbit and pork terrine to Cornish sardines and even a plate of Spanish delicacies. Although the ingredients are top-notch, the plates are sometimes a little too busy which perhaps explains the popularity of the simpler bar menu.

Closing times
Closed 23 December-
1 January and Monday
lunch except bank holidays

Prices
Meals: a la carte £ 24/42

Typical Dishes
Smoked mackerel pâté

Stone bass
with braised fennel

Dark chocolate,
Cointreau & basil
parfait

 East Putney. On-street parking.

54   **Angel & Crown**

**58 St Martin's Ln,
Strand, WC2N 4EA**
Tel.: (020)77485244
Website: www.theangelandcrown.com

VISA   **MC**   **AE**   **DC**

 **Sambrook's Junction Ale, Otter Amber, Adnams
Southwold Bitter and guest ales**

Tourist spots and good food are rarely enjoyed together and London is no exception, but fortunately the gastropub revolution is now creeping into the West End. The Angel & Crown is part of the Martin Brothers' portfolio which includes The Well and The Gun and here they've converted a handsome Victorian pub in the heart of theatre-land. The ground floor, with its pewter tankards hanging above the bar, is the sort of place you want to stand up in; most of the eating is done upstairs in the dining room. The menu wisely sticks to British dishes, with nothing to scare away the out-of-towners, and uses decent ingredients, so the pie may be venison and bone marrow and the sausages that go with the mash and onion gravy are made using wild boar.

Closing times
Closed 25 December
Prices
Meals: a la carte £ 23/34

Typical Dishes
Kiln-roast salmon, beetroot & crème fraîche
Roast fillet of Scottish sea trout
Dark chocolate parfait

 ⊖ *Leicester Square. On-street parking.*

55

Burger & Lobster

**29 Clarges St,
Mayfair, W1J 7EF**
Tel.: (020)74091699
Website: www.burgerandlobster.com

 No real ales offered

Around the corner from the Curzon cinema, in what was a pub called the Field, is a 'concept' so simple it borders on genius. The choice, if you didn't get the clue in the name, is between a burger, a lobster or a lobster roll, served with chips, salad and sauces, with either chocolate or lime mousse for dessert - that's it. You're given a numbered luggage tag if you want a tab at the bar; there are no menus to read through and no side dishes to choose. There's a small, well-chosen wine and cocktail list under headings B or L (work it out). The lobsters are Canadian; the burgers 10oz and the customers mostly men. Bookings aren't taken so get your name down on the list as soon as you arrive – it may well be a bunfight, but it's a very well organised one.

Closing times
Closed Christmas and bank holidays
bookings not accepted
Prices
Meals: £ 20

Typical Dishes
Half lobster
Beef burger & fries
Chocolate mousse

 ⊖ *Green Park. On-street parking.*

56   **Grazing Goat**

**6 New Quebec St,
Marylebone, W1H 7RQ**
Tel.: (020)77247243
Website: www.thegrazinggoat.co.uk

VISA   MC   AE   ◑

Meantime Brewery Ales

The Portman Estate, owners of some serious real estate in these parts and keen to raise the profile of their investment, encouraged an experienced pub operator more at home in Chelsea and Belgravia to venture a little further north and take over the old Bricklayers Arms. Renamed in homage to a past Lady Portman (who grazed goats in a field where the pub now stands as she was allergic to cows' milk), it is now a smart city facsimile of a country pub. It's first-come-first-served in the bar but you can book in the upstairs dining room. Pub classics are the order of the day, such as pies or Castle of Mey steaks, and Suffolk chicken is cooked on the rotisserie. The eight bedrooms are nicely furnished, with their bathrooms resembling Nordic saunas.

Closing times
Open daily
booking essential at dinner
Prices
Meals: a la carte £ 28/44
🛏 **8 rooms:** £ 195/225

Typical Dishes
Scallops with greengage pickle
Sea bream, caper & spring onion croquette
Chocolate espresso tart

⊖ Marble Arch. On-street parking.

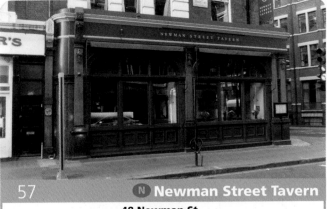

57  **Newman Street Tavern**

48 Newman St,
Regent's Park and Marylebone, W1T 1QQ
Tel.: (020)36671445
Website: www.newmanstreettavern.co.uk

VISA MC AE

Camden Town Camden Hell and Crate Brewery
Best Bitter

Provided it isn't preceded by "ye" and "olde", there's something very comforting about the word "tavern". The experienced foursome behind Newman Street Tavern chose the word deliberately as they wanted to create a genuinely warm and welcoming place for customers to come and celebrate British food – and they got it spot on. The menu has been thoughtfully compiled and, with its soused Cornish anchovies, Blackface lamb, game tea, and Banbury cakes, is instantly appealing. There are no short cuts in the kitchen: they do their own butchery, smoke their own fish, work closely with their suppliers and take issues of sustainability seriously. You can eat in the bustle of the bar or the charming and more sedate first floor dining room.

Closing times
Closed bank holidays
Prices
Meals: a la carte £ 23/39

Typical Dishes
Brown crab on toast
Blackface lamb with
sea succulents
Sticky toffee pudding

Goodge Street. On-street parking.

58   Only Running Footman

5 Charles St,
Mayfair, W1J 5DF
Tel.: (020)74992988
Website: www.therunningfootmanmayfair.com

VISA   **MC**   **AE**

 Wells Bombardier, Fuller's London Pride and Truman's IPA

Apparently the owners added 'only' to the title when they found out that theirs was the only pub in the land called 'The Running Footman'. Spread over several levels, it offers cookery demonstrations and private dinners along with its two floors of dining. Downstairs is where the action usually is, with its menu offering pub classics from steak sandwiches to fishcakes, but you can't book here and it's always packed. Upstairs is where you'll find a surprisingly formal dining room and here they do take reservations. Its menu is far more ambitious and European in its influence but the best dishes are still the simpler ones, with desserts a strength. You can't help feeling that you would be having a lot more fun below stairs, though.

Closing times
Open daily
Prices
Meals: a la carte £ 24/39

Typical Dishes
Bayonne ham with celeriac remoulade
Linguine of lobster with clams
Orange caramel custard

 ⊖ Green Park. On-street parking.

England • London

59   The Orange

**37 Pimlico Rd,
Victoria, SW1W 8NE**
Tel.: (020)78819844
Website: www.theorange.co.uk

VISA   M⑤   AE

 Meantime Brewery Ales and Adnams Ales

The former home of the Orange Brewery is a handsome pub that's as charming as its stucco-fronted façade suggests. The locals will no doubt have filled the bar, where the wood-burning oven is quite a feature, but it's still worth trying your luck to get one of the tables here or in the adjacent room; if you book ahead you'll be upstairs which is just as pleasantly decorated but a little more sedate. There's a clear Mediterranean bias to the menu which also includes plenty of salads along with spelt or wheat based pizzas which come with some original toppings; there are also roasts on a Sunday and pies for the traditionalists. Unusually for a London pub, there are bedrooms upstairs: these are stylish and comfortable.

Closing times
Open daily
Prices
Meals: a la carte £ 22/40
4 rooms: £ 195/225

Typical Dishes
Seared yellow fin tuna
Braised leg & grilled cutlet of lamb
Sticky toffee pudding

England • London

60   **Pantechnicon**

10 Motcomb St,
Belgravia, SW1X 8LA
Tel.: (020)77306074
Website: www.thepantechnicon.com

🚿 *VISA* 💳 AE ①

No real ales offered

It may be the very antithesis of the spit 'n' sawdust pub, but The Pantechnicon is still a very welcoming and busy local. The brightly run ground floor is crammed with tables and works on a first-come-first-served basis; upstairs you'll find a far more formal, Georgian style dining room and there's even a top floor cocktail bar – this is Belgravia after all. Wisely, the same menu is served throughout – an appealing mix of the refined and the comforting. Castle of Mey 28-day aged steaks and salt and chilli squid are the two most popular choices; home-smoked salmon, burgers and fish pie are also done well. The name comes from the horse-drawn wagons that once transported the belongings of locals to and from a repository on Motcomb Street.

Closing times
Closed 25 December
booking advisable
Prices
Meals: a la carte £ 27/63

Typical Dishes
Chilli salt squid
Rack of lamb, fennel &
broad beans
Chocolate, peanut &
caramel cake

 ⊖ *Knightsbridge. On-street parking.*

61
Portman

**51 Upper Berkeley St,
Marylebone, W1H 7QW**
Tel.: (020)77238996
Website: www.theportmanmarylebone.com

VISA   *MC*   *AE*

 Rebellion Ales

When it went by the name of The Masons Arms this pub was widely known for its gruesome history. It was here that the condemned, on their way to Tyburn Tree gallows, would take their last drink, which purportedly led to the phrase "one for the road". Reincarnated as The Portman, the pub these days boasts a less disreputable clientele who are more attracted by the quality of the cooking. Food is served all day and you can choose to eat in the busy ground floor bar or in the unexpectedly formal upstairs dining room, all thick-pile carpet and starched tablecloths. Fortunately, the style of food remains thoroughly down-to-earth and satisfying and is accompanied by a well-organised wine list and an interesting selection of cocktails.

Closing times
Open daily
Prices
Meals: £ 30/38
and a la carte £ 21/35

Typical Dishes
Asparagus with poached hen's egg

Bouillabaisse with saffron aioli

Chocolate mocha tart

⊖ Marble Arch. On-street parking.

Westminster

62 Prince Alfred & Formosa Dining Room

**5A Formosa St,
Bayswater and Maida Vale, W9 1EE**
Tel.: (020)72863287
Website: www.theprincealfred.com

 Young's Bitter and Wells Bombardier

The Prince Alfred is a wonderful example of a classic Victorian pub and its period features include ornate tiles, plate glass, panels and snugs. Unfortunately, the eating is done in the Formosa Dining Room extension on the side but at least it's a lively room and the open kitchen adds to the general bonhomie. There's more than a rustic edge to the appealing menu which will please all traditionalists; the mature steaks, pork belly and sticky toffee pudding are perennials but there are also dishes geared to those whose tastes are a tad more continental, such as sea bream with couscous and peppers. The service team could perhaps try revealing a little more personality but prices are kept realistic and the place still feels like a local.

Closing times
Open daily

Prices
Meals: £ 12 (weekdays) and a la carte £ 24/36

Typical Dishes
Pigeon breast
with swede & apricot
Twice-cooked crispy
pork belly
Sticky toffee pudding

Warwick Avenue. Parking by Warwick Avenue station (2min on foot).

England • London

63

Thomas Cubitt

**44 Elizabeth St,
Victoria, SW1W 9PA**
Tel.: (020)77306060
Website: www.thethomascubitt.co.uk

 Meantime Brewery Ales

The Thomas Cubitt is a pub of two halves: on the ground floor it's perennially busy and you can't book which means that if you haven't arrived by 7pm then you're too late to get a table. However, you can reserve a table upstairs, in a dining room that's a model of civility and tranquillity. Here, service comes courtesy of a young team where the girls are chatty and the men unafraid of corduroy. Downstairs you get fish and chips; here you get pan-fried fillet of brill with oyster beignet and truffled chips. The cooking is certainly skilled, quite elaborate in its construction and prettily presented. So, take your pick: upstairs can get a little pricey but is ideal for entertaining the in-laws; if out with friends then crowd in downstairs.

Closing times
Open daily
booking essential
Prices
Meals: a la carte £ 28/40

Typical Dishes
Carlingford rock oysters
Slow-cooked bavette & hollandaise
Chocolate & Guinness cake

 ⊖ Sloane Square. Parking meters in Elizabeth Street.

64

Waterway

**54 Formosa St,
Bayswater and Maida Vale, W9 2JU**
Tel.: (020)72663557
Website: www.thewaterway.co.uk

 Sharp's Doom Bar

It sits by the canal offering refreshment to passing narrowboaters, its large terrace gets besieged by drinkers and there's live music on a Thursday night – it sounds like a pub, it has the warmth and bustle of a pub, but it's all surprisingly smart. A bar occupies one side of the room and a restaurant the other – and there's no evidence anywhere of any spit or sawdust. The menu and cooking also sit somewhere between a restaurant and an urban gastropub, with dishes like rump of lamb with couscous sitting alongside more delicate offerings, such as scallops with pea purée, which reveal the kitchen's lighter touch. Desserts keep up the standard and prices are kept sensible. Service is youthful, bubbly and capable.

Closing times
Open daily
Prices
Meals: a la carte £ 23/39

Typical Dishes
Crayfish cocktail
Lemon sole with lemon butter
Eton mess

 Warwick Avenue. On-street parking.

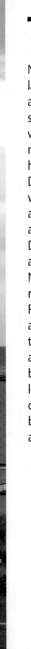

This region cradles some of England's wildest and most dramatic scenery typified by Northumberland National Park, a landscape of rolling purple moorlands and roaring rivers bursting with salmon and trout. Kielder Forest's mighty wilderness has been called "the country's most tranquil spot" while Bill Bryson has waxed lyrical upon the glories of Durham Cathedral. Those who love the wind in their hair are equally effusive about the eleven-mile footpath that accompanies the pounding waves of Durham's Heritage Coast; further north are the long, dune-backed beaches of Northumberland. Rambling across the region is Hadrian's Wall, 73 miles of iconic Roman history, while a modern slant on architectural celebrity is proffered by the Millennium Bridge, BALTIC Centre and Angel of the North. The famously bracing air whets hearty appetites for local Cheviot lamb, Coquetdale cheese or Holy Island oysters. And what could be more redolent of the North East than a breakfast of Craster kippers?

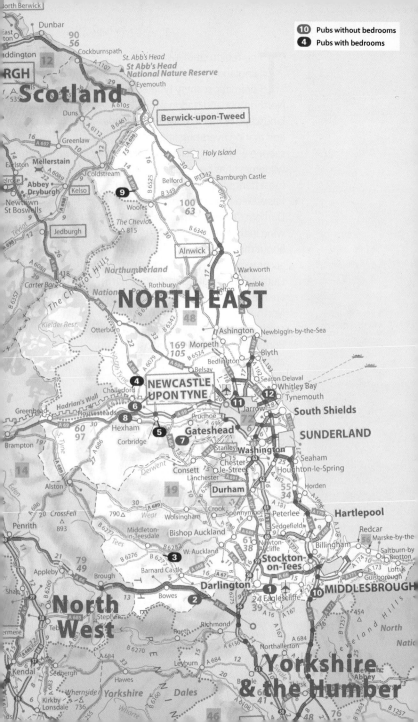

1 **Bay Horse**

45 The Green, Hurworth on Tees, DL2 2AA
Tel.: (01325)720663
Website: www.thebayhorsehurworth.com

🕍 *VISA* ⓜⓒ ⒜Ⓔ ⓓ

 Jennings Cumberland Ale, Captain Cook Slipway and Harviestoun Bitter & Twisted

Set on a long grassy street in an attractive village, this early 18C creamwashed pub is framed by colourful planters and hanging baskets, and boasts a pleasant rear terrace and garden. Drinkers and diners mingle amongst antique chairs, low stools and leather banquettes in the open-fired bar area and the relaxed, informal atmosphere continues through into the dining room. For special occasions the private first floor room definitely adds some style, with its 20 foot Victorian table and adjoining lounge. Menus offer something for everyone, featuring classics such as moules marinière, daube of beef or omelette Arnold Bennett, as well as familiar pub favourites. Dishes range in their presentation from simple and rustic to modern and intricate.

Closing times
Closed 25-26 December and Sunday dinner

Prices
Meals: £ 17 (lunch)/25 and a la carte £ 27/36

Typical Dishes
Mussels with white wine, cream & herbs

Daube of beef, steak & kidney pudding

Rice pudding with raisin & armagnac ice cream

🚗 *5.5 mi south of Darlington; signed off A 167; in the middle of the village. Parking.*

Hutton Magna

2

Oak Tree Inn

**Hutton Magna,
DL11 7HH**
Tel.: (01833)627371
Website: www.theoaktreehutton.co.uk

VISA MC

  Wells Bombardier, Timothy Taylor Landlord, Copper Dragon Best Bitter and Shepherd Neame Spitfire

They say good things come in small packages and that's definitely the case with this charming whitewashed pub. Found on the main street of a small hamlet, it consists of a single room with a proper old-fashioned counter, six wooden tables flanked by green settles and a bench table for the locals. Claire – who both serves the drinks and delivers the food – provides a warm welcome at the bar, while behind the scenes in the kitchen, Alastair single-handedly holds the fort. The short menu takes on a fairly formal format, offering generous portions of hearty, flavoursome cooking with a rustic British style and some subtle modern twists: you might find confit belly pork, onion and thyme tart, turbot with orange or Best End of lamb with artichokes.

Closing times
Closed 24-27 and 31 December, 1 January and Monday
dinner only
booking essential
Prices
Meals: a la carte £ 32/40

Typical Dishes
Lemon sole & crab tortellini
Fillet of beef with lovage mash
Coconut panna cotta

 7 mi southeast of Barnard Castle off A 66. Parking.

3   **Rose and Crown**

Romaldkirk,
DL12 9EB
Tel.: (01833)650213
Website: www.rose-and-crown.co.uk

VISA   MC   AE

🍺 **Black Sheep Best Bitter and Thwaites ales**

The Robinsons, who own nearby the Headlam Hall hotel, took over the running of this delightful Georgian inn when Chris and Alison Davy sold up after 23 years – but as the majority of the charming, chatty and helpful staff have remained, the transition was relatively smooth. The pub occupies a very pleasant spot overlooking three village greens and comes with a wonderfully characterful bar filled with horse brasses. On its other side is the somewhat misnamed 'brasserie', which offers a reassuringly familiar menu as well as afternoon tea, but most guests prefer the wood-panelled dining room with its list of classics. Bedrooms are individually decorated and well-equipped; those after more privacy and peace should ask for one in the annexe.

Closing times
Closed 23-27 December
Prices
Meals: a la carte £ 18/29
🛏 **14 rooms:** £ 95/175

Typical Dishes
Whitby crab fritter with lemon apple straws
Roast Best End of lamb with mini shepherd's pie
Chocolate tart with chantilly cream

🚗 3.5 mi southeast of Middleton-in-Teesdale on B 6277; on the village green, next to the church. Parking.

Barrasford

4 — **Barrasford Arms**

**Barrasford,
NE48 4AA**
Tel.: (01434)681237
Website: www.barrasfordarms.co.uk

 VISA **M©**

Wylam Gold Tankard, Cumberland Corby Ale and High House Brewery Auld Hemp

In the heart of the Northumbrian countryside, close to Kielder Water and Hadrian's Wall, sits this family-run 19C stone inn, providing an ideal base for exploring the North Tyne Valley. Retaining its traditional character, the pub provides the perfect home from home. The cosy fire is a huge draw, as are the regular vegetable, darts and quoits competitions, but the star attraction is the food. Menus differ between lunch and dinner; the former being a touch less formal. Local rib-eye is a permanent feature, as is the twice-baked cheese soufflé, and many come for the local game, which is handled deftly. The owner works closely with his suppliers to ensure that the ingredients remain tip-top. Comfortable bedrooms are sensibly priced.

Closing times
Closed 25-26 December, Sunday dinner, Monday lunch and bank holidays

Prices
Meals: £ 12 (weekday lunch) and a la carte £ 21/31

🛏 **7 rooms:** £ 67/87

Typical Dishes
Twice-baked cheddar cheese soufflé
Pork shoulder with Savoy cabbage, cider & apple
Sticky toffee pudding with vanilla ice cream

 7 mi north of Hexham signed off A 6079. Parking.

5 Duke of Wellington

**Newton,
Corbridge, NE43 7UL**
Tel.: (01661)844446
Website: www.thedukeofwellingtoninn.co.uk

 Mordue Spring Tide, Wylam Collingwood, Cullercoats Sugiboat Blond and Hadrian Border Tyneside Blond

Dating from the early 1600s, this is reputedly the oldest licensed premises in the county and, despite being tucked away down a twisty single track, it's clear that a good few people know about it. The first thing you'll notice as you approach is the great valley view and, when the sun's shining, a spot on the terrace is definitely the place to be. Inside it has a smart, modern country style, with a large, open-fired bar displaying stone walls and a more formal dining room with its tables already laid. Local eggs Benedict features at breakfast, after which there's a choice of two menus – one featuring pub classics, the other, more adventurous dishes such as saddle of roe deer. Stylish, luxurious bedrooms come with characterful exposed beams.

Closing times
Open daily
Prices
Meals: £ 14 (weekdays) and a la carte £ 23/35

7 rooms: £ 80/110

Typical Dishes
Ham knuckle ballotine
Braised lamb shank
Sticky Guinness pudding

3 mi east of Corbridge off A 69 in the centre of the village. Parking.

Great Whittington

6   **Queens Head Inn**

Great Whittington,
NE19 2HP
Tel.: (01434)672267
Website: www.thequeensheadinngw.co.uk

Wylam Ales and Black Sheep Best Bitter

A wonderful mural above the fire in the bar depicts the Queens Head Inn as it once was; in fact, this cosy room was at one time all that existed of what is considered by some to be the oldest inn in Northumberland. Its 400 year old thick brick walls have now been breached and the rear extension houses a smart dining room with a large skylight, heavy wood tables and bold, modern décor. Cooking is rooted in a traditional pub vein but has a refined edge – the ham hock terrine with homemade pease pudding is a hit, as is the seared squid from nearby North Shields. Regional produce plays a key role: the lamb and Galloway beef are from Tom Quiver's adjacent fields and the pork is local and free range. Dishes not only taste good but look good too.

Closing times
Closed Sunday dinner and Monday

Prices
Meals: a la carte £ 16/30

Typical Dishes
Braised pig's cheeks
Fish platter
Chocolate fondant

 6 mi north of Corbridge by A 68 off B 6318. Parking.

7   **Feathers Inn**

**Hedley on the Hill,
NE43 7SW**
Tel.: (01661)843607
Website: www.thefeathers.net

   VISA   **M©**

 Mordue Workie Ticket, Wylam Gold Tankard and Consett Ale Red Dust

All three rooms in this characterful village centre pub have their bookshelves crammed with cookbooks and their walls filled with photos of those who supply their produce, both of which suggest that this is a place which takes its food seriously. The kitchen certainly does things properly, whether that's making its own black pudding or preparing the popular game dishes. The food is generous in both flavour and size and seasonality plays a large part – the menu changes on a daily basis and it's worth exploring the selection of local cheeses. The pub has a warm and welcoming feel, thanks to its large central fireplace and stove and feels genuinely part of the local community. It also offers really nice views of the surrounding countryside.

Closing times
Closed first 2 weeks January
Prices
Meals: a la carte £ 20/29

Typical Dishes
Rhian's homemade black pudding

Roast haunch of Hedley roe deer with shepherd's pie

Sticky toffee pudding

England • North East • Northumberland

6 mi north of Consett by A 694, B 6309 and minor road. Parking.

Hexham

8 **Rat Inn**

**Anick,
Hexham, NE46 4LN**
Tel.: (01434)602814
Website: www.theratinn.com

 Wylam Ales, Hexhamshire Ales and Timothy Taylor Landlord

There are several suggestions as to how this 18C drovers' inn got its name – theories include rat catchers using it as a meeting place, a large rat once residing here and it being home to the local snitch during the Jacobite rebellion. Nobody actually knows the answer, so just sit back and enjoy the pleasant Tyne valley views. Situated in a small hillside hamlet, it's the perfect place to escape the rat race of the city, with its multi-levelled garden boasting arbours and picnic sets, and a traditional interior displaying wooden beams and an open range. The daily blackboard menu is concise but covers a good range of dishes, from pub classics like cottage pie to rib of beef for two to share. Produce is fresh, good quality and locally sourced.

Closing times
Closed
25 December, Monday except bank holidays and Sunday dinner

Prices
Meals: a la carte £ 19/36

Typical Dishes
Craster kipper pâté
Roast Northumberland rib of beef
Chocolate & Newcastle Brown Ale cake

 1.75 mi northeast of Hexham signposted off A 6079. Parking.

9 Red Lion Inn

**Main Rd,
Milfield, NE71 6JD**
Tel.: (01668)216224
Website: www.redlionmilfield.co.uk

 Black Sheep Best Bitter and guest ales

This classic stone pub started life as a mid-18C drovers' inn before becoming a stop-off point for the mail stagecoach between 1785 and 1835. It really is the heart of the village, so if you'd rather not catch up with the locals and the latest sporting events, head for the open-fired dining room instead of the bar. The menu has a traditional feel and offers plenty of choice, showcasing produce from both England and across the border. Dishes range from a prawn cocktail to scallops with black pudding; the Shetland mussels are not to be missed and the hearty homemade burger has now become a cult dish. Specials are chalked up the board and if you make it to pudding, you'll be rewarded with a tasty nursery selection. Bedrooms are fittingly homely.

Closing times
Closed 1 January, 25 December and dinner 31 December
booking advisable
Prices
Meals: a la carte £ 17/32
🛏 **2 rooms:** £ 30

Typical Dishes
Wild mushroom & garlic bruschetta
Steak & ale pie
Warm chocolate fudge cake

7 mi southeast of Coldstream by A 697. In the village centre. Parking.

Maltby

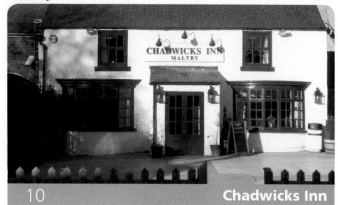

10 **Chadwicks Inn**

**High Ln,
Maltby, TS8 0BG**
Tel.: (01642)590300
Website: www.chadwicksinnmaltby.co.uk

 Wainstone Ales

Originally named The Pathfinder, this pub dates back over 200 years and was where the Spitfire pilots used to stop for a noggin before flying out on their missions. It's the only pub in the village, so you'll find regulars nursing their pints alongside those out for an evening meal. In warmer weather find a spot in the garden or on the sheltered patio area; in winter, head for the large open-fired bar or either of the two dining rooms with their smartly laid polished tables. The main à la carte features ambitious, intricate dishes, while a bistro menu of simpler offerings is available at lunch and in the early evening. The live acoustic sessions are becoming popular, as are the wine and tapas evenings. Service is friendly and fittingly formal.

Closing times
Closed 26 December,
1 January and Monday
booking advisable
Prices
Meals: £ 12/18 and a la carte £ 23/43

Typical Dishes
Shetland king scallops with tempura cockles
Wild sea bass with poached monkfish cheek
Chocolate ganache with roasted pineapple

 7 mi south of Middlesborough by A 19 and A 1045. Parking at rear.

11   Broad Chare

**25 Broad Chare,
Newcastle upon Tyne, NE1 3DQ**
Tel.: (0191)2112144
Website: www.thebroadchare.co.uk

VISA

 Wylam Angel, Gundog Top Dog and Thornbridge Jaipur

Owned by Terry Laybourne and set next to its sister operation Caffé Vivo, Broad Chare really hit the ground running. It's located on the quayside, close to the Millennium Bridge and, with its 'Proper Beer, Proper Food' motto, is a hit with the locals. The snug ground floor with its low level stool seating offers a choice of over 40 ales – some custom-made for the pub – and a bar snack menu featuring the likes of scotch eggs, cauliflower with curried mayonnaise and deep-fried pig's ears. Dining also takes place upstairs, where, along with this affectionately named 'Geordie Tapas', you'll find everything from an appealing 'on toast' selection to hearty daily specials such as steak and kidney pudding – all followed by tasty nursery puddings.

Closing times
Closed 25 December and Sunday dinner
booking advisable
Prices
Meals: a la carte £ 17/32

Typical Dishes
Cider-battered onions
Spicy blood pudding with apples
Monkey bread with toffee sauce

 Close to Millennium Bridge in Quayside area of city centre. On-street parking.

205

England • North East • Tyne and Wear

South Shields

12

Harbour Lights

**101 Lawe Rd,
South Shields, NE33 2AJ**
Tel.: (0191)4560124

Consett Brewery Steeltown and guest ales

Perched above the River Tyne, this pub offers great views past some old Victorian beacons and Russian cannons from the Crimean war, towards the Tynemouth Piers and the North Sea. It's run by a couple who grew up in the area and want to share their love of food, although drinkers are still welcome and you'll often find the darts or dominoes team playing over a pint or two. It's a simply furnished place, with a conservatory extension, and an open-plan bar and dining area where seafaring photos adorn the walls, recounting the local history. Menus offer pub classics like steak and kidney suet pudding, along with some more adventurous specials such as teriyaki salmon at weekends. Fish comes from the North Shields fish quay, visible on the river below.

Closing times
Open daily
Prices
Meals: £ 16 (lunch)
and a la carte £ 20/30

Typical Dishes
Tian of North Shields crab with tomato
Monkfish with spring onion butter
Sticky toffee pudding

 9 mi north of Sunderland by A 1018. Unrestricted on street parking.

206

Energised by Liverpool's swagger as 2008's European City of Culture, the north west feels like a region reborn. Dovetailed by the confident sophistication of a reinvigorated Manchester, the country's oldest industrial heartland boasts an impressive cultural profile. And yet arty urban centres are a million miles away from the rural grandeur of the region: trails and paths criss-cross the area all the way from the Solway Firth to Cheshire. Cumbria is a walker's paradise: from Hadrian's Wall to the glories of the Lake District, and along the vast shoreline of Morecambe Bay with its rich gathering of waders and wildfowl, there's a vivid contrast in scenery. The architectural landscape of the region covers the ages, too. Lancaster Castle reverberates to the footsteps of ancient soldiers, while Chester's walled city of medieval buildings is a true gem. Blackpool is now Europe's biggest seaside resort while the flavour of the north west is hotpot, black pudding and Morecambe Bay shrimps.

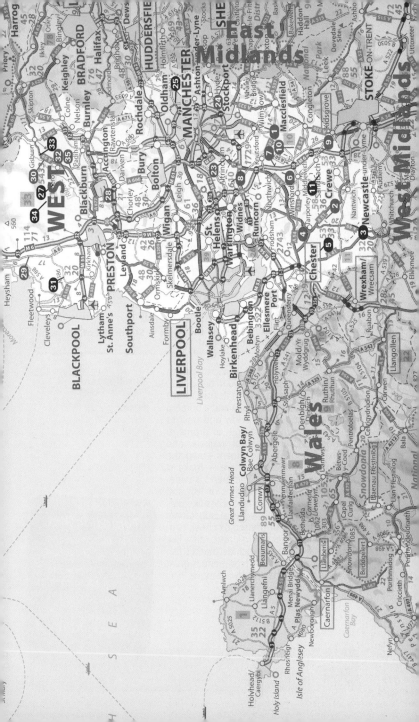

Alderley Edge

1

Wizard Inn

**Macclesfield Rd,
Alderley Edge, SK10 4UB**
Tel.: (01625)584000
Website: www.ainscoughs.co.uk

Thwaites Wainwright and Triple C, Storm Silk of Amnesia and Merlins The Wizard

With its flag floors, low wooden beams and open fires, this 200 year old pub is full of character and charm; its four rooms boasting a shabby-chic style and a homely, cosy feel. Being dog friendly and next to the famous Alderley Edge escarpment, it attracts its fair share of walkers, and its mix of drinkers and diners – and the resulting vibrant atmosphere – make it feel like a proper pub. The menu is wide-ranging, offering sandwiches or fish and meat platters and pub favourites like pies or burgers, as well as more substantial dishes such as slow-braised ox cheek with mash and the occasional retro dish like chicken Kiev. Specials include market fish of the day and the early bird menu is great value. Service is charmingly attentive.

Closing times
Closed 25 December

Prices
Meals: £ 10 (weekday dinner) and a la carte
£ 21/38

Typical Dishes
Venison scotch egg with pickled cabbage

Steak & Storm Ale suet pudding, triple cooked chips

Toffee apple oaty crumble with custard

 1.25 mi southeast of Alderley Edge on B 5087. Parking.

2 — Yew Tree Inn

Long Ln,
Spurstow, Bunbury, CW6 9RD
Tel.: (01829)260274
Website: www.theyewtreebunbury.com

 VISA **MC**

Stonehouse Station Bitter and guest ales

Once inside this handsome, part red brick, part black and white timbered pub, you'll find it isn't as big as you first thought – but there's room enough for one and all, whether that's locals with pints gathered to organise the latest village events or diners attending one of the regular themed evenings. Find a seat in the central bar or one of smaller rooms boasting wood and quarry tile flooring, mahogany panels and open fires. Extensive menus offer local and homemade produce, with dishes ranging from fish pie to braised ox cheeks; while the black pudding salad, chips in dripping and Cheshire brie for two are must tries. Come on a Friday to sample some lesser-known guest ales, accompanied by a small selection of British tapas dishes.

Closing times
Open daily
Prices
Meals: a la carte £ 20/33

Typical Dishes
Goujons of pollock with wasabi mayonnaise
Braised oxtail & celeriac lasagne with butter beans
Key lime posset

7.5 mi northwest of Nantwich by A 51, A 534 and A 49. Parking.

Cholmondeley

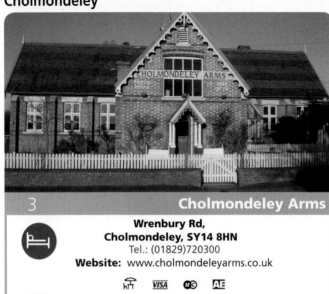

3 **Cholmondeley Arms**

**Wrenbury Rd,
Cholmondeley, SY14 8HN**
Tel.: (01829)720300
Website: www.cholmondeleyarms.co.uk

🛏️ 🍴 **VISA** **MC** **AE**

🍺 **Weetwood Ales, Salopian Shropshire Gold and
Coachouse Gunpowder Mild**

The Cholmondeley Arms started life in 1862 as the eponymous estate's schoolhouse and details like school blackboards, a section of 'old school favourites' on the menu and an ale called 'teacher's tipple' are a reminder that it spent more than a century as a place of learning. High vaulted ceilings and large windows let in lots of light, while roaring fires give the place a cosy, welcoming feel. The menu offers tasty, modern pub favourites like devilled lamb's kidneys on toast, stalker's venison pie or homemade lamb faggots. Cask beers come from within a 30 mile radius and gin-lovers will be in clover with over 140 to choose from, plus five types of tonic. Head to the Old Headmaster's House to sleep it all off in one of the 6 comfy bedrooms.

Closing times
Open daily
Prices
Meals: a la carte £ 21/35
🛏️ **6 rooms:** £ 75/90

Typical Dishes
Cheddar & leek rarebit
Baked cod loin with brown shrimps
Sticky spiced apple pancakes

 11 mi west of Nantwich by A51 and A 534 on A 49. Parking.

Cotebrook

4   Fox and Barrel

**Foxbank,
Cotebrook, CW6 9DZ**
Tel.: (01829)760529
Website: www.foxandbarrel.co.uk

 Weetwood Eastgate Ale and Deuchars IPA

With wood-panelled walls filled with framed pictures and shelves lined with books, you could be mistaken for thinking you're in a Brunning and Price pub, but then that's probably because the owners have both worked for the group in the past. The front bar with its open log fire is very much the drinkers' domain, while the smart terrace and large garden, complete with vintage tractor, attract one and all. Menus change virtually daily and offer plenty of originality and interest; you might find twice-baked cheese soufflé followed by loin of venison with spiced red cabbage, alongside old favourites like fish and chips. Dishes are generously proportioned, neatly presented and sensibly priced – and there's a good list of wines by the glass too.

Closing times
Closed dinner
25-26 December and
1 January

Prices
Meals: a la carte £ 16/36

Typical Dishes
Salmon roulade with
celeriac salad
Rump of lamb with
feta & black pudding
croquettes
Rhubarb & custard
panna cotta

On A 49 northeast of Tarporley. Parking.

England • North West • Cheshire

Higher Burwardsley

5

Pheasant Inn

**Higher Burwardsley,
CH3 9PF**
Tel.: (01829)770434
Website: www.thepheasantinn.co.uk

VISA MC AE

Weetwood Eastgate Ale, Cheshire Cat and Best Bitter

This well-run, modern pub is set atop a sandstone escarpment, with views across the Cheshire Plains to Wrexham and Liverpool. Outside space is plentiful, with various terraces and a garden. Inside feels fresh and clean with wooden floors, reclaimed beams and open fires. The snug is quite cosy; the dining room more formal – and the window tables are the first to be nabbed in either. The daily menu focuses on simple pub classics like ale, steak and mushroom pie, with some interesting specials, nibbles and deli boards to complement. The no-nonsense cooking has clear, gutsy flavours and the smartly dressed staff are keen to please. Spacious, beamed bedrooms are set in the main building; more modern rooms with views are located in the barn.

Closing times
Open daily
Prices
Meals: a la carte £ 19/40

12 rooms: £ 65/135

Typical Dishes
Goat's cheese croquette with Cumberland sauce
Pork fillet, confit belly & wild mushroom jus
White chocolate cheesecake

 2.5 mi southeast of Tattenhall. Parking.

6   **Duke of Portland**

**Penny's Ln,
Lach Dennis, CW9 8SY**
Tel.: (01606)46264
Website: www.dukeofportland.com

 **Marston's Pedigree, Jennings Cockerhoop,
Brakspear Oxford Gold**

This creamwashed inn sits on the main road through the village, welcoming drinkers and diners alike. The former tend to gather in the high-ceilinged main bar or the relaxing, leather-furnished lounge. The latter have two choices: a raised area close to the bar and – the more popular option – a smart, contemporary side room which features a mounted stag's head, shot in 1931 by the Duke of Portland. The lengthy à la carte menu offers dishes that won't scare the horses; expect fishcakes, chilli con carne, beef, Guinness and mushroom pie, or slow-roasted shoulder of Lune Valley lamb. Proper puddings include classics such as rum baba or Bramley apple crumble, while the good value set price Sunday lunch brings people from miles around.

Closing times
Open daily
Prices
Meals: a la carte £ 19/38

Typical Dishes
Beef carpaccio, rocket & parmesan
Sea bass fillets & piquant tomato sauce
Raspberry crème brûlée

Lower Peover

7

Bells of Peover

**The Cobbles,
Lower Peover, WA16 9PZ**
Tel.: (01565)722269
Website: www.thebellsofpeover.com

🍴 *VISA* 💳 AE

Robinsons Dizzy Blonde, Unicorn and XB

So, why does this refurbished 16C former coaching inn have the Stars and Stripes flying over it? Because, apparently, Generals Eisenhower and Patton were stationed nearby and were regulars. And the Bells? No, not from the church tower but the name of a family who once owned it. These days the pub offers keenly priced, flavourful food, with the likes of salads, burgers or a crisp belly pork sandwich at lunch; the menu expands in the evening to include dishes like pan-fried scallops, salt-baked fish or rabbit tortellini. You'll have to be quick to nab one of the three tables in the cosy, fire-lit bar, but there's always plenty of space in the three, tastefully furnished, contemporary dining rooms. Service is formal and knowledgeable.

Closing times
Closed Monday except bank holidays

Prices
Meals: £ 17 (lunch) and a la carte £ 23/39

Typical Dishes
Beetroot soup

Rump of lamb, aubergine caviar & couscous

Cherry Bakewell tart & milk ice cream

🚗 Off the B 5081, which runs through the village. Parking.

8   Church Green

**Higher Ln,
Lymm, WA13 0AP**
Tel.: (01925)752068
Website: www.thechurchgreen.co.uk

 Caledonian Golden XPA, Bank's Best Bitter, Black Sheep Ale and Theakston Lightfoot

England • North West • Cheshire

This double gable-fronted Victorian pub stands on the green next to St Mary's Church. Its experienced chef-owner, Aiden Byrne (who appeared on the Great British Menu) is supported by a well-structured team, who take pride in the pub's kitchen garden, which supplies everything from beetroot to soft fruits. The open-plan bar and restaurant are decorated in modern hues and there's a pleasant conservatory and attractive decked terrace to the rear. The appealing menu includes pub classics and a steak house section, where you choose a cut, then add sauce, garnish and any extras you want. There's a set tasting selection of more elaborate dishes on Saturday evenings and breakfast at the weekend, which includes a full English for children.

Closing times
Open daily
booking essential
Prices
Meals: a la carte £ 21/54

Typical Dishes
Pork belly with Lyonnaise potato

Breast of chicken with truffle macaroni

Lime cheesecake with roasted pineapple

 7 mi west of Altrincham by A 56. Parking.

Sandbach

9   **Old Hall**

**High St,
Sandbach, CW11 1AL**
Tel.: (01270)758170
Website: www.oldhall-sandbach.co.uk

 Brunning & Price Original Bitter, Redwillow Feckless and Three Tuns XXX

Testament to the strength of local feeling towards this black and white 17C former manor house is the fact that, having lain empty for several years, campaigning villagers managed to get it listed on the English Heritage 'buildings at risk' register. Eventually rescued from further decay by the current owners, total restoration has created a smart new look for the Old Hall's many rooms, whilst retaining the character that comes from original features like oak panelling and heavy timber beams. This is a proper pub with real ales aplenty and a daily menu which focuses on keenly priced pub classics; the no-frills style of cooking meaning that dishes like braised shoulder of lamb and steak and kidney pudding arrive exactly as they should.

Closing times
Open daily
Prices
Meals: a la carte £ 22/36

Typical Dishes
Game terrine with toasted brioche
Braised lamb shoulder with dauphinoise potatoes
Bread & butter pudding

 1.5 mi southwest of M 6 junction 17, off A 534. Parking.

10 Swettenham Arms

**Swettenham,
CW12 2LF**
Tel.: (01477)571284
Website: www.swettenhamarms.co.uk

VISA **MC** **AE**

Timothy Taylor Landlord, Beartown Brewery Kodiak Gold,
Moorhouse's Pride of Pendle

If you rely on your sat nav you may well end up in the middle of the local ford, but don't give up just yet, as this pub's well worth the search. Formerly a nunnery, it's been in the capable hands of the Cunninghams for many years now; although there's still the occasional ghostly sighting of a nun. Its beaten copper bar, welcoming open fireplaces and shiny horse brasses mean that tradition reigns, which is a surefire hit with both drinkers and diners. The seasonally changing menu provides plenty of choice, from sharing platters and satisfying pub classics to carefully prepared, well-presented restaurant-style dishes, such as rack of local lamb with basil mousse. Be sure to find time to stroll around the lavender meadow or the RHS arboretum.

Closing times
Open daily
Prices
Meals: a la carte £ 21/44

Typical Dishes
Smoked duck breast,
rhubarb & soft herb
salad
Bouillabaisse
Passion fruit soufflé
with pomegranate
sorbet

Between Holmes Chapel and Congleton, signposted off the A 54. Parking.

Warmingham

11

Bear's Paw

**School Ln,
Warmingham, CW11 3QN**
Tel.: (01270)526317
Website: www.thebearspaw.co.uk

VISA MC AE

**Weetwood Cheshire Cat, Eastgate Ale and Beartown
Kodiak Gold**

Sister to the Pheasant at Tattenhall is this handsome 19C inn; probably best described as very big and very, very busy. There's a spacious, semi wood panelled bar with two vast fireplaces and a huge array of local ales. The menu is also sizeable, with enough choice to please all appetites; from nibbles like flavoured chipolatas or olives to deli boards including charcuterie and cheese selections – all served with rustic bread and house chutney. Main dishes look to Europe for their inspiration, but it's the good old British favourites like fish and chips or steak and ale pie that win the day. You can cook your own steak on a hot stone – and make sure you try the Bear's Paw Sundae for dessert. Bedrooms are stylish and well worth the money.

Closing times
Open daily
Prices
Meals: a la carte £ 20/38
17 rooms: £ 95/140

Typical Dishes
King prawn pil pil
Pork belly with mustard mash, cider jus
Warm treacle tart with clotted cream

3.5 mi west of Sandbach by A 533. Parking.

12 **Drunken Duck Inn**

 **Barngates,
Ambleside, LA22 0NG**
Tel.: (01539)436347
Website: www.drunkenduckinn.co.uk

 Barngates Brewery Cat Nap, Cracker, Brathay Gold and Red Bull Terrier

Situated in the heart of the beautiful Lakeland countryside, this attractive inn takes its name from an old legend about a landlady, some ducks and a leaky beer barrel. The popular fire-lit bar is the cosiest place to sit, among hop bines, pictures of the hunt and old brewery advertisements; but there are also two more formal dining rooms. The same menu is served throughout, offering simple lunches and much more elaborate dinners, with prices to match; cooking is generous and service, attentive. Ales come from the on-site micro-brewery and are made with water from their own tarn. Boutique, country house bedrooms – some with patios – boast extremely comfy beds and country views. Afternoon tea can be taken in the lounge or residents' garden.

Closing times
Closed 25 December
booking essential
Prices
Meals: a la carte £ 25/47
17 rooms: £ 79/325

Typical Dishes
Wood pigeon, white onion soubise, garlic & parsley
Steamed halibut with asparagus, broad beans & lemon
Chocolate cake, Brathay Gold ice cream

3 mi southwest of Ambleside by A 593 and B 5286 on Tarn Hows road. By the crossroads at the top of Duck Hill. Parking.

Bowland Bridge

13   Hare and Hounds

**Bowland Bridge,
LA11 6NN**
Tel.: (015395)68333
Website: www.hareandhoundsbowlandbridge.co.uk

Tirrel Hair of the Dog, Loweswater Gold and Kirkby Lonsdale Ruskin's

This charming 17C Lakeland pub is situated in the delightful village of Bowland Bridge, where Arthur Ransome wrote the book 'Swallows and Amazons'. There's a large terrace with chunky wooden tables to the front, leading through into a rustic, open-fired inner with stone walls, black and white village photos and exposed beams draped with hop bines. Menus offer typical, hearty, pub-style dishes – such as homemade pies or Lakeland hotpot with black pudding and home-pickled cabbage – and much of the produce is locally sourced. There's also a fine selection of ales to choose from, including 'Hare of the Dog', which is specially brewed for them by a Lakeland brewery. Bedrooms are well-equipped and elegant with smart bathrooms; some have roll-top baths.

Closing times
Closed 25 December
Prices
Meals: a la carte £ 20/29
🛏 **3 rooms:** £ 75/165

Typical Dishes
Trio of lamb with apricot chutney

Beef and ale pie with potato gateau

Chocolate brownie with hot chocolate sauce

 7 mi south of Windermere signed off A 5074. In the village centre. Parking.

14 **Pig & Whistle**

**Cartmel,
LA11 6PL**
Tel.: (01539)536482
Website: www.pigandwhistlecartmel.co.uk

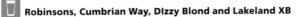

Robinsons, Cumbrian Way, Dizzy Blond and Lakeland XB

This pub might be run by the same owners as esteemed nearby restaurant L'Enclume but regulars can rest safe in the knowledge that this will stay a comfy, cosy village local; a place to while away the evening with a pint but also a place to come for a good meal. Situated close to the main square in the delightful Lakeland village of Cartmel, it looks, from the outside, rather like a row of terraced cottages, and with its three tiny rooms – with space for just 28 people – it certainly has an intimate feel. Menus are rooted in the traditional pub vein and cooking is honest and careful with bold, defined flavours. Satisfyingly, prices remain reasonable. The simple wine list features just 6 bottles, with the real ales taking pride of place.

Closing times
Closed Monday and Tuesday
Prices
Meals: a la carte £ 24/33

Typical Dishes
Crab soup
Steak & kidney pudding
Gooseberry & elderflower meringue

3 mi northwest of Grange-over-Sands. On-street parking.

Clifton

15 George and Dragon

**Clifton,
CA10 2ER**
Tel.: (01768)865381
Website: www.georgeanddragonclifton.co.uk

Lancaster Blonde, Hawkshead Bitter and Eden Gold

Consisting of 75,000 acres and covering much of Cumbria, the Lowther family estate includes properties ranging from a castellated mansion to this whitewashed coaching inn. Its characterful 18C bar features a flag floor, panelling and a wood burning stove, while the spacious restaurant takes on a more modern style, with its open kitchen and smart wood furnishings. When it comes to the food, it doesn't get more local than this, with vegetables from the kitchen garden, game from the surrounding moors and organic meats from the estate's farms. Appealing dishes might include twice-baked Cumbrian cheese soufflé, followed by Askham pork sausages or pan-fried wild sea bass. Modern bedrooms showcase furniture and paintings from the family's collection.

Closing times
Closed 26 December
Prices
Meals: a la carte £ 22/38
🛏 **12 rooms:** £ 79/155

Typical Dishes
Twice-baked cheese soufflé
Pan-fried venison liver with wild garlic mash
'Charlie's' chocolate pot

🚗 3 mi south of Penrith on A6. In centre of village. Parking.

16   Punch Bowl Inn

**Crosthwaite,
LA8 8HR**
Tel.: (01539)568237
Website: www.the-punchbowl.co.uk

 Barngates Cracker, Coniston Old Man and Winster Old School

Nestled among the hills in the heart of the picturesque Lyth Valley, this attractive 17C inn enjoys a truly delightful setting – and it's not just the views that are glorious, the pub itself is truly charming, with its antiques, cosy open fires and exposed wooden beams. Cooking has a classical base but displays some modern touches, and dishes display a degree of complexity that you wouldn't usually find in a pub. Dine in the rustic bar or, for more of an occasion, in the more formal restaurant. Smart, individually styled bedrooms boast good quality linen, roll-top baths and fluffy towels; 'Noble' features twin bath tubs and 'Danson' offers the best views. If you fancy sending a postcard, the reception also doubles as the village post office!

Closing times
Open daily
Prices
Meals: a la carte £ 22/40
9 rooms: £ 85/305

Typical Dishes
Twice-baked Lancashire cheese soufflé

Breast of guinea fowl with truffle gnocchi

Violet & blackberry crème brûlée

 5.25 mi west of Kendal by All Hallows Lane; next to the church. Parking.

Kirkby Lonsdale

17   **Sun Inn**

**6 Market St,
Kirkby Lonsdale, LA6 2AU**
Tel.: (015242)71965
Website: www.sun-inn.info

Hawkshead Brewery Bitter, Thwaites Wainwright and
Kirkby Lonsdale Monumental Blonde

This 17C inn's hands-on owners don't have to go far to find quality seasonal produce as it's literally on their doorstep, with the famous Churchmouse Cheese shop next door and a butcher's two doors down. Lunch sees a few pub classics like saddleback sausage and mash on offer, with a number of tapas-style small plates under the title 'meat, fishes, loaves and dishes'. Dinner is a more serious affair, with various different menus and dishes such as red leg partridge pithivier or slow-roasted shoulder of Lune Valley lamb. Well-lit, modern bedrooms boast quality linen and thoughtful extras like homemade flapjacks and fresh milk. Breakfasts are well worth getting up for, with delicious offerings like poached fruits and homemade granola.

Closing times
Closed Monday lunch

Prices
Meals: £ 27 (dinner)
and a la carte £ 20/29

🛏 **11 rooms:** £ 76/168

Typical Dishes
Asparagus with poached hen's egg

Lune Valley lamb with salsa verde

Lemon mess with citrus meringue

 In the centre of town. Long stay car park in Booth Rd.

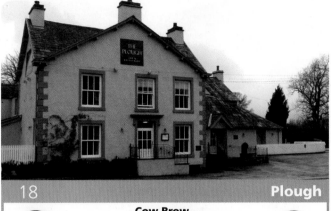

18

Plough

**Cow Brow,
Lupton, LA6 1PJ**
Tel.: (015395)67700
Website: www.theploughatlupton.co.uk

**Kirkby Lonsdale Monumental Blonde, Jennings
Cumberland Ale and Coniston Brewery Old Man Ale**

Younger sister to the Punch Bowl at Crosthwaite, the Plough is set on the main road that links the Lake District to North Yorkshire and, like its sister pub, is gaining a good reputation in the local area. There's a cosy, homely feel to the place, which is made up of two neutrally hued rooms filled with an assortment of quality antique tables and comfy sofas set around a wood burning stove. The cheery, knowledgeable team serve up a pleasing mix of pub and restaurant-style dishes: you'll find a selection of classics, alongside a list of tasty small plates – such as crispy whitebait or courgette fritters – that can be mixed and matched as you please with an enticing array of side dishes. Smart, individually styled bedrooms complete the picture.

Closing times
Open daily
Prices
Meals: a la carte £ 19/33
5 rooms: £ 95/195

Typical Dishes
Black pudding with apple & poached egg
Chargrilled sirloin steak
Lemon meringue pie & berry compote

 4.75 mi northwest of Kirkby Lonsdale on A 65. Parking.

Nether Burrow

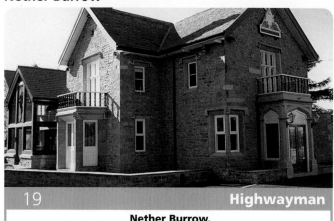

19 **Highwayman**

**Nether Burrow,
LA6 2RJ**
Tel.: (01524)273338
Website: www.highwaymaninn.co.uk

Thwaites Nutty Black, Lancaster Bomber and Wainwright

It's rumoured that this sizeable 18C coaching inn with its lovely terrace was once the midnight haunt of the local highwaymen. Set on the border of three counties – Cumbria, Lancashire and Yorkshire – it makes the most of its setting, with produce so local that a meal almost constitutes a regional geography lesson. The Lancashire hotpot is a signature dish, and you'll find bacon from Sillfield Farm and shrimps from Morecambe Bay, alongside seasonal classics like spring asparagus from Formby and game in winter. The rustic, no-nonsense approach to food means dishes are well-crafted and full of flavour; a similar approach to wine means you can bring your own and pay corkage.

Closing times
Closed Monday and 25 December.

Prices
Meals: a la carte £ 19/32

Typical Dishes
Sticky pork ribs
Lancashire hotpot
Rhubarb & apple crumble

 2 mi south of Kirkby Lonsdale by A 65 and A 683. Parking.

20   King's Head

**Ravenstonedale,
CA17 4NH**
Tel.: (01539)623050
Website: www.kings-head.com

VISA MC

Jennings Cumberland Ale, Eden Dark Knight, Tirril Old Faithful, Lancaster Blonde and Wychwood Hobgoblin

This whitewashed inn consists of four 17C cottages that were turned into a pub in late Victorian times – and have been owned by the same family since 1892. The pub's smartly refurbished interior features polished timbers, a flagged floor and a wood-burning stove; come summer, the garden fits the bill nicely, with a view out over the babbling beck and a wood inhabited by red squirrels. With a bounty of produce available on the pub's doorstep, the cooking here is, as you would expect, seriously seasonal; dishes like slow-roasted belly of pork, ale-battered cod, and venison and cranberry pie are well-prepared, appealingly presented and, most importantly of all, wonderfully tasty. Bedrooms are comfortable and elegant, with smart bathrooms.

Closing times
Closed 25 December
Prices
Meals: a la carte £ 20/33
🛏 **6 rooms:** £ 65/98

Typical Dishes
Cumberland cheese & onion soufflé
Venison & cranberry pie
White chocolate brûlée

England • North West • Cumbria

🚗 5 mi southwest of Kirkby Stephen signed off A 685. On edge of village. Small car park and parking opposite.

Troutbeck

21   Queen's Head

**Troutbeck,
LA23 1PW**
Tel.: (015394)32174
Website: www.queensheadtroutbeck.co.uk

🛏️   📶   *VISA*   MC   AE

🍺 **Robinsons Dizzy Blonde, Unicorn and Old Tom**

This passionately run pub is found in the most delightful of settings and makes a great stop off-point if you're heading for the Kirkstone Pass. It's amazingly characterful inside, consisting of a beamed bar with an unusual 'four-poster' counter – lined with a huge selection of whiskies – and several interlinking rooms which boast a vast array of memorabilia. Seating varies from heavy wooden settles to high-backed leather chairs but the best spot has to be on the terrace with its fantastic hill views. The large menu offers something for everyone, from traditional pub dishes to those with a more modern twist, and influences range from the Med to South Africa. Smart bedrooms boast strong comforts; rooms 10 and 11 have the best views.

Closing times
Open daily
Prices
Meals: a la carte £ 19/43
🛏️ **15 rooms:** £ 120/150

Typical Dishes
Goat's cheese & thyme
tortellini
Slow-braised lamb
shank
Chocolate
fondant with clotted
cream ice cream

 4 mi north of Windermere by A 592. Parking.

22

Brown Horse Inn

**Winster,
LA23 3NR**
Tel.: (015394)43443
Website: www.thebrownhorseinn.co.uk

 Winster Valley Brewery Old School, Dark Horse and Best Bitter

This simple coaching inn has always been popular with the locals; but even more so since the creation of its on-site brewery. It has a shabby-chic style, with flagged floors, antique dressers and a real mix of furniture. In one corner, a miniature model of the bar (made by one of the regulars) and a London Underground map of local pubs provide talking points; while the split-level terrace is a real draw. Seasonal menus feature produce from the fields out back and game comes from shoots they organise themselves. Dishes are designed with hungry walkers in mind; the blackboard specials are a little more adventurous and often include home-reared pork. Bedrooms are a mix of classical and boutique styles; the latter have French windows and terraces.

Closing times
Open daily
Prices
Meals: a la carte £ 19/36

9 rooms: £ 50/150

Typical Dishes
Black pudding, hen's egg, ventreche bacon

Chicken & haggis bon bon with wild mushrooms

Caramel panna cotta, honeycomb & popping candy

 4 mi south of Windermere by A 5074. Parking.

23 **Victoria**

**29 Stamford St,
Altrincham, WA14 1EX**
Tel.: (0161)6131855
Website: www.thevictoria-altrincham.co.uk

 Greene King Old Speckled Hen

The Victoria is a very traditional looking pub set in a quiet part of the town centre, with flower pots on the windowsills. Its appealing interior comes as a pleasant surprise; a single room with a wooden bar at its centre and half the tables left for drinkers; the other half laid up for diners. Lunchtime sees sandwiches, light bites and a few dishes from the evening à la carte, which are classically based but with a modern twist; maybe smoked duck crumpet, steak and kidney pudding or jugged wild rabbit. The emphasis is on locally sourced ingredients, so expect beef from Ashlea Farm, Pendrill's cheese and Dunham Massey Farm ice cream. There's a good value early evening set menu and friendly service from a young team.

Closing times
Closed 1 January, 26 December and Sunday dinner
bookings advisable at dinner

Prices
Meals: £ 14 (weekday dinner)/20 and a la carte £ 26/35

Typical Dishes
Smoked mackerel with ginger beer dressing

Pigeon breast with smoked bacon hash

Chocolate bread & butter pudding

 In centre of town. Pay & display parking outside; free at night.

24 **Oddfellows**

**Moor End Rd,
Mellor, SK6 5PT**
Tel.: (0161)4497826
Website: www.oddfellowsmellor.com

 Marston's Pedigree, Marble Manchester Bitter, Bollington Best, Moorhouse's Oddies Ale and Howard Town Wren's Nest

England • North West • Greater Manchester

A complete refurbishment by its new owners has given Oddies – as it is affectionately known by the locals – a light, uncluttered feel; while wood burning stoves and an eclectic assortment of furniture add an element of cosiness. Built into the side of a former stone quarry on a winding lane leading up into the hills, the Oddfellows proudly retains its identity as a pub, with its bar and its 5 hand pump beers the focal point of the room. An appealing, daily changing menu offers what they call 'British food with a modern twist'; this includes anything from a burger, fishcakes or a cheese and onion pie to sausage and mash or steak. Local suppliers are acknowledged on the menu, lamb comes from the owners' fields and bread is homemade.

Closing times
Closed Sunday dinner, Monday and Tuesday

Prices
Meals: a la carte £ 17/33

Typical Dishes
Oven-baked goat's cheese

Lamb rump with braised shoulder cottage pie

Lemon meringue tart

2.5 mi northwest of Marple by Marple Bridge and minor road. Parking.

235

Oldham

25   **White Hart Inn**

**51 Stockport Rd,
Lydgate, Oldham, OL4 4JJ**
Tel.: (01457)872566
Website: www.thewhitehart.co.uk

 Timothy Taylor Golden Best and Landlord, J.W. Lees and Copper Dragon Best Bitter

Set overlooking Saddleworth Moor, this stone-built inn has undergone various sympathetic extensions over the years; these are now home to a private dining room, a formal restaurant, a function room known as 'The Oak Room' and 12 bedrooms, named after local men of note. The bar boasts exposed beams, open fires and photos of the owner's travels; ironically, he once got thrown out of this pub for underage drinking before eventually buying it himself. Dishes such as potted rabbit or calves' liver sit alongside pub classics like sausage and mash on the brasserie menu, while the restaurant menu takes things to another level with choices such as cauliflower cappuccino with foie gras and chestnuts or galantine of guinea fowl with quails' eggs.

Closing times
Closed 26 December

Prices
Meals: £ 17 (lunch and early dinner) and a la carte £ 26/39

🛏 **12 rooms:** £ 95

Typical Dishes
Squab pigeon with dates & orange
Loin of spring lamb with sweetbreads
Iced vanilla cheesecake

 3 mi east of Oldham by A 669 on A 6050. Parking.

26 — Redwell Inn

Arkholme,
LA6 1BQ
Tel.: (015242)21240
Website: www.redwellinn.net

Guest ales from Tirril, Thwaites and Lancaster Breweries

England • North West • Lancashire

This attractive 16C stone inn takes its name from the well that stands to the rear of the pub, whose bricks gradually turned red over the years due to minerals leached from the water. It's one of those places that's a real family affair, with the son behind the scenes in the kitchen and his parents looking after the guests. The rustic bar boasts a few sofas, scrubbed tables and a wood burning stove, as well as a large display of homemade breads for sale, while the restaurant in the old coach house is a little more formal. The same menu is served throughout and offers something for everyone, from 'nibbles' such as a homemade scotch egg with HP sauce, to potted shrimps, Grandma Singleton's Lancashire cheese pasty or a classic fish pie.

Closing times
Closed 25 December, January and Monday-Wednesday

booking advisable

Prices
Meals: a la carte £ 19/41

Typical Dishes
Olive oil poached salmon
Sous-vide lamb rump
Belgian chocolate mousse

 9 mi southwest of Kirkby Lonsdale on B 6254. Parking.

Bashall Eaves

27   **Red Pump Inn**

**Clitheroe Rd,
Bashall Eaves, BB7 3DA**
Tel.: (01254)826227
Website: www.theredpumpinn.co.uk

**Moorhouse's Broomstick, Hawkshead Windermere Pale,
Ilkley Gold, Tirril Old Faithful and Cumberland Corby Blonde**

Dine in this pub's traditional restaurant or in the rustic bar. The fire-lit snug is a charming place to idle away an hour or two, while the valley sunsets make the terrace a fantastic place for a drink. Local produce features highly on the seasonal menus, with dishes like super slow roasted Pendle belly pork or hot-smoked Dunsop trout pâté. With local shoots in and around the Forest of Bowland, game is a speciality, so you'll also see dishes like venison ravioli and pan-fried breast of pheasant. Dessert might mean lemon sponge pudding or a selection of regional cheeses, and beers include local and guest ales, with Black Sheep on draught. Sleep in one of the spacious, modern bedrooms and wake up to views of Pendle Hill or Longridge Fell.

Closing times
Closed 1 week January, Monday except bank holidays and Tuesday in winter

Prices
Meals: £ 15 (weekdays) and a la carte £ 20/35

3 rooms: £ 65/115

Typical Dishes
Venison pithivier with beetroot & apple salad
Confit of local lamb with haggis & rösti
Liquorice-infused treacle tart

3 mi northwest of Clitheroe by B 6243 and minor road northwest. Parking.

28   **Clog & Billycock**

**Billinge End Rd,
Pleasington, Blackburn, BB2 6QB**
Tel.: (01254)201163
Website: www.theclogandbillycock.com

 VISA   **MC**   AE

Thwaites Original and Wainwright

This popular sandstone pub was originally called the Bay Horse, before being renamed after a fashion trend often sported by the former landlord – who liked to wear the quirky combination of clog shoes and a billycock hat. The addition of a large extension means the pub is now modern and open-plan. The neutrally hued walls are filled with photos of their local suppliers and the extensive menus offer a strong Lancastrian slant; you might find Morecambe Bay shrimps, Port of Lancaster smoked fish or Ribble Valley beef, alongside tasty sharing platters. Most produce comes from within 20 miles and suppliers are plotted on a map on the back of the menu. Cooking is rustic and generous; prices are realistic; and the service is friendly and organised.

Closing times
Closed 25 December

Prices
Meals: a la carte £ 19/33

Typical Dishes
Cod with marrowfat peas
Cheese & onion pie with sour cream
Rhubarb Bakewell tart

2 mi west of Blackburn, signed off A 677. Parking.

Ellel

29 | **Bay Horse Inn**

**Bay Horse Ln,
Bay Horse, Ellel, LA2 0HR**
Tel.: (01524)791204
Website: www.bayhorseinn.com

 Moorhouse's Pendle Witch, Thwaites Wainwright and Black Sheep Bitter

This pub is flanked by the A6 and M6, and just a stone's throw away from the main Euston to Glasgow railway line, so it's hard to believe how peaceful it is here. Burgundy walls, low beamed ceilings, a stone fireplace and characterful corner bar provide a cosy, welcoming atmosphere, while the brighter rear dining room overlooks an attractive summer terrace and a pleasant wooded garden. Seasonal menus offer traditional, tried-and-tested dishes and, since they've been passionate about supporting regional producers here long before it became fashionable to do so, you'll always find local offerings such as Higginson's pork and leek sausages, Swainson House Farm duck liver pâté or Cumbrian beef – with the Lancashire cheeseboard a speciality.

Closing times
Closed Sunday dinner in winter and Monday except bank holiday lunch

Prices
Meals: £ 18 (lunch) and a la carte £ 20/39

Typical Dishes
Black pudding with celeriac coleslaw
Slow-cooked duck, potato purée & red wine prunes
Bread & butter pudding

1.5 mi south by A 6 on Quernmore Rd. Parking.

30   **Duke of York Inn**

**Brow Top,
Grindleton, BB7 4QR**
Tel.: (01200)441266
Website: www.dukeofyorkgrindleton.com

 Lancaster Blonde and Timothy Taylors Landlord

This ivy-clad pub sits on the main road running through this pleasant hamlet, in the heart of the Trough of Bowland. If its character you're after, dine in the rustic bar with its flag floors and wood burning stove; the more modern alternative is the smart, airy dining room, adorned with wine bottles and a large mirror. The seasonal à la carte offers plenty of regional choices, with a decent selection of fish, often including lobster; the daily set menu is a steal – and there's a 5 or 7 course tasting option too. Produce is commendably local, with herbs from the chef-owner's garden – dishes might include Lancashire blue cheese soufflé, assiette of game or pan-roasted fillet of sea bass. Regular events include popular wine nights.

Closing times
Closed 25 December,
Monday except bank
holidays and Tuesday
following bank holidays

Prices
Meals: £ 16 (weekdays)
and a la carte £ 23/40

Typical Dishes
Scallops with black
pudding & pork belly
Loin of lamb & slow-
roast shoulder with
asparagus
Earl Grey & cardamom
panna cotta

3 mi northeast of Clitheroe signed off A 671. Parking.

Little Eccleston

31

Cartford Inn

**Cartford Ln,
Little Eccleston, PR3 0YP**
Tel.: (01995)670166
Website: www.thecartfordinn.co.uk

🛏 ☂ **VISA** **M©** **AE**

🍺 **Theakston Old Peculier, Moorhouse's Pride of Pendle and Bowland Ales**

This tiny 17C coaching inn can be found next to a small toll bridge by the Pilling Marshes, and is a great base for those who wish to explore Blackpool but would rather stay somewhere a little more peaceful. The owner played a major part in designing the bedrooms, which range from quirky to French farmhouse in style, and feature colourful glass fittings by a renowned local glassblower. When it comes to drinking or dining, find a seat in one of the cosy little rooms or on the pleasant terrace overlooking the river. Cooking is in the tried-and-tested vein and offers proper pub classics, with signature dishes – such as the Fleetwood fish pie, Pilling Marsh lamb hotpot, and oxtail and beef suet pudding – under the heading of 'Cartford Favourites'.

Closing times
Closed 25 December and Monday lunch except bank holidays

Prices
Meals: a la carte £ 19/39

🛏 **14 rooms:** £ 70/130

Typical Dishes
Pea panna cotta with goat's curd

Duck breast with Grand Marnier sauce

Salted caramel cheesecake

🚗 *7 mi east of Blackpool by A 585 and A 586. Parking.*

32

Three Fishes

**Mitton Rd,
Mitton, BB7 9PQ**
Tel.: (01254)826888
Website: www.thethreefishes.com

 VISA **MC** **AE**

Thwaites Wainwright, Bowland Bewery Hen Harrier and
Moorhouse's Blond Witch

From Morecambe Bay shrimps to Ribble Valley beef and Goosnargh chicken to Fleetwood fish, the menu here reads like a paean to Lancastrian produce. Regional specialities abound and local suppliers are celebrated as food heroes in the striking photos which adorn the pub's walls. The seasonally changing menus are extensive, meaning no matter how many times you come back, you can always try something new, and this is a truly family-friendly pub, with children's menus which pay much more than lip service to your little ones. Sunday lunch is popular, when a roast is also available – but this modern country inn is deservedly busy all week long, packed with people keen to try tasty, satisfying dishes made with the best the North West has to offer.

Closing times
Closed 25 December
Prices
Meals: a la carte £ 19/33

Typical Dishes
Bury black pudding with caramelised onion relish

Cod with spring greens & hollandaise sauce

Pineapple meringue with yoghurt & caramel sauce

2.5 mi northwest of Whalley on B 6246. Parking.

Sawley

33   Spread Eagle

Sawley,
BB7 4NH
Tel.: (01200)441202
Website: www.spreadeaglesawley.co.uk

 Moorhouse's Pride of Pendle, Thwaites Wainwright and Hetton Pale Ale

Its owners may have given the Spread Eagle a stylish makeover but it's still very much the local pub, at the heart of the community. Eat by the fire in the cosy bar, or for a touch more comfort, head for the spacious restaurant. Cooking is gutsy and flavourful, with plenty of pub favourites like fish and chips, sausage and mash or steak, all available in two sizes. There are platters and tapas-style nibbles, perfect for sharing, and a specials list – with dishes such as roast duck breast or rich game casserole – aptly entitled 'The Weather Report' because, just like the weather, they change daily. Comfortable bedrooms have smart, modern bathrooms; room 6 is one of the largest and features a mezzanine level with 'his and hers' sofas.

Closing times
Closed dinner 25 December and 1 January

Prices
Meals: a la carte £ 26/30

🛏 **7 rooms:** £ 70/135

Typical Dishes
Grilled Bury black pudding

Steamed smoked haddock

Chocolate & hazelnut meringue terrine

 4 mi north of Clitheroe by A 59. Parking.

34   **Inn at Whitewell**

**Forest of Bowland,
Whitewell, BB7 3AT**
Tel.: (01200)448222
Website: www.innatwhitewell.com

🛖   _VISA_   ⓂⒸ

Bowland Ales, Skipton Brewery Ales, Moorhouse's and
Timothy Taylor Ales

This 14C creeper-clad inn sits high on the banks of the River Hodder, in prime shooting and fishing country, in the heart of the Trough of Bowland. Antique furniture and a panoramic view of the valley make the spacious bar the most atmospheric place to sit. Other similarly styled rooms boast the character but not the view; for a more formal meal, head for a linen-laid table in the raised-level, valley-facing restaurant. Classic menus offer wholesome, regionally inspired dishes like Lancashire hotpot or fillet of local beef. Spacious bedrooms are split between the inn and nearby coach house – some are traditional in style with four-posters and antique baths; others are more contemporary. The well-stocked vintners sells cookbooks and guides.

Closing times
Open daily
Prices
Meals: a la carte £ 21/41
🛏 **23 rooms:** £ 88/240

Typical Dishes
Terrine of Goosnargh duckling
Confit shoulder of Lonk lamb
Chocolate brownie

 6 mi northwest of Clitheroe by B 6243. Parking.

Wiswell

35 **Freemasons**

**8 Vicarage Fold,
Wiswell, BB7 9DF**
Tel.: (01254)822218
Website: www.freemasonsatwiswell.com

 Three B's Honey B and Prospect Whatever

Charming, welcoming, warm and chatty are all adjectives which apply to the staff here, so it's no wonder that they're busy. Of course, smooth service counts for little if the food's not right; but here, again, the Freemasons comes up trumps. Chef Steven Smith has moved things on, and now offers refined, complex dishes with a hint of the 'pub classic' about them: think Goosnargh duck with Asian spices and duck hash, or custard tart with a rhubarb arctic roll. The first floor has a country house feel, with an elegant, antique-furnished dining area, as well as a comfortable lounge and two semi-private dining rooms. Flag floors, low beams and open fires feature downstairs, so dine here – alongside the regulars – for more of a 'pubby' vibe.

Closing times
Closed 2-14 January and Monday except bank holidays
Prices
Meals: £ 20 (lunch and early dinner) and a la carte £ 29/55

Typical Dishes
Scallops with gammon & pineapple
Chicken with black garlic & chargrilled spring vegetables
Amalfi lemon

 Signposted off A 671 east of Whalley. Some parking in the village.

The south east abounds in handsome historic houses once lived in by the likes of Disraeli and the Rothschilds, and it's no surprise that during the Plague it was to leafy Chalfont St Giles that John Milton fled. It is characterised by rolling hills such as the Chilterns with their ancient beechwoods, and the lilting North and South Downs, which cut a rural swathe across busy commuter belts. The film and television worlds sit easily here: Hambleden and Turville, in the Chilterns, are as used to the sound of the autocue as to the crunch of ramblers' boots. Meanwhile, James Bond's Aston Martin glistens in Beaulieu's Motor Museum, in the heart of the New Forest. Spinnaker Tower rivals HMS Victory for dominance of the Portsmouth skyline, while in Winchester, the Great Hall, home for 600 years to the Arthurian round table, nods acquaintance with the eleventh century Cathedral. Good food and drink is integral to the region, from Whitstable oysters and Dover sole to established vineyards.

Bray

1

Crown

High St,
Bray, SL6 2AH
Tel.: (01628)621936
Website: www.thecrownatbray.com

 Deuchars IPA, Wadworth 6X, Greene King IPA and Old Speckled Hen

Not content with owning just one pub in the village of Bray, Heston Blumenthal has added a second to his portfolio. This charmingly restored 16C building began life as two cottages and an old bike shop – hence the confusion with the doors as you approach; tip, head for the middle one. Drinkers mingle with diners beside roaring fires in the bar, sat amongst sturdy dark oak columns and below low beams; while next door there's a lighter, cottagey style dining room. Heston may be firmly involved in the compilation of the menu but that doesn't mean his young chef is kept from stamping his mark on the dishes. Cooking is robust, flavoursome and British in essence, ranging from ploughman's, through sausage and mash, to lemon sole with potted shrimps.

Closing times
Open daily
Prices
Meals: a la carte £ 23/38

Typical Dishes
Crispy cauliflower with warm cheese
Fish & chips
Brioche bread & butter pudding

 1 mi south of Maidenhead by A 308. Parking.

2 **Hinds Head**

High St,
Bray, SL6 2AB
Tel.: (01628)626151
Website: www.hindsheadbray.com

VISA MC AE D

Rebellion Ales

Set right in the heart of the pretty village of Bray, this charming pub boasts dark wood panelling and log fires, giving it a characterful, almost medieval feel. Although not far from its alma mater, The Fat Duck, it's light years away in terms of its menu. Heston Blumenthal might be famous for molecular gastronomy, but at The Hinds Head, the food is down-to-earth, with classic, comforting dishes like pea and ham soup or heartwarming oxtail and kidney pudding, and traditional desserts such as Eton mess or strawberry trifle. Dishes are fiercely British and big on flavour; rich, simple and satisfying. This is a proper pub and, as such, is busy with drinkers; the bar is the most atmospheric place to sit, although they don't take bookings here.

Closing times
Closed 25-26 December and Sunday dinner
booking essential

Prices
Meals: £ 22 (weekday lunch) and a la carte £ 32/52

Typical Dishes
Hash of snails
Veal chop with cabbage & onion, Reform sauce
Caramelised butter loaf with apple & Pomona

1 mi south of Maidenhead by A 308. Parking in 2 village car parks and opposite the pub.

3

Royal Oak

**Paley Street,
Bray, SL6 3JN**
Tel.: (01628)620541
Website: www.theroyaloakpaleystreet.com

ⱦ 🍇 *VISA* MC AE

🍺 **Fuller's London Pride**

Nick Parkinson is your host and his ability to put guests at ease is clearly one family trait he's inherited from his father, Sir Michael, whose famous encounters are captured in the photos on the walls. The characterful front bar is a great spot for a drink, while the rest of the beamed room and the extension are given over to dining. The chef is Dominic Chapman, son of West Country hotelier Kit, and, like his father, he champions British food. His cooking displays confidence and a commitment to quality, seasonal ingredients: fish is handled with particular aplomb and he also likes his game. The garden, with its elegantly manicured herb maze and water feature, is a pleasant place to sit, and the formal service provides a sense of occasion.

Closing times
Closed Sunday dinner
Prices
Meals: £ 25
(weekday lunch)
and a la carte £ 35/63

Typical Dishes
Wild rabbit lasagne
Peppered haunch of roe deer
Chocolate fondant with coffee ice cream

 3.5 mi southwest of Bray by A 308, A 330 and B 3024. Parking.

4 **Bladebone Inn**

**Chapel Row,
RG7 6PD**
Tel.: (01189)712326
Website: www.thebladeboneinn.com

 Mr Chubbs Lunchtime Bitter, Rebellion Smuggler & Wild Weather Stormbringer

The mysterious name apparently originates from prehistoric times, when an aggressive mammoth which roamed the surrounding plains was killed and buried. Many years later its bladebone was found on the banks of the River Kennet, dragged back to the inn and hoisted above the door; a gleaming gold version now hangs in its place. Thankfully, the inside of the pub is homelier than the name suggests, with a snug open-fired bar and dining room, and a terrace overlooking a rough garden where they grow more than 50 different herbs. The appealing menu offers everything from 'posh' fish finger sandwiches at lunch to rabbit with white and black pudding, or meaty local rump steaks with triple-cooked chips – along with some interesting wines by the glass.

Closing times
Open daily

Prices
Meals: £ 15
(weekday lunch)
and a la carte £ 25/38

Typical Dishes
Chicken liver parfait with pea, sauternes & malt

Local venison with red vegetables

Millefeuille of blackberry with wood sorrel

4 mi northeast of Thatcham by A4. Parking.

Cookham

5

White Oak

**Pound Ln,
Cookham, SL6 9QE**
Tel.: (01628)523043
Website: www.thewhiteoak.co.uk

🍴 *VISA* ⓜ© AE

🍺 Greene King Ales

Trifle – now there's a pud you want to see in a pub. OK, so it's had a little makeover here because it comes with lavender custard and crushed meringue, but it shows that this is a pub with an inherent understanding of what its customers want. There are Aubrey Allen's finest steaks, plenty of Cornish fish, classics like shepherd's pie and other choices with more European credentials such as duck confit – all prepared with care and understanding. Look out too for the 'Menu Auberge' – a great value daily menu. One could argue about whether this is a contemporary pub or a pubby restaurant, as it's set up quite formally, but what is in no doubt is the warmth of the welcome and the affection in which the place is held by its many regulars.

Closing times
Closed dinner Sunday and bank holidays

Prices
Meals: £ 12/35
and a la carte £ 23/54

Typical Dishes
Roast chicken ravioli, roast chicken juices

Pork belly, braised shin & purée potatoes

Hot brioche doughnuts

 Across the common. Parking.

6

Queen's Arms

**Newbury St,
East Garston, RG17 7ET**
Tel.: (01488)648757
Website: www.queensarmshotel.co.uk

VISA MC AE

Wadworth Henry's Original IPA

Nestled in the heart of racehorse country, this 18C inn encompasses all that is British. Framed prints and oils cover the walls, country pursuits can be arranged and don't be surprised to find yourself rubbing shoulders with a famous trainer or breeder. The bar has a satisfyingly rustic feel, with a stone floor, a mix of seating and a boar's head mounted above the fire; while the dining room, with its gleaming glassware, is a more formal affair. In keeping with the good old British surroundings, dishes are meaty and satisfying; you might find a hearty steak and ale pie, warming braised oxtail or some juicy local sausages, with the tasty game shot just over the road. Modern bedrooms are kitted out by leading clothing and countrywear companies.

Closing times
Closed 25 December
Prices
Meals: a la carte £ 24/36
8 rooms: £ 80/120

Typical Dishes
Pigeon breast salad
Rack of local lamb
Chocolate fondant

 3 mi southeast of Lambourn via Eastbury on Newbury Rd. Parking.

Frilsham

7 Pot Kiln

**Frilsham,
RG18 0XX**
Tel.: (01635)201366
Website: www.potkiln.org

VISA

West Berkshire Brick Kiln Bitter and Mr Chubb's
Lunchtime Bitter

Part of the old brickworks, The Pot Kiln originally provided refreshment for the workers digging clay from the surrounding fields. Head for the cosy bar and order a pint of specially commissioned Magg's Mild, Mr Chubbs or Brick Kiln beer, then follow the deliciously tempting aromas through to the dining area, where flavoursome British dishes arrive in unashamedly gutsy portions. Chef-owner Mike Robinson takes advantage of the pub's situation in the middle of prime hunting territory and shoots much of the game himself; so you might find pigeon salad followed by pavé of Lockinge fallow deer on the menu. If meat's not your thing, there's plenty of fish too, including local pike, trout and River Kennet crayfish. Service is particularly clued-up.

Closing times
Closed 25 December and
Tuesday

Prices
Meals: £ 14 (weekday lunch) and a la carte
£ 29/37

Typical Dishes
Pigeon, bacon & black
pudding salad
Pavé of venison
Brioche doughnuts

 6 mi northeast of Newbury by B 4009 to Hermitage and minor road. Parking.

8   **Belgian Arms**

**Holyport St,
Holyport, SL6 2JR**
Tel.: (01628)634468
Website: www.thebelgianarms.com

 Brakspear Bitter & Special and Marston's Pedigree

This pretty 17C, wisteria-clad inn is tucked away by the pond, just off the village green, and there can be few settings more appealing than this. The interior is characterised by old wooden beams and sloping floors, and the owners – one of whom is Nick Parkinson – have decorated it with photos of cricket, football and Nick's father, Sir Michael. There's no standing on ceremony here: this a gutsy local that's here to stay, with tasty pub dishes on the menu and ketchup bottles on the tables. If you're after something light, try appealing snacks such as sprats with aioli or Tamworth pork sausage rolls; the main menu, meanwhile, might feature braised leg of lamb or roast Cornish cod. It's a true locals' local, so there's always plenty going on.

Closing times
Closed Sunday dinner
Prices
Meals: a la carte £ 19/35

Typical Dishes
Cornish sardines on toast

Fish & chips, minted peas, tartare sauce

Raspberry knickerbocker glory

2.5 mi south of Maidenhead by A308 and Holyport Road. Just off village green by pond. Parking.

Stanford Dingley

9  **Bull Inn**

**Cock Ln,
Stanford Dingley, RG7 6LS**
Tel.: (01189)744582
Website: www.thebullinnstanforddingley.co.uk

**Black Sheep Best Bitter, West Berkshire Good Old Boy,
Andwell King John and Timothy Taylor Landlord**

Set at the very centre of the village of Stanford Dingley, the 15C Bull Inn has it all. It really is a family affair, with dad fixing the place up, mum adding some artistic touches and daughter, Laura, running the show. Locals and their dogs gather beside the fire in the rustic bar, while those wishing to eat head for the dining rooms with their dramatic red and silver stag antler wallpaper and trio of twinkling chandeliers. The bar menu offers light, pub-style dishes, while the main menu ranges from game terrine to steamed hake or braised pork cheeks. They also offer a good range of wines, and the 'beer tapas' – which allows you to sample three of the local ales in small glasses – is a nice touch. Comfortable bedrooms complete the picture.

Closing times
Open daily
Prices
Meals: a la carte £ 22/58
🛏 **5 rooms:** £ 60

Typical Dishes
Breast of wood pigeon with black pudding
Fillet of Cornish lemon sole
Amaretto zabaglione parfait

Midway between Newbury and Theale by A 4 and Chapel Row Rd. Parking.

10   Greene Oak

**Oakley Greene,
Windsor, SL4 5UW**
Tel.: (01753)864294
Website: www.thegreeneoak.co.uk

 VISA   MC   AE

Greene King IPA, Abbot Ale and Old Speckled Hen

It's set on a busy road junction, close to the Windsor racecourse, and is painted in an unusual shade of green, but don't let that put you off, as its pretty terrace and bright, modern interior more than make up for it. Smart polished wood and flag floors blend with sage-coloured furnishings and a friendly welcome is guaranteed. The experienced chef produces a constantly evolving array of generous, comforting dishes; if the local produce doesn't quite cut it, then he'll look further afield, so your Aberdeen Angus beef might come from Orkney, or you fish, from Newlyn. The tasty specials could include chicken and truffle terrine, scallops with squash risotto or wing of skate with lemon and caper butter; regular wine evenings feature.

Closing times
Open daily
booking advisable
Prices
Meals: £ 15/35
and a la carte £ 21/51

Typical Dishes
Scallops with chorizo & herb crust

Seared bavette with braised ox cheek & foie gras

Nougat & hazelnut parfait, poached rhubarb

3 mi west of Windsor by A 308 on B 3024 Dedworth Rd. Parking.

Yattendon

11 **Royal Oak**

**The Square,
Yattendon, RG18 0UF**
Tel.: (01635)201325
Website: www.royaloakyattendon.com

VISA **MC**

West Berkshire Good Old Boy

An eye-catching former coaching inn bursting with country charm, The Royal Oak manages to pull off the tricky feat of being both a true locals pub and a popular destination for foodies. While the picture perfect village and its proximity to the M4 could account in part for the pub's attraction to visitors, it's the cooking which really gets them travelling here from a distance. Honest British dishes might include devilled kidneys, potted shrimps or fish pie, while traditional puddings might be of the bread and butter or sticky toffee varieties. The beamed bar with its blazing log fires is at the pub's hub. There's also a lesser-used restaurant and a pleasant vine-covered terrace at the rear. Comfortable bedrooms boast a country house style.

Closing times
Open daily
booking advisable

Prices
Meals: £ 13
(weekday lunch)
and a la carte £ 24/39

10 rooms: £ 85/130

Typical Dishes
Devilled ox kidneys on toast
Roasted rack of lamb, boulangère potatoes
Lemon posset, shortbread

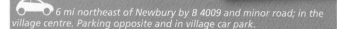

6 mi northeast of Newbury by B 4009 and minor road; in the village centre. Parking opposite and in village car park.

12

Crown

**Aylesbury Rd,
Cuddington, HP18 0BB**
Tel.: (01844)292222
Website: www.thecrowncuddington.co.uk

VISA _MC_ _AE_

🍺 **Fuller's London Pride and Adnams Best Bitter**

Set in the charming village of Cuddington, this Grade II listed 16C building is the very essence of a proper English pub. Whitewashed walls and an attractive thatched roof hide a traditionally styled interior with welcoming open fires, dancing candlelight and a multitude of bygone artefacts; while a loyal band of locals keep up the drinking trade and a friendly team set the tone. There's a blackboard of daily specials and an à la carte that changes with the seasons: so you'll find hearty comfort food in winter and lighter sandwiches and salads in the summer (the smoked haddock with Welsh rarebit is a hit); arrive early if you fancy one of these in a spot in the sun. Tuesday to Friday 'food nights' include steak, curry, pies and fish 'n' chips.

Closing times
Closed Sunday dinner
Prices
Meals: a la carte £ 20/35

Typical Dishes
Hoi sin duck &
poached pear salad
Slow-cooked Greek-
style shoulder of lamb
Raspberry & vanilla
cheesecake

🚗 _West of Aylesbury by A 418. Parking._

Denham

13 Swan Inn

**Village Rd,
Denham, UB9 5BH**
Tel.: (01895)832085
Website: www.swaninndenham.co.uk

Marlow Rebellion IPA and Caledonian Flying Scotsman

If you want to escape the hustle of London, this pub may well be the tranquil haven you're after. Close to the A40, M40 and M25 but in a secluded little world of its own, The Swan takes up prime position in this delightful village. Number three in the owner's collection, the Georgian red-brick building is fronted by beautiful cascades of wisteria and framed by manicured trees, with a secluded terrace and gardens to the rear. Menus change with the seasons but their signature bubble & squeak and rib-eye steak are mainstays. This is more than just typical pub food, so you might find confit duck with nutmeg boxty potato and sides such as such as leek, pancetta and parsley crumble. Satisfyingly, they open early for pre-Ascot or Wimbledon champagne.

Closing times
Closed 25-26 December
booking essential
Prices
Meals: a la carte £ 20/37

Typical Dishes
Rabbit rissoles with sweetcorn purée
Roast chicken with field mushrooms
Gooseberry and elderflower Eve's pudding

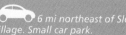 6 mi northeast of Slough by A 412; in the centre of the village. Small car park.

14   **Palmer Arms**

Village Rd,
Dorney, SL4 6QW
Tel.: (01628)666612
Website: www.thepalmerarms.com

Greene King IPA, Abbot Ale and guest ales

Despite its proximity to Windsor and the M4, this 15C pub feels like it's in a decidedly rural spot. It's run by a keen young couple, who have employed an equally enthusiastic chef, and the pub's huge popularity bears testament to the fact that they're doing things right: it's the food – not the furnishings – that's the focus here. Menus display a well-balanced mix of pub favourites and more adventurous dishes, with the likes of venison and black pudding sausage roll or macaroni with smoked Applewood cheese; while desserts feature heartwarming crumbles alongside more modern creations such as peanut butter mousse. There's also a large garden for lazy summer days and an upstairs private dining room with a lovely terrace and far-reaching views.

Closing times
Open daily
booking advisable
Prices
Meals: a la carte £ 20/36

Typical Dishes
Chilli beef salad
Sea bream with new potatoes
Peanut butter mousse & roast banana

 2.5 mi west of Eton on B 3026. Parking.

Fulmer

15 — Black Horse

**Windmill Rd,
Fulmer, SL3 6HD**
Tel.: (01753)663183
Website: www.theblackhorsefulmer.co.uk

 Greene King IPA

Originally a lodging house for the builders of the next door church – which dates from 1610 – this whitewashed village pub is the perfect place for a pint and a chat. It's got thick walls and cosy alcoves, a wood-burning stove, a large front terrace and a gem of a garden for sunny days. A pint is one thing, but you've not really experienced the Black Horse until you've stayed for a meal. The main dining area may feel quite formal and stylish, with its banquette seats and delightful portraits, but the white-shirted staff are only too eager to help guide you through the menu. Sharing boards are a popular choice, the 'small plates' section includes the classic sticky pork ribs, while mains could mean a steak, pork belly or a nice plump dover sole.

Closing times
Open daily
Prices
Meals: £ 13 (lunch)
and a la carte £ 21/36

Typical Dishes
Chicken liver parfait,
fig chutney
Fish pie
Apple & blackberry
crumble

2 mi south of Gerrards Cross in centre of village beside St James church. Parking.

16   **Three Oaks**

Austenwood Ln,
Gerrards Cross, SL9 8NL
Tel.: (01753)899016
Website: www.thethreeoaksgx.co.uk

    VISA   MC   AE

Greene King IPA, Fullers London Pride, Rebellion IPA and Smuggler

Turning into the car park and seeing all those smart cars makes you immediately aware that this isn't going to be your typical village local. Sharing the same owner as The White Oak in Cookham and The Greene Oak just outside Windsor, this revamped pub now attracts the local 'smart set'. There's a choice of dining room – go for the brighter one at the back as it looks out over the garden. Bright, enthusiastic service comes courtesy of local boys and girls, all dressed in black. The menu changes often but keeps things British and relatively safe as the customers clearly don't take to anything too unfamiliar. Expect the likes of home-cured salmon, roast lamb with mint jelly or chocolate brownie. There's also a good value lunch menu.

Closing times
Open daily
Prices
Meals: £ 12/35
and a la carte £ 22/49

Typical Dishes
Pulled pork, apple & ginger purée

Sea trout, wild garlic & caper butter

Apple galette with Granny Smith granite

0.75 mi northwest of the town by A 413 following signs for Gold Hill. Parking.

Great Missenden

17

Nags Head

**London Rd,
Great Missenden, HP16 0DG**
Tel.: (01494)862200
Website: www.nagsheadbucks.com

Sharp's Doom Bar, Marlow Rebellion IPA, Chilton Beechwood Bitter and Tring Jack O'Legs

This traditional 15C inn is run by the same team behind the Bricklayers Arms in Flaunden and is proving just as popular, so be sure to book ahead, especially at weekends. It has been made over, yet retains a wealth of original features: the two main dining areas have thick brick walls and exposed oak beams, while an extra helping of rusticity comes courtesy of the inglenook fireplace. Original menus mix Gallic charm with British classics, so you'll find things like foie gras or mushroom feuillette alongside eggs Benedict or sausage and mash; food is flavourful and service cheerful and keen. Stylish, modern bedrooms provide a comfortable night's sleep – number one is the best – and the tasty breakfast ensures you leave satiated in the morning.

Closing times
Open daily

Prices
Meals: £ 15 (weekdays) and a la carte £ 26/47

🛏 **5 rooms:** £ 75/115

Typical Dishes
Cornish crab & home-smoked salmon

Lamb brochette with crispy lamb croquettes

Chocolate & honey fondant

 1 mi southeast by A 413 turning at Chiltern Hospital. Parking.

18 **Queens Head**

**Pound Ln,
Little Marlow, SL7 3SR**
Tel.: (01628)482927
Website: www.marlowslittlesecret.co.uk

Fuller's London Pride, Sharp's Doom Bar and Rebellion Ales

Head towards Little Marlow's 12C church and, tucked away down a lane opposite the village's restored cattle pound, you'll find The Queens Head; a popular pub, with keen young partners at its helm and staff who provide poised, friendly service. Once a spit and sawdust sort of a place, its snug bar used to be a salting room and its priest hole makes it a popular place for filming. The garden gets into full swing during the summer months when hungry walkers gather to refuel. Lunch offers a quick fix with sandwiches, ploughman's and pub classics, as well as more refined dishes on the main à la carte – maybe scallops with black pudding, followed by Baileys brûlée. Menus change every 6-8 weeks and produce is from local farms, forages and shoots.

Closing times
Closed 25-26 December
Prices
Meals: a la carte £ 26/35

Typical Dishes
Curried smoked haddock & Whitley crab cake
Lamb rump with potato fondant
Earl Grey tea crème brûlée

 3 mi east of Marlow on A 4155 by Church Rd. Parking.

Long Crendon

19 **Mole & Chicken**

**Easington,
Long Crendon, HP18 8EY**
Tel.: (01844)208387
Website: www.themoleandchicken.co.uk

 **Hook Norton Hooky Bitter, Vale Brewery Easington Best
and Brill Amber**

If you're struggling to get your bearings, look to the rooftops for the weather vane depicting a mole and a chicken. This remote pub was built in 1831 as part of the local farm workers' estate and later took on the role of village store. The interior is charming, with wonky low ceilings, open fires, elegant prints and two squashy sofas, but the biggest draw is the large garden, which offers commanding views over the surrounding counties. The menu is a slightly curious affair, featuring classics such as rump of local lamb alongside more unusual offerings like Cornish sprats with aioli or pork belly laksa – with influences from the chef's travels in Asia and The Lebanon clear to see. The delightful modern bedrooms are in an adjoining house.

Closing times
Closed 25 December
Prices
Meals: £ 15 (weekdays)
and a la carte £ 26/40
5 rooms: £ 85

Typical Dishes
Devilled kidneys on toast
Pan-fried cod with brown shrimps & capers
Warm chocolate fondant

20 **Hand and Flowers**

**126 West St,
Marlow, SL7 2BP**
Tel.: (01628)482277
Website: www.thehandandflowers.co.uk

 Greene King Ales, Hardys & Hansons H and F Ale

With its softly lit interior, The Hand and Flowers glows enticingly, but it's not often you can drop in on the off-chance, as this is Marlow's not-so-well-kept secret. Low beamed ceilings, flagstone floors and a proper bar counter hint at its history, while the professional serving team are a clue as to the quality of the food. Cooking is of the highest order and the chef puts as much care and passion into a lasagne on the set lunch menu as a fillet of beef on the evening à la carte. The selection may be concise but dishes are refined and flavoursome, ingredients marry perfectly and the simple is turned into the sublime. Characterful cottage bedrooms are equally meticulous, boasting feature baths or showers; some even have outdoor jacuzzis.

Closing times
Closed 24-26 December, 1 January and Sunday dinner

booking essential

Prices
Meals: £ 20 (weekday lunch) and a la carte £ 42/64

🛏 **4 rooms:** £ 140/190

Typical Dishes
Smoked haddock omelette
Duck breast with duck fat chips & gravy
Tonka bean panna cotta

 On the western side of the town on A 4155. Parking.

Marlow

21 **Royal Oak**

**Frieth Rd,
Bovingdon Green, Marlow, SL7 2JF**
Tel.: (01628)488611
Website: www.royaloakmarlow.co.uk

 Rebellion Beer Co. IPA and Smuggler

Set less than 15mins from the M40 and M4, this part-17C pub is the ideal escape from the busy streets of London. As you approach, pleasant scents drift up from the herb garden, gentle 'chinks' emanate from the petanque pitch and the world feels at once more peaceful. While away the warmer days on the terrace or snuggle into pretty cushions beside the wood burning stove in winter, where rich fabrics and heritage colours provide a country-chic feel, and freshly cut flowers decorate the room. Not surprisingly, it's extremely popular and the eager team are often stretched to their limit. Cooking is British-led; you might find a slow-cooked ox cheek pasty or pork chops with salt and pepper squid. Wash these down with a pint of local Rebellion ale.

Closing times
Closed 25-26 December
Prices
Meals: a la carte £ 21/38

Typical Dishes
Open crab & bacon brioche club
Slow-cooked shin of beef cottage pie
Chocolate chip brownie with toasted marshmallow

1.25 mi west of Marlow by A 4155 and Bovingdon Green rd. Parking.

22   **Crooked Billet**

**2 Westbrook End,
Newton Longville, MK17 0DF**
Tel.: (01908)373936
Website: www.thebillet.co.uk

VISA MC AE

Greene King Abbot Ale, Wadworth 6X and Morland Old Speckled Hen

This charming 17C thatched pub is the last place you expect to find on the outskirts of Milton Keynes. Starting life as a farmhouse and later providing refreshments for passing farmers, it eventually evolved into the village pub. The interior is smart yet informal; the owner's artwork adorns the walls and a cheery bunch of locals prop up the bar. Over the last decade it's built up quite a reputation – so much so that you'll need to book. Emma heads the dedicated kitchen team, who create modern, seasonal dishes; lunch offers sandwiches or a three course à la carte and dinner introduces a 7 course tasting menu. Provenance is noted on the menu, as are wine recommendations, and ex-sommelier John happily guides you through the 200-strong wine list.

Closing times
Closed 25-26 December,
Sunday dinner and Monday
booking advisable

Prices
Meals: £ 21 (weekdays)
and a la carte £ 20/37

Typical Dishes
Scallops with smoked crispy bacon

Duck breast, sausage & crisp confit leg

Baked lemon & blueberry cheesecake

6 mi southwest of Milton Keynes by A 421. Parking.

Penn

23 **Old Queens Head**

**Hammersley Ln,
Penn, HP10 8EY**
Tel.: (01494)813371
Website: www.oldqueensheadpenn.co.uk

Greene King IPA and Ruddles County

This pub may not be quite as old as the ancient beech woodlands that surround it but it does have a part to play in the area's history. Legend has it that Lord Penn inherited the pub when he won a game of cards against Charles II. Whether this is true or not, no one knows, but it can be proved from the 1666 deeds that it was purchased by one of the King's physicians. Find a spot on the paved terrace or take in the view from the former barn – now the dining room; the surrounding rooms may be slightly newer but they continue the rustic theme. Big, hearty dishes are the order of the day – the bubble and squeak with oak smoked bacon, free range poached egg and hollandaise sauce is a perennial favourite. Come on a Saturday for a laid-back brunch.

Closing times
Closed 25-26 December

Prices
Meals: a la carte £ 20/36

Typical Dishes
Whiting fish finger
with pea purée
Slow-cooked
'Stockings Farm' pork
belly
Vanilla crème brûlée

4 mi northwest of junction 2 of M 40, via Beaconsfield and B 474. Parking.

24

Three Horseshoes Inn

**Bennett End,
Radnage, HP14 4EB**
Tel.: (01494)483273
Website: www.thethreehorseshoes.net

VISA MC

Brakspear Oxford Gold and Rebellion IPA

This 18C red-brick pub is set in a fantastic hillside location, deep in the countryside. The cosy bar with its attractive flag floor and inglenook fireplace is the place to be – although with space being limited, you might want to head to the restaurant, with its stunning beams and smart, minimalist feel. In warmer weather, make for the terrace, which boasts pleasant views over the duck pond to the hills beyond. Menus reflect the chef's background, so you'll find classically prepared dishes with the odd French touch. Lunch consists mainly of soups, salads and pâtés, while dinner offers a more formal à la carte and some lighter tapas dishes; the latter served in the bar and garden. Bedrooms are contemporary and lavish; Molières is the best.

Closing times
Open daily
Prices
Meals: £ 21 (weekdays) and a la carte £ 23/39

6 rooms: £ 80/150

Typical Dishes
Scallops with black pudding
Duck with Savoy cabbage & smoked bacon
Chocolate fondant

5 mi west of High Wycombe by A 40 and minor road north. Parking.

Seer Green

25 Jolly Cricketers

**24 Chalfont Rd,
Seer Green, HP9 2YG**
Tel.: (01494)676308
Website: www.thejollycricketers.co.uk

Fuller's London Pride, Rebellion IPA, Windsor & Eton Windsor Knot, Vale VPA and Chilton Ale

Somehow it's hard to imagine a pub called The Jolly Footballers. Indeed, no sport does nostalgia or evokes a spirit of bonhomie quite like cricket and this charming Victorian pub certainly does its bit for the gentleman's game: there's memorabilia aplenty, including signed cricket bats and Test Match programs, and even the menu comes divided into 'Openers, Main Play and Lower Order'. But this is also a pub where people come to eat. The kitchen nicely balances classic dishes with more modern choices, so seasonal asparagus could be followed by monkfish with Moroccan spices and, for dessert, a generously sized and satisfyingly filling fruit crumble. In winter, sit by the fireplace and count down the months until summer comes around again.

Closing times
Open daily
booking advisable
Prices
Meals: a la carte £ 25/43

Typical Dishes
Wild mushrooms & goat's cheese on toast

Breast of chicken, braised rabbit & pea purée

Apple crumble with hazelnuts & vanilla ice cream

 2.5 mi northeast of Beaconsfield off A 355. Parking.

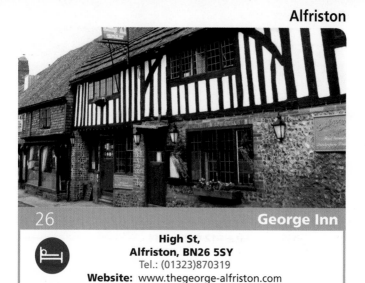

26 — **George Inn**

**High St,
Alfriston, BN26 5SY**
Tel.: (01323)870319
Website: www.thegeorge-alfriston.com

Greene King Abbot Ale, Dark Star Hop Head and Hardy & Hansons Olde Trip

If it's character you're after, you're in the right place. The picturesque village of Alfriston is on the Southdown Way and boasts its own cricket club, a group of bell ringers and this delightful 14C stone and timber pub. As characterful inside as out, it has vast inglenook fireplaces and more beams than you've ever seen before; there's even one on the floor! For dining, there's the choice between the rustic bar and another spacious, slightly more formal room. The traditional menu is chalked on the board and changes every 3 months, offering the likes of rustic sharing boards, pork tenderloin and slow-braised shoulder of lamb. Comfortable bedrooms have period charm; Bob Hall, named after a smuggler, boasts 13C wattle and daub murals.

Closing times
Closed 25-26 December
Prices
Meals: a la carte £ 22/34
6 rooms: £ 60/140

Typical Dishes
Glazed goat's cheese with roast vegetables

Pork belly with spring onion potato cake

Double-baked pistachio cheesecake

 Two public car parks (1min walk) and on-street parking.

27   **Ginger Dog**

12 College Pl,
Brighton, BN2 1HN
Tel.: (01273)620990
Website: www.gingermanrestaurants.com

VISA **MC** **AE**

 Harveys IPA, Long Man and Dark Star Ales

This charming Victorian pub has a pleasing shabby-chic, canine-theme, a welcoming atmosphere and a relaxed feel. Many of the original architectural features – such as the ornate woodwork – are juxtaposed with contemporary design touches; note the bowler hats unusually used as lampshades. Tables are smartly laid up behind the bar but you can eat anywhere. Fresh produce is to the fore on the menu, which is mostly British but with the odd nod to Italy, and could include local Rye Bay plaice with shrimps, scotch quail egg and black pudding salad or a proper trifle. Water and some delicious slices of bread are not only brought to the table without hesitation but aren't charged for either; and a ginger 'dog' biscuit is served with the coffee.

Closing times
Closed 25 December

Prices
Meals: £ 13 (lunch)
and a la carte £ 24/35

Typical Dishes
Dressed crab, tomato & basil salad

Butter roast chicken with Parma ham & potato terrine

Blueberry & frangipane tart

In heart of Kemp Town, just off Marine Parade (A 259) towards Lewes. Metered parking nearby.

28 Preston Park Tavern

**88 Havelock Rd,
Brighton, BN1 6GF**
Tel.: (01273)542271
Website: www.prestonparktavern.co.uk

 Harvey & Son Best Bitter and Longman's American Pale Ale

This majestic Victorian coaching inn, in a leafy residential area, is supposedly where the lords' and ladies' carriages were taken while they were at the beach. It's personally run by a charming couple, who have put their hearts and souls into restoring it. With polished wood floors and boldly decorated walls, it has a chic feel, and the smiley staff and delicious aromas only add to the welcoming atmosphere. Sit in the sunny gardens, on a comfy sofa in the bar or looking into the open kitchen from the restaurant. The concise menu alters twice daily and is driven by the latest local, ethical and sustainable ingredients; refined, confidently prepared dishes are well-balanced and bursting with flavour. Over 20 wines are available by the glass.

Closing times
Closed 25 December and 1 January

Prices
Meals: £ 13 (weekday lunch) and a la carte £ 22/31

Typical Dishes
Chicken & wild mushroom bon bons
Pork belly with bacon potatoes
Homemade doughnuts with chocolate dipping sauce

Off A 23 behind Preston Park. Unmetered on-street parking.

279

Chelwood Gate

29   **Red Lion**

Lewes Rd,
Chelwood Gate, RH17 7DE
Tel.: (01825)791609
Website: www.thecrown-horstedkeynes.co.uk

Harveys Sussex Best Bitter and Sharp's Doom Bar

No one is really sure whether this pub is in East Sussex or West Sussex, and the lion on its sign is white rather than red, but there's no such confusion when it comes to the food. Chef-owner Mark Raffan used to be head chef at Gravetye Manor – and this is a man who knows his capers from his cornichons. A local boy, he's gone back to his roots here, serving pub classics like steak, mushroom and ale pie, and fish and chips; with plenty of game in season and a beef Wellington that's fast becoming their signature dish. Locals – and their dogs – tend to congregate by the fire in the bar, but the best place to dine is in the conservatory, looking out onto the delightful terrace and garden which lie on the border of Ashdown Forest.

Closing times
Closed Sunday dinner and Monday except bank holidays

Prices
Meals: a la carte £ 23/34

Typical Dishes
Sea bass with soft shell crab tempura

Roast quail with black pudding & caper butter

Dark chocolate tart with pistachio ice cream

 On A 275 between Forest Row and Danehill. Parking.

30 **Jolly Sportsman**

**Chapel Ln,
East Chiltington, BN7 3BA**
Tel.: (01273)890400
Website: www.thejollysportsman.com

Dark Star Hophead and Harveys Sussex Best Bitter

England • South East • East Sussex

Down a myriad of country lanes, in a small hamlet, this grey clapperboard pub attracts locals in their droves. You're greeted by smoky aromas from an open fire and by a bubbly team; often even by the owner himself. Choose a spot in the cosy bar, in the warmly decorated red room or in the garden room with its concertina doors opening onto the large garden and terrace – and prepare for just as much choice when it comes to the food. There are interesting bar bites such as Cabezada and Guindillas, good value set menus, a rustic European-based à la carte and blackboard specials, which quickly come and go; many of the herbs and fruits come from the polytunnel outside. A very good wine list and plenty of cask ales, ciders and perries are on offer too.

Closing times
Closed 25 December
booking essential
Prices
Meals: £ 15/20
and a la carte £ 24/39

Typical Dishes
Goat's cheese and green olive mousse

Slow-cooked Middle White pork belly

Chocolate, cherry and espresso cake

5.5 mi northwest of Lewes by A 275 and B 2116 off Novington Lane. Parking.

Fletching

31 **Griffin Inn**

**Fletching,
TN22 3SS**
Tel.: (01825)722890
Website: www.thegriffininn.co.uk

Harveys Sussex Best Bitter, Hogs Back TEA, Rector's Revenge and Dark Star Hophead

Under the same ownership for over 30 years, this hugely characterful red and white brick coaching inn is the kind of place that every village wishes for. It boasts a linen-laid dining room, traditional wood-panelled bar and comfy 'Club Room' adorned with cricketing memorabilia, as well as a sizeable garden and terrace – with wood burning oven for sophisticated summer Sunday barbecues. A large freestanding blackboard in the bar offers a huge range of British and Italian classics, as well as some Spanish dishes, and there's a more structured à la carte available in the dining room. If you live locally, work it off by joining one of the pub's cricket teams; if not, follow narrow, sloping corridors to one of the individually decorated bedrooms.

Closing times
Closed 25 December

Prices
Meals: £ 25 and a la carte £ 25/43

13 rooms: £ 70/145

Typical Dishes
Pan-seared scallops with pea purée

Fillet of Sussex beef with roasted shallots

Dark chocolate terrine with orange ice cream

In centre of village. Parking.

32 **Ginger Pig**

3 Hove St,
Hove, BN3 2TR
Tel.: (01273)736123
Website: www.gingermanrestaurants.com

VISA MC AE D

Harveys Sussex Best Bitter and Fuller's London Pride

Set just off the seafront, this smart building displays a mortar relief of a ship above the entrance and a beautifully restored revolving door, harking back to its former days as the Ship Hotel. Inside you'll find a long wood-floored bar and a large dining room, and although they take bookings it's worth arriving early, especially at weekends. The à la carte offers precisely prepared, flavoursome British dishes – including plenty of vegetarian options – and there are great value set menus at both lunch and dinner, along with some good wine deals; order a coffee and it'll arrive with a quirky pig-shaped shortbread. They're used to being busy and service copes well under pressure, the only drawback being that it can lack a more personal touch.

Closing times
Closed 25 December

Prices
Meals: £ 13 (weekday lunch) and a la carte £ 23/35

Typical Dishes
Ceviche of scallops
Roast rump of lamb with braised shoulder
Banana & popcorn parfait

Off north side of shore road, Kingsway, A 259. NCP car park (2min walk) & parking meters (2hr maximum during day).

Rye

33

Ship Inn

**The Strand,
Rye, TN31 7DB**
Tel.: (01797)222233
Website: www.theshipinnrye.co.uk

 Harvey's Sussex Best Bitter, Old Dairy Gold Top and Whitstable Brewery Oyster Stout

Fittingly located at the bottom of Mermaid Street, The Ship Inn dates back to 1592, when it was used as a warehouse for impounding smuggled goods. This is a place that proves that smart surroundings aren't a prerequisite for good food. Modern pop art and boars' heads are dotted about the rooms, fairy lights are draped everywhere and if you sit on one of the battered sofas, don't be alarmed if you end up at a quirky angle or even falling through. The quality of the food then, comes as a surprise. Ingredients are well-sourced and preparation is careful. The result: flavoursome, rustic dishes that arrive in generous portions – maybe baked cod or soy-braised pork belly. Compact bedrooms display similarly wacky wallpapers and painted floors.

Closing times
Open daily
Prices
Meals: a la carte £ 22/34
10 rooms: £ 80/110

Typical Dishes
Rye Bay fish soup
Slow-roast pork belly with ragout of broad beans
Chocolate mousse

 Close to the Quayside. Local car park close by.

34

Bell

**High St,
Ticehurst, TN5 7AS**
Tel.: (01580)200234
Website: www.thebellinticehurst.com

VISA · MC · AE

Harveys Sussex Best Bitter and Old Dairy Gold Top

The lampshades are top hats, there are tubas in the loos and a pile of books appear to be holding up the beams: welcome to The Bell, a late 16C coaching inn which has been transformed into a quirky, shabby-chic pub with the emphasis firmly on the chic. There's a delightful snug, a bar with a vast inglenook, and a beautiful private dining room called 'the stable with a table'. Simple bar snacks might include burger and chips or pie and mash, while seasonal menus offer generous portions of proper pub food like local ham hock terrine, smoked salmon, a charred pork steak with orange sauce or a warming plum crumble. Seven rustic, individually styled bedrooms – each with their own silver birch tree – share the pub's idiosyncratic charm.

Closing times
Open daily
booking advisable
Prices
Meals: £ 14 (weekday lunch) and a la carte £ 22/39
7 rooms: £ 110/155

Typical Dishes
Smoked prawns with wild garlic mayonnaise
Chargrilled lamb cutlets with grilled vegetables
Lemon posset & shortbread

 In the centre of the village. Parking.

Baughurst

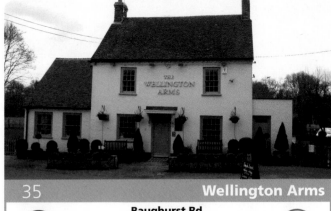

35 **Wellington Arms**

**Baughurst Rd,
Baughurst, RG26 5LP**
Tel.: (0118)9820110
Website: www.thewellingtonarms.com

 West Berkshire Good Old Boy and Mr Chubbs Lunchtime Bitter, Two
Cocks Cavalier and Round Head

If success is dependent on the effort put into sourcing local produce and making, growing and rearing everything possible, then The Wellington is a sure-fire winner. A smart, cream-washed building with box hedges framing the doorway, it has its own herb and vegetable beds, as well as its own sheep, pigs, chickens and bees; it comes as no surprise then, to discover eggs, honey and preserves for sale in the cosy quarry-tiled, low-beamed bar. Blackboard menus feature 6 dishes per course – which are rubbed off and replaced as produce runs out – and cooking is generous and satisfying, featuring dishes such as goat's cheese soufflé and beef from a farm just over the fields. Smart, rustic bedrooms come with sheepskin rugs and large beds.

Closing times
Closed Sunday dinner
booking essential

Prices
Meals: £ 16 (weekday lunch) and a la carte
£ 21/39

3 rooms: £ 130/200

Typical Dishes
Courgette flowers with ricotta & parmesan

Chargrilled pork chop & roasted aubergines

Rhubarb jelly, stem ginger ice cream

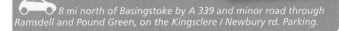

8 mi north of Basingstoke by A 339 and minor road through Ramsdell and Pound Green, on the Kingsclere / Newbury rd. Parking.

36 **Exchequer**

**Crondall Rd,
Crookham Village, GU51 5SU**
Tel.: (01252)615336
Website: www.exchequercrookham.co.uk

Hogsback TEA, Andwell Resolute and Ringwood Fortyniner

This pub has gone by many different monikers and its fortunes have changed as often as its name, but it's current owners seem to have hit on a winning formula. It has undergone a slick, modern facelift: as you enter there's an inviting drinkers' area, complete with a log burning stove; while further on it's divided into three, with two semi-private areas and a smart conservatory-style room. The menu offers gutsy British staples, with the likes of steak pie and crumble with custard, but there's also a nod to the East, courtesy of dishes such as prawn tempura. The blackboard best displays the kitchen's abilities – the well-crafted, boldly flavoured specials could include roast pheasant or grouse. Service is keen and completes the experience.

Closing times
Closed 25 December

Prices
Meals: a la carte £ 22/34

Typical Dishes
Roschip tea-smoked breast of duck
Lemon sole filled with salmon mousse
White chocolate & honeycomb cheesecake

 1 mi north off A 287 in centre of village. Parking.

Droxford

37

Bakers Arms

**High St,
Droxford, SO32 3PA**
Tel.: (01489)877533
Website: www.thebakersarmsdroxford.com

Bowman Ales

The owners met whilst working abroad on private yachts, eventually returning to their roots to run this roadside inn. Their experience, effort and enthusiasm have stood them in good stead: cooking is unfussy and filling, with an emphasis on locally sourced ingredients. They bake their own bread twice-daily and also grow some of the vegetables on the menu themselves. Main dishes might include venison steak or slow-cooked Hampshire beef, with puddings like pear crumble or treacle tart. The pub itself is pleasingly traditional with an open-plan bar, leather sofas and a roaring log fire; interesting decorative oddments include beer adverts and stag heads. Staff are friendly and polite, and the beer is from Droxford-based brewery, Bowman Ales.

Closing times
Open daily
Prices
Meals: £ 13 (weekdays)
and a la carte £ 24/32

Typical Dishes
Ham hock terrine with black pudding
Roasted venison with dauphinoise potatoes & game gravy
Chocolate fudge brownie

 6 mi north of Fareham by A 32. Parking.

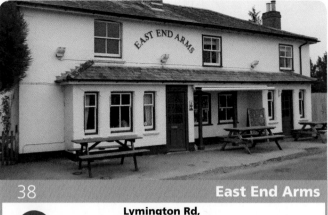

38

East End Arms

**Lymington Rd,
East End, SO41 5SY**
Tel.: (01590)626223
Website: www.eastendarms.co.uk

Marstons Best Bitter and Ringwood Fortyniner

Owned by John Illsley, bass guitarist of Dire Straits, this traditional country pub boasts a great display of black and white photos of legendary singers, musicians and celebrities from his personal collection. When he bought the place in the late '90s, the locals petitioned for him to keep the place the same, so you'll find a slightly shabby bar with cushioned pews, open fire and dart board, and a slightly smarter pine-furnished dining room behind. Menus are fairly concise, featuring local produce in satisfying, British-based dishes, which are listed in order of price. You might find whitebait followed by pigeon breast or maybe even shark loin. Service is polite if a little lacklustre. Modern, cottage-style bedrooms provide a smart contrast.

Closing times
Open daily
Prices
Meals: a la carte £ 18/39
5 rooms: £ 71/120

Typical Dishes
Scallops with artichoke purée & crisp pancetta
Sea bass with wild garlic & parmesan risotto
Chocolate fondant with caramel sauce

 3 mi east of Lymington by B 3054. Parking.

Hamble-le-Rice

39 **Bugle**

**High St,
Hamble-le-Rice, SO31 4HA**
Tel.: (023)80453000
Website: www.buglehamble.co.uk

🛉 *VISA* MC AE ⓘ

🍺 **Bowman Ales, Itchen Valley and Flowerpots**

This attractive whitewashed pub is set down a cobbled street in the coastal village of Hamble-le-Rice. It's popular with the sailing community – and is owned by a keen seafarer – and its terrace has pleasant views over Southampton Water. The pub menu is served in the bar and offers sandwiches, small plates such as salt and pepper squid or devilled whitebait – and pub classics like ale-battered fish and chips or home-cooked honey roast ham. The à la carte is available in the dining room and features more ambitious dishes such as seared local wood pigeon breast, slow-roast pork belly or whole roasted local plaice. Sporting events are popular thanks to the flat screen TVs; equally well-liked are the regular quiz nights and themed food evenings.

Closing times
Open daily
booking essential
Prices
Meals: a la carte £ 20/36

Typical Dishes
Rope-grown Scottish mussels
Pork with watercress champ & apple fritter
Apple crumble & custard

🚗 *7 mi southeast of Southampton by A 3024 or A 3025 and B 3397. Pay and display parking nearby.*

40   **Ⓝ Cricketers**

**The Green,
Hartley Wintney, RG27 8QB**
Tel.: (01252)842166
Website: www.thecricketers-hartleywintney.co.uk

 VISA **MC** **AE**

🍺 **Thwaites Wainwright, Caledonian Golden XPA and Theakston Old Peculier**

With its pillared entrance, creeping ivy and colourful hanging baskets, this attractive red brick property is every bit the quintessential British pub. It's tucked away to the side of Hartley Wintney's village green and the tables in front overlook what is thought to be the oldest continually played cricket pitch in the world. Fittingly, the daily changing menu focuses on local ingredients and good old pub classics, with the likes of Meon Valley steak or Berkshire free-range pork belly; but there are a few French influences to be found too, especially when it comes to dessert. Whether you sit in the intimate, bistro-style interior or out on the large rear terrace amongst the potted herbs, the atmosphere will be suitably relaxed and friendly.

Closing times
Closed dinner 25 December
Prices
Meals: a la carte £ 22/35

Typical Dishes
Scallops in a dill & white wine sauce
Spinach & ricotta tortellini
Warm chocolate fondant

🚗 *11 mi northeast of Basingstoke on A 30. Just south of the High St. by Hardings Ln. Restricted on-street parking.*

Highclere

41 **Yew Tree**

**Hollington Cross,
Andover Rd, Highclere, RG20 9SE**
Tel.: (01635)253360
Website: www.theyewtree.net

🍺 *VISA* 💳

Fuller's London Pride

Just down the road from Highclere Castle – the setting for Downton Abbey – is this pretty 17C inn, where you have to stoop to enter into the rustic interior, with its low beamed ceilings and original flagstone floors. The bar, with is leather sofas and roaring log fires, is a great spot for a drink and a snack, while the three dining rooms with their flickering candles provide a more intimate atmosphere. The menu is divided into 'small', 'medium' and 'large' dishes – for both main courses and desserts – and classically based recipes are given modern twists; there are some interesting vegetarian options too. In summer, relax on the pretty rear terrace. If you fancy staying overnight, bedrooms are cosy, with good mod cons and smart wet rooms.

Closing times
Open daily
Prices
Meals: a la carte £ 18/48
🛏 **8 rooms:** £ 95/120

Typical Dishes
Black pudding scotch egg
Fish & chips with mushy peas
Chocolate fondant with pistachio ice cream

🚗 *5 mi south of Newbury on A 343. Parking.*

England • South East • Hampshire

42

Hogget

**London Rd,
Hook, RG27 9JJ**
Tel.: (01256)763009
Website: www.thehogget.co.uk

VISA MC D

Ringwood Best Bitter, Marston's Pedigree and Wychwood Hobgoblin

You'll find this brightly painted pub at the junction of the A30 and the A287, with its busy bar, book-filled lounge and popular heated terrace. Wholesome, honest, flavourful cooking shows a real respect for the locally sourced ingredients, with sensibly priced dishes like Hampshire sausages and mash, beer-battered hake and chips or slow-cooked lamb shank alongside salads, snacks and grazing boards to share. Everything bar the bread and ice cream is homemade and they offer breakfast on Fridays, roasts on a Sunday – and cheery service every day of the week. Look out for members of the local football team who play on the field next door and meet for drinks after a game; the results board displays the many awards they've won since 1947.

Closing times
Closed 25-26 December

Prices
Meals: a la carte £ 18/33

Typical Dishes
Scallops with butternut squash

Duck breast with sherry reduction

Vanilla custard panna cotta

At the junction of A 30 and A 287. Parking.

Hook

43   Old House at Home

**Newnham Grn,
Hook, RG27 9AH**
Tel.: (01256)762222
Website: www.oldhousenewham.co.uk

VISA   MC   AE

🍺 **Wadworth 6X and Andwell Ruddy Date**

Tucked away in the corner of a picturesque green, you'll find this mid-19C former post office. Having survived two fires, the owners – one the daughter of cricket commentator 'Blowers' – have restored it nicely and it exudes warmth and charm aplenty. You'll find the local shooting party in most Fridays in season and some of the regulars make appearances at both lunch and dinner, while nearby businesspeople frequent the private rooms. The main room is split in two, with roaring fires on both sides, the original bar being cosier. Menus provide plenty of choice, from classic dishes such as slow-roast belly of pork with apple sauce or chargrilled minute steak with garlic and parsley butter to tempura of soft-shell crab or seared tuna sashimi.

Closing times
Closed Sunday dinner
booking advisable
Prices
Meals: a la carte £ 27/34

Typical Dishes
Pan-fried scallops
Slow-braised octopus stew
Trio of baby crème brûlée

Southwest 1.5 mi by A30 and Newnham Rd on edge of the green off Newnham Ln.

44   **Kings Arms**

**Romsey Rd,
Lockerley, SO51 OJF**
Tel.: (01794)340332
Website: www.kingsarmslockerley.co.uk

 Ringwood Best Bitter and Sharp's Doom Bar

Those who can call the Kings Arms their local are a lucky bunch. It's a cosy, friendly place which holds regular events with the villagers in mind: quiz nights and wine tasting, plus more unusual gatherings like a champagne lunch with a local guest speaker or children's pumpkin carving at Halloween. The garden is a cool place to hang out all year round, with its gentle stream and bridges, outdoor barbeque kitchen and funky wooden pods complete with heating, lighting, comfy seats and iPod docks. Food-wise, they keep things pleasingly simple and the tasty, hearty dishes are cooked with care. The 'full house sharing platter', with its meats, shellfish and salad, is great value – and game is a passion of the owner, so you'll find plenty in winter.

Closing times
Open daily
Prices
Meals: a la carte £ 19/32

Typical Dishes
Scallops, crab & sweetcorn
Cod with samphire & capers
Lemon parfait & honeycomb crumble

5.5 mi northwest of Romsey by A 3057 and B 3084 towards Awbridge. Parking.

295

Longparish

45 **Plough Inn**

**Longparish,
SP11 6PB**
Tel.: (01264)720358
Website: www.theploughinn.info

Ringwood Best Bitter, Timothy Taylor Landlord and Sharp's Doom Bar

Set in a lovely location in the Test Valley, this red brick and slate pub takes pride of place as the hub of this characterful village. It's owned by an experienced chef, who left the bright lights of London for a place of his own. Inside, it's pleasingly rustic, with a laid-back feel: there's a small bar to one side, a wine cave under the stairs and a cheese trolley sitting proudly in the corner – which is wheeled over for you to choose from if you're having a ploughman's. Menus are kept short and feature a likeable selection of flavoursome classics, which show a good respect for ingredients and are prepared in a modern way. This being prime fishing country, you are also more than welcome to bring your day's catch for the chef to prepare.

Closing times
Closed Sunday dinner
Prices
Meals: £ 12 (weekdays) and a la carte £ 21/37

Typical Dishes
Grilled sardines on toast

Butter-roasted cod, `English Breakfast'

Lemon meringue parfait

 7 mi east of Andover by A 303 and B 3048. Parking.

46   **Peat Spade Inn**

**Village St,
Longstock, SO20 6DR**
Tel.: (01264)810612
Website: www.peatspadeinn.co.uk

VISA   MC   AE   ◑

Flowerpots Bitter and Flack's Double Drop

Just north of Stockbridge, in the heart of the Test Valley, you'll come across the pretty village of Longstock and this charming 19C inn, where period furnishings and warming open fires are accompanied by flickering candlelight. Country pursuits are the name of the game, so you'll find plenty of shooters and fishermen inside, alongside local farm workers and those leisurely passing through. Menus offer generous, classically based dishes with bold flavours and a refined style; there might be Portland crab gratin, followed by free range chicken Kiev or risotto of autumn squash. Stylish bedrooms are split between the main building and the annexe, and there's a residents' lounge which overlooks the courtyard garden and its sunken fire-pit.

Closing times
Closed 25 December
booking essential
Prices
Meals: a la carte £ 25/40
8 rooms: £ 100/245

Typical Dishes
Wood pigeon breast
Shoulder of spring lamb with Savoy cabbage
Chocolate fondant

 1.5 mi north of Stockbridge on A 3507. Parking.

Lower Froyle

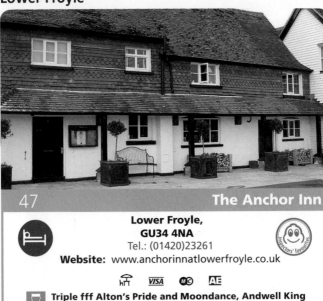

47

The Anchor Inn

**Lower Froyle,
GU34 4NA**
Tel.: (01420)23261
Website: www.anchorinnatlowerfroyle.co.uk

hiT   *VISA*   MO   AE

Triple fff Alton's Pride and Moondance, Andwell King John

With its origins firmly in the 14C, this part-whitewashed, part-tile hung pub boasts much more in the way of history than sister establishment, The Peat Spade Inn. Pretty countryside and a little pond set the scene and the interior doesn't disappoint, boasting characterful low-beamed olive green rooms and a pleasing mix of cushioned pews, benches and old chairs. Good-sized menus offer classic pub dishes with a refined edge and cooking is hearty and flavoursome; you might find jellied ham hock, followed by sirloin steak and jam roly poly to finish. Service is fittingly keen and friendly, and there's a concise but well-chosen wine list. Bedrooms are characterful but if you retire before closing, you may be able to hear a gentle hum from the bar.

Closing times
Closed 25 December
Prices
Meals: a la carte £ 24/44

🛏 **5 rooms:** £ 120/160

Typical Dishes
Portland crab mayonnaise

Loin of spring lamb with braised shoulder

Lemon meringue pie

 5 mi northeast of Alton by A 31. Parking.

Old Basing

48

Crown

**The Street,
Old Basing, RG24 7BW**
Tel.: (01256)321424
Website: www.thecrownoldbasing.com

VISA MC AE ◻

Fuller's London Pride, Andwell King John and Sharp's
Doom Bar

Away from the sprawl of Basingstoke lies lesser known Old Basing, home to the Tudor ruins of Basing House. Within the village you'll also find The Crown, which is now in the hands of two local chefs who gave it a lick of paint and set to the stoves. They may have started with a limited budget but their enthusiasm is palpable and they sensibly pay as much attention to the needs of the villagers just popping in for a drink as those coming for a meal. The menus come with a likeable simplicity and the classic, flavoursome food reveals a confident kitchen. Everything is homemade, from the bread to the fudge served with coffee; a good value lunch draws customers from the nearby business park and the concise dinner menu appeals to locals.

Closing times
Closed Sunday dinner
Prices
Meals: a la carte £ 22/33

Typical Dishes
Salad of Tunworth cheese with pear, celery & walnuts

Fish of the day with brown shrimp & caper butter

Earl Grey tea panna cotta

Parking. *East 2.5 mi by A 3010 following signs for Basing House.*

Otterbourne

49   White Horse

**Main Rd,
Otterbourne, SO21 2EQ**
Tel.: (01962)712830
Website: www.whitehorseotterbourne.co.uk

 Ringwood Best Bitter, Flowerpots Bitter and Timothy Taylor Landlord

This is a large pub which can get very busy, especially at weekends, so arrive early to bag a table. It's smart, with designer décor, arty photos, vintage adverts and leather sofas; one side is for drinkers, while the other side is set up for diners. When it comes to the menu, flexibility is key: have a bar snack like a pickled egg or some black pudding fritters; perhaps a lunchtime sandwich with some triple-cooked chips; a dish like chicken and leek pie or braised beef shin – or the full three courses. There are lovely local cheeses, bread from a nearby artisan baker, Sunday roasts and even afternoon teas. Add in a pleasant terrace and a young, friendly team, and it's not hard to see why the White Horse is once again the hub of the village.

Closing times
Open daily
Prices
Meals: a la carte £ 17/43

Typical Dishes
Ham hock terrine
Slow-roast lamb brisket
Sticky toffee pudding

NONE

 8.5 mi south of Winchester by B 3335 and minor roads. Parking.

England • South East • Hampshire

50   Purefoy Arms

**Alresford Rd,
Preston Candover, RG25 2EJ**
Tel.: (01256)389777
Website: www.thepurefoyarms.co.uk

 VISA

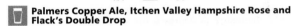 Palmers Copper Ale, Itchen Valley Hampshire Rose and
Flack's Double Drop

Don't be fooled by the somewhat austere façade; a charming young couple have totally restored this once crumbling pub, which was last rebuilt in the 1860s. It now comes with an attractive contemporary feel, although many of the original features have been retained. The daily changing menu, with its hints of Spain – especially in the bar nibbles – is very appealing. Some luxury ingredients may appear at weekends but the philosophy is tasty food at competitive prices and everything's homemade, including the bread. There are also dishes to share, such as the suckling pig, which requires pre-ordering. And the chocolates in the bar are courtesy of the owner's father, a retired chocolatier who has set up a studio in one of the barns.

Closing times
Closed 26 December,
1 January, Sunday dinner
and Monday

Prices
Meals: £ 18 (weekday lunch)
and a la carte £ 23/33

Typical Dishes
Razor clams with
Oloroso sherry &
Spanish onions
Dorset veal with white
asparagus & morels
Pistachio & olive oil
cake

6.5 mi north of New Alresford on B 3046 in centre of village.
Parking.

Romsey

England • South East • Hampshire

51   **Three Tuns**

**58 Middlebridge St,
Romsey, SO51 8HL**
Tel.: (01794)512639
Website: www.the3tunsromsey.co.uk

**Ringwood Fortyniner, Flack's Double Drop,
Wadworth St George & The Dragon and Upham Ales**

Having been through a number of mismanagements over the last few years, this charming pub, which dates from the 1720s, appears to have finally got the tenants it deserves. Tucked down a quiet road, it oozes charm from the moment you walk in. The low beamed bar with crackling fires is usually full of locals enjoying a drink and a 'small plate' like the homemade fishcakes. Beyond is a panelled room where you'll be offered well-priced and reassuringly 'proper' pub food, like steak and kidney pie or home-baked honey-glazed ham and eggs; while dishes like belly of pork with black pudding and Hampshire rhubarb crumble show that this is a kitchen with a deft touch. Service is pitched just right and is provided by a young and very hospitable team.

Closing times
Open daily
Prices
Meals: a la carte £ 22/33

Typical Dishes
Potted pheasant &
black pudding
Brixham sea bass
with new potatoes &
samphire
Pineapple `upside
down' sponge

 Towards the western end of the town, off the bypass. Parking.

302

52 White Star Tavern, Dining and Rooms

**28 Oxford St,
Southampton, SO14 3DJ**
Tel.: (023)80821990
Website: www.whitestartavern.co.uk

Itchen Valley Brewery White Star Ale and Sharp's Doom Bar

You can't miss this striking black pub with its oversized windows and smart pavement terrace. Set in the lively maritime district, it's provided nourishment and shelter for seafarers since the 19C, although you'll find a much more diverse mix of visitors nowadays. It's a spacious place, made up of several different areas organised around a central bar, and displays an eclectic combination of furniture. The à la carte offers a good choice of modern British main courses – finished off with proper old-fashioned puddings – but there's also a selection of tapas-style small plates on offer throughout the day; and they even open early for breakfast. Smart, modern bedrooms boast good facilities and are named after legendary White Star Liners.

Closing times
Closed 25-26 December
Prices
Meals: a la carte £ 19/40
14 rooms: £ 75/175

Typical Dishes
Scallops & crab with butter beans

Pork loin with braised leeks

Dark chocolate fondant

 Southeast of West Quay shopping centre, off Bernard Street. Parking meters directly outside and College St car park (2min walk).

Stockbridge

53   Greyhound on the Test

**31 High St,
Stockbridge, SO20 6EY**
Tel.: (01264)810833
Website: www.thegreyhoundonthetest.co.uk

🍴 *VISA* 💳 ⒜Ⓔ ⓪

Ringwood Best and Upham Ale

If ever there were a place close to J.R.Hartley's heart, it would have been Stockbridge: the River Test flows under the High Street and the oldest fishing club in England was founded here in 1882. This mustard-coloured pub plays its part too – head for the garden and you'll find over a mile of River Test fishing rights. At over 600 years old, it has plenty of character: low beams and wood burning stoves abound, and the elegant décor gives it a French bistro feel. When it comes to the food, there's a selection of well-presented, refined British classics. The good value set lunch keeps the regulars happy, local game and seafood are a feature, and the chef will happily cook your catch. Homely bedrooms have walk-in showers and quality bedding.

Closing times
Open daily
booking advisable

Prices
Meals: £ 18 (weekday lunch) and a la carte £ 23/44

🛏 **7 rooms:** £ 70/125

Typical Dishes
Braised cod cheeks with curried saffron sauce
Skate wing with caper butter
Nougatine glacé

 15 mi east of Salisbury by A 30. Parking.

54

Thomas Lord

**High St,
West Meon, GU32 1LN**
Tel.: (01730)829444
Website: www.thomaslord.co.uk

🍴 VISA MC AE

Upham Ales and Ringwood Best Bitter

This pub is named after the founder of Lord's Cricket Ground, who retired to and is buried in this village – so if you know your stump from your swing and your grubber from your googly, you should feel at home among the bats, county caps and other memorabilia making its home here. Three rooms display a worn, shabby-chic style, with open fires and soft seating; the snug has shelves of second-hand books for sale, with the proceeds going to community projects. Produce is almost exclusively local, with herbs and vegetables from the pub's kitchen garden. The concise menu of British dishes changes at least once a day, depending on what's freshly available and might include crab cakes, Hampshire rarebit, braised lamb or slow-cooked pork belly.

Closing times
Closed 25 December
Prices
Meals: a la carte £ 24/43

Typical Dishes
Potted confit chicken leg

Venison, ox cheek bread pudding & baked celeriac

Treacle tart, bay leaf ice cream

🚗 *9 mi west of Petersfield by A 272 and A 32 south. Parking.*

Winchester

55   No.5 Bridge Street

**5 Bridge St,
Winchester, SO23 OHN**
Tel.: (01962)863838
Website: www.no5bridgestreet.co.uk

🛜 *VISA* 🅜🅒 🅐🅔

🍺 **Ringwood Best Bitter and various guest ales**

Enter the town from the south and you can't miss this roadside pub by the busy main roundabout. A top-to-toe makeover has given the place a fashionable, modern feel and, come summer, the internal courtyard is a real boon. The front bar with its metal-topped tables is the best place for a drink – the humorous wine and cocktail list makes for a good read – or head to the dining room at the back for table service and a view of the chefs at work in the open kitchen. The menu is divided into various sections, including 'small plates', 'market plates', 'soups and salads' and 'British charcuterie and cheese', and dishes veer towards the Mediterranean in their influences. Simply styled, comfortable bedrooms – those at the front hear the road noise.

Closing times
Closed 25 December
Prices
Meals: a la carte £ 16/41
🛏 **6 rooms:** £ 90/125

Typical Dishes
Terrine of duck
Steak burger with triple-cooked chips
Rhubarb crème brûlée

In town centre. Pay and display parking nearby.

56 Wykeham Arms

**75 Kingsgate St,
Winchester, SO23 9PE**
Tel.: (01962)853834
Website: www.wykehamarmswinchester.co.uk

VISA **MC** **AE** **D**

🍺 **Fuller's London Pride & Seafarer, George Gale HSB and Flowerpots Goodens Gold**

This 18C red-brick inn might be hidden away but that doesn't stop a diverse collection of people from finding it. Tucked away on a cobbled street between the college and cathedral, it's named after Bishop William of Wykeham, who founded the former of these two establishments in the 14C. Made up of various characterful rooms, it's deceptively spacious, with an appealingly shabby style and an interesting display of curios; from old school uniform and ex-college desks to Nelson memorabilia, Bishop Pike's mitre and 1,700 tankards. Menus range from soups, pies and pastas through to more elaborate dishes such as lobster. Individually styled bedrooms boast good facilities; those upstairs are the most characterful, those opposite, the most peaceful.

Closing times
Open daily
booking essential

Prices
Meals: £ 18/35
and a la carte £ 25/43

🛏 **14 rooms:** £ 84/159

Typical Dishes
Ballotine of trout with poached quail's egg

Duck breast with potato & mustard croquettes

Bitter chocolate fondant

🚗 Near Winchester College (St Mary's). Access to car park via Canon Street only. Parking or street parking with permit.

Godshill

57 · Taverners

**High St,
Godshill, PO38 3HZ**
Tel.: (01983)840707
Website: www.thetavernersgodshill.co.uk

Sharp's Doom Bar, Yates Golden Ale and Goddards Fuggle Dee Dum

In a pretty – and often busy – little village, stands The Taverners, a pleasant whitewashed pub with a cosy, characterful bar and two deceptively large dining rooms. It's the kind of place that's all about the latest island ingredients and handmade, homemade everything. Out front, a blackboard asks for any surplus home-grown produce (in return for a local Taverners beer or two); to the rear, a large garden is home to chickens, herbs and veg; and inside, various boards display food miles and tables of what's in season when. Cooking is fresh and tasty, mixing traditional pub classics such as lamb burgers with more ambitious daily specials like sea bass fillets. The hand-raised pork pie is a speciality, as is "my nan's" lemon meringue pie.

Closing times
Closed first 3 weeks January

Prices
Meals: a la carte £ 18/26

Typical Dishes
Wild rabbit terrine with homemade piccalilli

Brownrigg duck breast with faggot & purple sprouting broccoli

Lemon meringue pie

 4 mi west of Shanklin by A 3020. Parking.

58 **New Inn**

Mill Rd,
Shalfleet, PO30 4NS
Tel.: (01983)531314
Website: www.thenew-inn.co.uk

Sharp's Doom Bar, Goddards Fuggle Dee Dum and Ringwood Best Bitter

This pub is tucked away on the main Newport to Yarmouth road and its name is somewhat of a misnomer, as there's been an inn here since 1743. It's full of character, with inglenook fireplaces, slate floors and simple, scrubbed wood tables. Things are also kept simple on the menu, where you'll find proper pub dishes like steak and ale pie, sausage and chips or salt beef salad with pickles; all proudly made with island produce. Locally landed fish and seafood feature in the summer months – when the decked terrace also comes into its own – and there are more adventurous specials chalked up on boards daily. Testimony to the pub's popularity is the fact that it's not unusual to see guests who've sailed over from the mainland especially for lunch!

Closing times
Open daily
Prices
Meals: a la carte £ 17/39

Typical Dishes
Grilled goat's cheese with apple & beetroot relish

Hake with cumin-roasted cauliflower

Double chocolate, date & almond tiffin

7 mi west of Newport on A 3054. Parking.

Biddenden

59   The Three Chimneys

**Hareplain Rd,
Biddenden, TN27 8LW**
Tel.: (01580)291472
Website: www.thethreechimneys.co.uk

 **Adnams Best, Old Dairy Brewery Red Top and Goody Ales
Penshurst Pale Ale**

This delightful pub dates back to 1420 and has all the character you would expect of a building its age. The low-beamed, dimly lit rooms have a truly old world feel and for sunnier days there's a conservatory, a garden and a charming terrace. Menus feature mainly British dishes, such as smoked haddock, finished off with nursery puddings like apple crumble; there are some tempting local wines, ciders and ales on offer too. The story surrounding the pub's name goes that French prisoners held at Sissinghurst Castle during the Seven Years' War were allowed to wander as far as the three lanes but were forbidden to pass the junction where the pub was sited. 'Les trois chemins' (the three roads) was then later mistranslated into 'The Three Chimneys'.

Closing times
Closed 25 and dinner
31 December
booking essential
Prices
Meals: a la carte £ 24/37

Typical Dishes
Cheddar rarebit with
Parma ham
Rump of lamb with
roasted squash
Chocolate & coffee
torte

 1.5 mi west by A 262. Parking.

60   **Five Bells Inn**

**Brabourne,
TN25 5LP**
Tel.: (01303)813334
Website: www.fivebellsinnbrabourne.com

 Goody Ales Good Health, Ripple Steam Brewery Best Bitter and Classic IPA, Gadds' No 3 and No 5

The original Five Bells Inn was set next to the church, but it was later relocated to this 16C former poorhouse, just a stone's throw from the Pilgrims Way. The pub's interior is a glorious candlelit hotchpotch: exposed beams burst with hop bines, open fires crackle, a gorgeous mermaid enhances the main fireplace and a host of butcher's blocks have been given a second life as tables. The gutsy menu ranges from eggs Benedict or a ploughman's to homemade beef burgers, wood-fired pizzas and fish from the local boats. If you fancy taking something home, produce from the menu is available to buy in the small deli; keep an eye out for the delicious pressed apple and pear juices. Service is chatty and welcoming, and the bedrooms, delightfully busy.

Closing times
Open daily
Prices
Meals: a la carte £ 23/39
4 rooms: £ 90/140

Typical Dishes
Scotch egg & black pudding with crackling
Oven-baked trawler pie
Chocolate, raspberry & pistachio slice

🚗 *5 mi east of Ashford by A 20. Parking.*

Chipstead

61   **George & Dragon**

**39 High St,
Chipstead, TN13 2RW**
Tel.: (01732)779019
Website: www.georgeanddragonchipstead.com

**Westerham Grasshopper and George's Marvellous
Medicine**

If it's character you're after, then this 400 year old inn on the edge of the village is the place to come. Outside there's a delightful mature garden with a large terrace, a children's play area and raised herb and salad beds. Inside, there's a lovely beamed bar where they serve a huge array of cocktails, and a charming first floor dining room with a sloping ceiling and wonky floor. Looking at the menu, there's no doubting you're in England: seasonal, regional ingredients feature in dishes such as bacon, kale and chestnut soup; celeriac and celery salad with English mustard dressing; and pork belly with apple sauce. The mature, 28-day hung steaks with triple-cooked chips are a perennial favourite, along with the steak sandwiches at lunch.

Closing times
Open daily
Prices
Meals: a la carte £ 19/34

Typical Dishes
Seared pigeon, pancetta, blackberry & cob nut
Pan-fried black bream with samphire
Dark chocolate & praline slice

 Located in the centre of the village. Parking.

62 **Dove Inn**

**Plum Pudding Ln,
Dargate, ME13 9HB**
Tel.: (01227)751360
Website: www.doveatdargate.co.uk

 VISA **MC** **AE**

 Shepherd Neame Ales

Set in the heart of a sleepy hamlet, in the delectable sounding Plum Pudding Lane, this attractive red-brick Victorian pub boasts well-tended gardens and three cosy rooms set with scrubbed pine tables. It's very much a locals pub and villagers pop in and out all day, especially at lunchtime and after work. Phillip, the chef-owner, began his training here at the age of 17 and returned over 10 years later to take the helm. Weekdays he offers a hugely appealing menu of enticing nibbles, pub classics and dishes like smoked cod macaroni: cooking is simple but executed with care and a light touch. Friday and Saturday things step up a gear with a concise, more ambitious menu and prices to match; you might find crab risotto or gurnard with chorizo.

Closing times
Closed first week January, 1 week February, Monday except bank holidays, Sunday dinner and Tuesday lunch
booking advisable
Prices
Meals: a la carte £ 24/37

Typical Dishes
Wild garlic risotto, pea shoots & truffle oil
Roast pork belly, smoked black pudding & apple sauce
Vanilla rice pudding

Between Faversham and Whitstable, south of A 299. Parking.

Goudhurst

63   **Goudhurst Inn**

**Cranbrook Rd,
Goudhurst, TN17 1DX**
Tel.: (01580)212605
Website: www.thegoudhurstinn.com

 Harvey's Sussex Best, Timothy Taylor Landlord and Sharp's Doom Bar

Anyone currently lamenting the state of their local should take heart from what happened to this pub. It was a down-at-heel place with something of a chequered past until a local chap bought it and did it up from top-to-toe, inside and out; and now it has resumed its place at the heart of village life. Vases of fresh flowers line the bar, the atmosphere is warm and friendly, the look remains suitably rustic and there's a lovely terrace at the back. The food is equally heartening and the kitchen goes local when it can – the wild boar sausages are from a local butcher, the scallops come from Rye and the lamb is from a nearby farm. Be sure to leave room for the gloriously 'proper' puds, like rhubarb crumble or sticky toffee pudding.

Closing times
Closed Sunday dinner
Prices
Meals: a la carte £ 21/37

Typical Dishes
Scallops with creamed Savoy cabbage
Confit of pork belly with watercress mashed potato
Baked chocolate tart

 In the centre of the village. Parking.

64 **Granville**

Street End,
Lower Hardres, CT4 7AL
Tel.: (01227)700402
Website: www.thegranvillecanterbury.com

 Shepherd Neame Master Brew and seasonal ales

This pub may not look as impressive as the Tudor warship it's named after but it definitely has the size. Set on a small village crossroads, it's a real family affair, with the owner's sister out front and her partner in the kitchen – and, like their other pub, The Sportsman, you can guarantee it'll be busy. With a high ceiling, exposed rafters and an open-plan layout, the interior is a touch Scandinavian; the sofas making a great spot for a quick snack, the hotchpotch of tables beyond being better for a proper meal. A constantly evolving blackboard menu offers unfussy dishes which arrive in generous, flavoursome portions; mostly on chunky wooden platters. Warm oiled pumpkin seeds come with the bread and veg originates from their allotment.

Closing times
Closed Sunday dinner and Monday

Prices
Meals: £ 16/20 and a la carte £ 24/35

Typical Dishes
Smoked salmon tart with beetroot relish

Roast leg & braised shoulder of lamb, mint sauce

Apple crème brûlée

 3 mi south of Canterbury on B 2068. Parking.

Milstead

65   **Red Lion**

Rawling St,
Milstead, ME9 0RT
Tel.: (01795)830279
Website: www.theredlionmilstead.co.uk

**Wells Bombardier, Adnams Southwold Bitter, Old Dairy
Copper Top and Canterbury The Miller's Ale**

A 'Red Lion' pub has stood on this spot since Victorian times; the current one belonging to a very capable and experienced couple, who have run numerous pubs in the area over the years. They like to get involved, so you'll find him hard at work in the kitchen and her leading the friendly, engaging service. It's a simple place, featuring a cosy, open-fired bar where the locals tend to gather and a dining room with rich red walls, benches and Lloyd Loom chairs. The ever-changing blackboard menu offers plenty of choice and the Gallic roots of the chef are clear to see; you might find French onion soup, homemade bouillabaisse, cassoulet of lamb shank and Provençale sauces. In true country style, dishes are honest, wholesome and richly flavoured.

Closing times
Closed Sunday and Monday
booking advisable
Prices
Meals: a la carte £ 17/39

Typical Dishes
Fish soup
Pan-fried calves'
liver with lime & sage
butter
Ginger parkin pudding

South of Sittingbourne signposted off the A 2. Parking.

England • South East • Kent

66   Three Mariners

**2 Church Rd,
Oare, ME13 0QA**
Tel.: (01795)533633
Website: www.thethreemarinersoare.co.uk

 Shepherd Neame Ales

If you've been negotiating the Saxon Shore Way, this 500 year old pub is the perfect place to refresh yourself, as there's a certain warmth and quirkiness about it, from the roaring fires to the smiley team. A constantly evolving à la carte offers an appealing mix of carefully prepared, flavoursome dishes like smoked pigeon salad or skate cheeks; while the set menus represent great value – the Walkers' Lunch might include potted duck, chicken pie and homemade ice cream, and the Business Lunch, Parma ham, sea bass and artisan cheeses. From starters to desserts, there's always plenty of local produce. Set in a sleepy hamlet, next to a small marina in the Swale channel, it offers pleasant views over the marshes to the estuary beyond.

Closing times
Closed dinner
24-25 December

Prices
Meals: £ 12/17 and a la carte £ 22/33

Typical Dishes
Beef carpaccio

Chargrilled fillet of wild sea bass with orange-glazed fennel

Passion fruit, mascarpone & mango mousse

1 mi northwest of Faversham by minor road or A 2 and B 2045. Parking.

Seasalter

67

The Sportsman

**Faversham Rd,
Seasalter, CT5 4BP**
Tel.: (01227)273370
Website: www.thesportsmanseasalter.co.uk

VISA MC

 Shepherd Neame Ales

Set on the edge of town, by the sea wall, the unassuming-looking Sportsman proves you should never judge a book by its cover, for while both its façade and its interior may appear rather modest, it's food is top-class. The daily blackboard menu is guided by what's seasonal and local, with meat from nearby Monkshill Farm and fish from the local day boats. Dishes feature just two or three top quality ingredients and are prepared with precision; flavours are extremely well-judged and presentation is original. The homemade bread, butter and salt are highlights and the roasted pork belly is a favourite. Arrive early if you want the full choice, as dishes disappear off the menu as produce is used up. A tasting menu can be requested when booking.

Closing times
Closed 25-26 December,
Sunday dinner and Monday
booking advisable
Prices
Meals: a la carte £ 33/40

Typical Dishes
Mussel & bacon
chowder
Thornback ray with
sherry vinegar
dressing
Warm chocolate
mousse

2 mi southwest of Whitstable by B 2205 following the coast road. Parking.

68 — George & Dragon

**Speldhurst Hill,
Speldhurst, TN3 0NN**
Tel.: (01892)863125
Website: www.speldhurst.com

Harveys Sussex Best Bitter, Larkins Traditional and
Brakspear Oxford Gold

Dating back to 1212, this timbered Wealden Hall house boasts an impressive beamed ceiling and displays an unusual Queen's post in the upstairs dining room (which is unfortunately only used at busier times). It's thought to be the second oldest pub in the country and, in the past, provided refreshment for the soldiers returning from Agincourt. It's a hugely appealing place, with several characterful flag floored rooms, vast inglenook fireplaces and a contrasting modern, landscaped terrace. Cooking is generous and strives to keep things local and organic, with menus offering a selection of pub classics alongside more elaborate dishes such as bacon-wrapped pheasant. The Groombridge belly pork and Ashdown Forest venison are best sellers.

Closing times
Open daily
Prices
Meals: £ 23/29
and a la carte £ 22/39

Typical Dishes
Pigeon breast on Puy lentils
Roast belly of pork with Groombridge apple compote
Pear tarte Tatin

 3.5 mi north of Royal Tunbridge Wells by A 26. Parking.

Stalisfield Green

69 **Plough**

**Stalisfield Green,
ME13 0HY**
Tel.: (01795)890256
Website: www.stalisfieldgreen.com

 VISA MC

 **Hopdaeman Ales, Whitstable Brewery Ales,
Kent Brewery Pale Ale and Old Dairy Gold Top**

The term 'rustic' could have been invented for this remotely set pub, with its thick walls, farming implements, exposed beams and hop bines. Sit at table 6 or 7 on either side of the open fire or go for table 10 – set almost in an inglenook – where you will be able to read a verse from the farmer's poem 'God Speed the Plough' on the wall. Evening candlelight only intensifies the 15C pub's charm – as do the pub's friendly and reassuring serving staff. Hearty portions of country-style cooking might include scallops with black pudding or grilled pork chops with apple sauce, but the braised brisket and mature local steaks are what most diners come for. Real ales are all brewed in the county and there's an impressive range of Kent wines too.

Closing times
Closed Monday except bank holidays

Prices
Meals: £ 14 (weekdays) and a la carte £ 25/36

Typical Dishes
Smoked haddock scotch egg
`Kentish Ranger' chicken & smoked bacon
Hot chocolate pudding

 7 mi southwest of Faversham by A 251. Parking.

70 **Pearson's Arms**

**The Horsebridge,
Sea Wall, Whitstable, CT5 1BT**
Tel.: (01227)773133
Website: www.pearsonsarmsbyrichardphillips.co.uk

 Gadds' Seasider, Harveys Sussex Best Bitter,
Whitstable Brewery IPA and Sharp's Doom Bar

With the Thames Estuary stretching out in front of it, this characterful pub is in a great spot. Exposed beams and wood floors provide a pleasant rustic style and contemporary furnishings add a touch of modernity. Enter into the bar for a pint from the next door brewery and snacks such as whitebait, jellied eels and crispy pigs' ears or head up to the dining room for superb water views and a more extensive selection of comforting dishes. You might find ham hock and parsley ballotine or lobster and prawn cocktail, followed by wild boar and apple sausages or an assiette of fruits der mer; with flavoursome Kentish produce to the fore. Service is friendly and copes well, and there's a great atmosphere, enhanced by live music every Tuesday.

Closing times
Closed Monday and dinner Sunday and Tuesday

Prices
Meals: £ 11 (weekday lunch) and a la carte
£ 23/37

Typical Dishes
Asparagus with deep-fried duck egg
Braised wild boar with apple purée
White chocolate cheesecake

 In centre of town on seafront. On-street parking nearby.

71   **Sweet Olive at The Chequers Inn**

**Baker St,
Aston Tirrold, OX11 9DD**
Tel.: (01235)851272
Website: www.sweet-olive.com

Fuller's London Pride and Brakspear Bitter

England • South East • Oxfordshire

A red-brick Victorian pub at the heart of an English village; cosy, welcoming and frequented by locals. What sets it apart is its decidedly Gallic feel, attributable in no small part to its French owners. One of the owners also happens to be the chef, so expect to see dishes like Mediterranean fish soup and onglet of beef on the menu; other staples include the more globally influenced tiger prawns in tempura or crispy duck salad, and the thoroughly British ox cheeks and mash or treacle sponge and custard. The old French wine boxes which bedeck the bar offer a clue as to wine list: most are from France, with many from the Alsace region, like one of the owners. Oenophiles will find plenty to get excited about on the separate fine wine list.

Closing times
Closed 2 weeks February, 3 weeks July, Sunday dinner and Wednesday
booking essential
Prices
Meals: a la carte £ 28/44

Typical Dishes
Tiger prawn salad with soy dressing
Escalope of roe deer with port wine sauce
Treacle sponge and custard

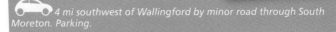

4 mi southwest of Wallingford by minor road through South Moreton. Parking.

72

Kings Head Inn

**The Green,
Bledington, OX7 6XQ**
Tel.: (01608)658365
Website: www.kingsheadinn.net

🍽 *VISA* **MC**

🍺 **Hook Norton Hooky Gold, Wye Valley Bitter and Purity Ales**

Sitting on a picturesque village green, bisected by a stream filled with bobbing ducks, this charming 16C former cider house provides the perfect backdrop for a holiday snap. The interior doesn't disappoint either: the large bar with its vast inglenook fireplace, solid stone floor and comfy, laid-back feel creates a wonderful atmosphere, and the cosy bedrooms – split between the pub and the courtyard – finish it all off perfectly. In keeping with the surroundings, menus are traditionally based, offering game in season and usually some fish-based specials on the blackboard; maybe crab and toast or Scottish mussels. Dishes on the main menu change weekly, and range from potted shrimps with beetroot to lamb chops with chickpeas and mozzarella.

Closing times
Open daily
Prices
Meals: a la carte £ 22/40
🛏 **12 rooms:** £ 75/135

Typical Dishes

Home-cured bresaola with rocket & parmesan

Corn-fed chicken breast with spiced sweet potato

Treacle tart

🚗 *4 mi southeast of Stow-on-the-Wold by A 436 and B 4450. Parking.*

Britwell Salome

73   **Red Lion**

**Britwell Salome,
OX49 5LG**
Tel.: (01491)613140
Website: www.theredlionbritwellsalome.co.uk

   VISA   **MC**

West Berkshire Mr. Chubbs Lunchtime Bitter, Loose Cannon
Abingdon Bridge, Rebellion IPA and Gun Dog Jack Spaniels

It may have had a few ups and downs over the years but the Red Lion is now back in capable hands and has once again established itself as a 'proper' village pub. It's next to the local cricket pitch and, fittingly, is decorated in deep red, with stags' heads and art by the owners on the walls. When it comes to the food, dishes are well-executed and interesting. There are lots of tasty nibbles – the homemade black pudding scotch egg is a must-try – and a daily deal offering the 'pie of the day' along with a pint of Mr Chubbs Bitter. There's always plenty of pork too, as whole beasts are delivered from the farm next door, and game is often a feature. The freshly churned ice creams are not to be missed and service is warm and friendly.

Closing times
Closed Sunday dinner, Monday and lunch Tuesday
booking essential

Prices
Meals: a la carte £ 21/38

Typical Dishes
Potted crab on toast
Beef shin & ale pie, hispi cabbage & mash
Vanilla panna cotta with poached rhubarb

 Midway between Watlington and Ewelme on B 4009. Parking.

74   **Trout at Tadpole Bridge**

**Buckland Marsh,
SN7 8RF**
Tel.: (01367)870382
Website: www.troutinn.co.uk

🛏   **VISA**   Ⓜ©

🍺 White Horse Wayland Smithy and Village Idiot, Ramsbury Trout Best Bitter and Loose Cannon Abingdon Pale Ale

If you fancy trying your hand at boating, then The Trout could be the pub for you. Set just off the Thames Path, it boasts a pleasant garden running down to the river, where, upon request, you'll find an electric punt, complete with picnic hamper; and six private moorings. It's a smart place but manages to retain a loyal band of drinkers, who congregate in the characterful flagstone bar; the diners sit beside them or in the airy back room. The concise main menu consists of classical Gallic dishes with the odd contemporary touch, supplemented by a blackboard of daily specials that often include seafood or game. It's a popular place, so you'll need to book but the cheery staff cope well under pressure. Comfortable bedrooms exceed expectations.

Closing times
Closed 25-26 December
Prices
Meals: a la carte £ 22/40
🛏 **6 rooms:** £ 85/160

Typical Dishes
Mackerel tartare with lime leaf dressing
Trio of Kelmscott pork, apple jelly & chard
Apple crumble

🚗 4.5 mi northeast of Faringdon by A 417 and A 420 on Brampton road. Parking.

Burford

75 | **Highway Inn**

**117 High St,
Burford, OX18 4RG**
Tel.: (01993)823661
Website: www.thehighwayinn.co.uk

Hook Norton Best Bitter, Butcombe Rare Breed, Wye Valley Dorothy Goodbody and Vale Aylesbury Duck

You might say that the Highway Inn's owners were meant to be: they were married in Burford and even spent their wedding night at this 15C inn. Twinkling lights in the trees draw you in – try to bag a table in one of the bay windows or close to the roaring fire. Cooking is as it should be, simple, honest and fresh, with pub dishes featuring alongside maybe roast Cornish gurnard or local game birds shot by the owner himself, while specials could include risotto, calves' liver or lamb shank. Desserts are delicious and far from dainty, with choices like bread and butter pudding or pear and blackberry crumble. Individually designed bedrooms have a classical style and good modern facilities; the courtyard rooms are ideal for those with dogs.

Closing times
Closed first 2 weeks January and 25-26 December
Prices
Meals: a la carte £ 19/39
9 rooms: £ 85/150

Typical Dishes
Potted Cornish crab with watercress
Smoked Kelmscott pork belly with garlic mash
Sticky ginger toffee pudding, vanilla ice cream

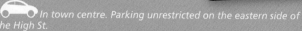 *In town centre. Parking unrestricted on the eastern side of the High St.*

76 **Lamb Inn**

**Sheep St,
Burford, OX18 4LR**
Tel.: (01993)823155
Website: www.cotswold-inns-hotels.co.uk/lamb

 Wickwar Cotswold Way and Hook Norton Old Hooky

Cosiness is a quality for which British pubs are renowned and this delightful pub – a collection of 15C weavers' cottages – certainly has 'snug' and 'warm' down pat. A pair of sitting rooms exude charm, with comfy armchairs, oil paintings and antiques; here and in the bar, the 'Garden and Fireside Menu' offers anything from prawn cocktail or ploughman's to pork chops and mash. In the elegant, candlelit dining room, things get more ambitious, with a tasting menu and an à la carte displaying classic dishes like ham hock and pea soup or rack of lamb; if meat from Ruby and White butchers is listed, be sure a cut ends up on your plate. The terrace and gardens make summer extra special and comfortable bedrooms have a loveliness all of their own.

Closing times
Open daily
Prices
Meals: £ 25/39
🛏 **17 rooms:** £ 150/310

Typical Dishes
Pigeon breast with butternut squash purée
Sea bass with crab tortellini
Chocolate fondant with hazelnut ice cream

🚗 *Parking at Bay Tree Hotel.*

Church Enstone

77 **Crown Inn**

**Mill Ln,
Church Enstone, OX7 4NN**
Tel.: (01608)677262
Website: www.crowninnenstone.co.uk

Hook Norton Hooky Bitter, Timothy Taylor Landlord and Sharp's Doom Bar

This 17C inn is found in among pretty stone houses in a picturesque village on the edge of the Cotswolds. It boasts a welcoming slate-floored conservatory, a beamed dining room and a rustic stone-walled bar – as well as a front terrace and a secluded garden for sunnier days. The chef-owner has built up quite a reputation for his seafood in these parts, so you'll find that some dishes – such as the fishcakes and the king scallop and bacon salad – are permanent fixtures, along with the locally renowned steak and Hooky ale pie. At lunch, the daily blackboard reads like a top ten of old pub favourites, with the likes of beer-battered cod and chips or pork sausages and mash; all of the meats, fruit and vegetables are sourced from the local farms.

Closing times
Closed 25-26 December,
1 January and Sunday dinner

Prices
Meals: £ 16 (lunch)
and a la carte £ 19/32

Typical Dishes
Scallop & bacon salad
Roast belly of pork, crackling & cider gravy
Baileys panna cotta, caramel ice cream

 3.5 mi southeast of Chipping Norton by A 44. Parking.

78   **N** **Chequers**

**Church Rd,
Churchill, OX7 6NJ**
Tel.: (01608)659393
Website: www.thechequerschurchill.com

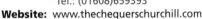

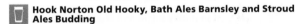

Hook Norton Old Hooky, Bath Ales Barnsley and Stroud Ales Budding

It may have an 'OX' postcode but this mellow sandstone pub, sitting proudly at the heart of the village, is clearly in Cotswold country. It's a vital part of the local community and the owners appear to have got the formula just right; it's filled with locals playing darts and the keen serving team exude as much warmth as the roaring fire in the inglenook. The bar is well-stocked with local ales, while the counter behind is filled with enticing hams and olives, just waiting to be nibbled on. Menus are firmly rooted in tradition, with hearty dishes such as ham hock and pease pudding, calves' liver and bacon or steaks cooked on the Josper grill. It's a popular place but there are always 6 tables left unreserved, for those without a booking.

Closing times
Closed 25 December and dinner 26 December and 1 January
Prices
Meals: a la carte £ 16/33

Typical Dishes
Twice-baked cheddar cheese soufflé

Baked sea bass, tomatoes, basil & anchovies

Marsala semifreddo

 3 mi southwest of Chipping Norton on B 4450. Parking.

East Hendred

79 Eyston Arms

**High St,
East Hendred, OX12 8JY**
Tel.: (01235)833320
Website: www.eystonarms.co.uk

ᴴᵀᵀ *VISA* **MC** **AE** **◑**

🍺 **Hook Norton Hooky Bitter and Wadworth 6X**

A pub has stood on this site for many years – although it was once much smaller and adjoined by estate workers' cottages, as this characterful village was, and still is, largely owned by the local estate. Inside, original tiled floors and exposed brickwork remain but it's been given a typical modern dining pub makeover with scrubbed tables and plenty of candles, along with caricatures of the locals and a great array of photos taken by the owner's daughter on her travels. Staff are warm and welcoming and as a result, they have gained a loyal local following. The menu offers a diverse range of dishes with influences from across the globe; maybe salad of wood pigeon with beetroot and goat's cheese, alongside lemongrass and chilli cured salmon.

Closing times
Closed 25 December and Sunday dinner

Prices
Meals: a la carte £ 27/39

Typical Dishes
Beetroot & vodka cured salmon

Calves' liver with bubble & squeak

Trio of lemon puddings

 4.5 mi east of Wantage by A 417. Parking.

**Filkins,
GL7 3JQ**
Tel.: (01367)860875
Website: www.thefiveallsfilkins.co.uk

🛖   *VISA*   ⓜⓒ

Brakspear Ales

The pub's curious logo refers to the fulfilment of the 5 human needs – the lawyer pleads for all, the parson prays for all, the soldier fights for all and the farmer pays for all, while at the centre, the devil governs all. When it comes to fulfilment, they certainly seem to have it covered here: there's an open-fired bar stocked with fine ales, where they serve snacks and takeaway burgers, and three large dining rooms furnished with antiques. There's also a terrace and a garden with an Aunt Sally area and, completing the picture, some cosy, modern bedrooms; and that's before even mentioning the food! Cooking is satisfyingly traditional, offering everything from potted shrimps with melba toast to a cured meat platter and hearty steaks.

Closing times
Closed 25 December and Sunday dinner
Prices
Meals: £ 20 and a la carte £ 26/43

🛏 **4 rooms:** £ 90/160

Typical Dishes
Stuffed courgette flower fritter

Pork belly with Jerusalem artichoke

Lavender & grappa panna cotta

🚗 *Midway between Burford and Lechlade-on-Thames. Parking.*

Fyfield

81

White Hart

**Main Rd,
Fyfield, OX13 5LW**
Tel.: (01865)390585
Website: www.whitehart-fyfield.com

**Hook Norton Hooky Bitter, Abingdon's Loose Cannon,
Sharp's Doom Bar and Loddon Hullabaloo**

This intriguing 15C chantry house displays many original features, including a two-storey, flag-floored hall with a vaulted ceiling (now the dining room), a minstrels' gallery and a secret tunnel; as well as a pleasant terrace and a cosy beamed bar with an inglenook fireplace. They make good use of the wealth of produce on their doorstep, so you'll find meat from nearby farms or estates; flour – for the homemade bread – from the local mill; and fruit and veg from the pub's own plot or the locals' gardens. Menus offer a diverse range of dishes – from sharing boards to slow-roast pork or tempura courgette flowers – and excellent desserts. Service is slick and friendly, and the annual beer festival and hog roast always makes for a great day out.

Closing times
Closed Monday except bank holidays

Prices
Meals: £ 20/30
and a la carte £ 27/40

Typical Dishes
Dippy Fyfield egg with crab toastie & brown shrimp

Assiette of Cotswold lamb with ratatouille

Roast pineapple with chilli & lime

 10 mi southwest of Oxford by A 420. Parking.

82   Bell at Hampton Poyle

**11 Oxford Rd,
Hampton Poyle, OX5 2QD**
Tel.: (01865)376242
Website: www.thebellathamptonpoyle.co.uk

VISA   *MC*   *AE*

🍺 **Hook Norton Hooky Bitter and Wye Valley Butty Bach**

Tiled flooring and a bright, fresh look make the Bell seem almost Mediterranean, which is not a style one usually associates with a pub in rural Oxfordshire, but it seems to work. The owners have made the kitchen a very visual element of the operation, with its wood-burning oven and large open-plan pass – and they've created a very accessible menu which covers all tastes: there's meze, homemade pizza, and seafood and charcuterie boards, as well as staples such as calves' liver and some decent steaks. They tweak it a little with the seasons and also strive to keep prices in check. If gin's your thing, they have the biggest selection in the world and if you've had too much to drive, there are smart bedrooms above the bar and in a small cottage.

Closing times
Open daily
Prices
Meals: a la carte £ 22/45

🛏 **9 rooms:** £ 95/145

Typical Dishes
Grilled king prawns with dips
Rib-eye steak & chips
Pimm's jelly with mint

🚗 *9 mi north of Oxford by A 34. Parking.*

83

Black Boy

**91 Old High St,
Headington, Oxford, OX3 9HT**
Tel.: (01865)741137
Website: www.theblackboy.uk.com

VISA **MC** **AE**

Hook Norton Old Hooky and St Austell Tribute

It's big and it's bold; it's The Black Boy. As well as having French roots, the chef did a long stint with Raymond Blanc, so it comes as no surprise that there's a Gallic edge to the essentially classic menu, but don't get the wrong idea; this is proper pub food, no messing, with unadorned mains, like braised pork belly or sausage and mash, for under a tenner. Bring some bling to your Black Boy burger by eating it in the small side restaurant; the low-lit bar is the less popular, but by no means less pleasant, alternative. There are homemade breads, mix and match tapas dishes and the roasts go down a storm on a Sunday. Tuesday is quiz night, Thursday is for jazz-lovers and Sunday mornings are when the kids can get creative in the kitchen.

Closing times
Closed 26 December and 1 January
Prices
Meals: a la carte £ 22/33

Typical Dishes
Chicken liver & foie gras parfait
Pork belly with thyme mash
Crème brûlée

East of Oxford off London Rd. On-street parking around the pub.

England • South East • Oxfordshire

84

Three Tuns

**5 Market Pl,
Henley-on-Thames, RG9 2AA**
Tel.: (01491)410138
Website: www.threetunshenley.co.uk

 VISA **MC** **AE**

Ringwood Fortyniner, Brakspear Bitter and Oxford Gold

This pretty, red-brick, town centre pub was originally three houses, one of which used to be a mortuary and, if you take a look above the central bar, you can still see the coffin drop. The atmosphere is far from deathly in this bijou inn, however; the best place to sit being among the drinkers in its lively, open-fired front bar (ask for table 10). The formal dining room has just four tables and is the place for a quieter, more intimate meal. There's something to please all palates on the seasonal menu, and traditional dishes like ham hock terrine or seafood pot au feu are well-presented, satisfying and full of flavour. Breads are homemade, meat comes from the butchers next door and there's an excellent value 2 course lunch menu Tues-Sat.

Closing times
Closed 25 December, Monday except bank holidays and Sunday dinner

Prices
Meals: £ 10/17
and a la carte £ 24/40

Typical Dishes
Homemade tagliolini with truffle butter
Guinea fowl with onion purée & thyme jus
Trio of ginger desserts

 In the centre of town. Local pay and display parking.

Kingham

85 **Kingham Plough**

**The Green,
Kingham, OX7 6YD**
Tel.: (01608)658327
Website: www.thekinghamplough.co.uk

ᴴᴛᴛ *VISA* ⓜⓒ

Hook Norton Ales and Wye Valley HPA

Set on the green of a beautifully unspoilt village in the Evenlode Valley, this pub boasts a rustic lounge-bar, a laid-back restaurant and an easy-going team. It's owned by Emily Watkins, former sous-chef at The Fat Duck, so you'll find the odd dish such as snails on toast that harks back to her Heston days; although the majority of dishes are rooted in a gutsy pub vein – albeit a very modern one. The bar menu offers tasty snacks such as scotched quails' eggs or Welsh rarebit, while the concise restaurant menu features the latest seasonal produce from foraging expeditions and nearby farms. Preparation is careful, slow cooking reigns and dishes evolve throughout the evening as new ingredients arrive. For the weary, 7 comfy bedrooms await.

Closing times
Closed 25 December
Prices
Meals: a la carte £ 28/47
🛏 **7 rooms:** £ 80/145

Typical Dishes
Cornish clam & white bean stew

Pigeon Wellington, confit shallots & curly kale

Milk chocolate & salted caramel pot

🚗 *In village centre. Parking.*

86   **Eagle Tavern**

**Little Coxwell,
SN7 7LW**
Tel.: (01367)241879
Website: www.eagletavern.co.uk

 VISA   MC   AE   ◑

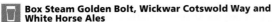 Box Steam Golden Bolt, Wickwar Cotswold Way and White Horse Ales

There's many a rural pub where a stranger walks through the door and the room falls silent; not so at the Eagle Tavern, where the locals welcome you with open arms. It was built in 1901 for the farmers of this sleepy hamlet and, although it might look slightly different nowadays, a convivial atmosphere still reigns. It's a spacious place with a homely bar and a dining room furnished in wood and wicker, and is run by a self-taught Slovakian chef, who cooks food he himself likes to eat. Dishes range from the simple to the ambitious – maybe a juicy burger with all the extras or home-salted beef brisket with piccalilli and rye bread crumble – and the local suppliers, like 'Paul's Poultry', are all named. Bedrooms are cosy and worth the money.

Closing times
Closed Sunday dinner and Monday

Prices
Meals: £ 22 (dinner) and a la carte £ 19/28

🛏 **6 rooms:** £ 60/90

Typical Dishes
Goat's curd with beetroot & honey

Rabbit sausage with gnocchi

Chocolate brownie & praline

 2.5 mi south of Faringdon by A 417. Parking in the village.

Maidensgrove

Five Horseshoes

**Maidensgrove,
RG9 6EX**
Tel.: (01491)641282
Website: www.thefivehorseshoes.co.uk

Brakspear Bitter and Oxford Gold

This charming 17C inn with delightful country views is set in the heart of walking country. When the weather's warm, make for the large garden and terrace, where on Fridays and Saturdays, they fire up the wood oven and bespoke pizzas are the name of the game. Inside, the two intimate rooms and large conservatory are warm and welcoming and also share the view; order a homemade ginger beer then seek out the small blackboard which lists the specials. The daily changing set menu represents the best value and cooking is wholesome and hearty, featuring plenty of meaty dishes, game in season and proper pudding like steamed treacle sponge. They like to keep things as local as possible here, so even the wines come from a vineyard just down the road.

Closing times
Open daily
Prices
Meals: £ 12 (weekdays) and a la carte £ 22/46

Typical Dishes
Home-smoked salmon with horseradish cream
Roast haunch of venison
Passion fruit & banana sorbet

6.25 mi northwest of Henley-on-Thames by A 4130, B 480 and Maidensgrove rd. Parking.

338

88 — **Old Swan**

**Minster Lovell,
OX29 0RN**
Tel.: (01993)774441
Website: www.oldswanandminstermill.com

VISA · MC · AE · ⑩

🍺 **Marston's Ales**

They may be a few hundred miles apart but the Old Swan and its sister, the Cary Arms, share a few things in common, including stylish accommodation and a passion for fresh, simply cooked food. The Old Swan is just the sort of place you expect to come across in Oxfordshire, with its smart parquet floor, roaring open fires and collection of horse brasses and Toby jugs. For summer there's boules and a giant chess set in the garden – set next to large herb plots which supply the pub all year round and contribute to unfussy pub classics and tasty daily specials from the Brixham day boats. Chic bedrooms are accessed via a winding staircase and display period furnishings, quality linens and the latest mod cons – some even boast feature bathrooms.

Closing times
Open daily
booking essential
Prices
Meals: a la carte £ 29/43
🛏 **16 rooms:** £ 135/375

Typical Dishes
Pressed wild rabbit terrine
Hobgoblin ale pie
Sticky toffee pudding

🚗 3.5 mi west of Witney by B 4047. Parking.

89   **Nut Tree**

**Main St,
Murcott, OX5 2RE**
Tel.: (01865)331253
Website: www.nuttreeinn.co.uk

Vale Best Bitter, Oxfordshire Pride and Sharp's Doom Bar

You want a tasty, top quality meal in good old pub surroundings: enter the Nut Tree. It's owned by a local and his wife, who have managed to retain a satisfyingly pubby feel in the cosy beamed bar, while also providing a more formal atmosphere in the smart restaurant. Appealing menus change constantly as the latest seasonal ingredients arrive and produce is organic, free range or wild wherever possible; there's always plenty of choice too, from baguettes and bar snacks to ambitious tasting selections. Breads and ice creams are homemade, salmon is smoked on-site and sausages and pork pies are for sale. Combinations are classical and satisfying, and to ensure only the freshest meats are used, they rear their own rare breed pigs out the back.

Closing times
Closed 27 December-
2 January, Sunday
dinner and Monday except
lunch bank holidays

Prices
Meals: £ 18 (weekday lunch)
and a la carte £ 32/51

Typical Dishes
Home-smoked
salmon with whipped
horseradish

Fillet of beef with
triple-cooked chips

Hot blood orange
soufflé

 7 mi from Bicester by A 41 east and south via Lower and Upper Arncott; at T-junction beyond the motorway turn right. Parking.

England • South East • Oxfordshire

90 **Magdalen Arms**

**243 Iffley Rd,
Oxford, OX4 1SJ**
Tel.: (01865)243159

VISA **MC** **DC**

Theakston Best Bitter, Caledonian Deuchars IPA,
XPA and Flying Scotsman

This battleship-grey pub is a relative newcomer to the established Oxford scene but it's already a hit with the locals. The place buzzes – even on a weeknight – and there's always something to keep you entertained, be it a board game or a turn on the bar billiards table. The spacious, open-plan interior boasts deep red walls, quirky old standard lamps and an eclectic collection of 1920s posters, while huge blackboards display nibbles and the twice daily changing menu. Order at the bar for a casual lunch or head through to the curtained-off dining room for table service. The experienced chef uses local ingredients to create tasty, good value dishes; perhaps pork and rabbit rillettes, braised ox cheek or seven hour lamb for five to share.

Closing times
Closed 2 weeks August,
24-26 December,
1 January, Monday lunch
and bank holidays

Prices
Meals: a la carte £ 17/32

Typical Dishes
Provençale-style fish
soup
Potato and ricotta
ravioli
Lemon polenta cake

 Southeast of city centre on A 4158. On-street parking.

91 Rickety Press

**67 Cranham St,
Oxford, OX2 6DE**
Tel.: (01865)424581
Website: www.thericketypress.com

Arkell's Wiltshire Gold, Moonlight and Kingsdown

Run by three old school friends, the Rickety Press is found in a highly residential area; its name a reference to the Oxford University Press, whose HQ was once close by. It's a friendly, shabby-chic kind of a place run by a professional team and has a conservatory, a large room filled with wooden pews and a cosy bar with a chessboard, a vast array of books and characterful reclaimed tables; stop here for a pint of Arkell's ale and a scotch egg, or a sandwich filled with Sandy Lane lamb or Cerne Abbas cheddar and chutney. The main menu changes every month and features vibrant, seasonal ingredients that provide plenty of flavour; you might find roast pumpkin and sage soup to start, followed by corn-fed chicken with rösti and wild mushrooms.

Closing times
Closed 25-27 December
Prices
Meals: a la carte £ 22/37

Typical Dishes
Dorset crab & tiger prawn cannelloni
Saddle of Cotswold lamb with a Provençale crust
Walnut, almond & honey tart

 Off Walton Street in Jericho. On-street parking.

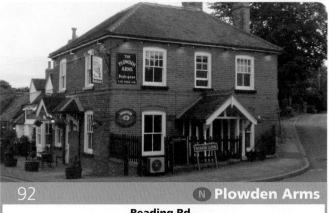

92   **Plowden Arms**

**Reading Rd,
Shiplake, RG9 4BX**
Tel.: (01189)402794
Website: www.plowdenarmsshiplake.co.uk

Brakspear Bitter, Ringwood Boondoggle and Fortyniner

This appealing pub sits close to Shiplake College and started life in the mid-18C as the Plough Hotel, but it was later renamed after an eminent local lawyer. It has a delightful garden and three different rooms where open fires, twinkling tea lights and hop bines set the scene. 1920s jazz music plays in the background and the air is one of relaxation. The experienced chef offers some interesting dishes: on the large blackboard you'll find snacks such as chicken scotch eggs or local chipolatas, alongside specials like red mullet with anchovy cream. The main menu, meanwhile, features a number of Eliza Acton influenced creations – maybe herrings in oatmeal or potted livers with pear chutney – with the inspiration for each dish listed beside it.

Closing times
Open daily
Prices
Meals: a la carte £ 18/37

Typical Dishes
Duck egg with brown shrimps & samphire

Salt cod, pease pudding, bacon & mustard sauce

Barley cream with blackcurrant compote

2 mi south of Henley-on-Thames on A 4155. Parking.

Shutford

93 **George & Dragon**

**Church Lane,
Shutford, OX15 6PG**
Tel.: (01295)780320
Website: www.thegeorgeanddragon.com

**Hook Norton Old Hooky, Fuller's London Pride,
Wychwood Hobgoblin and Wells Bombardier**

This pretty Grade II listed pub – set in an equally attractive village – dates back to the 13C and to this day, remains very much a community kind of a place; you'll find regular quizzes and events, along with a dedicated sports TV room. There are a handful of tables beside the impressive fireplace in the heart of the pub, with the remainder in the extension. Legend has it that it's haunted by ghosts and that a secret smugglers' tunnel links it to the nearby manor house; and if that's not enough, it's built into a hill, 12 foot beneath St Martin's Church, so when you order at the bar, you're as good as underground! Cooking is from a local boy returned home, and the tasty dishes display a refined simplicity and an appreciation for local produce.

Closing times
Open daily
Prices
Meals: £ 15
(weekday dinner)
and a la carte £ 20/38

Typical Dishes
Crab & apple tian
Rack of lamb, champ & buttered leeks
Rhubarb crème brûlée

Take B 4035 from Banbury Cross to Shipston and turn right after approx. 2 miles through North Newington. Parking on lane.

94

Wykham Arms

**Temple Mill Rd,
Sibford Gower, OX15 5RX**
Tel.: (01295)788808
Website: www.wykhamarms.co.uk

Purity Pure UBA, St Austell Tribute and Wye Valley Ales

If you're after a true village pub, the 17C Wykham Arms may well be it. Set down narrow lanes in the middle of the countryside, this thatched pub certainly plays its role in the community. It boasts attractive sand-coloured stone walls adorned with pretty climbing plants and a pleasant terrace with cast iron furniture. So as not to price out the locals, menus offer a range of dishes right through from light bites and bar snacks to the full three courses; so you might find Salcombe crab and mango salad or Brixham sea bream. Suppliers are proudly noted on the blackboard and the chef is only too happy to answer any questions. There's a good choice of wines and what better way to celebrate than with lobster and champagne on the terrace?

Closing times
Closed Monday except bank holidays
Prices
Meals: a la carte £ 23/32

Typical Dishes
Pan-fried squid with chorizo salad
Rump of Lighthorne lamb with bubble & squeak
Panna cotta with poached rhubarb

 8 mi west of Banbury by B 4035. Parking.

Sprigg's Alley

95 **Sir Charles Napier**

**Sprigs Holly,
Spriggs's Alley, OX39 4BX**
Tel.: (01494)483011
Website: www.sircharlesnapier.co.uk

 Wadworth 6X

Set in a small hamlet on the hillside, this attractive 18C flint pub might just have it all. The delightful terrace and gardens buzz with conversation in the warmer months, while sculptures of beasts and figures peer out from behind bushes or lie on the lawn. Inside yet more creatures hide about the place – and all are for sale. It's worth heading to the cosy bar with its open fires and comfy sofas, although the beamed dining room adorned with flowers and art is equally as charming. Cooking is refined and has a strong French accent, offering the likes of eel and foie gras terrine followed by noisette of venison or boeuf Bourguignon. Dishes are skilfully prepared and capture flavours to their full. A well-chosen wine list completes the picture.

Closing times
Closed 24-26 December, Sunday dinner and Monday except bank holidays
booking advisable

Prices
Meals: £ 18 (weekdays) and a la carte £ 38/56

Typical Dishes
Seared foie gras with endive marmalade
Yuzu-glazed duck
Chocolate and peanut terrine

 2.5 mi southeast of Chinnor by Bledlow Ridge rd. Parking.

96 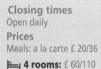 **Cherry Tree Inn**

**Stoke Row,
RG9 5QA**
Tel.: (01491)680430
Website: www.thelittleangel.co.uk

VISA **MC** **AE**

Brakspear Oxford Gold, Ordinary and Special

An attractive-looking pub with an attractive-sounding name: the trees in question no longer bear fruit but make sure you go for a wander to see the cherry orchard (now an ornamental garden) and the gilded 370ft well which were a gift from the Maharajah of Benares to this rural village 150 years ago. The wisteria-clad, 400 year old pub has a cosy, relaxing feel; its four intimate dining areas each with their own charm and character. Four stylish bedrooms beckon to the overnight guest but first enjoy a meal from the monthly changing à la carte or the seasonal, fish-based blackboard menu. Classic pub dishes like the popular handmade burgers sit alongside more modern creations; food is full of flavour and served by an attentive team.

Closing times
Open daily
Prices
Meals: a la carte £ 20/36
4 rooms: £ 60/110

Typical Dishes
Basil gnocchi with a tomato coulis
Rib-eye of Hereford beef
Lemon posset

*Between Henley-on-Thames and Wallingford off A 1430.
Parking.*

Stonor

97

Quince Tree

**Stonor,
RG9 6HE**
Tel.: (01491)639039
Website: www.thequincetree.com

🛖 *VISA* ⓂⒸ 🄰🄴 ⓄⒾ

🍺 **Marston's Ales**

This early 19C inn with its impressive brick façade can be found in a delightful setting, next to a country estate in a fold of the Chiltern Hills. Smart gardens lead to a sunny terrace, while inside it has a pleasant country-chic style, with leather banquettes and modern artwork featuring alongside exposed brick and oak timbers. There are a few leather bucket seats opposite the bar for drinkers but the focus here is on dining – either in the main room or the more formal restaurant. Menus offer an appealing range of dishes, from several varieties of sharing platters and pub classics with a twist to much more original, modern dishes such as spiced tagine of skate – and if you fancy taking something home, there's also a deli to the rear.

Closing times
Closed 25 December,
1 January and Sunday dinner
booking advisable

Prices
Meals: £ 14 (weekday lunch) and a la carte £ 24/35

Typical Dishes
Chicken liver & foie gras pâté
Cod with mixed seeds & golden raisin quinoa
Warm chocolate pot

 4 mi north of Henley-on-Thames by A 4130 on B 480. Parking.

Sutton Courtenay

98

Fish

**4 Appleford Rd,
Sutton Courtenay, OX14 4NQ**
Tel.: (01235)848242
Website: www.thefishatsuttoncourtenay.co.uk

 Greene King Abbot Ale

Its owners have brought a taste of France to Oxfordshire, so expect French pictures, French music and a largely French wine list, as well as French food and charming Gallic service. Feast on meaty terrines, escargots or moules marinière; such dishes mingle merrily with British classics like steak and kidney pie, Gressingham duck breast or fillet of lamb. L'entente cordiale continues on the dessert menu, with crème brûlée clamouring for your attention alongside treacle sponge. This is robust country cooking in its most classic form, with pretty much everything homemade using seasonal ingredients. Head to the rear of the pub for the lovely garden and conservatory, and be sure to ask Sebastian (one of the owners) for his wine recommendations.

Closing times
Closed January, Monday except bank holidays and Sunday dinner

Prices
Meals: £ 14 (weekdays) and a la carte £ 23/44

Typical Dishes
Chicken & prawn mayonnaise

Whole sea bream with crab & soft cheese

Chocolate délice with coffee ice cream & custard

 Between Abingdon and Didcot on B 4016. Parking.

England • South East • Oxfordshire

Swinbrook

99 Swan Inn

**Swinbrook,
OX18 4DY**
Tel.: (01993)823339
Website: www.theswanswinbrook.co.uk

🍺 **Hook Norton Hooky Bitter**

Set on the banks of a meandering river, The Swan Inn is a delightful place – so booking is a must. Outside, you'll find honey-coloured walls covered in wisteria and a lovely garden filled with fruit trees; while the interior boasts an open oak frame and exposed stone walls covered with old lithographs and handmade walking sticks. A well-versed team serve tasty dishes from the daily menu, which features the latest seasonal produce from nearby farms and estates. Cooking is fairly modern in style, with some dishes a contemporary take on older recipes; you might find roe deer carpaccio with truffled mayonnaise, fillet of bream with tandoori potatoes or baked ginger pudding with hot spiced treacle. Well-appointed bedrooms have a luxurious feel.

Closing times
Open daily
booking essential
Prices
Meals: a la carte £ 25/43
🛏 **6 rooms:** £ 65/180

Typical Dishes
Goat's cheese & tomato salad
Bavette steak with wild mushrooms
Tonka bean panna cotta

 3 mi northeast of Burford by A 40 and minor road north. Parking.

100   **Mole Inn**

**Toot Baldon,
OX44 9NG**
Tel.: (01865)340001
Website: www.themoleinn.com

 Hook Norton Old Hooky and White Horse Wayland Smithy

The Mole has made quite a name for itself in the area and deservedly so. Beautiful landscaped gardens and a pleasant terrace front the building, while inside, attractive beamed ceilings and exposed brick walls create a warm and welcoming atmosphere. The menu is equally appealing, catering for all tastes and appetites; you might find sautéed squid with linguine and chorizo, followed by twice-cooked belly of pork with gratin dauphinoise. Sourcing is a serious business and it's a case of 'first come, first served' if you want the full choice. The Tuesday grill and Wednesday fish night menus are decided the day before, so if there's something you've set your heart on, it's worth calling to reserve your dish. Service remains smooth under pressure.

Closing times
Closed 25 December
booking advisable

Prices
Meals: £ 20 and a la carte
£ 28/34

Typical Dishes
Curried risotto of smoked haddock

Slow-cooked blade of Oxfordshire beef

Treacle tart with Carnation milk ice cream

6 mi southeast of Oxford; between B 480 and A 4074. Parking.

Watlington

N Fat Fox Inn

**13 Shireburn St,
Watlington, OX49 5BU**
Tel.: (01491)613040
Website: www.thefatfoxinn.co.uk

 VISA **M©**

Ringwood Boondoggle, Brakspear Oxford Gold and Bitter

This pub was originally called the Fox and Hounds but there were so many other pubs of the same name in the surrounding villages that it became a little confusing; so the owners decided to hold a renaming competition and the Fat Fox was born. It's in the heart of a busy market village and dates from the 1800s and, although it's nothing fancy, is run with honesty and integrity by its experienced owners. The menu reflects what they themselves like to eat in a pub and covers all bases from potted mackerel or local rabbit broth to filling pheasant pie. Fight the cats for a spot on the sofas by the wood burning range in the buzzy bar or make for the slightly more formal dining room; afterwards, settle in for the night in one of the cosy bedrooms.

Closing times
Closed dinner 25 December and 1 January
Prices
Meals: a la carte £ 18/26
9 rooms: £ 79/109

Typical Dishes
Scotch egg with red onion marmalade
Baked pollock with lettuce & battered whelks
Coconut financier with apple crumble ice cream

 9 mi southwest of Thame by B 4012, A 40 and B 4009. Parking.

102 Killingworth Castle

**Glympton Rd,
Wootton, OX20 1EJ**
Tel.: (01993)811401
Website: www.thekillingworthcastle.com

Oxfordshire Churchill HPA, Compass Isis Pale and Shotover Prospect

This pub's name is slightly odd… first of all, it's nowhere near Killingworth, and secondly, there's no castle nearby! It's a large building dating from the 1500s and, after a year standing derelict, is now under the ownership of the Alexanders, who have set about returning it to its 'proper' pub status. Open fires, thick stone walls and old mix and match furniture provide a rustic feel, and black and white photos depicting its past adorn the walls. The chatty staff clearly know what they're doing and the food is great value, especially the dish of the day. The main menu follows the seasons and provides plenty of interest, offering the likes of sticky pork belly or lamb with truffle mash. You will leave feeling suitably fortified.

Closing times
Open daily
Prices
Meals: a la carte £ 21/33

Typical Dishes
Salmon, monkfish & crab cakes

Roasted loin of lamb with grain mustard sauce

Almond & honey frangipane tart

3.5 mi northwest of Woodstock by Hensington Rd and Banbury Rd on B 4027. Parking.

Abinger Common

103   **Abinger Hatch**

**Abinger Ln,
Abinger Common, RH5 6HZ**
Tel.: (01306)730737
Website: www.theabingerhatch.com

Ringwood Best Bitter, Sambrook's Wandle Ale, Sharp's Orchard

Deep in the Surrey hills and in prime walking country sits this attractive and lovingly restored 18C inn. With its low beams, leather sofas and roaring log fires it oozes country gentility and the newspapers, magazines and board games show that someone here has an eye for detail. A short à la carte and a good value set menu make way for greater choice by the end of the week; the country cooking is fresh, satisfying and a perfect match for the surroundings, be it charcuterie on a board, a lamb pie or a gooseberry fool. Lunchtime salads prove popular, as do the Sunday roasts, and in summer, the outside bar and kitchen – complete with wood-burning oven and a barbecue – are a real hit. Come on a Saturday for a game of croquet on the lower lawn.

Closing times
Open daily
Prices
Meals: a la carte £ 18/24

Typical Dishes
White onion & thyme soup
Grilled mackerel, chorizo & lentils
Chocolate & hazelnut brownie

 Between Guildford and Dorking off A 25 in village centre. Parking.

104 **Swan Inn**

**Petworth Rd,
Chiddingfold, GU8 4TY**
Tel.: (01428)684688
Website: www.theswaninnchiddingfold.com

 Surrey Hills Shere Drop and Adnams Southwold Bitter

The elegant tile-hung façade of the Swan Inn hints at its 200 year old heritage, although following a fire in 2003, it's interior is now of a more contemporary vintage. The pub's latest owners moved here from Knightsbridge, swapping the bustling city streets for a more sedate pace of life. Lunchtime sees the Surrey set popping in for maybe Maryland crab cakes or the 'terrine of the day', while the à la carte changes daily depending on the latest local produce available. The experienced owners keep a keen eye over proceedings and cool, contemporary bedrooms complete the picture. Wandering round the green it's hard to believe that eleven glass works once stood here, supplying many of the country's finest buildings, including St Stephen's Chapel.

Closing times
Open daily
Prices
Meals: a la carte £ 22/39
10 rooms: £ 100/180

Typical Dishes
Poached pear, stilton & rocket salad
Grilled sea bream with harissa & couscous
Strawberry & vanilla panna cotta with shortbread

 On A 283 on the eastern side of the village. Parking.

Cranleigh

105 Richard Onslow

**113-117 High St,
Cranleigh, GU6 8AU**
Tel.: (01483)274922
Website: www.therichardonslow.co.uk

Sharp's Doom Bar and Surrey Hills Shere Drop

This laid-back pub on the high street is named after a former MP, whose family once owned the nearby National Trust property Clandon Park. The whole place has been refurbished, which is clear to see as you enter through the bar and into the large, airy dining room. Venture round the counter and through a small door however, and the locals bar provides a complete contrast, with its beams, brick fireplace and cosy feel. The all-day menu offers everything from pub classics and deli boards to daily specials and a roast of the day; dishes are straightforward but carefully prepared and very tasty. Whether you're here for breakfast or retiring to one of the stylish bedrooms last thing at night, you'll be well looked after by the friendly team.

Closing times
Closed 25 December

Prices
Meals: £ 15 (lunch)
and a la carte £ 17/39

10 rooms: £ 65/85

Typical Dishes
Beef carpaccio with shallots
Wood pigeon Kiev with pomegranate salad
Steamed ginger pudding

 On the high street in the middle of town. Parking for overnight guests only.

106   Queen's Head

**The Street,
East Clandon, GU4 7RY**
Tel.: (01483)222332
Website: www.queensheadeastclandon.co.uk

 Hogs Back Brewery, Surrey Hills Brewery and Queen's Head Ales

Part of a group of 3 properties run by two lifelong friends, this charming 17C pub is one of those places where you can create a different experience each time you come. It's divided into four rooms and each has its own unique style, with furnishings ranging from the traditional to the modern: one room has an inglenook fireplace, another, a stove guarded by an old musket; some have bovine-themed pictures and others, faux beams; there's also a lovely terrace to consider, along with a large garden, where village celebrations are held. The simple menu offers something for everyone, from sharing boards or potted ham hock to steak and ale pie or a roast; there's also a large blackboard of daily specials. The tasty salad and veggies are home-grown.

Closing times
Open daily
Prices
Meals: a la carte £ 22/34

Typical Dishes
Tempura tiger prawns
Steak, ale & mushroom pie
Chocolate & walnut brownie

 Between Guildford and East Horsley off A 246. Parking.

Forest Green

107   Parrot Inn

**Forest Green,
RH5 5RZ**
Tel.: (01306)621339
Website: www.theparrot.co.uk

**Ringwood Best & Old Thumper, Fuller's London Pride &
Seafarers and Tillingbourne Falls Gold**

When a pub sells its own home-grown and homemade produce – bread, cheese, cakes and preserves, as well as eggs and meat from its own farm – you can be pretty much guaranteed that their cooking is going to be fresh and full of flavour. With well-priced, generously proportioned dishes such as vegetable and stilton pie or pork belly with chorizo and baked butter bean, the Parrot certainly doesn't disappoint. This is a pub where they make their own black pudding and aren't afraid to serve less well-known offerings such as oyster sausages or mutton. The 300 year old pub's interior is traditional, with plenty of character in the form of exposed brick, flag floors and low wooden beams. Sup real ale as you watch a cricket match on the green.

Closing times
Closed 25 December and Sunday dinner
Prices
Meals: a la carte £ 21/35

Typical Dishes
Scallops with black pudding
Home Farm pork rump with cabbage
Steamed marmalade pudding with custard

 8 mi south of Dorking by A 24, A 29 and B 2126 west. Parking.

108 **Three Horseshoes**

**25 Shepperton Rd,
Laleham, TW18 1SE**
Tel.: (01784)455014
Website: www.3horseshoeslaleham.co.uk

Fuller's London Pride and Spring Sprinter, George Gale Ales

There's not much left of this pub's 17C origins – but who cares when they've done such a good job of modernising it? Prop up the long bar with the locals or sit in the cosy, poster-lined snug, the rear dining room or the Garden room; each is furnished with leather chairs and chunky wood tables, its walls filled with interesting photos and pictures. If the sun is out, then you should be too: grab a watering can (your table number) and head for the pretty walled garden. The menu's also got something for everyone – perhaps you're after a light offering like a sandwich or a salad, or maybe a meaty main course such as calves' liver and bacon. They've got pub classics covered, sharing plates for those 'à deux' and specials on the blackboard too.

Closing times
Closed 26 December

Prices
Meals: £ 17/31
and a la carte £ 22/33

Typical Dishes
Wild mushrooms on toast
Guinea fowl, rosemary polenta & red cabbage
Passion fruit crème brûlée

2.5 mi southeast of junction 13 of M 25 by A 30, A 308 and B 376. Parking.

Lower Eashing

109 **Stag on the River**

**Lower Eashing Rd,
Lower Eashing, GU7 2QG**
Tel.: (01483)421568
Website: www.stagontherivereashing.co.uk

 Hogs Back TEA, Surrey Hills Shere Drop and Stag on the River Spring Ale

Perched on the banks of the River Wey, this pretty little 16C pub was once a mill and its smartly furnished terrace overlooks the old millstream. This isn't the kind of spot you just happen to stumble upon, so you can guarantee a large number of those around you are from the local area. You'll need to arrive early if you want a choice of table, be it on the terrace or beside the roaring fire in the appealing beamed and quarry-tiled interior. The menu ranges from sandwiches and pub classics to more interesting dishes such as a fish platter, French-style beef burger or chateaubriand for 2; the haddock and bacon rarebit fishcakes are also worth a try. Attractively appointed, modern bedrooms come with a complimentary bottle of locally brewed beer.

Closing times
Open daily
Prices
Meals: a la carte £ 25/33
7 rooms: £ 65/110

Typical Dishes
Duck scotch egg with mustard sauce
Lemon sole fillet with lemon mascarpone & prawns
Choux bun with salted caramel

 1.75 mi west of Godalming by A 3100 and Eashing Lane. Parking.

110   **Old Plough**

**2 Station Rd,
Stoke D'Abernon, KT11 3BN**
Tel.: (01932)862244
Website: www.oldploughcobham.co.uk

🛏   **VISA**   **MC**   **AE**

Fuller's London Pride & Spring Sprinter, Surrey Hills Shere Drop and George Gale Seafarers

The fourth venture for this small pub group, the Old Plough has been smartly done up, once again becoming a welcoming sight for those journeying home from the station. It's managed to retain a satisfyingly pubby feel, thanks to an open-fired bar filled with comfy chairs and chunky wood furnishings in the restaurant. The menu is the same wherever you sit and offers starters such as wild mushroom and spinach tart or duck liver terrine with spiced plum chutney, followed by main courses of thyme rotisserie chicken, French fish stew or tagliatelli with tomato and black olive sauce. At lunchtime you'll find the likes of bubble and squeak, devilled lamb's kidneys on toast or a crab & mayo sandwich, and sharing dishes are on offer throughout the day.

Closing times
Open daily
Prices
Meals: a la carte £ 22/34

Typical Dishes
Serrano ham & roasted artichoke salad

Pan-fried sea bream, spinach, lemon & caper butter

Sunken chocolate & almond cake

Between Cobham and Leatherhead on A 245. Parking.

Tilford

tagged **England • South East • Surrey**

111   Duke of Cambridge

**Tilford Rd,
Tilford, GU10 2DD**
Tel.: (01252)792236
Website: www.dukeofcambridgetilford.co.uk

VISA   *MC*   *AE*

Hogs Back TEA, Surrey Hills Shere Drop and Ringwood Fortyniner

This 18C pub may be well-known to local dog walkers but isn't somewhere you're likely to just stumble upon by chance, as it's hidden away in the heart of the forest. Despite a refurbishment, it retains a pleasantly rustic feel, with a small, flag-floored bar, a cosy snug and neatly laid wooden tables filling the rest of the room; there's also an appealing heated terrace covered by an impressive oak-beamed roof – a great vantage point if you have children who want to visit the large play area. Menus offer everything from deli boards to share and old pub classics like steak and ale pie, to a few more adventurous dishes such as sea bass with chorizo, red onion and tomato fricassee; there are some interesting dishes for children too.

Closing times
Closed 25 December
Prices
Meals: a la carte £ 24/33

Typical Dishes
Salt duck with sesame vinaigrette

Seared sea bass with tomato salsa & Serrano ham

Lemon posset with lavender & almond shortbread

 Between Farnham and Godalming, signed off B 3001. Parking.

362

112   **Onslow Arms**

**The Street,
West Clandon, GU4 7TE**
Tel.: (01483)222447
Website: www.onslowarmsclandon.co.uk

Sharp's Cornish Coaster, Surrey Hills Shere Drop and Tillingbourne Brewery Ales

Following in the footsteps of the group's first two pubs, the Onslow Arms has been taken back to its roots and re-established as a proper village pub. It has undergone a smart refurbishment but wooden beams, open fires and copper artefacts still give a glimpse as to its true age – although nobody seems to know exactly when it was built. Locals prop up the bar or sit at the high tables opposite, while diners head for the restaurant, but wherever you sit, the menu's the same. It's a popular spot with the local workers and ladies who lunch, so you'll find sharing platters and light bites in the middle of the day and more sophisticated dishes in the evening; maybe lemon and thyme rotisserie chicken or braised Gressingham duck with parsnip mash.

Closing times
Closed 26 December
Prices
Meals: a la carte £ 18/42

Typical Dishes
Pork belly & wild mushroom terrine
21-day aged fillet steak
Sticky toffee pudding

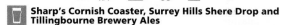

4.75 mi northeast of Guildford by A 25 on A 247. Parking.

113 The Inn @ West End

**42 Guildford Rd,
West End, GU24 9PW**
Tel.: (01276)858652
Website: www.the-inn.co.uk

 Fuller's London Pride and Seafarers, Sharp's Cornish Coaster

It's not the best-looking pub in the world – but what it lacks in rustic charm, it more than makes up for in personality; its lively atmosphere and genuine hospitality being two of the reasons it's always so busy. Another big draw is the food: there's something for everyone on the menu, from sandwiches and pub classics like sausage and mash to dishes like lobster Caesar salad and deep-fried poached egg; with fish specials and plenty of game in season. Portions are generous and flavours robust, with global influences, good quality ingredients and some original touches. The owners also have a wine shop in the car park, so it comes as no surprise to find an interesting list of well-chosen wines, strong on pinot noir and claret.

Closing times
Open daily
Prices
Meals: £ 14/28
and a la carte £ 27/44

Typical Dishes
Marinated game strips with cranberry dressing
Pan-fried calves' liver with caramelised apple sauce
South African vinegar pudding

 2.5 mi southeast of junction 3 of M 3 on A 322. Parking.

114 Queen's Head

**1 Bridge Rd,
Weybridge, KT13 8XS**
Tel.: (01932)839820
Website: www.whitebrasserie.com

🛖 *VISA* Ⓜ️Ⓒ

🍺 **Fuller's London Pride and Sharp's Doom Bar**

It was built in the mid-1700s as a coach house but the Queen's Head has also spent time as a courthouse, complete with gallows. An appealing whitewashed building with a small terrace and patio, it's been lovingly restored and, with its series of snug little rooms, warming open fires and a pewter bar, can't fail to impress. Menus offer French brasserie classics alongside British pub staples: start with snails in garlic butter, potted pork or a smoked fish board, followed by steamed Loch Fyne mussels, beef stroganoff, venison sausages or chargrilled steak – which you can watch being cooked in the open kitchen. There's also a good value set menu and a well-chosen wine list; sit in the spacious restaurant if you fancy a more formal experience.

Closing times
Closed 25 December

Prices
Meals: £ 12/17
and a la carte £ 21/41

Typical Dishes
Hot-smoked salmon with horseradish cream

Rack of Southdown lamb with gratin dauphinoise

Waffle with caramelised apples

🚗 In town centre, just off B 374 (Heath Rd). Limited parking (12 spaces).

Windlesham

115

Brickmakers

Chertsey Rd,
Windlesham, GU20 6HT
Tel.: (01276)472267
Website: www.thebrickmakerswindlesham.co.uk

 Fuller's London Pride, Courage Best Bitter and Sharp's Doom Bar

The name of this 400 year old pub comes from its popularity with workers from the nearby former brickmaking works, who would pop in for a pint on their way home – beamed ceilings, wooden floors and open fires provide appropriate levels of charm and rusticity for a pub of such a noble age. Regulars head for the leather sofas by the bar, while those wanting a touch more formality with their food choose a seat at one of the linen-clad tables in the conservatory. One menu serves all areas but evolves between lunch and dinner; sandwiches, lighter bites and pub classics making way for more substantial dishes such as calves' liver or twice-cooked pork belly. Come summer, the garden is the place to be, with its picnic tables, gazebo and heaters.

Closing times
Open daily
Prices
Meals: £ 24 (dinner)
and a la carte £ 20/31

Typical Dishes
Duck egg with English asparagus & soldiers
Shoulder of lamb with prunes
Dorset apple cake & custard

 1 mi east on B 386. Parking.

116

Red Lion

**High St,
Horsell, GU21 4SS**
Tel.: (01483)768497
Website: www.redlionhorsell.co.uk

🏠 *VISA* ⓜⓒ ▲Ε

Fuller's London Pride, St Austell Tribute and Caledonian Flying Scotsman

Set in a residential area but just five minutes from the centre of Woking, the Red Lion ticks all the boxes for the locals – and for visitors too. When the weather's right, make for the pleasant rear terrace or landscaped garden; if you've work to do, head for a sofa beside the open fire in the bar and make use of the wi-fi; and if you're hungry, take a seat in the rustic beamed dining room amongst the Brooklands racing memorabilia. The menu offers something for everyone, from sandwiches and pub classics to more interesting dishes such as warm duck and orange salad, sweet potato and aubergine tagine or pressed chicken terrine with chorizo butter and peperonata. It's a deservedly popular place, so book a table or make sure you arrive early.

Closing times
Closed 26 December
booking advisable
Prices
Meals: a la carte £ 22/34

Typical Dishes
Seafood thermidor
Chicken with fennel & chorizo, tarragon jus
Baked New York cheesecake

1.5 mi northwest of Woking by Brewery Rd and Church Hill. Parking.

Burpham

117   George & Dragon Inn

Main St,
Burpham, BN18 9RR
Tel.: (01903)883131
Website: www.gdinn.co.uk

Arundel Brewery Sussex Gold, Old Ale and Special Bitter and Greene King IPA

The George and Dragon stands close to the green in the peaceful hamlet of Burpham, which borders the South Downs National Park. Such a good old English name is perfectly fitting for a pub that's been trading since 1736 and the associations don't end there. The menu features British classics, with a concise à la carte offering the likes of rib-eye steak, rump of lamb and game from the local estate – supplemented by a list of pub favourites and daily specials which are chalked on the board. The laid-back, classically styled interior is divided in two: there's a fairly formal linen-laid dining room and a rustic bar with scrubbed wood tables and a large brick fireplace; exposed beams, twinkling church candles and local art feature throughout.

Closing times
Open daily
Prices
Meals: £ 13/16
and a la carte £ 24/34

Typical Dishes
Mussels with cider & thyme
Cod with bacon mash & shellfish cream
Triple chocolate brownie

3 mi northeast of Arundel by A 27.

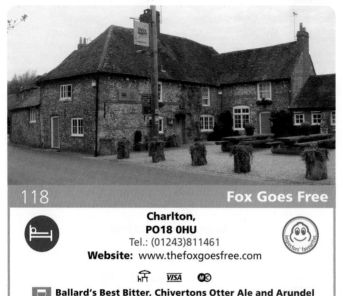

118   **Fox Goes Free**

**Charlton,
PO18 0HU**
Tel.: (01243)811461
Website: www.thefoxgoesfree.com

VISA   **MC**

Ballard's Best Bitter, Chivertons Otter Ale and Arundel
The Fox Goes Free

Set in the beautiful South Downs countryside, close to Goodwood, this charming 17C flint pub was once the haunt of William III and his Royal Hunting Party. It boasts a superb garden and terrace with lovely outlooks and retains most of its original features, including exposed stone walls, low beamed ceilings, brick floors, inglenook fires and even an old bread oven. There are three dining areas, two with waiter service and one where you order at the bar; behind which you'll find a good selection of hand-pulled ales. Dishes range from simple pub classics on the bar menu to an à la carte featuring local pork chops, braised venison shank or steak and kidney pie for two. Bedrooms are clean and unfussy; those above the pub have low ceilings.

Closing times
Open daily
Prices
Meals: a la carte £ 26/32
🛏 **5 rooms:** £ 65/175

Typical Dishes
Smoked salmon with rocket & pesto

Slow-cooked pork belly with cauliflower cheese

Sticky toffee pudding with caramel sauce

🚗 Midway between Chichester and Midhurst off the A 286.
Parking.

East Lavant

119 — Royal Oak Inn

**Pook Ln,
East Lavant, PO18 0AX**
Tel.: (01243)527434
Website: www.royaloakeastlavant.co.uk

Sharp's Doom Bar, Skinner's Betty Stogs and Arundel Gold

Set in the heart of the village, among some stunning properties, this 18C inn boasts a small outside seating area with immaculately kept planters and a welcoming interior filled with exposed stone, brick and wood. There's a really relaxing feel to the place but you'll have to make like the locals and arrive early if you want to bag a sofa or a spot by the fire. Although combinations may be classical, cooking is fairly refined. There are always some interesting vegetarian options, steaks play an important role and there's a good selection of cheese. Produce is delivered from Smithfield, Billingsgate and Covent Garden, and you'll find a fine selection of wines by the glass. Spacious bedrooms are very comfy and well-equipped; breakfast is a treat.

Closing times
Open daily
Prices
Meals: £ 17 (lunch) and a la carte £ 27/44

8 rooms: £ 90/340

Typical Dishes
Taste of salmon & crab
Cheek & braised shoulder of pork with home-cured bacon
Dark chocolate & orange fondant

 Off A 286 after the humpback bridge. Parking.

Halfway Bridge

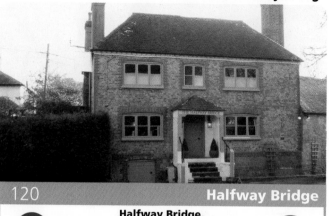

120 — Halfway Bridge

Halfway Bridge,
GU28 9BP
Tel.: (01798)861281
Website: www.halfwaybridge.co.uk

   VISA   MC   AE

 Langham Best Bitter, Sharp's Doom Bar and Long Man Long Blond

Dating from the 17C and set on the edge of the Cowdray Park polo grounds, the Halfway Bridge looks like the quintessential Sussex pub with its brick and flint exterior. Its owners, who also have the Crab & Lobster in Sidlesham, have given it a sympathetic overhaul so that the cosy interior comes with oodles of charm. The bar, with its open fireplace and old pictures of the inn, is a great place to sit, and overnight guests just need to stroll up the road for a couple of minutes to get to the converted stables which house the country-chic bedrooms. The menu offers a good range of classically based dishes presented in quite a modern style; influences could come from Morocco, France or Italy and puds are nursery-style with a twist.

Closing times
Open daily

Prices
Meals: £ 20 and a la carte £ 29/50

🛏 **7 rooms:** £ 80/190

Typical Dishes
Kiln-smoked potted salmon

Belly of pork with bubble & squeak

Clementine sponge pudding

 Between Petworth and Midhurst on A 272. Parking.

Henfield

121

Ginger Fox

**Muddleswood Rd,
Albourne, Henfield, BN6 9EA**
Tel.: (01273)857888
Website: www.gingermanrestaurants.com

Harveys Ales and Sharp's Doom Bar

The first thing you notice is the pub's charming thatch – spot the fox running across it and you know you've come to the right place. The play area in the garden is a reassuring sight for parents; base yourself in 'the den' and you can keep an eye on your children as you eat. A monthly changing menu offers good value, flavoursome dishes; there's the occasional pub classic like beef and ale pie, but dishes are generally more akin to those served in a restaurant; perhaps crispy lamb sweetbreads, scallops with onion purée, roast partridge or wild halibut with sprouting broccoli. The vegetarian tasting plate will please any herbivores in your party and desserts are a highlight, so save space for some doughnuts or a slice of Bakewell tart.

Closing times
Closed 25 December
Prices
Meals: a la carte £ 25/35

Typical Dishes
Pig's head terrine with pistachio nuts
Roasted rump of lamb with lamb croquettes
Caramelised white chocolate mousse

 3 mi southwest of Henfield on A 281. Parking.

122 Duke of Cumberland Arms

**Henley,
GU27 3HQ**
Tel.: (01428)652280
Website: www.dukeofcumberland.com

  Harveys Sussex Best Bitter, Langham Best Bitter and Hip Hop

A hidden gem affectionately known as The Duke, this 16C hillside pub nestles in pretty tiered gardens with trickling streams, trout ponds and a splendid view over the South Downs. The pub's interior is as enchanting as the garden, with a cosy beamed, fire-lit front bar and an open plan, flag-floored dining area – and the charming staff provide efficient service. An appealing menu offers carefully prepared, seasonal dishes; lunch is a two course affair, with choices like fish and chips or braised ox cheeks, a selection of organic baguettes and homely puddings like hot chocolate fondant. Dinner shifts up a gear with the full three courses; dishes might include potted pheasant with cranberry compote or pork belly with apple and Calvados glaze.

Closing times
Closed 25-26 December and dinner Sunday-Monday

Prices
Meals: a la carte £ 32/48

Typical Dishes
Ricotta & wild garlic ravioli

Hake with caviar & chive velouté

Chocolate & salted caramel torte

 2.75 mi north of Midhurst off A 286. Parking.

Lurgashall

123   **Noah's Ark Inn**

**The Green,
Lurgashall, GU28 9ET**
Tel.: (01428)707346
Website: www.noahsarkinn.co.uk

ħŦ   **VISA**   **MC**   **AE**   **D**

🍺 **Greene King Ales and guest ales**

This quintessentially English pub is found in a picturesque location on the village green, next to the church – its large garden overlooking the cricket pitch. Rumour has it that the pub was once accessed by a narrow path over a moat, where visitors had to go in two-by-two, hence its unusual name. The gloriously rustic interior is divided into four rooms: the bar, offering a good selection of real ales; a large, baronial-style room with a tiled floor, exposed beams and a wood-burning stove; and two dining rooms with scrubbed tables and a large inglenook fireplace. Menus offer something for everyone, from prawn and chilli broth to chicken liver parfait; ale-battered fish to pan-fried fillet of cod studded with Parma ham. Portions are generous.

Closing times
Open daily
Prices
Meals: a la carte £ 21/35

Typical Dishes
Blue cheese rarebit
Roast guinea fowl suprême
Apple charlotte with vanilla ice cream

Between Petworth and Chiddingfold off the A 283. Parking.

124

Earl of March

**Mid Lavant,
PO18 0BQ**
Tel.: (01243)533993
Website: www.theearlofmarch.com

 Harveys Ales

This 18C inn offers the perfect blend of country character and contemporary styling, boasting a wood burning stove and cosy sofas in the bar, a smart restaurant, and a relaxed feel throughout. Its terrace affords amazing views of the South Downs, with the main stand at Goodwood racecourse in the distance, and its private dining room changes use seasonally; home to shooting parties in winter and serving champagne and seafood in summer. The owner spent time as executive head chef at The Ritz, so expect good quality, seasonal produce; dishes are British and mainly classical in style, and might include vegetable soup, lamb chops, pan-fried fillet of Sussex beef or Gressingham duck breast. Desserts are old favourites like sticky toffee pudding.

Closing times
Open daily
Prices
Meals: £ 19 (lunch and early dinner) and a la carte £ 24/38

Typical Dishes
Pea & mint bavarois
Loin of venison with celeriac dauphinoise
White chocolate & rhubarb panna cotta

125 Badgers

**Coultershaw Bridge,
Petworth, GU28 0JF**
Tel.: (01798)342651
Website: www.badgerspetworth.co.uk

Young's Ales and Skinner's Betty Stogs

This white-painted pub close to the River Rother has a satisfyingly homely feel. Log fires blaze in the grate, fresh flowers are dotted about the place and in the evening, candles flicker. A beautiful oak-panelled bar boasts carvings from its former 'Badger and Honeypot' days, while black and white photos depict its original railway inn-carnation. You'll also find an attentive, cheery team and a truly intimate single table alcove. Menus are rather eclectic; offering robust, flavoursome cooking with international influences. You could find anything from lamb's liver or bubble and squeak to prawns with Cajun spices or Spanish fish casserole – while in summer, lobsters picked from the tank are a favourite. Bedrooms aren't currently recommendable.

Closing times
Closed 25 December
Prices
Meals: a la carte £ 22/37

Typical Dishes
Baked camembert, red onion marmalade
Pork fillet with apricots
Chocolate mousse torte

 2 mi south of Petworth by A 285 at Coultershaw Bridge. Parking.

126 — **Chequers Inn**

Rowhook,
RH12 3PY
Tel.: (01403)790480
Website: www.thechequersrowhook.com

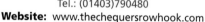 **Hogs Back TEA, Upman Brewery Punter and Harveys Sussex Best Bitter**

As you step inside you're instantly surrounded by the oaky aroma of an open fire and the murmur of the day's tales being recounted by groups of cheery locals. The origins of this inn can be traced back to the 15C, which comes as no surprise when you look around the charming stone-floored bar, but there's also a slightly unusual corrugated dining room extension (formerly the village hall), a large paved terrace and spacious garden. The experienced chef-owner loves the hands-on approach, so he's often out in the woods foraging for wild mushrooms and tracking down game, or out in the garden gathering the latest yield; maybe artichoke, pears or greengages. Classically based menus display a good understanding of how best to prepare ingredients.

Closing times
Closed 25 December and Sunday dinner

Prices
Meals: a la carte £ 26/40

Typical Dishes

Scallops on parsnip & vanilla purée

Hake with spinach & porcini cream

Ginger steamed pudding

 3 mi west of Horsham by A 281. Parking.

Sidlesham

127 | **Crab & Lobster**

**Mill Ln,
Sidlesham, PO20 7NB**
Tel.: (01243)641233
Website: www.crab-lobster.co.uk

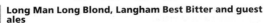

Long Man Long Blond, Langham Best Bitter and guest ales

This historic inn, with its pretty gardens, is superbly located within the striking landscape of Pagham Harbour Nature Reserve; a marshy haven for wildlife, particularly birds. Sympathetically modernised, it retains a flagged floor, open fires and the odd beam; there are a few tables for drinkers but, being a dining pub, most tables are laid up for eating. The well-presented dishes are very much at the restaurant end of the scale; perhaps saffron-scented seafood risotto with seared scallops and crab mascarpone or poached fillet of halibut on a sweetcorn and spring onion chowder – although lunch also sees lighter options like sandwiches and salads. Comfortable bedrooms have a modern, minimalist style; one has a garden and an open-fired stove.

Closing times
Open daily
booking advisable

Prices
Meals: £ 20 (weekday lunch) and a la carte £ 30/51

5 rooms: £ 80/250

Typical Dishes
Scallops with broad beans, peas & pancetta
Fillet of halibut with Selsey crab
Cherry Bakewell tart

5 mi south of Chichester by B 2145, then turn right into Rookery Lane. Parking.

128 — Horse Guards Inn

**Upperton Rd,
Tillington, GU28 9AF**
Tel.: (01798)342332
Website: www.thehorseguardsinn.co.uk

 Harveys Sussex Best, Hammerpot Shooting Star and Langham Hip Hop

In an elevated spot in the heart of a quiet village sits this pretty mid-17C inn, with views over Rother valley and the South Downs from its lovely lavender-filled garden. Happily, it's equally charming inside, with its low beams, fireplaces, period features and fresh flowers. Specialities and the names of suppliers are chalked up on the blackboard and there's a good mix of the rustic, like wild mushrooms on toast, and the more elaborate, like stone bass with roast fennel. Local seafood is handled with skill and some of the vegetables and salads come from their own patch. The staff are young, chatty and willing, and contribute considerably to the charm. There are three simple bedrooms available; families can book the cottage opposite.

Closing times
Closed 25 December
Prices
Meals: a la carte £ 19/38
3 rooms: £ 85/130

Typical Dishes
Warm salad of smoked sprats
Roast baby chicken with greens
Chocolate St. Emilion torte

 Just off A 272 in heart of the village. Unrestricted on-street parking.

West Ashling

129　　　　　　　　　　　　**Richmond Arms**

**Mill Rd,
West Ashling, PO18 8EA**
Tel.: (01243)572046
Website: www.therichmondarms.co.uk

🍽 *VISA* 🅜🅒

🍺 **Harveys ales**

This appealing, laid-back country pub is found at the foot of the South Downs, opposite a duck pond in a lovely little village; look out for the colourful decoy ducks they sometimes race. In warmer weather, try for one of the handful of tables outside, amongst the colourful hanging baskets; otherwise, head inside, where you'll find fresh flowers and a blackboard listing enticing nibbles such as halloumi chips or ham sliced on the antique slicing machine. The main menu is European in base and offers plenty of appeal; game comes from the family estate in Anglesey, and there's a delightful rotisserie and a Japanese robata grill used to cook local mature steaks. Freshly made desserts include some tasty sorbets. Two luxurious bedrooms are above.

Closing times
Closed Easter, last week July, last week October, 24 December-11 January, Sunday dinner, Monday and Tuesday

Prices
Meals: a la carte £ 25/39

🛏 **2 rooms:** £ 95/125

Typical Dishes
Venison scotch egg
Slow-cooked beef brisket with dripping chips
Pistachio crème brûlée

🚗 *4.5 mi northwest of Chichester, located on far side of village pond. Parking.*

130

Cat Inn

**Queen's Sq,
West Hoathly, RH19 4PP**
Tel.: (01342)810369
Website: www.catinn.co.uk

VISA **MC**

Harveys Ales, Larkins Traditional and Black Cat Original

Set in an idyllic village and only four centuries younger than the 11C church it overlooks, The Cat is very much a village pub, where you'll find locals relaxing by the inglenook with a pint. There are beamed ceilings, pewter tankards, open fires and plenty of corners in which to get cosy; one of these even contains a surprisingly deep well. Run by an experienced owner who cut his teeth at Gravetye Manor just down the road, it can get very busy; but, full or not, the friendly service doesn't falter. Cooking focuses on tasty pub classics and is carefully executed and good value; dishes might include roast belly of pork, Rye Bay lemon sole or steak, mushroom and ale pie. Four tastefully decorated bedrooms complete the picture.

Closing times
Closed 25 December and Sunday dinner

Prices
Meals: a la carte £ 22/39

4 rooms: £ 90/150

Typical Dishes
Black pudding scotch egg

Steak, mushroom & ale pie

Steamed ginger sponge

Between East Grinstead and Haywards Heath off B 2028; follow signs for the church. Parking.

Six hundred miles of relentlessly breathtaking coastline pound the majestic South West, assuring it of a dramatic backdrop whatever the season. Its prestige is bolstered by four UNESCO World Heritage sites: one of them is Dorset's spectacular Jurassic Coast, which includes the 180 billion pebbles of Chesil Beach. Further north, Dartmoor and Exmoor embody the region's untamed beauty. The built environment may be of a more recent time line, but examples are still impressive, ranging from thirteenth century Lacock, home of many a filmed costume drama, to Elizabethan Longleat with its Capability Brown designed parkland, and late Victorian Lanhydrock, "the great house of Cornwall". The same county boasts its very own "theatre under the stars", The Minack, where the drama of nature collides with the drama of the written word. Days out in this unforgettable region come complete with pasties and a pint of local ale, or freshly caught lobster, scallops or mussels enjoyed along the quay.

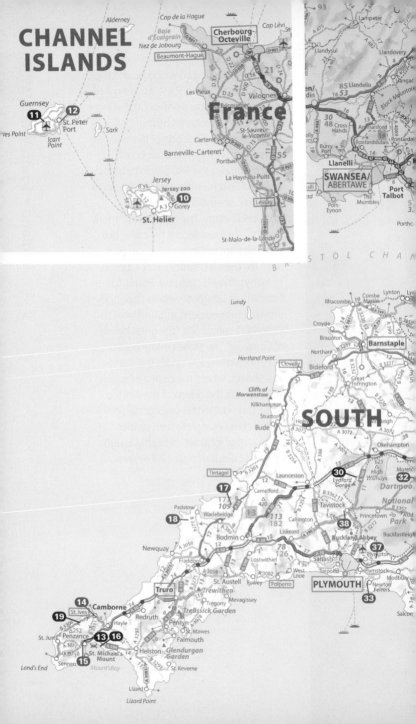

10 Pubs without bedrooms

16 Pubs with bedrooms

Bath

1 **Chequers**

50 Rivers St,
Bath, BA1 2QA
Tel.: (01225)360017
Website: www.thechequersbath.com

Butcombe Bitter and Bath Ales Gem

Set in a smart residential street amid elegant Georgian terraces, the Chequers isn't far from its sister, the Marlborough Tavern. They may look similar from the outside but cross the thresholds and you'll see each has something different to offer. The Chequers has some pubby character with its simple tables, parquet floor and central bar but it's also been smartened up with a bright paint job. The cooking is fairly sophisticated and presentation, elaborate, so alongside robust pub favourites you might find starters of beetroot and caraway cured salmon or salt cod fishcake with Bath pig chorizo, followed by red wine braised beef cheek or stuffed chicken breast with fondant potato. Lunch is good value and desserts offer something a little different.

Closing times
Open daily

Prices
Meals: £ 12 (weekday lunch) and a la carte £ 23/42

Typical Dishes
Citrus-cured mackerel
Chicken pie & chips
Burnt rhubarb custard

 Close to The Royal Crescent, off Upper Church St. Parking bays opposite.

England • South West • Bath and North East Somerset

2 **Marlborough Tavern**

35 Marlborough Buildings, Bath, BA1 2LY
Tel.: (01225)423731
Website: www.marlborough-tavern.com

 Butcombe Ales and Boxstream Brewery Ales

On the eastern edge of Victoria Park, only a stone's throw from the Royal Crescent, sits this 18C pub, surrounded by grand terraced properties. Despite its traditional outer appearance, it's surprisingly chic and fashionable inside, boasting a modern, open-plan interior, boldly patterned wallpapers and contemporary art; not forgetting a rather pleasant walled terrace to the rear. At lunch they offer sandwiches, pub classics and a good value set menu, while dinner steps things up a gear with some interesting specials. The chef sources ingredients carefully and lists suppliers on the back of the menu; there might be potted Wiltshire game, followed by south coast plaice with Cornish samphire, finished off with local raspberry pavlova ice cream.

Closing times
Closed 25 December

Prices
Meals: £ 15 (lunch)
and a la carte £ 22/44

Typical Dishes
Diver-caught scallops
Loin of Neston Park venison
Dark chocolate pot

 East side of Royal Victoria Park. Parking bays opposite.

3 | **White Hart**

**Widcombe Hill,
Bath, BA2 6AA**
Tel.: (01225)338053
Website: www.whitehartbath.co.uk

Butcombe Bitter and Rare Breed, Sharp's Red Ale

Situated close to the railway, just over the river, The White Hart has a real neighbourhood feel. It attracts a loyal local following, so get here early or book ahead as it fills up quickly. Food-wise, the mantra here is 'keep it simple', with the sourcing of ingredients afforded paramount importance. Portions are large and cooking, hearty, with dishes like baked fillet of pork wrapped in bacon, breast of chicken with lentils or whole baked sea bass with lime, ginger and chilli butter. Most people have a main dish and share a side and a dessert, but the smaller tapas plates are also very popular. The pub has a rustic feel, with scrubbed wooden floors and worn wooden tables and the rear terrace is a great spot in warmer weather.

Closing times
Closed 25-26 December, Sunday dinner and bank holidays
booking essential at dinner

Prices
Meals: £ 13 (weekday lunch) and a la carte £ 24/34

Typical Dishes
Pheasant breast with orange salad
Sea bream fillet with potted shrimp butter
Rhubarb, apple & plum crumble

 On southern side of the city just off A 36. On-street parking.

4 Albion Public House and Dining Rooms

**Boyces Ave,
Clifton Village, Bristol, BS8 4AA**
Tel.: (0117)9733522
Website: www.thealbionclifton.co.uk

 St Austell Brewery Ales and Otter Bitter

Tucked away down a cobbled street in a fashionable neighbourhood quarter, the trendy 17C Albion is exactly as a pub should be – fun, friendly and casual – with an equal split of drinkers and those out for a relaxed meal. Cooking is highly seasonal and the unfussy British menu changes as new produce arrives. Dishes are straightforward and satisfying, and range from fish fingers to Iberico pork with roasted peppers or T-bone for two to share, with everything made in-house, including the rustic bread and nibbles like salt cod fritters. Booking is imperative, as drinkers multiply throughout the evening; if the weather's fine then the benches outside on the terrace make a pleasant spot to take in the comings and goings of the area.

Closing times
Closed 25-26 December
booking essential
Prices
Meals: a la carte £ 20/31

Typical Dishes
Home-smoked salmon with prawn & citrus salsa

Pan-fried pork, apple & black pudding rösti

Chocolate parfait, praline crisp & orange cream

In Clifton Village. Parking in Victoria Square or surrounding roads.

Bristol

5 Kensington Arms

**35-37 Stanley Rd,
Bristol, BS6 6NP**
Tel.: (0117)9446444
Website: www.thekensingtonarms.co.uk

 Greene King Ales

The crest of the Royal Borough of Kensington and Chelsea swings on the board outside, proclaiming the motto 'quam bonum in unum habitare': what a good thing it is to dwell together in unity – and with this pub at the heart of the neighbourhood, what a good thing indeed. With its charming Victorian style, large wood-floored bar and impressive high-ceilinged dining room, you could be mistaken for thinking someone had simply picked up a London pub and dropped it down here. Menus change daily and have a strong British base, featuring maybe buttered asparagus or calves' liver and bacon. Seasons play an important role, so you'll find hearty, nourishing dishes and proper homemade puddings in the colder months. Service is particularly warm.

Closing times
Closed 25-26 December and Sunday dinner

Prices
Meals: £ 15 (lunch) and a la carte £ 22/43

Typical Dishes
Grilled octopus, fennel & cucumber

Megrim sole, brown shrimp & crème fraîche

Chocolate fondant with salted caramel ice cream

 In city centre. Unrestricted parking outside pub and in nearby streets.

6

Pump House

Merchants Rd,
Bristol, BS8 4PZ
Tel.: (0117)9272229
Website: www.the-pumphouse.com

VISA MC AE

Butcombe Bitter, Bath Ales Gem, St Austell Tribute and Otter Ale

Standing proudly on the quayside, this Victorian building was once a pumping station for the adjacent docks; evidence of which can be seen through its cavernous interior, in the form of exposed stone walls, quarry tiled floors and original pipework. When the sun's out, sit on the terrace and watch the boats; on colder days head for the large bar or one of the many sofas or tables dotted about over various different levels. The same menu is offered throughout, featuring sandwiches and pub classics alongside some much more elaborate modern dishes such as roast turbot with fennel and a caper and raison vinaigrette or smoked eel with egg, mustard and apples. Textures and flavours are well-balanced and the wine list is comprehensive.

Closing times
Closed 25 December, Sunday dinner and Monday

Prices
Meals: a la carte £ 27/38

Typical Dishes
Ballotine of rabbit with carrot & walnut
Saddle of venison, polenta and onion purée
Lemon marshmallow parfait

On the eastern side of the docks. Parking.

Chew Magna

7

Pony & Trap

**Knowle Hill,
Newtown, Chew Magna, BS40 8TQ**
Tel.: (01275)332627
Website: www.theponyandtrap.co.uk

 VISA **MC**

 Butcombe Ales and Sharp's Doom Bar

With this whitewashed pub on their doorstep, the inhabitants of this tiny hamlet have plenty to smile about. The rear garden with its rolling countryside views is the place to be but the cosy stone-walled bar and oversized dining room windows make it just as welcoming whatever the weather. To say the food is local and seasonal is an understatement: the menu is written twice a day; meats are locally sourced and hung; fish comes from the nearby Chew Valley smokehouse; and eggs are collected from their own chickens out the back. The passionate chef keeps his cooking rooted firmly in the classical British vein, flavours are clean and clear, and the lamb '2 ways' is establishing itself as a firm favourite. Service can sometimes be a little subdued.

Closing times
Closed Monday except December and bank holidays and Sunday dinner
booking essential
Prices
Meals: a la carte £ 23/39

Typical Dishes
Beetroot salad with ewe's curd
Beef with swede purée & ox tongue
Fennel crème brûlée

 1.5 mi south of the village; follow signs for Bishop Stuttard. Parking.

8 — Wheatsheaf

Combe Hay,
BA2 7EG
Tel.: (01225)833504
Website: www.wheatsheafcombehay.com

VISA **MC**

Butcombe Ales

The Wheatsheaf began life as a farmhouse in 1576. Centuries and several seamless additions later, it boasts chic, über-modern styling typified by delightful pink flocked wallpaper and vivid artwork, and a relaxed atmosphere helped on its way by open fires, comfy low sofas and an abundance of books and magazines – not forgetting Milo and Brie, the pub's friendly resident spaniels. The flavourful, seasonal food is presented in a contemporary style – often on slate plates – and dishes might include homemade fish pie, game broth or slow-roasted belly pork with black pudding; with desserts such as chocolate fondant or almond and prune cake. Bedrooms follow the pub's lead, with a spacious, contemporary feel and an emphasis firmly on quality.

Closing times
Closed 1 week January, 24-25 December, Sunday dinner and Monday except bank holidays

Prices
Meals: £ 15 (weekday lunch) and a la carte £ 21/40

Typical Dishes
Seared foie gras with Yorkshire pudding
Duck breast with chorizo & red pepper
Treacle tart, lemon curd ice cream

England • South West • Bath and North East Somerset

 Signposted off A 367, 5 mi south of Bath. Parking.

Monkton Combe

9   **Wheelwrights Arms**

**Church Ln,
Monkton Combe, BA2 7HB**
Tel.: (01225)722287
Website: www.wheelwrightsarms.co.uk

Butcombe Bitter and Sharp's Cornish Coaster

If you're after a spot of peace and quiet, make a beeline for the sleepy village of Monkton Combe, where you can relax to the sound of birdsong at this charming inn. Formerly a private residence, it's made up of two buildings, which have attractive parquet floors, exposed stone walls and welcoming open fires. Classical menus offer a wide range of dishes from sharing plates and good value set lunches to tasty three course dinners. You might find blue cheese, almond and spinach tart, followed by sea bass with ratatouille or rabbit and pork braised in cider. Specials consist mainly of fish and to finish, the treacle tart is always a good bet. Set in the old carpenter's workshop, individually designed bedrooms are modern with rustic overtones.

Closing times
Open daily
Prices
Meals: £ 12
(weekday lunch)
and a la carte £ 22/33

7 rooms: £ 75/150

Typical Dishes
Home-cured salmon
Loin of Mendip lamb
Sticky toffee pudding

 2 mi southeast of Bath city centre by A 3062. Parking.

10   Bass and Lobster

Gorey Coast Rd,
Gorey, JE3 6EU
Tel.: (01534)859590
Website: www.bassandlobster.com

 No real ales offered

This bright, modern pub, set close to the sandy beach, has smartly laid wooden tables, a mock wooden floor, some banquette seating and a small decked terrace. Having lived and worked on the island for many years, the experienced owner has built up a network of local suppliers and uses these whenever possible. Fresh seafood and shellfish dominate the seasonal menu and dishes are simply cooked and immensely flavourful: try the roast fillet of sea bass, the Chancre crab linguine with prawns or some fantastic steely oysters. Wonderfully earthy Jersey Royals make a great side dish and the prices also bring a smile to one's face, with the lunch menu representing particularly good value. Smooth service comes from a friendly European team.

Closing times
Closed Monday lunch and Sunday in summer and Monday dinner in winter

Prices
Meals: £ 13/21
and a la carte £ 27/40

Typical Dishes
Lobster risotto cake with grilled asparagus

Sea bass with Jersey Royals & local scallops

White chocolate & passion fruit cheesecake

On the coast road. Parking.

Kings Mills (Guernsey)

11   Fleur du Jardin

**Grand Moulins,
Kings Mills, GY5 7JT**
Tel.: (01481)257996
Website: www.fleurdujardin.com

VISA   MC   AE   DC

Bucktrouts Ales

Set in a small hamlet, not far from the sea, this attractive inn started life as a several stone cottages. The first thing you'll notice is the stylish terrace and lovely landscaped garden, and it will come as no surprise that they host regular summer BBQs. Pleasingly, the interior lives up to every expectation too, with its series of charming, adjoining rooms, rustic beams, exposed stone walls and open fires. When it comes to dining, the regularly changing menu ranges from homemade burgers to sea bass with pesto potatoes; specials feature tasty island seafood and every dish is prepared with care and a lightness of touch. Completing the picture are stylish New England themed bedrooms with luxury bathrooms – there's even a heated outdoor pool.

Closing times
Closed dinner 25 December and 1 January

Prices
Meals: a la carte £ 20/33

11 rooms: £ 65/185

Typical Dishes
Salt & pepper squid
Corn-fed chicken breast with pesto mash
Treacle tart

In the centre of the village. Parking.

12   **Swan Inn**

**St Julian's Ave,
St Peter Port, GY1 1WA**
Tel.: (01481)728969

Randall's Patois

With its smart, bottle-green façade, this pub wouldn't look out of place in London, although its tightly packed, shabby-chic interior might not go down so well. It's very passionately and personally run by a gregarious French owner, and his enthusiasm can be felt throughout the place. On the ground floor there's a traditional bar complete with a coal fire, some booths and walls filled with sporting paraphernalia; above, there's a more sedate dining room with polished wood tables and leather chairs. Both the choice of dishes and the portions themselves are large, and tempting as it may be, you're unlikely to make it through all three courses. Dishes stick mainly to tried-and-tested pub classics but you'll find a few Asian influences too.

Closing times
Closed 25 December, Sunday in winter and bank holiday Mondays

Prices
Meals: a la carte £ 20/22

Typical Dishes
Home-smoked chicken with wild mushrooms
Lobster & scallop thermidor
Lemon posset

St Julian's Ave is opposite South Quay. Parking on South Quay (50yds).

Gulval

13 **Coldstreamer**

**Gulval,
TR18 3BB**
Tel.: (01736)362072
Website: www.coldstreamer-penzance.co.uk

Skinner's Spriggan Ale, Bays Topsail and guest ales

This handsome pub is set in the heart of Gulval and, like much of the village, was built by the Bolitho family. Following the death in service of Harry Bolitho it was given to the Coldstream Association, before being taken over by two local brothers. It's a spacious place, boasting a bright dining room and a large bar adorned with Coldstream Guards memorabilia. The concise, seasonal menu features fish from Newlyn, meat from Penzance and products from the village's now retired Smoker, and cooking is clean, generous and modern; lunch might offer salt cod fritters and dinner, more elaborate dishes like lamb rump with caramelised shallots. May sees an asparagus menu and the regular wine dinners prove popular. Bedrooms are fresh and well-appointed.

Closing times
Closed 25-26 December

Prices
Meals: £ 15/21
and a la carte £ 21/34

🛏 **3 rooms:** £ 60/85

Typical Dishes
Smoked mackerel cakes
Pork loin with rhubarb & apple compote
Sticky toffee pudding

1.25 mi northeast of Penzance off A 30 in centre of village. Plenty of parking in the square.

14   **Halsetown Inn**

**Halsetown St Ives,
TR26 3NA**
Tel.: (01736)795583
Website: www.hasletowninn.co.uk

🍴   *VISA*   Ⓜ©

Sharp's Doom Bar and Skinner's Betty Stogs

'Proper pub, thoughtful food' is their strapline and it sums up this endearingly quirky place pretty well. It's a bit scruffy from the outside and fairly modest inside, but it's got character and more importantly, it's got soul. There are various little adjoining areas where you can eat – find a spot in front of the bar or on the terrace at the back, which is a real suntrap. The kitchen tends to eschew the usual pub classics and instead offers an interesting selection of dishes enlivened with some global flavours, with a particular nod towards the Mediterranean – and the prices are good too. They even plough their own furrow on Sundays when, in lieu of a traditional lunch, they operate their own burger van in the car park.

Closing times
Closed Sunday dinner
Prices
Meals: a la carte £ 21/30

Typical Dishes
St Ives Bay crab
Twice-cooked pork with smoked mackerel croquette
Chocolate pâté

🚗 *1.5 mi southwest of St Ives on B 3311. Parking.*

Newlyn

15 **Tolcarne Inn**

**Tolcarne Pl,
Newlyn, TR18 5PR**
Tel.: (01736)363074
Website: www.tolcarneinn.co.uk

Skinner's Betty Stogs

Having been flooded a number of times over the years, this unremarkable looking but refreshingly unaffected 19C pub is now protected by a tall sea wall – it's a shame it hides the view of Mount's Bay, but at least it keeps the wind off the terrace. Inside, things are cosy and traditional with a wood-burner at one end keeping the drinkers warm, and the rest of the place laid out for eating. The owner-chef is an experienced chap who cooks with intelligence and care. Being in Newlyn and within a literal stone's throw from the boats, it's no surprise that fish and shellfish are the stars of the show. The blackboard changes daily and you can always expect wonderfully fresh and uncomplicated dishes that deliver plenty of flavour.

Closing times
Open daily
Prices
Meals: a la carte £ 20/34

Typical Dishes
Scallops with lentils & coriander
Turbot, pork confit & black pudding
White chocolate & salt lemon cheesecake

 By the sea wall in the centre of town. Parking.

16   **Victoria Inn**

**Perranuthnoe,
TR20 9NP**
Tel.: (01736)710309
Website: www.victoriainn-penzance.co.uk

🍴   *VISA*   Ⓜ©

🍺 **Keltek Brewery and Cornish Chough Serpentine**

Simple but characterful, with a cosy, homely feel, this pink-washed inn sits in the heart of the village and appeals to drinkers and diners alike. Its owners are keen for it to remain a proper pub, so you'll see locals here for a beer alongside families who've hot-footed it in from the beach for lunch, sand between their toes. The menu offers sandwiches and soups as well as wholesome pub classics – like ham, free range eggs and real chips – and choices such as honey-roasted Cornish duck breast or roasted whole lemon sole with asparagus and new potatoes. Dishes are tasty and the chef-owner – a local boy returned home – is proud to showcase local produce. The terrace provides a pleasant suntrap and two modest bedrooms are situated above the pub.

Closing times
Closed 25-26 December,
1 January, Monday in winter
and Sunday dinner

Prices
Meals: a la carte £ 22/32

🛏 **2 rooms:** £ 50

Typical Dishes
Seafood & shellfish on garlic toast

Cornish cod with champ potato

Rhubarb & almond trifle

 3 mi east of Marazion, south of A 394. Parking.

St Kew

17   **St Kew Inn**

St Kew,
PL30 3HB
Tel.: (01208)841259
Website: www.stkewinn.co.uk

St Austell HSD, Proper Job and Tribute

St Kew Inn was built in the 15C to serve the masons who constructed the magnificent next door church and boasts flag floors, stone walls and wooden beams. It sits in a quintessentially English location and its attractive front garden is as much of a draw as the pub itself, come the warmer weather. A massive electric umbrella means that sudden summer showers are not a problem, and there are heaters too, should it turn nippy. Cooking is fresh and tasty, with a wide range of appealing, good value dishes from which to choose; lunch means choices like Fowey mussels, Welsh rarebit, corned beef hash and a range of sandwiches, while dinner offers similar (minus the sandwiches), plus perhaps some grilled lemon sole or pan-fried lamb's liver.

Closing times
Open daily
Prices
Meals: a la carte £ 23/36

Typical Dishes
Mackerel on red onion & parmesan toast
Chicken & mushroom pie
Coconut crème caramel

 3 mi northeast of Wadebridge by A 39 and minor road north. Parking.

St Merryn

18   Cornish Arms

**Churchtown,
St Merryn, PL28 8ND**
Tel.: (01841)532700
Website: www.rickstein.com

 St Austell Ales

Rick Stein liked his local so much that he bought the lease on it! Instead of then heading down the 'gastropub' route, he has sensibly kept things simple, with a nicely priced menu of pub classics like a ploughman's, scampi or sausage and mash. Summer means an influx of tourists, who enjoy the local seafood specials, Sunday roasts and nursery puddings and there are plenty of events like pub quizzes, curry nights and live music to keep the regulars happy in winter. Service is chirpy and cheerful, the bar, beamed and cosy, and the dining area, light and airy. The wine list offers a well-priced selection, with plenty to choose from by the glass or carafe – and keep a look-out for the man himself, who still pops in for a pint from time to time.

Closing times
Open daily
bookings not accepted
Prices
Meals: a la carte £ 20/29

Typical Dishes
Cornish mussels with bread & butter
Tywardreath sausages with mash & onion gravy
Sticky toffee pudding

 2.5 mi west of Padstow on B 3276. Parking.

Zennor

19 **Gurnard's Head**

**Treen,
Zennor, TR26 3DE**
Tel.: (01736)796928
Website: www.gurnardshead.co.uk

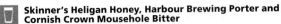

Skinner's Heligan Honey, Harbour Brewing Porter and Cornish Crown Mousehole Bitter

Set in a remote location, surrounded by nothing but fields and livestock, the Gurnard's Head provides a warm welcome that sets you immediately at your ease. It's dog-friendly, with stone floors and shabby-chic décor, while blazing fires and brightly coloured walls help create a relaxed, cosy feel. The menu relies on regional produce, including some locally foraged ingredients. Dishes might include pigeon with celeriac purée and mushroom jus, gurnard with braised fennel and scallop velouté or orange and mascarpone mousse with date sponge; while the wine list includes a very interesting selection by the glass. Service is friendly and remains calm even when it's busy. Extremely comfortable beds feature good quality linen and colourful throws.

Closing times
Closed 24-25 December and 4 days early January
booking advisable

Prices
Meals: £ 15 (lunch)
and a la carte £ 25/33

🛏 **7 rooms:** £ 85/170

Typical Dishes
Garlic soup
with scallop & grapes
Pork tenderloin with
cheek, cider & apple
Dark chocolate terrine
with popcorn ice
cream

 7.5 mi west of St Ives on B 3306. Parking.

20

Cary Arms

**Babbacombe Beach,
Torquay, TQ1 3LX**
Tel.: (01803)327110
Website: www.caryarms.co.uk

🍴 *VISA* 💳 AE ⓓ

🍺 **Otter Ale, Bays Topsail and Hunter's Pheasant Plucker**

Set in an idyllic spot on the English Riviera, The Cary Arms is built into the rocks, with terraces down to the shore and far-reaching views. Its boutique-chic, New England style bedrooms come with stunning bathrooms complete with roll-top baths; the stylish, ultra-comfy residents lounge continues the nautical theme, and there's even a spa room for treatments. If the rooms are all about luxury, the food, by contrast, is straightforward in style; we're talking reasonably priced pub dishes of simply cooked fish and meats. At the hub of the operation is its atmospheric stone and slate floored bar where you're served by chatty staff; in summer, there's also a wood burning pizza oven on the terrace, to make the most of the wonderful location.

Closing times
Open daily
Prices
Meals: a la carte £ 24/40

🛏 **8 rooms:** £ 125/275

Typical Dishes
Goat's cheese panna cotta
Brixham battered fish & chips
Trio of chocolate

🚗 2.75 mi northeast of Torquay by A 379. Chargeable parking at adjacent beach car park.

Bampton

21   **Swan**

**Station Rd,
Bampton, EX16 9NG**
Tel.: (01398)332248
Website: www.theswan.co

VISA **MC**

Red Rock Brewery Devon Coast and Devon Storm, Exe Valley Dob's Best Bitter and St Austell Proper Job

The Swan's history can be traced back to 1450, when it provided accommodation for craftsmen working on the local church. The original inglenook fireplace and bread oven remain in situ but, aside from that, it has a modern, open-plan layout and a fresh, new feel; if you fancy a more intimate experience, head for the upstairs dining room. When it comes to the food, it sticks to unfussy pub classics, with the likes of homemade soup or whitebait, followed by pies, steaks or liver and bacon – finished off with comforting old school desserts like treacle pudding. Dishes arrive neatly presented on wooden boards, with fish originating from Devon and Cornwall, and meats from nearby Waterhouse Farm. Smart, modern bedrooms are found on the 2nd floor.

Closing times
Closed 25-26 December and Monday

Prices
Meals: a la carte £ 19/33

🛏 **3 rooms:** £ 60/85

Typical Dishes
Soused Cornish herrings
Fillet of cod with textures of carrot & cumin
White chocolate cheesecake

 6 mi north of Tiverton by A 396 and B 3190. Just out of village centre. Public car park opposite.

22

N **Normandy Arms**

Chapel St,
Blackawton, TQ9 7BN
Tel.: (01803)712884
Website: www.normandyarms.co.uk

VISA **MC** **AE**

Otter Ales

This pretty pub takes its name from the American occupation of this part of Devon prior to the Normandy landings – and is now under the command of a keen young couple with lots of experience. You'll find local drinkers on the sofas by the wood burning stove and those eating, in the bar or the small dining room with its colourful artwork. Reka looks after things out front, while Andrew does the cooking. Lunch sticks mainly to familiar pub dishes, such as a homemade scotch egg or a ploughman's, while dinner could see loin of lamb en croute or roasted plaice on the bone. Cooking is carefully done, ingredients are local and flavours are distinct. Come for the International Festival of Wormcharming and stay in one of the pleasant bedrooms.

Closing times
Closed January, Sunday dinner and Monday

Prices
Meals: £ 18 (weekday dinner) and a la carte £ 24/37

3 rooms: £ 85/95

Typical Dishes
Chicken liver parfait
Mackerel with Heritage tomatoes
Hot chocolate mousse

5.5 mi west of Dartmouth signposted off A 3122. Parking.

Brampford Speke

23   Lazy Toad Inn

**Brampford Speke,
EX5 5DP**
Tel.: (01392)841591
Website: www.thelazytoadinn.co.uk

Palmers 200, Otter Ale and Branscombe Brewery Ales

This sweet little Grade II listed pub has charming bedrooms, oak-beamed ceilings and slate floors and is set in an equally attractive village not far from the River Exe. In summer, head for the beautiful walled garden or lovely cobbled courtyard – once used by the local farrier and wheelwright. If you're paying a flying visit, opt for a real ale or a glass of Mo's homemade blackcurrant cordial, along with some tasty pork scratchings; if you've got longer, choose from the interesting Asian-inspired main menu. Much of the produce, including the pak choi, comes from their polytunnel just across the car park; visit in the spring and you can also sample lamb raised on their smallholding. Prices are kept keen by the chefs' more unusual choices of cuts.

Closing times
Closed 3 weeks January, Sunday dinner, Monday and bank holidays

Prices
Meals: a la carte £ 23/36

3 rooms: £ 58/100

Typical Dishes
Cornish crab soufflé with crab cappuccino
Cod with squid ink tagliatelle
Pear & walnut frangipane tart with custard

 5 mi north of Exeter by A 377. Parking.

24

Rusty Bike

**67 Howell Rd,
Exeter, EX4 4LZ**
Tel.: (01392)214440
Website: www.rustybike-exeter.co.uk

 O'Hanlan's Yellow Hammer and Exeter Ferryman

This small backstreet boozer was closed for 7 years before larger-than-life owner Hamish transformed it into a destination dining pub. It's made up of three rustic rooms with wood floors, reclaimed furniture and an eclectic mix of art, while to pass the time, there are magazines, board games and a vintage table football game. When it comes to the food, all produce is sourced from within 20 miles or is from their nearby farm; complete beasts are brought in and all parts of the animals are used, so you'll find the likes of pig's head terrine or carpaccio of beef. Dishes are hearty and satisfying, with the home-bred pork being particularly popular. They also cure their own meats and make their own cider, which features alongside other local beers.

Closing times
Closed lunch Monday-Wednesday
Prices
Meals: a la carte £ 22/37

Typical Dishes
Locally shot pigeon
Rare breed suckling pig belly
Peanut butter parfait

 On edge of city centre. Metered on-street parking nearby.

Exton

25 **Puffing Billy**

**Station Rd,
Exton, EX3 0PR**
Tel.: (01392)877888
Website: www.thepuffingbilly.co.uk

 Otter Ale & Exmoor Gold

You'd think this was a typical old railway inn: set right on the street, with a whitewashed exterior and the name of a train. Venture inside and you're in for a shock, for the reality is a bright, modern and open-plan country dining pub, with high vaulted ceilings, a semi-circular bar and a friendly, welcoming atmosphere. An eclectic menu offers tasty, globally influenced dishes such as squid, prawn and chorizo chowder, alongside local specialities like pan-roasted Devon beef rump or rack of West Country lamb. If you like to be where the atmosphere is, sit close to the bar; if it's a quiet meal you're after, head for the far end instead. Trainspotters should take a seat by the window to watch the engines chug along the scenic coastline.

Closing times
Open daily
Prices
Meals: £ 16 (weekdays) and a la carte £ 20/37

Typical Dishes
Wild mushroom arancini with celeriac velouté
Slow-cooked beef short ribs in Exmoor Ale
Lemon bavarois

Brown tourist sign off A 376 to Exmouth, 3 mi from junction 30 of M 5. Parking.

26

Holt

**178 High St,
Honiton, EX14 1LA**
Tel.: (01404)47707
Website: www.theholt-honiton.com

VISA MC AE

Otter Brewery Ales

This is a family owned and run pub, where the passion for food and drink is almost palpable. Angus McCaig oversees goings-on in the Holt's kitchen, while brother Joe works out front; their parents meanwhile run the well-known Otter Brewery down the road. Sustainable, regional produce is the central tenet of their ethos with everything cooked in-house and meats and fish cured and smoked on-site. Oft-changing, eco-friendly menus are printed on paper made from recycled hops and list rustic dishes like slow-roasted pork belly or seared lamb rump, with tapas and sandwiches also available at lunch. The smoked pint of prawns is a real winner – and try the tasting rack: a third of a pint of three Otter Brewery ales, matched with recommended dishes.

Closing times
Closed 25-26 December, 1 January, Sunday and Monday

Prices
Meals: a la carte £ 21/32

Typical Dishes
Smoked haddock scotch egg
Lamb rump with crisp breast & mint jus
Chocolate brownie

At lower end of High Street. Dowell Street car park (2min walk).

Honiton

27

Railway

**Queen St,
Honiton, EX14 1HE**
Tel.: (01404)47976
Website: www.therailwayhoniton.co.uk

 **Branscombe Vale Branoc, St Austell Tribute
and Bath Ales Gem**

This smart, modern pub offers authentic Mediterranean cooking at affordable prices; a combination patently pleasing the people in this East Devon market town. Touches like the Bibendum statues and various cookery books dotted around suggest a serious approach, underlined by the open kitchen and the pub's strapline, 'Every plate a picture of freshness and flavour'. Nibble on olive oil dipped bread while you read the menu, where classics like fritto misto sit alongside homemade pastas, brick-fired pizzas and steaks; the warm Sicilian tart is a house favourite and specials might include seared scallops or wild boar terrine. An eclectic wine list and an olive oil top-up service add to the fun and comfortable bedrooms complete the picture.

Closing times
Closed 25-26 December,
Sunday and Monday
Prices
Meals: a la carte £ 21/32
3 rooms: £ 70/90

Typical Dishes
Fritto misto
Rib-eye of beef
Lemon tart

 2min off the High Street, via New Street. Parking.

England • South West • Devon

28   **Bickley Mill Inn**

**Stoneycombe,
Kingskerswell, TQ12 5LN**
Tel.: (01803)873201
Website: www.bickleymill.co.uk

📶   **VISA**   **MC**   **AE**

🍺 **Bays Gold, Teignworthy Ales and Hunters Ale**

This converted former flour mill is the last place you expect to find as you drive down winding country lanes and past a large quarry. You're greeted by a huge decked terrace, gardens built into rocky banks and a contemporary entranceway and, despite the rustic furnishings, large open fireplaces and cosy bar, it feels decidedly modern inside too. Menus are keenly priced and, for the most part, take on a simple, traditional style; you might find king prawn cocktail or devilled kidneys on toast, followed by shepherd's pie with cheddar and leek mash, home-baked ham and free range eggs or caramelised duck breast with balsamic and honey glaze. Individually designed bedrooms are bold and stylish; Riviera, with its private balcony, is one of the best.

Closing times
Open daily
Prices
Meals: a la carte £ 20/30

🛏 **12 rooms:** £ 65/100

Typical Dishes
Smoked salmon, apple & celeriac salad

Duck breast, white bean & juniper jus

White chocolate parfait

 3 mi south of Newton Abbot by A 380 and minor road east. Parking.

Knowstone

29   Masons Arms

**Knowstone,
EX36 4RY**
Tel.: (01398)341231
Website: www.masonsarmsdevon.co.uk

☂   *VISA*   ⓜⓒ   AE

🍺 **Cotleigh Tawny Ale**

This pretty thatched inn is set in a secluded village in the beautiful foothills of Exmoor. Built in the 13C by the masons who also constructed the village church, it exudes rural charm, featuring a cosy, beamed bar with an inglenook fireplace that plays host to the locals. Cooking is more sophisticated than you'd expect to find in most pubs, with canapés and petit fours served alongside attractively presented British and French classics such as Devon beef fillet or monkfish loin, which have the pronounced, assured flavours that come from using the finest of local produce. Dine beneath a celestial ceiling mural in the bright rear dining room, with delightful views out over the rolling hills towards Exmoor. Charming service complements the food.

Closing times
Closed first week January,
1 week mid February,
1 week August-September,
Sunday dinner and Monday
booking essential

Prices
Meals: £ 25 (lunch)
and a la carte £ 35/47

Typical Dishes
Croquette of ham
hock
Corn-fed chicken with
tarragon ravioli
Mango parfait with
coconut sorbet

🚗 *7 mi southeast of South Molton by A 361; opposite the village church. Parking.*

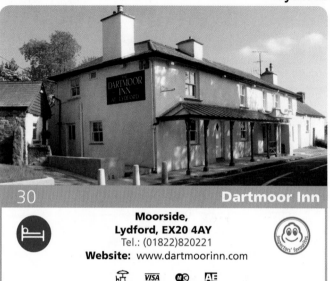

30 | **Dartmoor Inn**

**Moorside,
Lydford, EX20 4AY**
Tel.: (01822)820221
Website: www.dartmoorinn.com

📶 *VISA* Ⓜ️ 🅰️🅴

🍺 **Otter Ale and St Austell Tribute**

England • South West • Devon

A pub might have a snazzy new look or a barrel-load of special offers on but it's the feel of a place which dictates whether you'll want to spend time there – this cosy, rustic pub being a case in point. The exterior is rather non-descript but the owners offer a genuinely warm welcome, the local staff are friendly and a there's a buzzing air of satisfaction. The numerous rooms are decorated in a shabby-chic style: the one with the wood-burning stove is the most popular; another houses a little boutique selling linen, jewellery and the like. Classic dishes like liver and onions or slow-cooked belly pork are satisfying and full of flavour; for less expensive options, take a look on the blackboard menu. Spacious bedrooms have a French feel.

Closing times
Closed Sunday dinner and Monday lunch except bank holidays

Prices
Meals: £ 18 (weekdays) and a la carte £ 22/35

🛏 **3 rooms:** £ 75/115

Typical Dishes
Pork cheeks with star anise sauce
Slow-cooked beef short-rib
Lemon & ginger panna cotta

 8.5 mi northeast of Tavistock on A 386. Parking.

Marldon

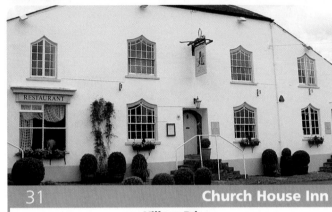

31 **Church House Inn**

**Village Rd,
Marldon, TQ3 1SL**
Tel.: (01803)558279
Website: www.churchhousemarldon.com

**St Austell Tribute, Teignworthy Gun Dog, Bays Topsail
and Dartmoor Jail Ale**

The Church House Inn was originally built in the 17C to provide accommodation for stone masons constructing the nearby church; it was rebuilt in the 18C and still displays some of its eye-catching, original Strawberry Hill Gothic windows. Inside, it's fresh and simple, with a formally laid restaurant and a bar offering locally brewed beer; there are beams, open fires and plenty of nooks and crannies in which to settle, and local art hangs on the walls. The multitude of menus can be a little confusing, with different blackboards offering everything from tapas and sharing plates to vegetarian dishes and wines by the glass, but once you've decided what to go for, you'll find the cooking hearty and comforting and the service, friendly and helpful.

Closing times
Closed dinner
25-26 December
Prices
Meals: a la carte £ 22/39

Typical Dishes
Brixham mussels
Pan-fried pork loin with black pudding
Plum & almond frangipane tart

 Between Torquay and Paignton off A 380. Parking.

32 **White Horse Inn**

**7 George St,
Moretonhampstead, TQ13 8PG**
Tel.: (01647)440242
Website: www.thehorsedartmoor.co.uk

**Dartmoor Legend and IPA, Otter Brewery Otter Ale,
O'Hanlans Yellow Hammer and Teignworthy Reel Ale**

It's hard to believe that this pub, in the heart of rural Dartmoor, was semi-derelict when its owners took it on. While locals gather in the bar to watch the sport, diners head for rustic, flag-floored rooms created from the converted stable and barn; or out to the sunny, Mediterranean-style courtyard. With an actor-turned-chef at the helm you might expect some melodrama in the kitchen; you won't get this, but you will get tasty, unfussy dishes with more than a hint of Italy – think homemade sliced focaccia or crab linguine, with the odd pub classic like fish and chips thrown in for good measure. Authentic, thin crust pizzas come from a custom-built oven, while desserts such as burnt toffee panna cotta finish your meal off with a flourish.

Closing times
Closed 25 December,
Sunday and Monday lunch

Prices
Meals: a la carte £ 18/38

Typical Dishes
Home-cured venison bresaola
Skewer of monkfish & scallops
Trio of ice creams

 In heart of village. Two car parks within 1min walk.

Noss Mayo

33   **Ship Inn**

**Noss Mayo,
PL8 1EW**
Tel.: (01752)872387
Website: www.nossmayo.com

St Austell Tribute, Dartmoor Jail Ale and Otter Amber

Wonderful waterside views are one of the main attractions of this fine pub, set in a peaceful spot on the south side of the Yealm Estuary. It's well run, large and very busy, with friendly staff who cope admirably under pressure. Its oldest part dates from the 18C and its characterful interior features wooden floors and open fires, while its collection of maritime memorabilia, including numerous old photographs, gives a tangible sense of seafaring history. The menu offers pub classics such as rib-eye steak or sausage and mash, followed by tried-and-tested desserts like bread and butter pudding. The wine list is well-presented, with a good selection by the glass. Be careful where you park your car because time and tide wait for no man!

Closing times
Open daily
Prices
Meals: a la carte £ 21/32

Typical Dishes
Flat mushroom glazed with Welsh rarebit
John Dory with salsa verde
Sticky toffee pudding with butterscotch sauce

10.5 mi southeast of Plymouth; signed off A 379; turn right onto B 3186. Restricted parking, particularly at high tide.

34

Jack in the Green

**London Rd,
Rockbeare, EX5 2EE**
Tel.: (01404)822240
Website: www.jackinthegreen.uk.com

 🍺 *VISA* **MC**

Otter Ale, Butcombe Bitter and Sharp's Doom Bar

With its unassuming whitewashed exterior, this is a place that you could easily pass by – but if you did, you'd be missing out. Inside it's warm and welcoming, both in its décor and in the friendliness of its team, with the larger-than-life owner ensuring that the locals are kept 'in-the-know' by sending out newsletters and recipe cards. They take a very serious approach towards their cooking and have been supporting local producers long before it became the fashion. There's a vast array of menus to mix and match between, so you can start with an old pub classic, move on to a more modern, restaurant-style dish and then return to a tasty, old-school favourite for dessert; the six highlighted dishes make up the 'Totally Devon' set menu.

Closing times
Closed 25 December-
3 January

Prices
Meals: £ 25 and a la carte
£ 18/35

Typical Dishes
Sea bass in Thai broth
Duck breast, confit blood orange & potato fondant
Lemongrass panna cotta

 7.25 mi east of Exeter by A 30 and Clyst Honiton rd. Parking.

Slapton

35   **Tower Inn**

**Church Rd,
Slapton, TQ7 2PN**
Tel.: (01548)580216
Website: www.thetowerinn.com

🍺 Otter Bitter, St Austell Proper Job, Sharp's Doom Bar and Butcombe Bitter

Leave your car in the car park as you enter the village and make the 10 minute walk up the hill: not only is it the easiest place to park but it's also a pleasant stroll. Built in 1347 as cottages for the workers building the next door chantry, the pub is now overlooked by the ruins of the former tower. It's a charming place, boasting dark red walls, polished tables and roaring fires, not forgetting fresh flowers and flickering candles. Menus differ from lunch to dinner and change every 3 months. It's pub food with an extra little twist; nothing gimmicky, just good cooking that adds something a little different – so your lunchtime fish and chips might come in vodka batter and your evening sea bass, with crab dumplings. Simple bedrooms await.

Closing times
Closed first 2 weeks January and Sunday dinner in winter

Prices
Meals: a la carte £ 21/32

🛏 **3 rooms:** £ 60/90

Typical Dishes
Potted slow-cooked pork

Barnsley chop with sautéed kidneys & sweetbreads

Steamed date & walnut pudding

6 mi southwest of Dartmouth by A 379. Parking with exceptionally narrow access.

36 **Millbrook Inn**

**South Pool,
TQ7 2RW**
Tel.: (01548)531581
Website: www.millbrookinnsouthpool.co.uk

 Red Rock Ales

You'll find this characterful, shabby-chic pub squeezed in between the houses on a narrow village street. Low beamed ceilings and an open fire create a cosy atmosphere and two terraces provide a pleasant alternative come summer. It's very passionately run: they use olive oil from their farm in Andalucía and sell fresh, local produce 24hrs a day in the 'Veg Shed'. Cooking is traditional and hearty with some Mediterranean influences; you might find potted South Devon crab, bouillabaisse or Chateaubriand with pomme pont neuf and béarnaise sauce. The blackboard offers a good value set menu and if you're in a group, you can order 72 hours ahead for a whole roast suckling pig. They host regular live music nights and guest chefs feature in winter.

Closing times
Open daily

Prices
Meals: £ 12 (weekday lunch) and a la carte
£ 24/45

Typical Dishes
Pan-fried foie gras with walnut dressing

Fillet steak with tartiflette

Coconut parfait with Malibu jelly

5.5 mi southeast of Kingsbridge off A 379. On-street parking in the village.

Sparkwell

37 Treby Arms

**Sparkwell,
PL7 5DD**
Tel.: (01752)837363
Website: www.thetrebyarms.co.uk

 VISA

Dartmoor Jail Ale, IPA and Legend, St Austell Tribute

It may be hidden away in a tiny hamlet but the Treby Arms is a very popular place, so you'll need to book ahead. It was built by Isambard Kingdom Brunel for workers constructing the nearby Plymouth-Cornwall train bridge in the 1850s, and is now owned by Anton and his wife Clare. Since winning 'MasterChef', their name and the pub's reputation have spread like wildfire; but despite its fame, it still welcomes the locals, who linger over their tankards and enticing nibbles in the cosy bar. There's the odd pub classic to be found on the main menu but the majority of dishes are creative and modern. Cooking is skilled and careful, offering the likes of asparagus with a pistachio-crusted egg or pork crackling coated king prawns with chorizo dressing.

Closing times
Closed 25-26 December and 1 January
booking essential

Prices
Meals: £ 16 (lunch) and a la carte £ 27/45

Typical Dishes
Asparagus, pistachio crusted egg, onion purée

Bream with clam & crayfish beurre blanc

Cardamom panna cotta

 10 mi east of Plymouth signposted off A 38. Parking.

38   **Cornish Arms**

**15 West St,
Tavistock, PL19 8AN**
Tel.: (01822)612145
Website: www.thecornisharmstavistock.co.uk

VISA **M©**

St Austell Proper Job, Tribute and Dartmoor Best

It might have been refurbished but the Cornish Arms is still a pleasingly traditional pub. It's run in partnership by the St Austell brewery and local lad John Hooker, and has a warm, welcoming feel. The quarry-tiled bar is usually filled with regulars playing darts, watching the football or sitting at simple wooden tables snacking on homemade sausage rolls or fishcakes; a few steps up, is the equally relaxed restaurant. The talented, ambitious chef prepares both carefully crafted classics – like braised ox cheek with horseradish, mash and beef gravy – and more elaborate offerings such as fillet of stone bass with potted shrimp, bisque and braised lettuce. Desserts are sophisticated and a treat for both the eyes and the stomach.

Closing times
Closed dinner 24 December
Prices
Meals: a la carte £ 23/42

Typical Dishes
Braised pork cheek with hogs pudding
Roast ling with asparagus & chicken jus
Banana loaf with peanut & salted caramel

In the centre of town. Parking.

Buckhorn Weston

Stapleton Arms

**Church Hill,
Buckhorn Weston, SP8 5HS**
Tel.: (01963)370396
Website: www.thestapletonarms.com

Butcombe Bitter and Moor Revival

A welcoming, well-run pub, with a homely, shabby-chic style, its rustic, wood-floored bar offering the obligatory comfy sofas and open fire, and its brightly painted dining room being the more formal option. Menus showcase pub classics like beer-battered haddock with triple-cooked chips or pork loin with mash and greens, with the occasional international influence also putting in an appearance. Snacks like pork pie, scotch egg and biltong can be wrapped up to take home; they hold monthly themed dinners and even craft and cookery mornings for kids. Bedrooms are spacious with Egyptian cotton linen, smart bathrooms and a mix of modern and antique furnishings – and you can keep your packing light as they also provide maps, wellies and picnics.

Closing times
Closed 25 and 26 December
Prices
Meals: a la carte £ 24/34
4 rooms: £ 72/120

Typical Dishes
Pea, mint & broad bean frittata
Lamb cutlet with mange tout
Chocolate & peanut butter tart

 7 mi west of Shaftesbury by A 30 and minor road north. Parking.

40

New Inn

**14 Long St,
Cerne Abbas, DT2 7JF**
Tel.: (01300)341274
Website: www.thenewinncerneabbas.co.uk

VISA **MC**

Palmers Ales

The picture postcard village of Cerne Abbas is overlooked by the famous Chalk Giant – and this 16C former coaching inn is another impressively sized and rather ancient village landmark. Its décor is traditional, with exposed beams and dark wood tables, but a little revamp has made it slightly less cluttered than it once was. Apart from a few midday sandwiches, the same menu is offered at lunch and dinner. Expect a mix of traditional and more modern dishes – good pub grub with no unnecessary fuss, just freshly prepared, ably cooked and using locally sourced ingredients. A pleasant landscaped courtyard leads out to the pub's vast back garden with its delightful apple trees. Bedrooms are stylish; some are in the converted stable block.

Closing times
Open daily
Prices
Meals: a la carte £ 22/44

12 rooms: £ 75/160

Typical Dishes
Seared Lyme Bay scallops & cured cauliflower
Glazed Cracknell duck with fondant potato
Plate of mini puddings

In the centre of the village. On-street parking.

Fontmell Magna

41   **Fontmell**

Fontmell Magna,
SP7 0PA
Tel.: (01747)811441
Website: www.thefontmell.com

Keystone Ales, Salisbury Ales and Sharps Brewery Ales

Stylish, modern pub in a small hamlet, with a comfy bar – complete with an open fire and a piano – and a spacious dining room, which straddles the brook below. Sit in the latter of the two rooms, surrounded by shelves filled with books, knick-knacks and wine bottles, and keep an eye out for the visiting otters. The concise daily menu offers an eclectic mix of carefully executed dishes, ranging from homely pub classics to those that display Mediterranean and even some Thai influences. You might find Dorset lamb and black pudding suet pudding or Sicilian-style linguine alla Norma, and on Sundays, the likes of kedgeree and eggs Benedict on the simpler 'Supper' menu. Smart bedrooms are named after butterflies; one has a roll-top bath in the room.

Closing times
Closed 26 December

Prices
Meals: £ 16 (weekdays)/19 and a la carte £ 22/41

6 rooms: £ 85/155

Typical Dishes
Seafood tapas
Creedy Carver duck breast with leg croquette
Lemon posset, hazelnut & Amaretto crumble

4.75 mi south of Shaftesbury on A 350 in centre of village. Parking.

42 | **Three Horseshoes Inn**

**Powerstock,
DT6 3TF**
Tel.: (01308)485328
Website: www.threeshoesdorset.co.uk

VISA MC

Palmers Ales

It's all about the food here at The 'Shoes. Granted, the pub occupies a lovely spot on the edge of the Dorset Downs but looks-wise, there's really not much here to write home about. A glance at the menu will explain the pub's growing reputation, however – it all sounds so appealing that it's a dilemma deciding what to choose. Great ingredients go into the dishes, which come with a proper pubby earthiness, whether that's wild boar scotch eggs, deep-fried rabbit with coleslaw or a veal and bone marrow burger. The day's fish specials are chalked up on the blackboard and they make their own breads, ice creams, chutneys and pickles. Prices are sensible and the triple-cooked chips are worth the journey alone. Bedrooms are simple but spacious.

Closing times
Closed 25 December and Monday in winter
Prices
Meals: a la carte £ 22/38
3 rooms: £ 75/95

Typical Dishes
Wild boar scotch quail egg
Lamb rump with sweetbreads, peas & gnocchi
Rhubarb Queen of puddings

5.5 mi northeast of Bridport by A 3066. Parking.

Sydling St Nicholas

43   Greyhound

**26 High St,
Sydling St Nicholas, DT2 9DP**
Tel.: (01300)341303
Website: www.dorsetgreyhound.co.uk

VISA   MC   O

Plain Ales Innspiration

Take a walk past lovely flint and thatch houses, along the banks of a gurgling trout stream, past the church where Hardy's 'Far From The Madding Crowd' was filmed and up Breakheart Hill – and you'll be rewarded with one of the prettiest views in Dorset. If you're staying in one of the smart, modern bedrooms of the Greyhound Inn you can borrow fishing nets and torches to make the most of your exploration, while wellies are available for one and all. Sit over a south west ale in the rustic bar or make for the conservatory or linen-laid dining room with its sunken well. Dishes are modern and seasonal; you might find oxtail faggot with foie gras, followed by Gilthead bream with squid bolognaise or saddle of red deer with beetroot fondant.

Closing times
Open daily
Prices
Meals: a la carte £ 23/39
6 rooms: £ 80/100

Typical Dishes
Scallops, rocket pesto & pancetta
Confit lamb shoulder, shepherd's pie
Double chocolate brownie, vanilla bean ice cream

6 mi north of Dorchester by A 37. Parking.

44   **N** **Rose & Crown**

🛏️ **Trent, Sherborne, DT9 4SL**
Tel.: (01935)850776
Website: www.roseandcrowntrent.co.uk

📶 *VISA* 💳 **AE** **D**

🍺 **Wadworth's Ales & Butcombe Bitter**

This pretty part-thatched pub dates back to the 14C, when it was built to house the workers constructing the spire of the adjacent church. With its open-fired lounge and a bar complete with a grandfather clock, it has plenty of rustic charm, but on a sunny day you can't beat a spot in the conservatory, which opens out onto the garden. The young chef offers a plethora of menus: lunch sees light bites, platters and pub classics, while dinner consists of British dishes with ambitious modern twists; although there's also a simpler 'supper' menu. Bedrooms, in the old cow shed, have country-chic décor and terraces with views. What really makes this pub stand out, however, is the friendly service – nothing is ever too much trouble for the team.

Closing times
Open daily
Prices
Meals: a la carte £ 20/32
🛏️ **3 rooms:** £ 70/110

Typical Dishes
`Ham, egg & peas'
Slow-cooked lamb's neck with Provençale vegetables
Lemon millefeuille

🚗 *4 mi northwest of Sherborne signposted off B 3148. In village centre opposite church. Parking.*

Barnsley

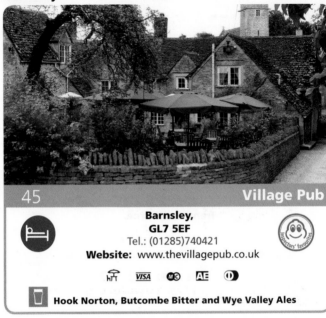

45 **Village Pub**

**Barnsley,
GL7 5EF**
Tel.: (01285)740421
Website: www.thevillagepub.co.uk

Hook Norton, Butcombe Bitter and Wye Valley Ales

One of the trailblazers of the gastro-revolution, the Village Pub ran out of steam somewhat in the late noughties but, now under the expert guidance of Calcot Manor, is once again on the up. With an interior straight out of any country homes magazine, it's got that cosy, open-fired, village pub vibe down to a tee. The daily changing menu exudes modern appeal; nibbles like sea trout blinis are an irresistible teaser, there are starters like homemade country terrine, mains like braised lamb hotpot and comforting desserts such as treacle tart. Meat comes from within a 30 mile radius, with charcuterie often from Highgrove and vegetables from partner Barnsley House just up the road. Bedrooms are individually styled; No. Six has a four-poster.

Closing times
Open daily
Prices
Meals: a la carte £ 24/36
6 rooms: £ 130/160

Typical Dishes
Baked goat's cheese with tomato salad
Braised lamb shoulder & pickled red cabbage
Rice pudding

 4 mi northeast of Cirencester on B 4425. Parking.

England • South West • Gloucestershire

46   **Horse & Groom**

**Bourton-on-the-Hill,
GL56 9AQ**
Tel.: (01386)700413
Website: www.horseandgroom.info

   VISA   **MC**

Goffs Jouster, Purity Mad Goose, Stroud Organic Ale and Prescott Hill Climb

Having grown up working in their parents' pub, brothers Will and Tom jumped at the chance to start their own venture when this listed Georgian building came on the market. Built from honey-coloured Cotswold stone, it's set on the main street of a pretty village high on the hillside, and features stylish bedrooms and lovely country views. Study the daily blackboard menu then order at the bar, but bear in mind it's a popular place, so you'll need to have booked or be willing to wait. The food is good value, fresh and flavoursome; expect the likes of parmesan and rosemary crumbed sardine fillets, pan-roast skate wing or braised blade of Dexter beef. Beers are passionately described and a thoughtful wine list offers plenty by the glass.

Closing times
Closed 25, 31 December and Sunday dinner
booking essential
Prices
Meals: a la carte £ 22/33
5 rooms: £ 80/170

Typical Dishes
Home-cured salt beef
Pork & chorizo meatballs
'Granny G's' toffee meringue

 2 mi west of Moreton-in-Marsh by A 44. Parking.

Cheltenham

47 **N** Royal Oak

**The Burgage,
Prestbury, Cheltenham, GL52 3DL**
Tel.: (01242)522344
Website: www.royal-oak-prestbury.co.uk

Timothy Taylor Landlord, Purity Mad Goose, Wye Valley HPA and Severn Valley Session

If you recognise the name of the pub's cricket team, it's because it's christened after batting legend Tom Graveney – who also happens to a be a previous landlord. Turn left and you'll discover a bar with a worn floor, a wood-burning stove and plenty of framed sporting prints; turn right and you'll find a dark wood furnished dining room with an open fire, red walls filled with an array of jugs and vessels, and several blackboards announcing the month's events. Lunch offers tasty, satisfying dishes such as kedgeree or duck hash with bubble and squeak, while dinner steps things up with the likes of goat's cheese and beetroot terrine or rump of lamb with baby onions. The large garden is a hit, with its patio heaters and 'Pavilion' function room.

Closing times
Closed 25-26 December
Prices
Meals: a la carte £ 23/30

Typical Dishes
Seared scallops with seafood gratin
Pan-fried duck breast with redcurrant sauce
Bakewell tart & custard

2 mi northeast towards racecourse by Prestbury Rd and New Barn Ln. On-street parking.

England • South West • Gloucestershire

48 | **Eight Bells Inn**

**Church St,
Chipping Campden, GL55 6JG**
Tel.: (01386)840371
Website: www.eightbellsinn.co.uk

VISA **MC**

Hook Norton Hooky Bitter, Purity Mad Goose, Wye Valley HPA and Goffs Jouster

If you're following the Cotswold Way Walk, this 14C pub, close to the historic high street of this old wool merchant's town, is well worth a visit. It originally accommodated the stonemasons working on St James's church, and later stored the eight bells from the church tower. Rebuilt in the 17C using the original stone and timbers, it has retained a good old community feel, welcoming drinkers and diners alike. The four neighbouring counties are represented behind the bar in their ale selection and they even offer scrumpy and perry on tap. Cooking is traditionally British – pies are the real thing, puddings are gloriously homemade and specials are just that, so arrive early if you want the full choice. Bedrooms combine character with mod cons.

Closing times
Closed 25 December
Prices
Meals: a la carte £ 25/37
7 rooms: £ 60/125

Typical Dishes
Home-smoked sea trout pâté
Lamb, garlic, rosemary & oregano burger
Banana & walnut sponge pudding

 In centre of town. Unrestricted parking on road.

England • South West • Gloucestershire

Cockleford

49 The Green Dragon Inn

**Cockleford,
GL53 9NW**
Tel.: (01242)870271
Website: www.green-dragon-inn.co.uk

**Sharp's Doom Bar, Butcombe Bitter, Hook Norton Hooky
and Otter Bitter**

This characterful stone pub can be found nestled in a peaceful country lane that borders the grounds of the Cowley Manor hotel. The surrounding area is serious walking territory, so at lunchtime you'll find plenty of ramblers tucking into hearty burgers or sausages – alongside others sampling some of the more unusual dishes, such as deep-fried pheasant and chestnut samosas or sea bass baked in a banana leaf. Huge open fireplaces are a focal point in two of the rooms and what better way to start the day than breakfast by a roaring fire? Keep an eye out for the carved mice that hide among the woodwork – the hallmark of Robert 'Mouseman' Thompson. Bedrooms are simple and modern; the St George suite is the best and boasts a super king sized bed.

Closing times
Closed dinner 25-26 December and 1 January
booking essential
Prices
Meals: a la carte £ 24/36

9 rooms: £ 70/175

Typical Dishes
Minted lamb kofta meatballs

Maple syrup glazed pork with sweet potato wedges

Sticky toffee pudding with butterscotch sauce

 5 mi south of Cheltenham by A 435. Parking.

50   **Ebrington Arms**

Ebrington,
GL55 6NH
Tel.: (01386)593223
Website: www.theebringtonarms.co.uk

 Prescott Hill Climb, Uley Bitter, Stroud Budding and North Cotswold Windrush

This 17C inn snuggles into a charming chocolate box village in the glorious Cotswold countryside; its beamed, flag-floored bar with blazing log fire providing the hub from which locals and visitors come and go, while owners Claire and Jim oversee proceedings with humour and grace. The smart dining rooms provide an intimate atmosphere for a meal, while the delightful sloping garden is the place to be in good weather. Monthly menus offer hearty, robust dishes like ham hock terrine, rump of lamb or roast breast of guinea fowl, with game to the fore in season and fresh fruit and veg supplied by village farms. Comfortable bedrooms come with countryside views and plenty of thoughtful extras; Room 3 has a four-poster and Room 4, a claw-foot bath.

Closing times
Open daily
Prices
Meals: a la carte £ 21/33
5 rooms: £ 120/150

Typical Dishes
Confit duck & foie gras croquettes

Pan-roasted lamb shank with Parmentier potatoes

Chocolate & raspberry tart

 2 mi east of Chipping Campden by B 4035. Parking.

Gretton

51 **Royal Oak**

Gretton,
GL54 5EP
Tel.: (01242)604999
Website: www.royaloakgretton.co.uk

 Brakspear Oxford Gold, Wye Valley HPA and Old Pie Factory Bitter

There's no doubt that the selling point of this pub is its large garden: aside from being a great place to sit and eat – especially in the barbecue season – it offers plenty to keep you occupied. Children are kept busy watching the chickens or in the play area, while those of more mature years can sit back and appreciate the chug of the trains passing by on the Gloucestershire-Warwickshire Steam Railway; sporty individuals can even don their shorts and make for the tennis court! Inside, there's a nice bar and two snug dining rooms but head for the conservatory to be rewarded with the best views. The experienced owner has good local connections when it comes to sourcing his produce and the dishes are honest and traditionally based.

Closing times
Open daily
Prices
Meals: a la carte £ 20/32

Typical Dishes
Pork belly with celeriac coleslaw & green apple purée
Lemon sole with fennel & salsa verde
Sticky toffee pudding with caramel sauce

 On the edge of the village, 2 mi northwest of Winchcombe. Parking

Lower Oddington

52   **Fox Inn**

**Lower Oddington,
GL56 0UR**
Tel.: (01451)870555
Website: www.foxinn.net

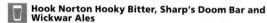

Hook Norton Hooky Bitter, Sharp's Doom Bar and Wickwar Ales

Lying at the heart of a peaceful Cotswold village is this creeper-clad, quintessentially English pub; personally run by a cheery owner. Its five rooms each have their own character; the Old Kitchen, with its solid stone walls and thick stone floor is the best. The lovely garden has plenty of seating for those long, sunny summer afternoons, while the wood burning stoves make cold winter days desirable. Wherever you sit, Mr Fox is never too far away, be he a wall-mounted head, a cartoon or a cuddly toy, as featured in the three comfy bedrooms. The daily changing menu keeps things fresh, with British classics like local steak or lemon curd syllabub alongside dishes of a more Mediterranean bent, like sliced Bayonne ham with celeriac remoulade.

Closing times
Open daily
booking essential
Prices
Meals: £ 17 and a la carte
£ 24/37

3 rooms: £ 75/110

Typical Dishes
Bath chap with scotch quail's eggs
Slow-cooked ox cheek & tongue
Baked Alaska

 3 mi east of Stow-on-the-Wold by A 436. Parking.

Lower Slaughter

53 Bar at Slaughters Country Inn

**Lower Slaughter,
GL54 2HS**
Tel.: (01451)822143
Website: www.theslaughtersinn.co.uk

🛋️ *VISA* **MC** **AE**

🍺 Marstons Ales

Its name might not conjure up the loveliest of thoughts but Lower Slaughter is actually one of the prettiest and most idyllic of the Cotswold villages. At its heart, beside the river, stands a fine light-stone hotel with cosy bedrooms – once a 'crammer' school for Eton College – and within it, you'll find a trio of rooms that make up the bar; chock-full of character, with wonky low ceilings and stone floors. To accompany the selection of juices and real ales, you'll find an appealing menu of wholesome dishes, offering everything from field mushrooms on toast to the pie of the day; while puddings stray from the norm with the likes of crème caramel with poached autumn fruits. Have afternoon tea on the beautiful terrace overlooking the gardens.

Closing times
Open daily
Prices
Meals: a la carte £ 21/43

🛏️ **26 rooms:** £ 80/265

Typical Dishes
Roast pigeon, morel dressing
Flat iron steak, watercress & house fries
Baked Alaska

🚗 1.75 mi northwest of Bourton-on-the-Water by A 429, in grounds of Slaughters Country Inn. Parking.

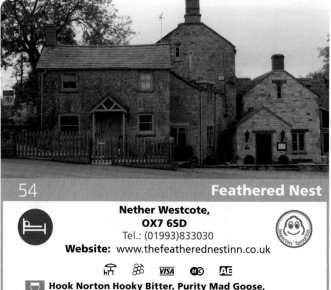

54 · **Feathered Nest**

**Nether Westcote,
OX7 6SD**
Tel.: (01993)833030
Website: www.thefeatherednestinn.co.uk

🛏 🍺 VISA MC AE

Hook Norton Hooky Bitter, Purity Mad Goose,
Ringwood Fortyniner and Prescott Hill Climb

Set in a small hamlet, this pub has really come into its own under its latest owners, who spent several years in Portugal gaining experience in the hospitality industry. It's the type of place that offers something for everyone, with a laid-back bar, a rustic snug, a casual conservatory and a formal dining room. Sit on quirky bar stools made from horse saddles and sample dishes such as smoked mackerel on toast, or head through to the elegant antique tables for more complex offerings such as black pudding and ham hock or wild venison with bacon and cabbage – not forgetting a list of over 200 wines. Once fully sated, make for a comfy bedroom complete with antique furnishings, quality linens and a smart roll-top bath. The views are superb.

Closing times
Closed 25 December
booking advisable

Prices
Meals: £ 20 (weekday lunch) and a la carte £ 39/52

🛏 **4 rooms:** £ 105/200

Typical Dishes
Red mullet with artichoke & vegetable broth
Grouse with cabbage, bacon & pickled celeriac
Passion fruit parfait

4.75 mi southeast of Stow-on-the-Wold by A 429 and A 424. Parking.

England • South West • Gloucestershire

Northleach

55 **Wheatsheaf Inn**

**West End,
Northleach, GL50 3EZ**
Tel.: (01451)860244
Website: www.cotswoldswheatsheaf.com

Hobsons Best, Otter Amber and Oxfordshire Churchill

The owners of this smartly refurbished, 17C coaching inn also own the old cottage next door, where you'll find simple, modern bedrooms with some quirky touches; some have baths in the rooms and most are furnished with interesting finds from French flea markets. The pub itself is similarly styled, with a stone-floored, open-fired bar in the centre and a dining room on either side – look out for the semi-private 'Poker Table' table in the alcove – and the tiered terrace provides plenty of extra space when the weather's good. The same menu is available throughout, offering classical dishes and something to suit every taste. If you fancy getting a bit more involved in local life, they hold a monthly book club and occasional jazz evenings.

Closing times
Open daily
Prices
Meals: £ 13
(weekday lunch)
and a la carte £ 25/84

14 rooms: £ 130/200

Typical Dishes
Twice-baked cheddar soufflé
Rump of Cotswold lamb
Warm treacle tart

 In centre of town. Parking.

56

Churchill Arms

Paxford,
GL55 6XH
Tel.: (01386)594000
Website: www.thechurchillarms.com

 Hook Norton Hooky Bitter, Otter Bitter and Wye Valley HPA

Despite a troubled past few years, this traditional Cotswold stone inn is on the up. Set in a picture postcard location, it boasts views over pretty stone houses, the nearby church and rolling open fields; as well as a charming interior with exposed beams, stone floors and a large wood burning stove. The enclosed rear garden is popular in summer, especially on a Thursday night, when you'll find the locals playing the old Oxfordshire game 'Aunt Sally'. Cooking displays a real mix of influences, ranging from unfussy pub classics such as faggots or apple crumble to more restaurant-style dishes like sea bass with crab beignets. Bedrooms are cosy with good country views but be aware that silence doesn't reign until the pub doors close.

Closing times
Closed 25 December
Prices
Meals: a la carte £ 23/36
4 rooms: £ 60/100

Typical Dishes
Seared scallop with Bury black pudding

Rump of lamb with artichoke, tomato & olive

Vanilla panna cotta with salted caramel

 3 mi east of Chipping Campden by B 4035. On-street parking.

England • South West • Gloucestershire

Piff's Elm

57 **Gloucester Old Spot**

**Tewkesbury Rd,
Piff's Elm, GL51 9SY**
Tel.: (01242)680321
Website: www.thegloucesteroldspot.co.uk

 VISA

 Purity Mad Goose, Timothy Taylor Landlord, Wye Valley Butty Bach and Butcombe Rarebreed

There's no denying that British pub names are a varied and interesting bunch. This little beauty used to be called the ubiquitous 'Swan' but now its moniker has more meaning, as its owners specialise in rare breed pork; enjoy such delights as crispy Old Spot pig's cheeks, rolled and boned belly pork, or pork T-bone steak. If you don't fancy pig, fret not: there are plenty of other tasty offerings on the seasonal menu, from a crusty lunchtime cob filled with roast lamb and mint & cucumber relish to pan-fried sea bass with seared squid and prawns. The atmosphere is cosy and relaxing and the staff, cheery and welcoming – although it was not ever thus: there used to be a hanging post in the garden where many miscreants met their demise.

Closing times
Open daily
Prices
Meals: £ 13 (lunch)
and a la carte £ 24/33

Typical Dishes
Wood pigeon with Stornoway black pudding
Old Spot pork with kidney, mustard sauce
Chocolate brownie tart, blackberry ice cream

4 mi northwest on A 4019, midway between Cheltenham and Tewkesbury. Parking.

58 | **The Bell**

**Sapperton,
GL7 6LE**
Tel.: (01285)760298
Website: www.bellsapperton.co.uk

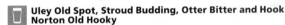

Uley Old Spot, Stroud Budding, Otter Bitter and Hook Norton Old Hooky

On a warm summer's day head for this pretty village, where, above the road, you can relax amongst the neatly-lawned gardens and paved terraces of this charming pub. Exposed stone and wooden beams feature throughout and colourful modern art adorns the walls. The wide-ranging menu offers a selection of comforting British dishes, with the odd international influence here and there. Lunch offers the likes of salads and steaks, dinner boasts some more substantial offerings and the blackboard specials consist mainly of seafood. Cooking is refined yet rustic and a glance at the back of the menu assures you of the local or regional origins of the produce used. Completing the package is an interesting wine list and friendly, well-paced service.

Closing times
Closed 25 December and Sunday dinner January-mid February

Prices
Meals: a la carte £ 18/40

Typical Dishes
Hand-picked crab with salmon skin biscuit
Trout, broad beans & Jersey Royals
Buttermilk & elderflower pudding

5 mi west of Cirencester by A 419. Parking.

Southrop

59 — **Swan**

**Southrop,
GL7 3NU**
Tel.: (01367)850205
Website: www.theswanatsouthrop.co.uk

VISA MC AE O

Sharp's Doom Bar and Stroud Organic Ale

There are few more charming Cotswold villages than Southrop and it's here you'll find the equally delightful Swan. This 17C Virginia creeper covered inn comes with characterful beamed dining rooms, open fires and assorted objets d'art. It also plays a key role in the community; you'll always find plenty of locals in the snug bar and there's even a skittle alley at the back. Cooking is firmly British based and features produce from the extensive gardens; you might find vegetable tempura with daikon salad or roast breast of guinea fowl with pea purée. Just down the road, they have three delightful cottages (min. 2 night stay), and if you're feeling particularly inspired after your meal, you can always enrol at the owners' nearby cookery school.

Closing times
Open daily
Prices
Meals: £ 17 (weekdays)
and a la carte £ 26/45

3 rooms: £ 120

Typical Dishes
Home-cured bresaola with toasted almonds

John Dory with lovage, lemon & green olive relish

Chocolate fondant

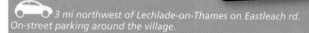

3 mi northwest of Lechlade-on-Thames on Eastleach rd. On-street parking around the village.

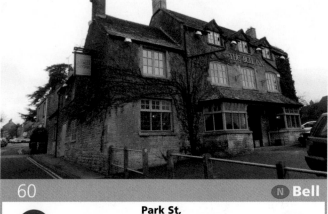

60 **Bell**

**Park St,
Stow-on-the-Wold, GL54 1AJ**
Tel.: (01451)870916
Website: www.thebellatstow.com

 VISA **MC**

Fuller's London Pride, Hook Norton Old Hooky and Cotswold Brewery Bell at Stow Bitter

If you're looking for a good base from which to explore the Cotswolds, then this smart inn could well fit the bill – although, as it offers pretty much everything under one roof, you may be reluctant to ever actually leave. It's been given a new lease of life by an experienced restaurateur and comes with the prerequisite open fires and stone floors. Staff are pleasant and welcoming and there's bags of choice on the menu – parfaits, terrines, pies, slow-cooked meats and mature steaks from the local butcher – along with a continually changing fish board. For dessert, the romantically inclined can share a chocolate fondue and get dipping with their strawberries, before retiring to one of the comfy bedrooms; ask for one with a country view.

Closing times
Closed 1 week May
Prices
Meals: a la carte £ 21/35
5 rooms: £ 70/120

Typical Dishes
Corned beef & caramelised onion hash

Roasted cod with broad beans & bacon

Treacle slice with marmalade mascarpone

In the centre of the town. Parking.

Tetbury

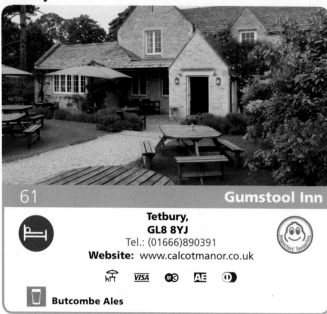

61 **Gumstool Inn**

**Tetbury,
GL8 8YJ**
Tel.: (01666)890391
Website: www.calcotmanor.co.uk

VISA MC AE O

Butcombe Ales

Set in the grounds of the stylish Calcot Manor Hotel, on a 700 year old estate, this converted farm out-building is now an attractive country pub. With wood-panelled walls, flag flooring and modern furnishings, it successfully combines classic country style with contemporary chic. It's warm and cosy in winter, bright and airy in the spring and the paved terrace is ideal in summer. The monthly menu is seasonal, rustic and hearty, but also accommodates for lighter appetites by offering some scaled-down main courses; while the extensive daily specials provide some interesting choices. Service is polite and friendly but make sure you are courteous in return – as in the past miscreants were placed on the local gumstool and ducked in the pond.

Closing times
Open daily
booking essential
Prices
Meals: a la carte £ 21/30
35 rooms: £ 252/385

Typical Dishes
Warm crab & leek tart
Beer-battered fish & chips
Vanilla panna cotta

 3.5 mi west of Tetbury on A 4135, in grounds of Calcot Manor Hotel. Parking.

62   **Trouble House**

**Cirencester Rd,
Tetbury, GL8 8SG**
Tel.: (01666)502206
Website: www.troublehousetetbury.co.uk

 Wadworth Henry's Original IPA, 6X and Horizon

The 'trouble' in the pub's name refers to rumours of old hauntings but no ghosts have been seen here for a while; well apart from Liam, the chef, who turned up in the kitchen again four years after leaving. The busy roadside setting isn't ideal and the exterior may not seem all that appealing but it's worth stopping off here for the warm welcome and tasty food. The interior has a shabby, homely style and there's a characterful, ultra-low beam in the bar; a place where the owners encourage the locals to come and drink. Dishes range from sardines on toast to more ambitious offerings like rib of beef roasted in hay for two to share; and the Salcombe crab gratin and duck fat chips are favourites. The daily specials usually feature fish.

Closing times
Closed 25 December, Sunday dinner and Monday

Prices
Meals: £ 12 (weekday lunch) and a la carte £ 20/39

Typical Dishes
Mussel chowder, aioli & croutons

Pot-roasted pork shoulder with tartiflette

Steamed lemon sponge, honey lavender ice cream

2 mi northeast on A 433. Parking.

Weston-sub-Edge

63 **Seagrave Arms**

**Friday St,
Weston-sub-Edge, GL55 6QH**
Tel.: (01386)840192
Website: www.seagravearms.co.uk

🏠 *VISA* **MC** **AE**

Hook Norton Old Hooky, Cotswold Shepherds Delight &
Cask, Bath Spa and North Cotswold Windrush

This part-Georgian coach house is located just a couple of miles out of Chipping Campden and has been attractively refurbished by its 'ex-London-restaurant' owners. It's pleasingly compact and cosy; be sure to grab a seat by the fire in the bar before moving on to one of the wood-furnished dining rooms. Service is polite and fairly formal – even in the bar drinks are brought to your table – and the food follows suit, with a concise menu of restaurant rather than pub-style dishes. Cooking is ambitious and complex, offering the likes of baked foie gras beignets, neck of lamb with sweetbreads, veal noisettes with salted fennel, and white chocolate parfait. Split between the pub and an outbuilding, bedrooms are stylish, modern and well-equipped.

Closing times
Closed first week January, Sunday dinner November-March and Monday

Prices
Meals: a la carte £ 25/37

🛏 **8 rooms:** £ 95/125

Typical Dishes
Home-smoked chicken
& ham hock terrine
Duo of Old Spot pork,
black pudding & apple
Sticky toffee pudding

 3 mi northwest of Chipping Campden. Parking

64 **Lion Inn**

**North St,
Winchcombe, GL54 5PS**
Tel.: (01242)603300
Website: www.thelioninnwinchcombe.co.uk

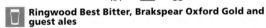 **Ringwood Best Bitter, Brakspear Oxford Gold and guest ales**

You'll find this bijou Cotswold stone inn in the heart of a historic town close to Sudeley Castle. It dates from the 15C and has been transformed from 'spit and sawdust' to 'country chic'. Turn left for the bar and snug – a great place for a pint and the papers – or right for the flagstone-floored restaurant. Here you'll find a concise, balanced menu where freshness is key. For lunch try a seafood or farmer's platter; at dinner the chef's classical culinary background is evident in dishes that have a certain sophistication and pleasingly complementary flavours. The staff take pride in their work and have the confidence of youth, so tend not to wilt under pressure. The stylish bedrooms come with biscuits and board games instead of TVs.

Closing times
Open daily
booking advisable

Prices
Meals: £ 12 (weekday lunch) and a la carte £ 26/39

6 rooms: £ 110/180

Typical Dishes
Treacle-cured salmon
Lemon sole with crayfish tails
Lemon posset with raspberries

In the town centre off the High St. Small pay and display public car park at the rear accessed via Chandos St.

Batcombe

65   Three Horseshoes Inn

**Batcombe,
BA4 6HE**
Tel.: (01749)850359
Website: www.thethreehorseshoesinn.com

VISA **MC** **AE**

Butcombe Bitter, Plain Ales Innocence, Moor Brewery Revival, Wild Beer Co Seasonal Best

Despite being hidden away in a small hamlet off the beaten track, this is a pub that's well-known in the area. Its enthusiastic owners know the score when it comes to running successful pubs and have injected a new lease of life into the place. The characterful interior has exposed beams and in winter, a fire roars in the inglenook. The three horseshoes in the pub's name refer back to a time when the building was a blacksmith's; the old forge would have been where the dining room now stands. The menu isn't large but covers all bases, from pork pies and pub classics to the likes of duck with orange sauce and pork belly with Savoy cabbage. Leave room for some of the excellent cheeses, then retire to one of the comfy, simply furnished bedrooms.

Closing times
Closed 25 December
Prices
Meals: a la carte £ 18/34
3 rooms: £ 60/85

Typical Dishes
Ham hock & leek terrine
Slow-roast belly of Somerset pork
Crème brûlée with shortbread

Midway between Castle Cary and Frome, signed off A 359; tucked away behind the church. Parking.

66 **Queens Arms**

**Corton Denham,
DT9 4LR**
Tel.: (01963)220317
Website: www.thequeensarms.com

 **Bath Barnsley Gem, Timothy Taylor Landlord,
Moor's Ales, Cheddar Ales and Dark Star Ales**

Aside from the enticing range of bar nibbles, The Queens Arms divides its food between two menus: on the first are classic pub dishes like a ploughman's or sausage and mash; on the other you'll find a more interesting array of dishes – perhaps confit duck leg, foie gras and Puy lentil terrine or bream en papillote with chilli, basil, coriander and udon noodles. There's an appealing selection of apple juices and ciders and they also have a great range of whiskies and beers; wine and beer pairings are suggested and the pub also holds regular regional beer festivals. With open fires and a hotchpotch of tables including a glass-topped cartwheel, there's a relaxed, bohemian feel – and service follows suit. Bedrooms are modern, with good facilities.

Closing times
Open daily
booking advisable
Prices
Meals: a la carte £ 27/35
8 rooms: £ 80/120

Typical Dishes
Brown crab crème brûlée

Seared pork fillet & smoked belly

Dark chocolate torte with raspberry sorbet

3 mi north of Sherborne by B 3145 and minor road west.
Parking.

451

Dulverton

67

Woods

**4 Banks Sq,
Dulverton, TA22 9BU**
Tel.: (01398)324007
Website: www.woodsdulverton.co.uk

 St Austell Dartmoor and Red Rock Devon Coast

It doesn't look much like a pub – in fact, with its shop window still in situ, it looks more like the bakery it once was – but its cosy, hugely characterful interior soon allays any doubts: a fire blazes in the hearth, locals prop up the bar and wooden beams abound, while the walls are lined with rustic oddments ranging from agricultural implements to hunting paraphernalia and even a pair of antlers. Carefully prepared, tasty dishes offer more than the usual pub fare: you might find seared steak or pancetta and black pudding salad at lunch, and the likes of scallops with cauliflower purée or chicken ballotine with wild garlic mousse at dinner. Provenance is taken seriously here, with quality local produce including meat from the owner's farm.

Closing times
Closed dinner 26 December and 1 January
Prices
Meals: a la carte £ 22/34

Typical Dishes
Chicken liver parfait & red onion jam
Belly pork with smoked champ
Chocolate mousse

 In the centre of the town. Pay and display parking close by.

68 Lord Poulett Arms

**High St,
Hinton St George, TA17 8SE**
Tel.: (01460)73149
Website: www.lordpoulettarms.com

 VISA **MC**

Otter Ale, Branscombe Vale Branoc and Cotleigh Tawny Owl

The Lord Poulett offers everything you could possibly want from a pub. A picture perfect, lavender-framed terrace overlooks a boules pitch to a wild, untamed secret garden, while inside lovely old tables and squashy armchairs are set in a detailed country interior filled with hops and glowing candles. The kitchen creates a traditional British menu with a modern edge and local produce abounds; you might find ham hock terrine with cider and apple jelly or Lyme bay crab fritters with chilli apple compote. Lunch offers some lighter dishes, the daily specials are a feature and to finish, you'll find West Country cheeses and tempting desserts. Bedrooms are smart and stylish: two boast feature baths and they all have Roberts radios instead of TVs.

Closing times
Closed 25-26 December and 1 January

Prices
Meals: a la carte £ 21/38

4 rooms: £ 60/95

Typical Dishes
Dorset Blue Vinny cheesecake
Cider battered fish & chips
Chocolate & salted caramel tart

3 mi northwest of Crewkerne signposted off A 356. Free parking on the high street.

Holcombe

69 **Holcombe Inn**

**Stratton Rd,
Holcombe, BA3 5EB**
Tel.: (01761)232478
Website: www.holcombeinn.co.uk

VISA MC

Otter Ale and Bath Ales Gem

Set deep in the heart of the Somerset countryside, on the edge of a small village, the 17C Holcombe Inn provides all the charm you'd expect of a building its age, with exposed beams, flag floors and cosy open fires. Come summer, the large garden with its lovely southerly aspect makes a great place to sit and as you unwind, you feel as if you really have escaped to the middle of nowhere. Satisfyingly, this is a place that has a good reputation for its food too, with menus offering quite a range of dishes, from good old pub classics like homemade pie of the day to more sophisticated offerings like ballotine of local chicken or pork belly with black pudding. Bedrooms are luxuriously appointed and some boast views over Downside Abbey.

Closing times
Open daily
Prices
Meals: a la carte £ 19/32
🛏 **7 rooms:** £ 65/110

Typical Dishes
Mackerel with beetroot & horseradish

Loin of rabbit with confit leg

Baked Alaska with raspberries

Between Radstock and Shepton Mallet off the A 367. On the western edge of the village on Stratton-on-the-Fosse rd. Parking.

70   **Old Inn**

Holton,
BA9 8AR
Tel.: (01963)32002
Website: www.theoldinnholton.co.uk

 Wessex Brewery, Potters and Kilmington Best

The owner of nearby Clinger Farm always fancied being a chef but never realised his dream. Instead, he bought this 400 year old village pub, added a large, modern restaurant and now delights in seeing the kitchen make good use of his own farm produce, be it Gloucester Old Spot, lamb, corn-fed chicken, or apples and pears; you can even buy his eggs as you leave. The menu is kept short and to the point and the star of the show is the Josper grill, used to chargrill the assorted cuts of meat, as well as the fish from the Brixham day boats. Portions are not for the fainthearted and dishes deliver big, gutsy flavours. The wine list is decidedly Old World, focuses on a limited number of growers and offers a decent selection by the glass.

Closing times
Closed Sunday dinner
Prices
Meals: a la carte £ 20/36

Typical Dishes
Scottish salmon with dill cream
Fillet of beef with chips
Plum crumble tart

Just off the A 303 to the west of Wincanton on A 357. Parking.

Long Ashton

71   **Bird in Hand**

**17 Weston Rd,
Long Ashton, BS41 9LA**
Tel.: (01275)395222
Website: www.bird-in-hand.co.uk

 St Austell Tribute, Boxsteam Piston Broke, Bath Ales Gem and various Guest Ales

When the owner of the Pump House pub found out his own local was going to close, he did what any panicking regular would like to do – and bought the place! This tiny country pub – a complete contrast to his first venture – boasts slightly wacky décor, with an antelope's head and walls covered with pages from Mrs Beeton's Book of Household Management. Lunchtimes are usually fairly quiet, so they offer a concise menu of classics such as tomatoes on toast or home-baked ham and local eggs; while dinner adds more interesting dishes like onglet steak with oxtail and bone marrow or roast fillet, faggot and belly of suckling lamb. Cooking is tasty, carefully executed and keeps things simple, letting the British ingredients speak for themselves.

Closing times
Closed 25 December
booking essential at dinner
Prices
Meals: a la carte £ 20/30

Typical Dishes
Game Terrine
Wild Devon river trout, cucumber & sorrel
Chocolate cake & salted caramel

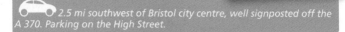

2.5 mi southwest of Bristol city centre, well signposted off the A 370. Parking on the High Street.

72

Devonshire Arms

**Long Sutton,
TA10 9LP**
Tel.: (01458)241271
Website: www.thedevonshirearms.com

VISA MC

Moor Beers, Otter Brewery Ales, Hopback Crop Circle and Cheddar Ales Potholer

This spacious Grade II listed hunting lodge is set right on the village green and has a contemporary interior, with a relaxing, open-plan bar and more formal dining room. The chef is Russian and his menu, appealingly eclectic, with plenty of fish and locally sourced meats. It has a French bias but includes influences from all over Europe, so expect to see words like bresaola, brûlée, clafoutis and chorizo, as you whet your appetite with nibbles like fresh olives or pistachios. Main dishes could include local chicken livers, pollock with pan-fried squid or veal burger with hand-cut chips, while dessert might mean homemade ice cream or dark chocolate fondant. The extremely comfortable bedrooms boast excellent quality linen and toiletries.

Closing times
Closed 25-26 December and 1 January
Prices
Meals: a la carte £ 24/42
🛏 **9 rooms:** £ 80/135

Typical Dishes
Pigeon breast with pancetta
Gilthead bream with wild garlic gnocchi
Treacle tart with vanilla ice cream

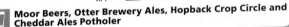
4 mi east of Langport by A 372. Parking.

Tarr Steps

73 **Tarr Farm Inn**

Tarr Steps,
TA22 9PY
Tel.: (01643)851507
Website: www.tarrfarm.co.uk

VISA

Exmoor Ale and St Austell Tribute & Proper Job

Arrive on the wrong side of the river and you might get a shock – you'll be able to see the pub but, unless you have a 4x4, contending with the water isn't an option. That said, if you've travelled by foot then there's no better way to approach than by crossing the 17 spans of the charming 1000 BC, stone-slab clapper bridge. The setting is nothing short of idyllic: birds sing in the trees and cool, clear water gurgles under the bridge. If the sun's out, head for the garden for a spot of afternoon tea; if the rain's lashing down, make for the narrow, beamed bar or the cosy restaurant. Menus provide plenty of choice, from potted shrimps and sharing boards through to rack of Exmoor lamb or Devon Ruby steak. Bedrooms are comfy and well-equipped.

Closing times
Closed 1-10 February
Prices
Meals: a la carte £ 20/39
9 rooms: £ 75/150

Typical Dishes
Scallops with apple & walnut salad
Duck breast, fondant potato, honey & thyme sauce
Pineapple soufflé

 Signed off B 3223 Dulverton to Exford road. Parking.

Blue Ball Inn

74

**Triscombe,
TA4 3HE**
Tel.: (01984)618242
Website: www.blueballinn.info

Quantock Brewery Rorke's Drift and Exmoor Stag

This characterful thatched former barn is located in the beautiful Quantock Hills; it dates from the 15C and boasts a cosy, rustic feel, with exposed rafters, open fires, a tartan carpet and stags' heads. Lunchtime sandwiches, 'posh' ploughman's and classics like guinea fowl and mushroom pie or sausage and mash provide fuel for passing walkers; dinner sees well-presented, modern dishes with a touch of originality – perhaps linguine with hare bolognese or pork cutlet with braised cheek – and the bacon and black pudding scotch egg is a favourite at either sitting. Behind the pub, you'll find a lovely tiered garden and a skittle alley, while the pretty annexe contains three comfortable, stylish bedrooms named 'Pheasant', 'Hind' and 'Stag'.

Closing times
Closed 25-26 December,
dinner 1 January, Monday
and Sunday dinner in
autumn and winter

Prices
Meals: a la carte £ 26/38

🛏 **3 rooms:** £ 55/110

Typical Dishes
Black pudding & bacon
scotch egg
Pork confit and loin
with tartiflette
Duck egg custard tart

 Between Taunton and Williton off the A 358. Parking.

Wedmore

75

Swan

**Cheddar Rd,
Wedmore, BS28 4EQ**
Tel.: (01934)710337
Website: www.theswanwedmore.com

VISA MC

Bath Ales Gem, Otter Bitter and Cheddar Ales Potholer

If good British ingredients that match the seasons and unfussy, flavoursome dishes are your thing, then this 18C coaching inn is the place for you. The chef previously worked at River Cottage and his time there shows, so expect the likes of smoked mackerel pâté or ham, cheddar and parsley croquettes, followed by braised pheasant with juniper and thyme or short rib of beef with Swan cured bacon and January King cabbage. Inside it's spacious and airy: there's a large bar with bare floorboards and simple wooden tables; a cosy little area with rugs and leather furniture; and, past the open kitchen and display of home-baked breads, a comfortable dining room – be sure to book, as it's a rightly popular place. Stylish bedrooms complete the picture.

Closing times
Closed 25 December and Sunday dinner
booking essential
Prices
Meals: a la carte £ 22/38
6 rooms: £ 85/120

Typical Dishes
Home-cured bresaola with marinated kohlrabi
Pan-fried hake with salsa verde & beetroot
Apple & almond cake

 In the centre of the town. Parking.

England • South West • Somerset

76

Rising Sun Inn

**West Bagborough,
TA4 3EF**
Tel.: (01823)432575
Website: www.risingsuninn.info

 Exmoor Ale, Butcombe and St Austell Proper Job

Sitting on the side of a hill in the Quantocks, the Rising Sun Inn looks like a traditional country pub. Inside however, you'll discover that although there's the odd beam and a pleasing mix of old tables and chairs, it's also pretty modern, with smart slate floors and bright artwork helping to keep the mood light. It's not a big place but there are several rooms in which to sit: the piano room – complete with pianola; the snug, hidden away at the back; the first floor gallery; or, of course, the bar. Menus offer plenty of choice, featuring typical pub-style light bites and more sophisticated classics, from calves' liver and bacon to pork belly with cider sauce or rack of lamb with mint jus. Upstairs, two contemporary bedrooms offer great views.

Closing times
Closed 25 December

Prices
Meals: a la carte £ 20/36

🛏 **2 rooms:** £ 65

Typical Dishes
Baked feta cheese with dates
Pork belly with caramelised apple & cider jus
Sticky toffee pudding

 10.5 mi northwest of Taunton, off A 358. On-street parking

West Pennard

77 **Apple Tree Inn**

**West Pennard,
BA6 8ND**
Tel.: (01749)890060
Website: www.appletreeglastonbury.co.uk

Exmoor Gold and Hound Dog, Palmers Copper Ale and Butcombe Bitter

Many speed past this unassuming pub without giving it a second glance but, if you're after a bite to eat, you'd do well to stop here. The blackboards list sandwiches, good old pub classics and tasty homemade snacks such as pork scratchings, while the main menu offers accomplished braises and confits that are packed with flavour, alongside a few more innovative dishes; maybe brûléed wild mushroom parfait or poached pear with blue cheese and walnut ice cream. It's a small but cosy place, with beams, flagged floors and a skittle alley, and is run by a talented young couple. You'll find the locals relaxing on the sofas, while the diners gravitate towards the open fire or the smallest of the dining rooms with its characterful thatched bar.

Closing times
Closed 7-14 January,
25 December and Monday
except bank holiday lunch

Prices
Meals: £ 12/20 and a la carte
£ 21/34

Typical Dishes
Cornish squid
with garlic mayonnaise
Chicken in red wine
with wild mushrooms
Vanilla bean panna
cotta

 4.5 mi east of Glastonbury on A 361. Parking.

78 — Royal Oak Inn

**Halse Ln,
Winsford, TA24 7JE**
Tel.: (01643)851455
Website: www.royaloakexmoor.co.uk

 Exmoor Fox, Gold and Antler

Mind the pheasants as you navigate the winding lanes of Exmoor towards this charming little village where, beside the ford, you'll find a delightful 12C former farmhouse and dairy. Turn left into the dining room or right, through the rustic bar – with its small gathering of locals and their dogs – into the wood-furnished dining area. There's both a bar and restaurant menu, although you can choose from either wherever you sit, as well as from the specials chalked on a board above the fireplace. Dishes are tasty and satisfying, offering tarts and parfaits, followed by well-executed pub and British classics, with tempting desserts to finish. Spacious, country bedrooms come with huge bathrooms and rain showers; most have four-poster beds.

Closing times
Open daily
Prices
Meals: a la carte £ 22/35
8 rooms: £ 75/140

Typical Dishes
Deep-fried Somerset brie with rhubarb relish
Cornish lobster & crayfish risotto
White chocolate panna cotta

 5 mi north of Dulverton off B 3223. Parking.

Bishopstone

79

Royal Oak

**Cues Ln,
Bishopstone, SN6 8PP**
Tel.: (01793)790481
Website: www.royaloakbishopstone.co.uk

Arkell's Wiltshire Gold and Donnington BB

At the rurally set Royal Oak, where the décor is rustic and open fires create a relaxing feel, they assert that 'great food starts off with good farming' – and they're not wrong. Of course, it helps that the nearby organic farm which supplies it is owned by Helen Browning, who also owns the pub. The menu changes twice daily, according to which ingredients are fresh, local and in season: these might include berries or nettles foraged from the local hedgerows; veal, pork or beef from the farm; and vegetables provided by local growers in exchange for dinner vouchers. Less local are ingredients like cannellini beans and unfiltered extra virgin olive oil; these come from the Abruzzo region of Italy, courtesy of the chef, who has a house there.

Closing times
Open daily
Prices
Meals: a la carte £ 23/40

Typical Dishes
Country pork terrine
Beef & mushroom pie
Lemon posset

 6 mi east of Swindon on B 4057. Parking.

80

The Northey

**Bath Rd,
Box, SN13 8AE**
Tel.: (01225)742333
Website: www.ohhcompany.co.uk

Wadworth Ales

Having passed from one generation of Warburtons to the next, this traditional-looking coaching inn is a real family affair. It's a sizeable place, with an open-plan interior and fairly modern styling: the bar boasting low level seating and vivid artwork; the large rear dining room, heavy wooden furniture and a more formal feel. The chef has extensive experience countrywide, so you can rest assured that the appealing monthly menus are as good as they sound. Dishes are unfussy, seasonal and British, and everything is made on the premises, including the bread. There are tasty local steaks and, with seafood arriving fresh from Cornwall, the fish dishes – particularly the mussels – are a strength. Smart, contemporary bedrooms have bathrooms to match.

Closing times
Closed 25-26 December
Prices
Meals: a la carte £ 23/49
5 rooms: £ 89/160

Typical Dishes
Pan-fried scallops with lemon risotto

Calves' liver & bacon with honey-roast carrots

Steamed lemon pudding

 4.75 mi northeast of Bath on A 4. Parking.

Broughton Gifford

81

The Fox

**The Street,
Broughton Gifford, SN12 8PN**
Tel.: (01225)782949
Website: www.thefox-broughtongifford.co.uk

Bath Ales Gem, Otter Bitter, Fuller's London Pride and Butcombe Bitter

Raising the profile of this pub, both locally and farther afield, has been a labour of love for its young owner, Alex. He's given it one of those clever refurbishments that cost a lot of money but make everything look largely unchanged. It lies at the heart of the community and sponsors the local football team. There's always a great choice of beer on draught but the real surprise is out back: there are raised beds of salad leaves, rhubarb, herbs and fruits, and behind these, you'll find chickens and a pigsty. In a move towards self-sufficiency, the kitchen also makes its own sausages and dries its own meat for the excellent charcuterie dishes. And what does Alex do on his day off? He goes foraging for more local produce.

Closing times
Closed 26-27 December, 1-2 January and Sunday dinner

Prices
Meals: £ 16 (lunch) and a la carte £ 25/44

Typical Dishes
Pork belly croquettes
Fillet of cod, peas, samphire & onions
Rum panna cotta & rhubarb jelly

 Between Bradford-on-Avon and Melksham off B 3107. Parking.

82

Ship Inn

**Burcombe Ln,
Burcombe, SP2 0EJ**
Tel.: (01722)743182
Website: www.theshipburcombe.co.uk

 VISA **MC** **AE**

 Wadworth 6X, Butcombe Bitter and Ringwood Best Bitter

If you find yourself anywhere near the delightful village of Burcombe on a sunny summer's day, be sure to make your way to this charming 17C pub. Its riverside garden is just the place to linger over a leisurely lunch, with only the wind in the trees and the quack of the local ducks to disturb the silence. If you arrived too late to nab a table, then head inside; with its open fire, low oak beams and chunky wood furniture, the pub itself is an equally enchanting place to dine. The seasonal menu offers honest portions of traditional dishes; perhaps pan-fried pigeon breast, homemade fishcakes, pot-roasted lamb shank or smoked fish kedgeree. 'Lunchtime bites' offer a lighter alternative and the twice-daily changing specials board adds interest.

Closing times
Closed 25 December

Prices
Meals: a la carte £ 23/38

Typical Dishes
Smoked haddock & leek gratin

Fishcakes with tartare sauce

Baked vanilla cheesecake

5.25 mi west of Salisbury by A 36 off A 30. Parking.

Compton Bassett

83 **White Horse Inn**

**Compton Bassett,
SN11 8RG**
Tel.: (01249)813118
Website: www.whitehorse-comptonbassett.co.uk

**Bath Ales Gem, Wadworth 6X, Sharp's Doom Bar,
Timothy Taylor Landlord**

The White Horse Inn dates back to 1780 and is named after the hillside carving at nearby Cherhill Down. The cosy bar with its wood burning stove and jolly atmosphere is where you'll find the regulars, while diners head for the more formal room next door. It's the kind of place that offers genuine hospitality, with Tara's bubbly personality and Danny's all-encompassing menu helping to draw customers from far and wide. You might find a croque monsieur or homemade cheeseburger at lunchtime, alongside more ambitious dishes on the à la carte, maybe salmon gravadlax, Blue Vinny soufflé, roast monkfish or loin of venison from their own farm. Head outside, beyond the large garden and skittle alley, and you'll find simple, well-priced bedrooms.

Closing times
Closed 2-9 January, Sunday dinner and Monday
Prices
Meals: a la carte £ 21/39
8 rooms: £ 65/105

Typical Dishes
Home-smoked salmon with horseradish
Fillet of local venison
Dark chocolate & Grand Marnier mousse

 4 mi east of Calne signposted off A 4. Parking.

84

Methuen Arms

**2 High St,
Corsham, SN13 0HB**
Tel.: (01249)717060
Website: www.themethuenarms.com

VISA **MC** **AE**

Butcombe Bitter, Wadworth 6X, Otter Amber Ale,
St Austell Proper Job and Moles Landlord

This 17C coaching inn stands in the heart of an attractive little town and is named after the family who own nearby Corsham Court. It's run by experienced owners Martin and Debbie, who place great emphasis on the quality of their food. You can eat anywhere: in the 'Little Room' by the bar; in the 'Nott Room' with its flagged floor and open fire; or in the characterful restaurant with its penny farthing and exposed stone walls. Lunch sees everything from a grilled aubergine and melted cheese sandwich to deep-fried squid with harissa mayonnaise, while dinner steps things up a gear with the likes of local venison with beetroot and spelt risotto or herb-crusted Cornish brill with leeks, chorizo and mussels. Comfy, boutique-style bedrooms await.

Closing times
Open daily
Prices
Meals: £ 16/25
and a la carte £ 25/48

🛏 **21 rooms:** £ 80/180

Typical Dishes
Crispy belly pork & black pudding

Pot-roasted beef cheek with spelt & beetroot

Poached Yorkshire rhubarb with toasted pistachios

 In the centre of the town. Parking.

Cricklade

85 **Red Lion**

**74 High St,
Cricklade, SN6 6DD**
Tel.: (01793)750776
Website: www.theredlioncricklade.co.uk

🛏

☂ **VISA** Ⓜ©

🍺 **Butcombe Bitter, Wadworth 6X and Hop Kettle Ales**

Just off the Thames path, you'll find this traditional 17C inn. With a cosy, low-beamed interior crammed full of bric-a-brac, it looks like a proper pub; and pleasingly, it adopts a good old English attitude too. The bar serves 4 regular and 5 guest ales, as well as 30 speciality bottled beers, which can be sampled while tucking into a pub classic, dog at feet. Next door is a small but airy stone-walled dining room boasting a beautiful carved slab. Here you'll find classical dishes such as oysters, venison stew and treacle tart, with beer recommendations for every dish. Produce is fresh and extremely local – and if you're down a pound or two, they'll accept some home-grown fruit or veg as payment. Comfy, modern bedrooms are in the old stables.

Closing times
Open daily
Prices
Meals: a la carte £ 19/37

🛏 **5 rooms:** £ 80

Typical Dishes
Brawn & caper terrine
Pan-fried
mullet, squid ink,
mussels & cider
Rhubarb & pistachio
Eton mess

🚗 At the eastern end of the High St. Unrestricted parking on the High St.

86 **Bath Arms**

**Clay St,
Crockerton, BA12 8AJ**
Tel.: (01985)212262
Website: www.batharmscrockerton.co.uk

 Hobdens Crockerton Classic and Potters Ale

The Bath Arms offers a warm welcome, open fires, plenty of country appeal, and a wealth of outdoor space. It's part of the Longleat Estate and is run with a passion by local boy Dean Carr, who returned from his culinary experiences in the Big Smoke to put some love back into this community pub. The menus offer something for everyone, from filled baguettes or shepherd's pie to dishes such as fillet of red mullet with fennel salad or slow-braised rabbit with polenta and bacon; not forgetting favourites like the fishcakes or the now legendary sticky beef with braised red cabbage. Traditional desserts like tarte Tatin round things off nicely – and there are two ultra-spacious, contemporary bedrooms should you wish to stay the night.

Closing times
Closed dinner
25-26 December

Prices
Meals: a la carte £ 18/29

2 rooms: £ 80/110

Typical Dishes
Crab mayonnaise with crostini
Sticky beef with braised red cabbage
Lemon curd cheesecake

2 mi south of Warminster just off A 350 on Shearwater rd. Parking.

Crudwell

87   **Potting Shed Pub**

**The Street,
Crudwell, SN16 9EW**
Tel.: (01666)577833
Website: www.thepottingshedpub.com

Timothy Taylor Landlord, Bath Ales Gem and Butcombe Gold

Despite its contemporary name and décor, the Potting Shed is very much a proper pub, where locals gather for a pint and a chat. Situated opposite its sister establishment, the Rectory Hotel, it consists of five spacious, light-filled rooms, with open fires and a relaxing feel. The pub's large gardens provide it with an abundance of fresh, seasonal herbs and vegetables – and the horticultural theme continues inside, with trowel door knobs, wheelbarrow lights and fork and spade pump handles. Monthly changing menus offer fresh, satisfying dishes like local trout, wild rabbit fettuccine and apple and blackberry crumble. Lollipops on the bar ensure that the kids are kept happy, while dog biscuits do the same for your four-legged friends.

Closing times
Open daily
Prices
Meals: a la carte £ 23/36

Typical Dishes
Pan-fried scallops with minted pea purée
Herb-crusted rack of lamb
Coconut pavlova with passion fruit sorbet

 4 mi north of Malmesbury by A 429. Parking.

88 **The Forester**

**Lower St,
Donhead St Andrew, SP7 9EE**
Tel.: (01747)828038
Website: www.theforesterdonheadstandrew.co.uk

 Butcombe Bitter and Otter Best Bitter

England • South West • Wiltshire

Hidden down narrow lanes in a delightful Wiltshire village, this 13C thatched pub has a gloriously rustic feel. Exposed stone walls feature throughout and vast open fires ensure that it's always cosy. There's a lovely bar crammed with cookery books, and two main dining areas – one in a cleverly added extension that's perfectly in keeping. The experienced owners take a very hands-on approach and, along with the chef, are passionate about using good country ingredients, with meats coming from local farms and estates and fish from the Brixham day boats. Menus change with the seasons and there's always a daily 3 course set selection dedicated to seafood. Dishes are well-prepared and flavoursome, with a classical country base and a refined edge.

Closing times
Closed Sunday dinner

Prices
Meals: £ 17 (weekdays) and a la carte £ 23/36

Typical Dishes
Carpaccio of Aberdeen Angus
Trio of Wiltshire rabbit with spinach
Iced mojito parfait

5 mi east of Shaftesbury by A 30. Parking.

East Chisenbury

89 Red Lion Freehouse

**East Chisenbury,
SN9 6AQ**
Tel.: (01980)671124
Website: www.redlionfreehouse.com

[VISA] [MC] [◐]

Keystone, Ramsbury, Stonehenge and Plain Ales

Enthusiastically run, cosy, and proudly impervious to the trend for designer pubs, the Red Lion is a charming thatched property with a pretty little garden, in a tiny hamlet on the edge of Salisbury Plain. Seven simple wooden tables are set around the bar, a wood burner crouches in the inglenook and exposed beams lend a reassuringly solid air. The daily à la carte features down-to-earth dishes that are stunning in their simplicity, precisely composed and packed with flavour; this might include wild boar terrine, coq au vin or roast partridge. The resident Springer Spaniel often welcomes you with a wag of his tail and service is equally convivial. Set opposite, smart, well-equipped bedrooms come with private terraces; most have river views.

Closing times
Open daily
booking advisable
Prices
Meals: a la carte £ 27/42
🛏 **5 rooms:** £ 100/200

Typical Dishes
Chicken liver pâté with Madeira jelly

Cod with mussels, Bombay potatoes and curry velouté

Beer genoese with honeyed Guinness cream

 The village is between Pewsey and Amesbury off the A 345. Parking.

90

Three Daggers

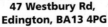

**47 Westbury Rd,
Edington, BA13 4PG**
Tel.: (01380)830940
Website: www.threedaggers.co.uk

🏝 *VISA* 💳

🍺 **Three Daggers Dagger Ale and Dagger Edge**

Originally named after the local landowners, this pub has been refurbished and reborn as the 'Three Daggers' – a reference to the insignia on the Paulet family's coat of arms. It's an attractive place, with a large conservatory overlooking the garden, and the original beams and flagstones are still in place, so the character quotient remains high. When it comes to the food, there's something for everyone: a homemade soup, the 'pie of the day' or a local lamb burger; and the sharing plates – the Huntsman's and the Fisherman's – prove extremely popular. They have their own farm shop and brew their own beers too, so are pretty self-sufficient. Charming bedrooms feature bespoke oak furnishings and you're given free reign of the farmhouse kitchen.

Closing times
Open daily
Prices
Meals: £ 12 (lunch)
and a la carte £ 21/38

🛏 **3 rooms:** £ 80/150

Typical Dishes
Wild mushrooms with garlic & thyme
Fish pie
Sticky toffee pudding

 4 mi east of Westbury on B 3098. Parking.

Foxham

91   **Ⓝ Foxham Inn**

**Foxham,
SN15 4NQ**
Tel.: (01249)740665
Website: www.thefoxhaminn.co.uk

⛱ **VISA** **ⓂⒸ**

🍺 **Butcombe Bitter and Ramsbury Kennet Valley**

Located in a sleepy Wiltshire village, the family-run Foxham Inn is a secret that the locals have clearly been trying to keep to themselves. For pleasant views over the fields and paddocks, bag a seat on the semi-covered terrace; on colder days, make for the cosy bar with its scrubbed pine tables, old church pews and wood burning stove, or if you fancy some live cooking action, head through to the airy extension, where you can look into the kitchen. The menu offers a good range of dishes at a uniform price for each course, along with sandwiches and paninis at lunch. Everything from the condiments to the ice creams is homemade and flavours are clear and defined. The regular gourmet nights are a hit and two homely bedrooms complete the picture.

Closing times
Closed 2 weeks early January and Monday
booking advisable

Prices
Meals: a la carte £ 24/28

🛏 **2 rooms:** £ 65

Typical Dishes
Crispy quail's eggs, black pudding & pickled mushrooms
Roast pigeon with rabbit
Trio of chocolate

7 mi northeast of Chippenham signposted off B 4069 in centre of village. Parking.

92

Angel Inn

**High St,
Heytesbury, BA12 0ED**
Tel.: (01985)840330
Website: www.theangelheytesbury.co.uk

Wadworth 6X and Ringwood Best

This pretty looking, family-run pub has a typically English feel; its spacious bar is home to wood fires and comfy sofas and the beamed dining room is packed with locals discussing the shoot, dogs by their sides. Two further dining areas have a more formal feel, with exposed brickwork and open fires adding an air of rusticity. Menus change as and when, depending on what produce is freshly available; maybe English parsnip and sherry soup or wild duck, pheasant and rabbit terrine to start, followed by braised lamb's liver or roasted pork belly in cider. The sharing boards are firm favourites, and simple pub classics might include homemade faggots and the ever-popular steak and kidney pie. Bedrooms are currently too modest to recommend.

Closing times
Open daily
Prices
Meals: a la carte £ 19/38

Typical Dishes
Scallop, bacon & gruyère gratin
Pork fillet Wellington
Caramel parfait

4 mi southeast of Warminster on A 36. Parking.

Horningsham

93 Bath Arms

**Longleat,
Horningsham, BA12 7LY**
Tel.: (01985)844308
Website: www.batharms.co.uk

VISA M©

Wessex Horningsham Pride and Golden Apostle

This pub is found within the Longleat Estate and boasts a rustic, dog-friendly bar with an open fireplace, a grand main dining room and a delightful terrace – witness to some impressive sunsets. Appealing menus offer everything from light dishes, salads and sandwiches through to main courses like stuffed saddle of rabbit or braised shoulder of lamb. The sharing plate is popular and the fishcakes are a veritable institution. Much of the produce comes from the estate (game, specialist cheeses and even flavoured organic vodkas) and they rear pigs and even have their own vegetable garden. Staff clearly enjoy their work and are willing to go the extra mile for their customers. Quirky, individually themed bedrooms offer good levels of comfort.

Closing times
Open daily
Prices
Meals: a la carte £ 29/37

🛏 **16 rooms:** £ 75/185

Typical Dishes
Oyster beignets with cucumber raita
Creedy Carver duck breast with wild mushrooms
Dark chocolate mousse

3 mi southwest of Warminster by A 362 and minor road, adjacent to the Longleat Safari Park. Parking.

94 **Wheatsheaf at Oaksey**

**Wheatsheaf Ln,
Oaksey, SN16 9TB**
Tel.: (01666)577348
Website: www.thewheatsheafatoaksey.co.uk

VISA **MC** **AE** **D**

Sharp's Doom Bar, Fuller's London Pride and Timothy Taylor Landlord

This is very much a community pub – it's popular with the locals and the chef-owner and his son even cook lunch for children at the village school. With its vast open fireplace, low leather sofas and magazines, the bar is the best place to sit. The rear dining room is the more modern alternative and the 'red hot' snug with its burlesque pictures is perfect for smaller parties. The chef's classical background means dishes like cep risotto or shoulder of local lamb on the regularly changing menu, alongside pub classics with a twist, like breaded fish or pork suet pudding. There are 10 varieties of burger, including one made with Wagyu beef and, to finish, artisan cheeses and desserts like chilled vanilla rice pudding or dark chocolate soufflé.

Closing times
Closed Sunday dinner and Monday

Prices
Meals: a la carte £ 19/35

Typical Dishes
Pheasant & poached bantam egg
Spiced mango free-range chicken
Chocolate brownie & vanilla ice cream

🚗 *6 mi north of Malmesbury, signed off A 429. Parking.*

Ramsbury

95

Bell

**The Square,
Ramsbury, SN8 2PE**
Tel.: (01672)520230
Website: www.thebellramsbury.com

Ramsbury Brewery Ales and guest ales

Despite an extensive refurbishment, this charming 16C building has managed to retain plenty of its original pubby character, particularly in its open-fired bar, where you'll find hop-covered beams and a menu of old pub favourites. If you're looking for the bell the pub's named after, you'll find it hanging in the fireplace of the crisply laid dining room. Here you can sit on smart tartan banquettes and enjoy a more sophisticated atmosphere, dining on ambitious, accomplished dishes such as crispy fried duck egg with chorizo and tomato salsa, followed by local estate venison with carrot and celeriac purées. At the back, 'Café Bella' is a popular meeting place for the locals, while stylish, well-appointed bedrooms welcome those staying over.

Closing times
Closed 25 December

Prices
Meals: £ 19 (weekday lunch)/25 and a la carte £ 25/37

9 rooms: £ 110/150

Typical Dishes
Pan-fried foie gras with apricot & hazelnut crunch

28-day aged rump of beef with oxtail

Lemon meringue parfait

 4 mi northwest of Hungerford signposted off B 4192. Parking.

96 **George & Dragon**

**High St,
Rowde, SN10 2PN**
Tel.: (01380)723053
Website: www.thegeorgeanddragonrowde.co.uk

VISA **MC** **D**

Butcombe Bitter, Sharp's Doom Bar and Kennet & Avon Dundas

This 16C coaching inn has a rustic feel throughout; its cosy inner boasting solid stone floors, wooden beams and open fires. There's a strong emphasis on seafood, with fish delivered daily from Cornwall to ensure it arrives on your plate in tip-top condition. That the menu is written anew each day also speaks volumes about the pub's take on food; seafood dishes could be a plate of fishy hors d'oeuvres, pan-fried cod with bacon or a whole grilled lemon sole; more meaty choices might include rack of lamb or roast fillet of beef. Some dishes come in two sizes and can be taken as either a starter or a main course. There is also a good value set three course menu. Old-world charm meets modern facilities in the individually designed bedrooms.

Closing times
Closed Sunday dinner

Prices
Meals: £ 17 (weekdays)/20 and a la carte £ 19/41

3 rooms: £ 75/115

Typical Dishes
Baked potted crab
Chargrilled scallops with belly pork & black pudding
Chocolate & orange bread & butter pudding

 2 mi northwest of Devizes on A 342. Parking.

Tisbury

97 — Beckford Arms

**Fonthill Gifford,
Tisbury, SP3 6PX**
Tel.: (01747)870385
Website: www.beckfordarms.com

 ⛱ *VISA* ⓂⒸ

🍺 **Butcombe Bitter and Keystone Ales**

Set next to the 10,000 acre Fonthill Estate, this charming 18C inn offers something a little different. There's a delightful terrace and a large garden – complete with hammocks, a petanque pitch and a dog bath – not forgetting a beamed dining room, a rustic bar and a lovely country house sitting room, where films are screened on Sunday nights. Tasty, unfussy cooking relies on excellent ingredients, with the daily menu offering classics and country-style fare such as roast partridge or pork with Morteau sausage, while for a snack, the homemade pork scratchings are a hit. Tastefully furnished bedrooms offer thoughtful comforts and, if you like to be out-and-about, the charming young team gladly provide hampers and arrange fishing and shooting trips.

Closing times
Closed 25 December
booking essential
Prices
Meals: a la carte £ 23/32
🛏 **10 rooms:** £ 95/175

Typical Dishes
Duck liver parfait with plum purée
Confit of Creedy Carver duck leg
Rhubarb & pear trifle with vanilla cream

Between Shaftesbury and Warminster signposted off A 350. Parking.

98   **King John Inn**

Tollard Royal,
SP5 5PS
Tel.: (01725)516207
Website: www.kingjohninn.co.uk

VISA

Butcombe Adam Henson's Rare Breed

The beautiful black and white hunting photos that line the walls of this creeper-clad Victorian pub are a clue both to its clientele and to its menus. The sofas are a popular place to relax with a drink after a day's shooting, before enjoying locally stalked venison or whole roast grouse at one of the scrubbed wooden tables. Other dishes on the classically based menus might include homemade chicken Kiev, steak and chips or oxtail and pumpkin ravioli; fish is regularly brought up from the coast and the soufflés and home-baked bread are fast becoming trademarks. Like the open-plan, fire-lit interior, the service is relaxed and informal. There's also a wine shop and comfy, stylish bedrooms which blend antique furniture with modern facilities.

Closing times
Closed 25 December
Prices
Meals: a la carte £ 27/34
8 rooms: £ 110/170

Typical Dishes
Sole & smoked eel ravioli

Lamb chops & saddle with chorizo & kale

Apple doughnuts with toffee sauce

5 mi southeast of Shaftesbury on B 3081. Parking.

Upper South Wraxall

99 **Longs Arms**

**Upper South Wraxall,
BA15 2SB**
Tel.: (01225)864450
Website: www.thelongsarms.com

Wadworth Henry's Original IPA, 6X and Malt & Hops

The appetite for British food shows no sign of abating, particularly in British pubs. How apt it is to see traditional dishes like goats' scrumpets or crispy tongue and pickles in a pub like this – named after local landowners, the Long family, in whose manor house Sir Walter Raleigh allegedly smoked the first tobacco in England. The only smoking that goes on nowadays is that of meat and fish in the pub's own smokehouse. Meat is hung and butchered on-site, there's a kitchen garden and everything is made in-house, including bread, ice cream, feta cheese, faggots, black pudding and haggis. Service is warm and friendly and the pub itself is bursting with character; think exposed Bath stone walls, bay windows, a woodburner and flagged floors.

Closing times
Closed 2 weeks January-February, Sunday dinner and Monday
booking essential
Prices
Meals: a la carte £ 22/35

Typical Dishes
Smoked salmon with pickled cucumber

Venison loin, English asparagus, St George mushrooms

Valrhona chocolate & salted caramel tart

3 mi north of Bradford-on-Avon by A 363, signed off B 3109. In centre of village opposite the church. Parking.

100 **Bridge Inn**

**Upper Woodford,
SP4 6NU**
Tel.: (01722)782323
Website: www.thebridgewoodford.co.uk

VISA MC AE

Hopback Summer Lightning, Wadworth 6X and Ringwood Best Bitter

Situated in the Woodford Valley, a few miles south of Stonehenge, the aptly named Bridge Inn stands on the banks of the Avon, overlooking the river crossing; its garden, with picnic tables from which to watch the swans and ducks, an alfresco diner's delight. The pub is modern, with a light, airy feel. Its relaxed atmosphere means that locals with dogs rub shoulders with diners, and you can peek through the glass windows to see the chefs hard at work in the kitchen. Lunch sees a light bites menu of interesting sandwiches, while the à la carte offers dishes such as fishcakes, pot-roasted lamb shank or the popular pork belly. This is the sister pub to the Ship Inn at Burcombe; get your hands on a loyalty card and you can reap the benefits at both.

Closing times
Closed 25 December
and Sunday dinner
January-February

Prices
Meals: a la carte £ 23/38

Typical Dishes
Breaded whitebait
with tartare sauce
Pressed pork belly with
gratin dauphinoise
White chocolate &
Baileys cheesecake

North of Salisbury off A 360; follow signs for The Woodfords. Parking.

Upton Scudamore

101 **Angel Inn**

**Upton Scudamore,
BA12 0AG**
Tel.: (01985)213225
Website: www.theangelinn.co.uk

🛏 ⛱ *VISA* Ⓜ©

🍺 **Butcombe Bitter and Wadworth 6X**

It may be the dependable village local, but things have moved on at the Angel Inn. True, it looks the same from the outside, but inside it's been flipped back-to-front and the bar's been moved from the upper to the lower level. There's no need to panic though – the large dining room still has a pleasant, cottage-like feel, while the lovely garden and terrace are as appealing as ever, providing a wonderful suntrap. Menus are fairly formal and not your typical pub grub; you might find home-cured gravadlax, roasted venison steak or salt-cured duck breast, with plenty of specials – usually fish – on the board. Lunch offers a good value set menu and puddings are of the good old-fashioned variety. Individually themed bedrooms are cosy and well-kept.

Closing times
Open daily
Prices
Meals: £ 10 (weekday lunch) and a la carte £ 24/34

🛏 **10 rooms:** £ 85/95

Typical Dishes
Terrine of chicken & ham
Braised beef with duxelle potato
Dark chocolate mousse

North of Warminster signed off A 350. Parking.

102 **Weymouth Arms**

**12 Emwell St,
Warminster, BA12 8JA**
Tel.: (01985)216995
Website: www.weymoutharms.co.uk

 Butcombe Gold and Bitter

If you fancy a slice of history with your lunch, you won't be disappointed. This Grade II listed building started life as a private home (round the back, an archway is inscribed with '1771 D.C.', as the house once belonged to Daniel Capel, a well-known clothier); in the 19C it became a lodging house and, a century later, was turned into a public house. It's immensely characterful, displaying original wood panelling, antiques and lithographs, as well as two fireplaces originally intended for nearby Longleat House (Lord Weymouth of Longleat was once a frequent visitor). Cooking is fittingly traditional, with fresh ingredients featuring in dishes such as chicken liver pâté and apple and pear crumble. Cosy bedrooms have charming original fittings.

Closing times
Closed Sunday dinner and Monday lunch
Prices
Meals: a la carte £ 21/37
6 rooms: £ 65/85

Typical Dishes
Risotto of crayfish tails
Sticky belly of pork, pig's cheek croquette & apple sauce
Chocolate pot with flapjack

0.25 mi west by High St, Silver St and George St. Pay and display car park adjacent.

West Overton

103   **Bell**

**Bath Rd,
West Overton, SN8 1QD**
Tel.: (01672)861099
Website: www.thebellwestoverton.co.uk

Moles Best, Ramsbury Flint Knapper, Box Steam Golden Bolt and Three Castles Saxon Archer

One way to improve any walk, apart from having proper shoes and fair weather, is to end up at a decent pub. If you've been out on the Cherhill Downs, then pop into the Bell at West Overton. The pub was rescued by a local couple, who realised a dream by buying it, but who were also sensible enough to hire an experienced pair to run it. The same menu is served in the bar and restaurant, and the latter is far from stuffy, as they don't want to scare anyone away. What the pub may lack in character, it makes up for in the quality of its cooking. There's an appealing blend of pub classics and dishes of a Mediterranean bent, such as crispy fried squid or Cornish bream with chorizo and olives. Presentation is modern but not at the expense of flavour.

Closing times
Closed Monday except bank holidays

Prices
Meals: £ 15 (weekdays) and a la carte £ 22/42

Typical Dishes
Venison, wild boar & pistachio pâté

Rump of lamb with chorizo & butternut squash

Hot chocolate & walnut fondant

 4 mi west of Marlborough on A 4. Parking.

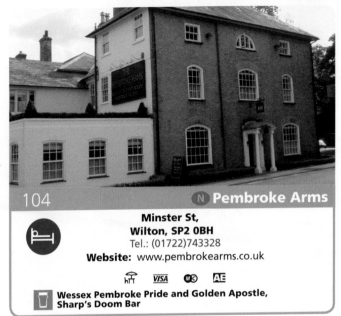

104 **Pembroke Arms**

**Minster St,
Wilton, SP2 0BH**
Tel.: (01722)743328
Website: www.pembrokearms.co.uk

VISA MC AE

Wessex Pembroke Pride and Golden Apostle,
Sharp's Doom Bar

This 18C inn is named after the Earl of Pembroke, whose country seat, Wilton House, sits just across the road. Many of its original architectural features remain and it has a relaxed, individual style: the bar is filled with stag heads, display cases of fish and old coach lanterns, while the dining room features rug-covered floorboards, chunky wood furnishings and windows framed by French floral fabrics. The menu offers an array of British dishes, with a few pub favourites at lunch and the likes of Old Spot pork chop or sea bass with spinach and prawn salsa verde at dinner; and whatever the time of day, there's always the 'Pembroke Pie', with its regularly changing filling. Bedrooms are quirky – some of the furniture is from Rajasthan.

Closing times
Open daily
Prices
Meals: a la carte £ 27/37

9 rooms: £ 65/160

Typical Dishes
Applewood cheese croquettes
The 'Pembroke Pie'
Pear panna cotta

3 mi west of Salisbury off A 36. Parking.

The names Gas Street Basin, Custard Factory and Mailbox may not win any awards for exoticism, but these are the cutting edge quarters fuelling the rise of modern day Birmingham, at the heart of a region evolving from its grimy factory gate image. Even the Ironbridge Gorge, the cradle of the Industrial Revolution, is better known these days as a fascinatingly picturesque tourist attraction. The old urban landscapes dot a region of delightful unspoilt countryside with extensive areas of open moorland and hills, where stands Middle Earth, in the shape of Shropshire's iconic Wrekin hill, true inspiration of Tolkien. Shakespeare Country abounds in pretty villages, such as Henley-in-Arden, Shipston-on-Stour and Alcester, where redbrick, half-timbered and Georgian buildings capture the eye. Taste buds are catered for courtesy of a host of local specialities, not least fruits from the Vale of Evesham and mouth-watering meats from the hills near the renowned gastro town of Ludlow.

Belbroughton

1   **The Queens**

**Queens Hill,
Belbroughton, DY9 ODU**
Tel.: (01562)730276
Website: www.thequeensbelbroughton.co.uk

Marston's Pedigree, Ringwood Boondoggle and monthly guest ales

Dating from the 16C, The Queens has been around nearly as long as the millstones in the wall dividing it from the brook. The pub might have been refurbished but its traditional look and feel remains – a conscious effort by the owners to respect the locals' preferences. There's a bar with some nice leather benches for drinkers, and three small rooms neatly laid for dining. Food plays a substantial role here: in true pub style you can get a hearty steak and ale pie but you'll also find the likes of steamed cod with Parma ham, tomatoes and black olives, showing the chef's passion for classical flavours. Dishes are attractively presented and more refined than their descriptions imply. Come in September for the village's annual scarecrow festival.

Closing times
Closed 25 December
bookings advisable at dinner
Prices
Meals: £ 18 and a la carte £ 23/36

Typical Dishes
Scallop ravioli with caviar cream
Medallions of beef with field mushrooms & rösti potato
Chocolate & mint pots

 Between Stourbridge and Bromsgrove off A 491. Parking.

Royal Forester

2

**Callow Hill,
DY14 9XW**
Tel.: (01299)266286
Website: www.royalforesterinn.co.uk

Wye Valley HPA and Butty Bach, Greene King Abbot Ale

Dating back to 1411, The Royal Forester is reputedly one of the oldest pubs in Worcestershire and, despite its modern feel, retains a rustic richness of character typified by the dining room's exposed stone walls. Cooking is flavourful, simple in style and reasonably priced, although side dishes can push the bill up. The regularly changing menu explains what's in season, with pork from their own pigs and ingredients like local venison or honey supplied by regulars in exchange for dinner credits. The atmosphere is easy-going and added to by the tinkling of the grand piano in the bright bar. Food-themed bedrooms are fresh and modern, while chauffeur service in a VW camper van is available for locals wanting a drink with their meal.

Closing times
Open daily
Prices
Meals: a la carte £ 22/40
7 rooms: £ 65/99

Typical Dishes
Scallops with Jerusalem artichoke velouté
Rump of lamb & wild garlic gnocchi
Dark chocolate tart

 3 mi southwest of Bewdley. Parking.

England • West Midlands • Hereford and Worcester

3 — Bell & Cross

**Holy Cross,
Clent, DY9 9QL**
Tel.: (01562)730319
Website: www.bellandcrossclent.co.uk

**Timothy Taylor Landlord, Wye Valley HPA and
Sharp's Doom Bar**

Set down a maze of narrow lanes, the Bell & Cross stands at what the locals call 'the old crossroads'. Colourful window boxes greet you at the front and round the back there's a spacious, well-kept lawn boasting lovely country views. The inside is made up of a series of rooms; the bar with its red leather banquettes and listed counter is particularly characterful. Football mementoes adorn the hall, harking back to the time when the owner cooked for the England football squad – but it's unlikely that they were given as much choice on their menus: there's sarnies, light bites and pub classics, and some more substantial dishes on the à la carte; not forgetting a set menu and some blackboard specials too. Influences range from Asia to the Med.

Closing times
Closed 25 December and dinner 26 December and 1 January

Prices
Meals: £ 14 (weekdays) and a la carte £ 21/34

Typical Dishes
Pressed pork & mushroom terrine
Pork belly, spring cabbage & cider sauce
Chocolate & salted caramel crème brûlée

Between Stourbridge and Bromsgrove off northbound A 491; the pub is on the left hand side in Holy Cross. Parking.

4

Chequers

Kidderminster Rd, Cutnall Green, WR9 0PJ
Tel.: (01299)851292
Website: www.chequerscutnallgreen.co.uk

Wye Valley HPA, Marstons Banks Bitter and Sharp's Doom Bar

If football's your thing, then make for the "Players' Lounge" of this lightly washed roadside pub and sit among photos of the old England team and Roger, the owner, who was their chef for 21 years. Despite the fact that rich burgundy colours and modern furnishings have been introduced, the exposed beams and original wood and quarry-tiled floors maintain a cosy, traditional feel – furthered by a collection of timeless food items such as Colman's mustard, Lyle's golden syrup, and HP and Worcestershire sauces, displayed on shelves above the bar. The large menus are mainly Asian-led but also offer a good selection of light bites and pub classics, while some more adventurous fish and offal-based specials are chalked up on the board every day.

Closing times
Closed 25 December, dinner 26 December and 1 January
Prices
Meals: £ 14 (weekdays) and a la carte £ 20/34

Typical Dishes
Smoked salmon with horseradish cream

Slow-cooked pork belly with rhubarb confit

Rice pudding with shortbread crumble

 3 mi north of Droitwich Spa on A 442. Parking.

Eldersfield

5 **Butchers Arms**

Lime Street,
Eldersfield, GL19 4NX
Tel.: (01452)840381
Website: www.thebutchersarms.net

 VISA MC

 Wye Valley Ales, Wickwar Ales and St Austell Tribute

Apart from the modern sign swinging outside, this pub remains as traditional as ever. Two small rooms display original beams, part-oak flooring and a wood burning stove, while dried hops hang from the bar and memorabilia adorns the walls. A few of the small wooden tables are left for the local drinkers, while the rest are set for around 20 or so diners. With only one person in the kitchen the menu is understandably quite concise but it changes regularly – sometimes even from service to service – and despite the lack of man-power, everything from the bread to the ice cream is homemade. Many of the ingredients are extremely local and the kitchen makes clever use less obvious cuts of meat, such as pigs' cheeks, in thoughtful and tasty dishes.

Closing times
Closed 2 weeks early January, 2 weeks late August, Sunday dinner, Monday, lunch Tuesday to Thursday and bank holidays

booking essential

Prices
Meals: a la carte £ 37/47

Typical Dishes
Middle White pig's cheek with black pudding
Roast turbot & saffron risotto
Praline and pistachio macaroons, pistachio ice cream.

 8.5 mi north of Gloucester by A 417 and signposted off B 4211. Parking.

6   **White Hart**

Hartlebury,
DY11 7TD
Tel.: (01299)250286
Website: www.thewhitehartinhartlebury.co.uk

 Timothy Taylor Landlord, Sharp's Doom Bar and Hobsons Best Bitter

Once a run-down old pub, the White Hart is now the pride and joy of owners Simon and Venetia, who have established it as a proper village local, where regulars watch TV from brown leather sofas and play on the games machine in the bar. If you're dining, head for the bright, contemporary dining room or out onto the terrace on warmer days. Dishes are carefully prepared, classically based and rely on quality produce; you'll find light offerings such as baked camembert at lunch, along with some good value pub classics, while dinner features the likes of chicken, port and bacon pâté followed by loin of pork with champ potatoes and sage cream. They hold regular curry and pizza nights, as well as an annual beer festival with a barbecue and live music.

Closing times
Open daily
Prices
Meals: £ 15 (lunch)
and a la carte £ 21/34

Typical Dishes

Spiced sweet potato & coconut soup

Gressingham duck, spring cabbage & fondant potato

Tagliatelle of almonds, lemon & honey

 4 mi south of Kidderminster, village signposted off A 449. Parking.

England ● West Midlands ● Hereford and Worcester

Titley

7   **Stagg Inn**

Titley,
HR5 3RL
Tel.: (01544)230221
Website: www.thestagg.co.uk

🛏   *VISA*   **MC**   **AE**

🍺 **Wye Valley Butty Bach and Ludlow Gold**

Situated at the meeting point of two former drovers' roads, this characterful part-medieval, part-Victorian pub was once called 'The Balance', as it marked the point where farmers would stop to weigh their wool. Inside, it's delightfully cosy – one room was once a butcher's shop and another still displays an old bread oven. Cooking is fittingly straightforward, relying on classically based recipes, careful preparation and top quality produce; menus are short, simple and to the point; and the dishes themselves are truly satisfying. The owners are keen to promote the area and serve local beers, ciders and unusual vodkas – such as potato or marmalade flavour. Bedrooms in the pub are snug but can be noisy; opt for one in the former vicarage.

Closing times
Closed 2 weeks January-February, first 2 weeks November, 25-26 December, Sunday dinner and Monday
booking essential

Prices
Meals: a la carte £ 26/43
🛏 **6 rooms:** £ 75/140

Typical Dishes
Lambs' sweetbreads, black pudding & walnut crumb
Herefordshire rump steak & chips
Bread & butter pudding

 3.5 mi northeast of Kington on B 4355. Parking.

8

Mill Race

**Walford,
HR9 5QS**
Tel.: (01989)562891
Website: www.millrace.info

🍺 **Wye Valley Brewery Ales and Butcombe Brewery Ales**

England • West Midlands • Hereford and Worcester

This isn't the kind of place you expect to find in a small country village but the locals aren't complaining. It doesn't really look like a pub, either outside or in, save for the bar counter; you enter via a Gothic-style door, pass a board pinpointing their suppliers and head towards the chefs hard at work in the semi open-plan kitchen. You'll find regulars standing around the bar, pint in hand, and local families out for the night in the darker, slate-floored areas. Cooking is fairly simple, letting the ingredients speak for themselves, and the small team flit about, coping well when it's busy – which it usually is. They hold regular theme nights, with pizzas cooked outside on the rear terrace, and they even do food and wine to take away.

Closing times
Open daily
Prices
Meals: a la carte £ 21/32

Typical Dishes
Field mushrooms on
sourdough toast
Wye Valley beef cheek
Trio of rhubarb

🚗 *3 mi south of Ross-on-Wye by B 4234. Parking.*

9 **Butchers Arms**

Woolhope,
HR1 4RF
Tel.: (01432)860281
Website: www.butchersarmswoolhope.co.uk

Wye Valley Bitter and Butty Bach, Hereford Brewery HLA and Three Tuns XXX

Hidden away deep in the countryside, this half-timbered 16C inn boasts a characterful interior with open fires, wattle walls and beams slung so low you're forced to duck. Saws and pitchforks hang from the walls, while the pretty garden, with its babbling brook and weeping willow, offers delightful views over farmland. Chef-owner Stephen Bull was one of the pioneers of modern British cooking, so expect the daily menu to offer simple sounding, classically based dishes like Goodrich Middle White sausages, mash and onion gravy or his speciality twice-baked soufflé – meticulously executed and full of flavour. A focus on regional produce means that lamb comes from over the road, fruit and veg from nearby farms and herbs from their own garden.

Closing times
Closed 1 week January, 25 December, Sunday dinner and Monday except bank holidays

Prices
Meals: a la carte £ 21/31

Typical Dishes
Pigeon breast with celeriac purée

Confit duck leg, apple & sultana compote

Warm ginger cake, treacle toffee ice cream

 9 mi north of Ross-on-Wye by A 449 and B 4224. Parking.

10 **Feathers at Brockton**

**Brockton,
TF13 6JR**
Tel.: (01746)785202
Website: www.feathersatbrockton.co.uk

Hobsons Best Bitter and Six Bells Brewery ales

Set on the edge of the village in an area popular with walkers, this rustic 16C pub is snug and warm with homely décor, open fires, exposed beams and thick stone walls; a more modern feature is its gift shop which sells quirky home accessories. This is a personally run place and the atmosphere is relaxing and unpretentious, with the focus firmly on the food. Having learnt his trade in London, chef-owner Paul returned to Shropshire to open the Feathers back in 2004 – and his tasty cooking has been attracting customers ever since. Mainly traditional in style, with some Mediterranean influences, dishes make use of local produce and might include corn-fed chicken breast, shoulder of lamb or steak and ale pie. Old school puddings follow.

Closing times
Closed 26 December, 1 January, Monday and lunch Tuesday

Prices
Meals: £ 13 (lunch and early dinner) and a la carte £ 21/33

Typical Dishes
Garlic king prawns with lemon

Slow-cooked pork belly, apple chutney & crackling

Warm chocolate fondant

 5 mi southwest of Much Wenlock on B 4378. Parking.

Burlton

11

Burlton Inn

**Burlton,
SY4 5TB**
Tel.: (01939)270284
Website: www.burltoninn.com

🍴 **VISA** **MC** **AE**

🍺 Robinsons Ales

Set on a busy road in a small village between Ellesmere and Shrewsbury, this traditional 18C whitewashed inn welcomes you with a colourful flower display. Since the current owners took over it has undergone a transformation – most notably a terrace, fountain and landscaped garden have been added. It's a characterful place with exposed beams, tiled floors, scrubbed pine tables and some soft seating by a wood burning stove. To one side there's a dining area but you can eat throughout; although it can get busy in the bar with local drinkers, especially on a Friday. The straightforward lunch menu offers snacks and pub classics, while in the evening some more adventurous dishes appear too. Neat, wood-furnished bedrooms boast spacious bathrooms.

Closing times
Closed 25-26 December
Prices
Meals: a la carte £ 18/41
🛏 **6 rooms:** £ 68/95

Typical Dishes
Crayfish salad
Slow-cooked beef cheek
Espresso crème brûlée

8 mi north of Shrewsbury on A 528. Parking.

12

Sun Inn

**Marton,
SY21 8JP**
Tel.: (01938)561211
Website: www.suninn.org.uk

 VISA **MC**

Hobsons Best Bitter

A welcoming country pub on the English-Welsh border, the Sun Inn is a family affair, with father and son in the kitchen, their respective spouses looking after the customers and even the grandchildren helping out on occasion. It's not a plush place but it's cosy enough, with a fire-lit bar on one side and a brightly painted dining room on the other; the locals certainly seem to like it – you'll find them enjoying a game of dominoes or puzzling it out at one of the regular quiz nights. The concise menu offers tasty, satisfying and comforting home-cooked dishes, so expect rich, creamy homemade soups, steak and ale pie, delicious homemade faggots with mash and peas, and sticky toffee pudding – and make sure you try the excellent fish specials.

Closing times
Closed Sunday dinner and lunch Monday-Tuesday

Prices
Meals: a la carte £ 21/30

Typical Dishes
Tea-smoked salmon, chicory & fennel salad
Roast guinea fowl with wild mushrooms
White chocolate & raspberry cheesecake

 8.5 mi southeast of Welshpool on B 4386. Parking.

Alstonefield

13   **George**

**Alstonefield,
DE6 2FX**
Tel.: (01335)310205
Website: www.thegeorgeatalstonefield.com

 **Marston's Pedigree and Burton Bitter, Jennings
Cumberland Ale and Brakspear Oxford Gold**

The moment you walk in the George, feel the warmth from the roaring fires and start to soak up the cosy, relaxed atmosphere, you just know that it's going to be good. A traditional pub set on the village green, it's simply furnished, with stone floors, scrubbed wooden tables and pictures of locals on the walls. The bubbly manager – the third generation of her family to have owned the pub – brings a woman's touch to the place, with the latest fashion mags for flicking through and candles and fresh flowers on every table. Like the décor, the food is simple but well done. The menus change daily according to the produce available; the team use local suppliers where possible and also grow some of their own vegetables in the garden.

Closing times
Closed 25 December
Prices
Meals: a la carte £ 23/45

Typical Dishes
Scallops, pancetta & cauliflower purée

Loin of lamb with asparagus & peas

Vanilla panna cotta, summer fruit compote

 7.5 mi north of Ashbourne by A 515. Parking.

14   **The Trooper**

**Watling St,
Wall, WS14 0AN**
Tel.: (01543)480413
Website: www.thetrooperwall.co.uk

Marston's Pedigree, Greene King IPA, Holden's Golden Glow and guest ales

With the A5 starting life as the Roman military road to north Wales, and the hamlet of Wall playing host to what was once an important forces' staging post, it seems fitting that this pub should be named The Trooper. Open fires welcome you into the lounge, where you'll find locals sitting around the central bar, and to the rear, the extension leads out onto a huge terrace with a garden beyond. There's plenty of offer when it comes to the food. The main menu features restaurant-style dishes – with 28-day aged Kobe beef the speciality and local Packlington pork a permanent feature – supplemented by pub favourites such as gammon and eggs at lunchtime. A friendly, experienced team oversee things; the first Sunday of the month is live band night.

Closing times
Open daily
Prices
Meals: a la carte £ 25/50

Typical Dishes
Scallops with cumin spiced cauliflower
Canon of venison with vanilla parsnip purée
Triple chocolate brownie

Just south of Lichfield off A 5127, adjacent to the A 5. Parking.

15

King's Head

**21 Bearley Rd,
Aston Cantlow, B95 6HY**
Tel.: (01789)488242
Website: www.thekh.co.uk

Purity Pure Gold and Mad Goose, Greene King Abbot Ale

Set close to the Cotswolds, in the picturesque village of Aston Cantlow, is the 13C Norman church where Shakespeare's parents were married; and they are thought to have had their wedding breakfast at this attractive ivy-clad inn. The timbered bar is hugely characterful – the experienced owner has decorated it with contemporary black and white photos he took himself – and behind that, is a chic, country-style restaurant in pastel shades. Menus focus on the classics but there's the odd modern twist, so your pork might come with a cheek bon bon or your lamb, with Bombay potato and yoghurt dressing. Regular duck suppers celebrate the pub's past, when during wartime rationing the landlord was allowed to serve duck, as he reared his own.

Closing times
Open daily
Prices
Meals: a la carte £ 20/36

Typical Dishes
Duck leg confit with chorizo
Fillet of sea bass with chilli & crab
Sticky toffee pudding with vanilla ice cream

 6 mi northwest of Stratford-upon-Avon, signposted off A 46. Parking.

16 **Chequers Inn**

**91 Banbury Rd,
Ettington, CV37 7SR**
Tel.: (01789)740387
Website: www.the-chequers-ettington.co.uk

 Greene King IPA, St Austell Tribute and Box Steam Tunnel Vision

The signs outside scream country gastropub but to assume so would be off the mark; with its chandeliers, brushed velvet furniture and round-backed Regency chairs, this place is anything but formulaic. The open-fired bar is a popular spot with villagers, no doubt pleased with the large selection of beers as well as their local's transformation from run down boozer to smart, contemporary inn. When it comes to the cooking, the menus display a broad international style. There are good old British classics like prawn cocktail, cauliflower cheese and ham hock with bubble and squeak, alongside dishes of a more global persuasion, like rabbit rigatoni, salami platters and other Asian-influenced offerings. Friendly service completes the package.

Closing times
Closed Sunday dinner and Monday
Prices
Meals: a la carte £ 22/33

Typical Dishes
Tiger prawn cocktail with Bloody Mary mayo
Herb-crusted lamb shoulder
Chocolate croissant bread & butter pudding

Southeast of Stratford-upon-Avon where the A 422 crosses the A 429. Parking.

Great Wolford

17 **Fox & Hounds Inn**

**Great Wolford,
CV36 5NQ**
Tel.: (01608)674220
Website: www.thefoxandhoundsinn.com

⛱ *VISA* **MC**

🍺 **Hook Norton Hooky Bitter and Purity Pure UBU**

This unpretentious pub lies at the heart of a small village which, in turn, is nestled in the rolling Cotswold Hills. Built in 1540 from local stone, it's a traditional English country inn – small, cosy and characterful – with flagged floors, a large inglenook fireplace and hops hanging from low beamed ceilings. With the owner out front and her son in the kitchen, it's very much a family affair. Menus are chalked up on the board daily and feature largely rustic pub fare, alongside a few more modern dishes. The chef is passionate about local produce, sourcing Chastleton beef, venison from Todenham and game from nearby shoots; while the bread, bacon and sausages are all made in-house. Simple, pine-furnished bedrooms offer country views.

Closing times
Closed first 2 weeks January, Sunday dinner and Monday
Prices
Meals: a la carte £ 24/38
🛏 **3 rooms:** £ 60/80

Typical Dishes
Cured mackerel, pickled radish, samphire & cucumber

Pork belly & homemade black pudding

Yoghurt panna cotta

🚗 4 mi northeast of Moreton-in-Marsh signposted off A 44. Parking.

18 **Bluebell**

93 High St,
Henley-in-Arden, B95 5AT
Tel.: (01564)793049
Website: www.bluebellhenley.co.uk

 Purity Mad Goose, Church End Ales and Hook Norton Old Hooky

This part-timbered building on the high street is not your usual kind of pub. True, it comes with exposed beams, open fires and mix and match chairs – but some of those chairs have French-style gilding, and one of the rooms has grey padded walls and sumptuous curtains fringed with peacock feathers. This mix of rustic character and formal elegance seems to be a hit with the customers, as does the wide-ranging selection of wines, beers, cocktails and tasty British dishes. The experienced chef uses the best local suppliers and cooking is honest and seasonal, with dishes ranging from fish and chips to pot-roast pheasant; there's also a good value set menu to consider. Puddings are more modern and could include crème brûlée with blackcurrant sorbet.

Closing times
Open daily
Prices
Meals: £ 15/23
and a la carte £ 26/34

Typical Dishes
Velouté of Cornish mussels & saffron

Barbary duck breast with Madeira sauce

Treacle tart with clotted cream ice cream

 8 mi northwest of Stratford-upon-Avon on A 3400. Parking.

Henley-in-Arden

19   Crabmill

**Preston Bagot,
Henley-in-Arden, B95 5EE**
Tel.: (01926)843342
Website: www.thecrabmill.co.uk

🏠 *VISA* Ⓜ⊚

**Greene King Abbot Ale, Purity Pure UBU and Fuller's
London Pride**

This characterful timbered pub is the ideal place to kick back and relax, whether you sit in the lawned garden, on the peaceful terrace or inside the pub itself. It's made up of various beamed snugs and lounges, which are fitted out with a mixture of traditional old wood furnishings and contemporary leather chairs set at black wood tables. You can eat anywhere but if you're tucked away in a corner and it's busy – which it usually is – you may need to flag down one of the team to place your order. The good-sized à la carte offers modern Mediterranean-influenced dishes; start with a tasty sharing plate and move on to one of the interesting main courses, maybe venison pavé, sweet potato and corned beef hash or ostrich fillet wrapped in Serrano ham.

Closing times
Closed Sunday dinner
booking essential

Prices
Meals: £ 14 (weekdays)
and a la carte £ 21/37

Typical Dishes
Serrano ham with burrata & compressed melon

Rack of lamb with samphire & pan haggerty

Raspberry & honey panna cotta

 1 mi east of Henley-in-Arden on A 4189. Parking.

20   **Red Lion**

**Main St,
Hunningham, CV33 9DY**
Tel.: (01926)632715
Website: www.redlionhunningham.co.uk

📶   *VISA*   ⓂⒸ   🅰🅴

🍺 **Greene King Abbot Ale and IPA, Timothy Taylor Landlord and Oakham JHB**

Set close to the River Leam – and sometimes, in the past, underneath it – this charming, part-17C timbered inn has been lovingly restored. In summer, don't be surprised to find groups of stripy deckchairs down at the end of the garden by the water's edge and maybe a huge inflatable cinema screen or a festival taking place in the adjoining fields. Inside you'll discover a keen, welcoming team, over 300 framed American comics and a ceiling-mounted air pipe that delivers orders to the kitchen. The daily menu offers well-crafted, unfussy pub fare with the occasional modern touch; you might find haddock and prawn fishcakes, black pudding salad or carpaccio of mid-Shires veal; order at the bar next to the case of tempting, locally made pork pies.

Closing times
Open daily
Prices
Meals: a la carte £ 19/32

Typical Dishes
Breaded terrine of mushroom & spinach
Roasted fillet of cod
Dulce de leche crème brûlée

🚗 *6.25 mi northeast of Royal Leamington Spa by A 425 off B 4455. Parking.*

Ilmington

21 **Howard Arms**

**Lower Green,
Ilmington, CV36 4LT**
Tel.: (01608)682226
Website: www.howardarms.com

VISA **MC** **AE**

Purity Pure Gold and Hook Norton Old Hooky

This 400 year old Cotswold stone inn, set on a peaceful village green, is the very essence of an English country pub. Bright flower displays welcome you at the front, and round the back there's a small garden and terrace. Inside, you'll find the expected stone-faced walls, exposed beams, flagged floors and a huge inglenook fireplace, and a mix of chairs, pews and benches; there's also a raised-level dining room with a large dresser and fully laid dark wood tables. Blackboards are dotted about the place, displaying hearty dishes that are mainly British-based; you might find braised beef and ale pie or calves' liver and bacon. Featuring antique furniture, the original bedrooms are warm and cosy; those in the extension are more contemporary.

Closing times
Open daily
Prices
Meals: a la carte £ 21/47
8 rooms: £ 85/145

Typical Dishes
Scallops with pea shoots
Pot-roasted brisket & creamed potato
Rosewater and buttermilk panna cotta

Between Stratford-upon-Avon and Moreton-in-Marsh signposted off A 429. Parking.

22   **Boot Inn**

**Old Warwick Rd,
Lapworth, B94 6JU**
Tel.: (01564)782464
Website: www.bootinnlapworth.co.uk

 Fuller's London Pride, Purity Pure UBU and Marstons EPA

Whether you're hastening down the M40 or pottering along on a narrow boat, it's worth stopping off at this large, buzzy red-brick pub. Set close to the junction of the Grand Union and Stratford-upon-Avon canals, it draws in a mixed crowd – from the young to the old, businesspeople to pleasure seekers – and you may well wonder where they all come from. With its traditional quarry-floored bar, modern first floor restaurant and large terrace complete with a barbecue, it's deservedly popular, so booking is a must. Dishes vary greatly, from sandwiches, a picnic board and sharing plates through to more sophisticated specials. The crispy oriental duck salad and the bubble and squeak are mainstays, and influences range from Britain to the Med and Asia.

Closing times
Open daily
booking essential
Prices
Meals: £ 17 (weekdays)
and a la carte £ 21/34

Typical Dishes
Crispy duck salad with mango & lime
Breast of duck with ginger carrots
White chocolate & cranberry brownie

2 mi southeast of Hockley Heath on B 4439; on the left hand side just before the village. Parking.

515

Long Compton

23

Red Lion

**Main St,
Long Compton, CV36 5JS**
Tel.: (01608)684221
Website: www.redlion-longcompton.co.uk

VISA **MO** **AE** **D**

Adnams Broadside and Hook Norton Ales

With its flag floors and log fires, this 18C former coaching inn has the character of a country pub, and its stylish interior boasts a warm, modern feel. The seasonal menu offers classic pub dishes like homemade steak and Hook Norton pie, pan-fried calves' liver or fish and chips, with old favourites like rhubarb crumble or warm chocolate fudge cake for dessert. These are tasty, home-cooked dishes from the tried-and-tested school of cooking – so if you're after something a little more adventurous, try the daily specials board instead. Staff are pleasant and smartly attired; Cocoa, the chocolate Labrador, also gives a warm welcome. Bedrooms may be slightly on the small side, but are stylish and contemporary, with a good level of facilities.

Closing times
Open daily
Prices
Meals: a la carte £ 25/33
5 rooms: £ 60/140

Typical Dishes
Twice-baked smoked salmon soufflé
Chargrilled rib-eye steak
Spiced rhubarb fool

 Between Chipping Norton and Shipston-on-Stour on A 3400. Parking.

24 **Stag**

**Welsh Rd,
Offchurch, CV33 9AQ**
Tel.: (01926)425801
Website: www.thestagatoffchurch.com

🏠 *VISA* MC AE

🍺 **Warwickshire Beer Co Ales, Hook Norton Hooky Bitter
and Purity Pure UBU**

Charles and Nigel may have won over the villagers before they even started, by distributing tasty home-baked bread to mark their arrival, but newcomers seem just as taken with this 16C thatched pub. Inside it's surprisingly contemporary, boasting a boldly coloured bar and two modern dining rooms: the first – adorned with deer antlers and animal heads – is cosy, beamed and wood-panelled; the second, overlooking the garden, boasts funky fabrics, large mirrors and dark Venetian blinds. The extensive menu changes with the seasons, offering generous, classically based dishes – maybe haddock fishcakes or pan-fried calves' liver – and the antipasti and charcuterie sharing plates are a hit. Service is efficient and copes well under pressure.

Closing times
Open daily
Prices
Meals: a la carte £ 23/39

Typical Dishes
Curried crab
mayonnaise on toast
Cod with brown
shrimps, clams & cider
Pear & cardamom
tarte Tatin

🚗 *3.5 mi east of Royal Lemington Spa signposted off A 425.
Parking.*

25   **Orange Tree**

**Warwick Rd,
Chadwick End, B93 0BN**
Tel.: (01564)785364
Website: www.lovelypubs.co.uk

 Purity Pure UBU and Greene King IPA

'Hoof, fin, fur, feather and flour' is painted on both the front and back of this pub, giving some idea of what to expect: yes there is beer here but it's the food that really excites, and you'll find plenty of options under each heading, plus more under slightly less catchy ones such as 'grazing and sharing' or 'starters and salads'. Influences are global, with some adventurous combinations, so expect dishes like salmon tataki with mouli, spring onions, pickled ginger, soy and wasabi or pan-fried guinea fowl with salami, thyme and sage, toasted almonds and lemon and basil mash. This impressively smart pub has a unique, 'ski chalet meets New England' style: cosy, rustic and contemporary by turns, with a bit of kitsch thrown in for good measure.

Closing times
Closed 25 December and Sunday dinner
booking advisable
Prices
Meals: a la carte £ 21/37

Typical Dishes
Red onion, beetroot & goat's cheese tart

Flat iron steak, Café de Paris butter

Ginger sticky toffee pudding with coconut ice cream

 On A 4141 midway between Solihull and Warwick. Parking.

England's biggest county has a lot of room for the spectacular; it encapsulates the idea of desolate beauty. The bracing winds of the Dales whistle through glorious meadows and deep, winding valleys, while the vast moors are fringed with picturesque country towns like Thirsk, Helmsley and Pickering. Further south the charming Wolds roll towards the sea, enhanced by such Georgian gems as Beverley and Howden. Popular history sits easily here: York continues to enchant with its ancient walls and Gothic Minster, but, owing to its Brontë links, visitors descend on the cobbled street village of Haworth with as much enthusiasm. Steam railways criss-cross the region's bluff contours, while drivers get a more streamlined thrill on the Humber Bridge. Yorkshire's food and drink emporiums range from quaintly traditional landmarks like the country tearoom and fish and chip shops proudly proclaiming to be the best in England, to warm and characterful pubs serving heart-warming local specialities.

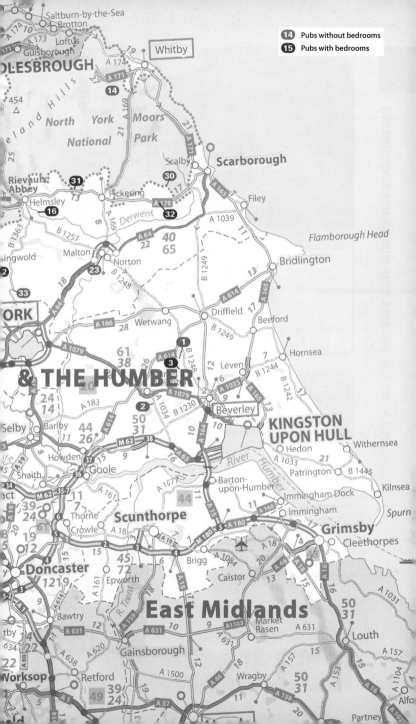

Lund

1   **Wellington Inn**

**19 The Green,
Lund, YO25 9TE**
Tel.: (01377)217294
Website: www.thewellingtoninn.co.uk

 Theakston Best Bitter, Timothy Taylor Landlord and Copper Dragon Golden Pippin

They may have called their company 'Warm Beer and Lousy Food' but that couldn't be further from the truth at the 'Welly', where they offer a good array of well-kept Yorkshire ales and an extensive range of dishes that capture the imagination. At lunch the blackboard 'Baaa…r Menu' lists appealing dishes such as warm crab and samphire tart or calves' liver and bacon, while in the evening there's a large à la carte offering the likes of loin of venison with parsnip boulangère or pork belly with scallops and hot and sour sauce. Dishes are generous, flavoursome and feature good quality ingredients. Eat next to an open fire in one of the beamed bars or in one of the numerous dining rooms, where you'll be served by a smart, efficient team.

Closing times
Closed 25 December,
1 January and Monday

Prices
Meals: a la carte £ 27/40

Typical Dishes
Rabbit, leek & bacon
pudding
Beef fillet with blue
cheese butter
Hazelnut tart with
Nutella ice cream

 10 mi northwest of Beverley just off B 1248. Parking.

2 **Star**

King St,
Sancton, YO43 4QP
Tel.: (01430)827269
Website: www.thestaratsancton.co.uk

 Black Sheep Best Bitter, Wold Top Best Bitter, Copper Dragon Golden Pippin and York Brewery Yorkshire Terrier

Owners Ben and Lindsay bought this once down-at-heel pub in the small village of Sancton over ten years ago and have since set about establishing and expanding it into the place you see before you today. There's a cosy, slightly rustic bar – its counter topped with homemade nibbles – where the locals like to come for a pint and maybe sausage and mash or a steak and ale pie. There are also two rooms with upholstered banquettes, smart wood-topped tables and plush carpets, which make up the restaurant; here you'll find a good value 'Yorkshire Lunch' menu and an à la carte offering hearty, boldly flavoured dishes which display a little more imagination. Every dish proudly lists the main ingredient's grower or supplier – all local, of course.

Closing times
Closed Monday

Prices
Meals: £ 16 (weekday lunch) and a la carte £ 21/44

Typical Dishes
Scallops with bacon
Rack of Yorkshire lamb with wine juices
Miniature Yorkshire rhubarb desserts

2 miles south of Market Weighton in centre of village on A 1034. Parking.

South Dalton

3

Pipe and Glass Inn

**West End,
South Dalton, HU17 7PN**
Tel.: (01430)810246
Website: www.pipeandglass.co.uk

Black Sheep Best Bitter, Great Yorkshire Brewery Two
Chefs, Wold Top, Old Mill and York Brewery seasonal ales

Very personally run by its experienced owners – he cooks, while she looks after front of house – the Pipe and Glass Inn is a deservedly popular place. Grab a drink and a seat beside the log burner or head straight for a table in the contemporary dining room to enjoy food that's carefully executed, big on flavour and generously proportioned. Dishes are made with local, seasonal and traceable produce, and might include venison and juniper suet pudding or roast loin of red deer; desserts like the Pipe and Glass chocolate plate (subtitled 'Five reasons to love chocolate') continue the decadent theme. Luxurious bedrooms are equipped with the latest mod cons and have their own patios overlooking the estate woodland; breakfast is served in your room.

Closing times
Closed 2 weeks January, Sunday dinner and Monday except bank holidays

Prices
Meals: a la carte £ 21/51

2 rooms: £ 160

Typical Dishes
Potted Gloucester Old Spot pork
Roast turbot with monkfish cheek fritter
Rhubarb trifle with East Yorkshire sugar cakes

5 mi northwest of Beverley by A 164, B 1248 and side road west. Parking.

4 Crab and Lobster

**Dishforth Rd,
Asenby, YO7 3QL**
Tel.: (01845)577286
Website: www.crabandlobster.com

VISA MC AE D

Hambleton Bitter and Copper Dragon Golden Pippin

From the moment you set eyes on this pub, you'll realise it's no ordinary place. Old advertisements and lobster pots hang from the walls, thatched crabs and lobsters sit on the roof and even the umbrellas are thatched. Inside it's just as quirky, with charming exposed beams hung with knick-knacks aplenty and all kinds of characterful memorabilia strewn over every surface The menu, unsurprisingly, features plenty of seafood, with the likes of fish soup, fishcakes, fish pie, shellfish and lobster; alongside traditional British favourites such as cheese soufflé, pork cheek confit and crusted loin of lamb. Split between an 18C Georgian Manor and log cabins, the stylish bedrooms are themed around world-famous hotels; some boast private hot tubs.

Closing times
Open daily
Prices
Meals: £ 20 (lunch)
and a la carte £ 28/46
17 rooms: £ 90/160

Typical Dishes
Yorkshire game terrine
Swordfish loin with curried king prawns
Sticky date pudding

4 mi southwest of Thirsk by B 1448 and A 168. Parking.

Aysgarth

5 George and Dragon Inn

**Aysgarth,
DL8 3AD**
Tel.: (01969)663358
Website: www.georgeanddragonaysgarth.co.uk

Yorkshire Dales Brewing Company George and Dragon and Swinacote, Rudgate Hop and Glory

Set in the heart of prime walking country, close to the breathtaking waterfalls of the River Ure, this 17C coaching inn makes the perfect base for exploring Wensleydale. This is a proper pub in all senses of the word: there's not a plasma screen in sight and if you've made yourself comfy in the laid-back bar, you're welcome to settle in for the night. The large restaurant winds its way around the front of the building, first taking on a French brasserie style and then ending up in a Victorian themed room; there's also a patio with great views of Pen Hill. Unfussy pub classics include plenty of local meats, game and old-fashioned puddings and there's a good value early evening menu. Bedrooms are comfy and well-priced; some boast whirlpool baths.

Closing times
Closed 3 weeks January
Prices
Meals: £ 14 (lunch) and a la carte £ 20/33
7 rooms: £ 40/120

Typical Dishes
Whitby crab risotto
Venison haunch with pressed potato, shallot & carrot
Sticky date & banana cake

 7 mi west of Leyburn by A 684. Parking.

6 · Malt Shovel

**Main St,
Brearton, HG3 3BX**
Tel.: (01423)862929
Website: www.themaltshovelbrearton.co.uk

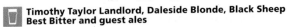

Timothy Taylor Landlord, Daleside Blonde, Black Sheep
Best Bitter and guest ales

The Bleiker family are best known for their successful smokehouse but Jürg, the founder, has left his sons-in-law in charge and moved on to combine his family's two greatest loves – food and music. The Malt Shovel is a rather quirky, shabby-chic pub boasting a panelled, fire-lit bar, an opera-themed 'Red Room', an elegant 'Green Room' and a conservatory. There's a small kiln outside the kitchen and whatever meat, game or fish is in season will be smoking away. Dishes are largely classical with continental flavours, so will feature the likes of moules frites or Wiener schnitzel, with some smaller tapas-style plates available at lunch. Most Sundays they host jazz sessions and from time to time son D'Arcy and wife Anna give the odd opera recital.

Closing times
Closed 25 December,
1 January and Sunday dinner

Prices
Meals: £ 14 (lunch and early dinner) and a la carte £ 26/43

Typical Dishes
Malt Shovel smokie
Slow-cooked Old Spot, red cabbage & crackling
Yorkshire rhubarb & orange crumble

 4 mi east of Ripley by B 6165 and Brearton road. Parking.

England • Yorkshire and The Humber • North Yorkshire

Broughton

7

Bull

**Broughton,
BD23 3AE**
Tel.: (01756)792065
Website: www.thebullatbroughton.com

Copper Dragon Golden Pippin and Hetton Pale Ale

The Bull is a member of the Ribble Valley Inns group – but don't expect some sort of faceless corporate brand – this is the bourgeoning pub company set up by Nigel Haworth and Craig Bancroft, co-proprietors of Lancashire's celebrated Northcote. They have led the way in promoting the specialities of their region and the Bull is no different. Expect real ales, local meats and cheeses, as well as traditional British dishes, rediscovered classics and the sort of puddings that make you feel patriotic. The Bull is an appropriate moniker as this pub is big and solid looking. It's at the side of Broughton Hall and is made up of assorted snugs and spaces, with beams, stone floors and log fires. It's cosy in winter and charming on a summer's day.

Closing times
Closed 25 December and Monday
Prices
Meals: a la carte £ 20/32

Typical Dishes
Gloucester Old Spot crispy pork croquette
Veal kidneys with mushroom sauce & garlic mash
Baked Alaska

3 mi west of Skipton on A 59. In the grounds of Broughton Hall Country Park Estate. Parking.

8

Red Lion

**Burnsall,
BD23 6BU**
Tel.: (01756)720204
Website: www.redlion.co.uk

🛜 *VISA* Ⓜ︎Ⓒ

Theakston Best Bitter, Dark Horse Hetton Pale Ale and Ilkley Brewery Joshua Jane

This appealing stone inn sits at the heart of a small rural community on the banks of the River Wharfe. It has a warm yet worn feel, which isn't all that surprising when you learn that it has cellars dating back to the 12C and a wood-panelled bar from its 16C ferryman's inn days. There's plenty of choice when it comes to where to sit – the cosy bar with its copper-topped counter, the laid-back lounge or the more formally dressed dining room. The choice of food is similarly wide, with a bar menu of pub favourites; an à la carte featuring local lamb in spring, East Coast fish in summer and game in winter; and a blackboard of daily specials. Bedrooms are traditional with modern overtones – those in the nearby manor house are the most contemporary.

Closing times
Open daily
Prices
Meals: a la carte £ 20/37
🛏 **25 rooms:** £ 60/158

Typical Dishes
Crispy beetroot salad
Wood pigeon with plum sauce
Bread & butter pudding

England • Yorkshire and The Humber • North Yorkshire

🚗 *7 mi north of Bolton Abbey by B 6160. Parking.*

Carthorpe

9 **Fox and Hounds**

**Carthorpe,
DL8 2LG**
Tel.: (01845)567433
Website: www.foxandhoundscarthorpe.co.uk

Black Sheep Bitter and Theakstons Best

It may be just a few minutes from the A1 but this traditional stone pub is a true country local. It's been in the same family since 1983 and is now run by hands-on couple Vincent and Helen. It's a fairly small place: to one side there's a stone-walled, open-fired bar; to the other, a neatly laid dining room with an array of equine paraphernalia, farming implements and blacksmith's tools filling the walls. Good-sized menus offer unfussy, home-cooked dishes; choose something from the daily changing blackboards, maybe ham hock terrine with piccalilli, followed by a satisfying steak and kidney short crust pie. Fruit and vegetables are from Snape, meats from Bedale and fish, from Hartlepool. Local, organic and homemade products are also for sale.

Closing times
Closed first 2 weeks January,
25 December,
and Monday

Prices
Meals: £ 15 (weekdays)
and a la carte £ 21/42

Typical Dishes
Grilled pear & Parma ham with balsamic
Sea bass on stir-fried vegetables
Plum tart with vanilla ice cream

9 mi north of Ripon by minor road via Wath and Kirklington. Parking.

10   Ye Old Sun Inn

**Main St,
Colton, LS24 8EP**
Tel.: (01904)744261
Website: www.yeoldsuninn.co.uk

Black Sheep Best Bitter, Timothy Taylor Landlord and Ilkley Brewery Ilkley Gold

The demise of many a local post office has highlighted their importance in the local community, but Ye Old Sun Inn is a good example of how significant a role the pub plays in local life. This family-run inn does it all: from selling homemade produce from its small deli to holding cookery demonstrations. It's also a great ambassador for local suppliers, several of whom are name-checked on the menu. The open fires and rustic feel make this a very popular place with the local community, although race days at the Knavesmire bring a regular invasion of interlopers. The menus change monthly and are as seasonal as ever. Those not from these parts can take advantage of the three very smart bedrooms in the recently acquired house next door.

Closing times
Closed 26 and 31 December
Prices
Meals: £ 20 and a la carte £ 20/39

3 rooms: £ 75

Typical Dishes
Crab scotch egg
Poached plaice with pickled grapes
Banana pudding & chocolate sauce

England • Yorkshire and The Humber • North Yorkshire

 3 mi northeast of Tadcaster by A 659 and A 64. Parking.

Constable Burton

11   **Wyvill Arms**

**Constable Burton,
DL8 5LH**
Tel.: (01677)450581
Website: www.thewyvillarms.co.uk

🍴 **VISA** **MC**

🍺 **Theakston Best Bitter and Wensleydale West Keeper**

As you approach this ivy-clad stone pub you might recognise the large Elizabethan stately home immediately in front it; that's if you're a fan of the 2006 film Wind in the Willows. To the rear you'll find pleasant gardens and a small sitting area; while inside classical décor and rustically themed furnishings provide a warm, intimate feel. For dining, there's the choice of a small open-fired bar, a stone-floored area with banquettes and a more formal room with high-backed chairs. There's plenty of choice on the menu too, which features local, traceable produce in carefully prepared, classical dishes. You'll find tasty mature steaks, daily fish specials and Nigel's Yorkshire puddings are a must on Sundays. Bedrooms are simple but well-kept.

Closing times
Closed Monday except bank holidays
Prices
Meals: a la carte £ 21/37
🛏 **4 rooms:** £ 65/125

Typical Dishes
Pigeon with black pudding & blackcurrant
Herb-crusted lamb with dauphinoise potatoes
Mascarpone cheesecake

 3.5 mi east of Leyburn on A 684. Parking.

12   **Durham Ox**

**Westway,
Crayke, YO61 4TE**
Tel.: (01347)821506
Website: www.thedurhamox.com

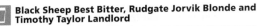

Black Sheep Best Bitter, Rudgate Jorvik Blonde and Timothy Taylor Landlord

Set in a sleepy little hamlet, next to Crayke Castle, the 300 year old Durham Ox is a bustling, family-run pub which boasts pleasant views over the vale of York and up to the medieval church. You'll receive a warm welcome whether you sit in the carved wood panelled bar with its vast inglenook fireplace or more formal beamed dining room; but when the weather's right, head straight for the rear courtyard, as this is definitely the place to be. The regularly changing menu features plenty of fresh seafood, steaks and Crayke game; as well as tasty chicken from the rotisserie. Set in converted farm cottages, the cosy bedrooms display original brickwork and quarry tiling; some are suites, some are set over two floors and some have jacuzzis.

Closing times
Closed 25 December
booking essential
Prices
Meals: a la carte £ 24/38
5 rooms: £ 80/150

Typical Dishes
Crab cocktail, avocado
& apple salad
Steak frites
Taste of lemon

 2 mi east of Easingwold on Helmsley rd. Parking.

East Witton

13

Blue Lion

**East Witton,
DL8 4SN**
Tel.: (01969)624273
Website: www.thebluelion.co.uk

 VISA **MC**

Black Sheep Ales and Theakstons Best Bitter

Set in a delightful village, this former coaching inn boasts a truly rustic interior, pleasingly untouched by the minimalist makeover brigade. Dine in the flag-floored bar or in the high-ceilinged, wood-floored dining room; either way you'll sit at a polished wooden table in the glow of candlelight and enjoy unfussy, hearty cooking made from local produce. The menu is chalked up above the fire in the bar and dishes might include homemade pork pie, cassoulet of duck leg or roast wild venison. The wine list is of particular note and offers bottles at a wide range of prices. Bedrooms in the main house are furnished with antiques, including a four-poster in Room 3, while the rooms in the converted stable are more contemporary in style.

Closing times
Open daily
booking essential
Prices
Meals: £ 16/29
and a la carte £ 25/48

15 rooms: £ 69/145

Typical Dishes
Curried crab cakes
Pan-fried beef fillet with braised shin
Pear tart with vanilla ice cream

 3 mi southeast of Leyburn on A 6108. Parking.

14   Wheatsheaf Inn

Egton,
YO21 1TZ
Tel.: (01947)895271
Website: www.wheatsheafegton.com

 Black Sheep Bitter, Timothy Taylor Landlord and Cropton Ales

This late 19C inn is located at the centre of a delightful stone-built hamlet on the edge of the picturesque North Yorkshire Moors. There's a small garden and several rooms filled with framed prints and lithographs of hunting scenes, along with a delightful snug that boasts a lovely range – that acts as an open fire – and chunky tables crafted by one of the locals from thick slices of oak cut at the Castle Howard Estate. Menus offer a real taste of Yorkshire, utilising fresh produce from just outside the door, so you'll find the likes of lamb's kidneys, local steak, Whitby scampi and game shot within two miles, all accompanied by triple-cooked chips. It really is a family affair here, with mum cooking and her husband and daughter out front.

Closing times
Closed 25 December and Monday
light lunch
Prices
Meals: a la carte £ 20/26

Typical Dishes
Lamb's kidney with bacon & redcurrant

Chicken with tallegio cheese, Parma ham & basil

Ginger sticky toffee pudding

Felixkirk

15   **Carpenter's Arms**

**Felixkirk,
YO7 2DP**
Tel.: (01845)537369
Website: www.thecarpentersarmsfelixkirk.com

🍽 **VISA** **MC** **AE**

🍺 **Black Sheep Bitter and Timothy Taylor Landlord**

Mentioned in the Domesday Book, Felixkirk's claim to fame is that it was once a local Commandery of the Knights Hospitallers of St John of Jerusalem. Dating back to the 18C, the Carpenter's Arms may not be quite as old, but it really is a good old village pub, so you'll often find local groups such as the bell ringers in. When it comes to dining, there's a choice of blackboard specials or dishes from the seasonal main menu, which offers everything from gammon or venison casserole to sea bass with ratatouille. Be sure to save room for pudding before the steep climb back up Sutton Bank; if you don't fancy the ascent, spend the night under a duck down duvet in a well-equipped, stylishly appointed bedroom, overlooking the Vale of Mowbray.

Closing times
Open daily
Prices
Meals: a la carte £ 21/39
🛏 **10 rooms:** £ 99/185

Typical Dishes
Baked queen scallops with gruyère & cheddar
Rack of spicy & sticky ribs
Pear Bakewell tart

🚗 Signposted off A 170, 3 mi northeast of Thirsk. Parking.

16 **Star Inn**

**High St,
Harome, YO62 5JE**
Tel.: (01439)770397
Website: www.thestaratharome.co.uk

VISA **MC**

Black Sheep Ale and Great Yorkshire Brewery Two Chefs

Head for the main low-ceilinged bar with its open fire, photo-filled walls and award-laden shelves, then grab the kidney-shaped Mousey Thompson table for the best seat in the house; alternatively try the rustic middle room, or the brighter, brasserie-like restaurant. This thatched 14C pub also has a delightful terrace, and a kitchen garden which provides some of the produce to be found on its comprehensive, seasonal menu of generously proportioned classic dishes. Other ingredients won't have travelled much further, so you'll find trout from Pickering, apples from Ampleforth, roast Whitby turbot or saddle of Harome-shot deer. Stylish bedrooms come with unique features: one has a snooker table and another, a suspended bed.

Closing times
Closed Monday lunch except bank holidays
booking essential
Prices
Meals: £ 25 (weekdays) and a la carte £ 30/56
8 rooms: £ 160/270

Typical Dishes
Risotto of wild garlic with cured pancetta
Halibut with Yorkshire Blue rarebit
Steamed lemon thyme sponge

England • Yorkshire and The Humber • North Yorkshire

 2.75 mi southeast of Helmsley by A 170. Parking.

Helperby

17   Oak Tree Inn

**Raskelf Rd,
Helperby, YO61 2PH**
Tel.: (01423)789189
Website: www.theoaktreehelperby.com

Black Sheep Bitter, Timothy Taylor Landlord & Golden Best, Yorkshire Brewery Ales and Rudgate Ales

Don't let the Brafferton Helperby sign confuse you – this did, in fact, start life as two even smaller villages; The Oak Tree being in the latter of the two. Younger sister to the Durham Ox and the Carpenters Arms, this is a place of two halves: there's a large bar, a tap room and two snugs, while in the old hay barn there's a smart dining room with large windows overlooking a terrace. The same menu is available throughout, offering hearty, generous dishes which use ingredients from small local suppliers; everything from the bread to the petit fours is homemade and combinations are familiar and comforting. If you're in a rush, pizzas and wines are also available to take away. Service is charming. Smart, modern bedrooms boast jacuzzi baths.

Closing times
Open daily
Prices
Meals: a la carte £ 20/33
🛏 **6 rooms:** £ 80/150

Typical Dishes
Onion & Black Sheep Ale soup
Duo of Yorkshire Dales lamb
Old-fashioned treacle sponge

 5 mi northeast of Boroughbridge on T-junction entering village. Parking.

18   **Angel Inn**

**Hetton,
BD23 6LT**
Tel.: (01756)730263
Website: www.angelhetton.co.uk

Black Sheep Ale, Timothy Taylor Landlord and Hetton Pale Ale

This 18C stone inn might be in a rural location but it's gained quite a reputation over the years. It's a characterful place, featuring old beams and roaring log fires, and the well-drilled team cope with the numbers proficiently. Bookings are only taken from 12-12:30 and 6-6:30pm; if you miss this, join the group of drinkers at the bar, waiting for their name to reach the top of the list. The seasonal menu offers an extensive range of hearty dishes crafted from local produce, alongside Yorkshire tapas, a good value midweek set selection and a list of daily specials; for a more formal experience, head to one of the smart dining rooms. Regular events include cookery classes and themed evenings. Bedrooms are found in the nearby 'Barn Lodgings'.

Closing times
Closed 4 days January
booking essential
Prices
Meals: a la carte £ 26/43
9 rooms: £ 125/190

Typical Dishes
Hay-smoked duck breast
Roast lamb chump with barley & spelt
Rhubarb three-ways

 5.75 mi north of Skipton by B 6265. Parking.

Kirkby Fleetham

19 **Black Horse Inn**

**Lumley Ln,
Kirkby Fleetham, DL7 0SH**
Tel.: (01609)749010
Website: www.blackhorsekirkbyfleetham.com

Black Sheep Ale, Copper Dragon Golden Pippin & Pennine Real Blonde

Originally called 'The Salutation', this 18C pub was reputedly renamed after a highwayman rode away on his black horse with a local landowner's daughter. Inside it's been subtly modernised – it still has its original beams but now also a smart flagged floor. Drinkers and diners sit alongside one another in the candlelit bar, with its Welsh dresser and cushion-filled benches but there's a dedicated dining room too, with painted tables and high-backed chairs. The same menu is served throughout, ranging from sharing boards to flavoursome British classics that are a step above your usual pub fare; maybe Yorkshire game pie or oxtail casserole. Stylish bedrooms come with designer bathrooms; if the weather's good, head outside for a game of quoits.

Closing times
Open daily
booking advisable
Prices
Meals: a la carte £ 21/32
7 rooms: £ 60/100

Typical Dishes
Fishcakes & tartare hollandaise
Confit duck leg with bubble & squeak
Cherry chocolate bar

Midway between Catterick and Northallerton signposted off B 6271. Parking.

20 Charles Bathurst Inn

**Langthwaite,
DL11 6EN**
Tel.: (01748)884567
Website: www.cbinn.co.uk

**Black Sheep Ales, Theakston Best Bitter and Rudgate
Brewery Ales**

This characterful 18C hostelry is named after a local land and lead mine owner, and former resident. Sitting on the edge of the Pennine way, high in the hills of Arkengarthdale, it boasts commanding views over the surrounding countryside and is so remotely set, that the only sound you'll hear is the 'clink' of quoits being thrown in the garden. Inside you're greeted by open fires, various timbered snugs and a charming dining room hung with old monochrome photos and sepia lithographs. Unusually inscribed on a mirror, the daily menu offers refined yet hearty classical British dishes, with the likes of asparagus and Wensleydale tart, followed by local meats; maybe fillet of beef on oxtail terrine. Bedrooms are spacious and extremely comfy.

Closing times
Closed 25 December
Prices
Meals: a la carte £ 21/35
19 rooms: £ 81/125

Typical Dishes
Homemade scotch egg
Braised Swaledale lamb shank with lentils
White chocolate panna cotta

 3.25 mi northwest of Reeth on Langthwaite rd. Parking.

England • Yorkshire and The Humber • North Yorkshire

Leyburn

21 **Sandpiper Inn**

Market Pl,
Leyburn, DL8 5AT
Tel.: (01969)622206
Website: www.sandpiperinn.co.uk

VISA MC AE ◉

🍺 **Black Sheep Ales, Rudgate Ales and Copper Dragon Ales**

A friendly Yorkshire welcome is extended to the Dale walkers who come to refuel at this stone-built, part-16C pub, situated just off the main square. Visitors can rest their blistered feet by the fire in the split-level, beamed bar, or plump for a seat in the more characterful dining room. A small enclosed terrace out the back provides a third alternative for when it's sunny, but you'll have to come inside to read the blackboard menus, found hanging on the walls amidst the general clutter of decorative pictures, books and ornaments. Subtle, refined cooking offers a modern take on the classics, so expect dishes like ham hock terrine and piccalilli, pressed Dales lamb or slow-cooked Wensleydale beef. Two homely bedrooms are on the first floor.

Closing times
Closed Monday
Prices
Meals: a la carte £ 26/41
🛏 **2 rooms:** £ 75/90

Typical Dishes
Belly pork with scallops & cauliflower
Venison on a pearl barley risotto
Assiette of desserts

🚗 *In town centre. Limited parking available in the Market Place.*

22 **Punch Bowl Inn**

**Low Row,
DL11 6PF**
Tel.: (01748)886233
Website: www.pbinn.co.uk

Black Sheep Ales, Theakston Best Bitter and Timothy Taylor Landlord

This traditional 17C stone-built inn's rustic exterior is a complete contrast to its modernised, shabby-chic style interior, with its open fires and scrubbed wooden tables. It's a popular stop-off point for walkers, who refuel on classic dishes like duck liver parfait, braised local lamb shank or beef and red wine casserole; but don't go looking for a paper menu, since dishes are listed on mirrors in the bar. There's a selection of filled ciabatta at lunchtime, tasty desserts such as spiced apple tart and custard, and bi-monthly steak nights which prove popular with the villagers. Supremely comfortable bedrooms are decorated in a fresh, modern style; all of them have views over Swaledale, while the superior rooms are more spacious.

Closing times
Closed 25 December
Prices
Meals: a la carte £ 20/34
11 rooms: £ 80/115

Typical Dishes
Chicken liver parfait with red onion confit
Sirloin steak with Swaledale blue cheese salad
Yorkshire parkin

4 mi west of Reeth on B 6270. Parking.

Malton

23 New Malton

2-4 Market Pl,
Malton, YO17 7LX
Tel.: (01653)693998
Website: www.thenewmalton.co.uk

VISA **MC**

Wold Top Bitter, Rudgate Ruby Mild, Daleside Leg Over and Treboom Drum Beat

This 18C stone building has been serving the market town of Malton for many years, first as a pub, then a tea room and later, as a tapas restaurant – and now it's back as a pub again. There are three different rooms, all with open fires, reclaimed furniture and black and white photos of old town scenes, a style which is clearly a hit with the locals. The good-sized menu offers hearty pub classics with the occasional adventurous dish thrown in, and cooking is unfussy and flavoursome with an appealing Northern bias; the toad in the hole is particularly popular. Beers change regularly and food is served all day, every day; you're meant to order at the bar but if you catch one of the friendly team walking by, they'll happily save you the trip.

Closing times
Closed 25-26 December and 1 January
Prices
Meals: a la carte £ 18/32

Typical Dishes
Scallops with smoked cauliflower purée
Free range chicken & ham pie
Glazed lemon tart

In centre of town, ample on-street parking.

24 **Punch Bowl Inn**

Marton cum Grafton, YO51 9QY

Tel.: (01423)322519

Website: www.thepunchbowlmartoncumgrafton.com

Timothy Taylor Landlord and Black Sheep Best Bitter

You won't find Marton cum Grafton on your map because it's two villages which have slowly joined together over the years. What you will find is this delightful whitewashed inn, which part-dates from the 14C and is the fourth in the area to have been taken over by these experienced owners. It has a strange, almost crescent shape, with a small seating area in front, a lovely terrace behind and various little rooms with open fires and old beams; not forgetting a private room with wine glass chandeliers. The all-encompassing, seasonal menu features local produce and includes a seafood platter and a 'Yorkshire board', along with excellent fish and chips and a great rib-eye steak; from 5.30-7 they offer the 'Magnificent Seven' – 7 dishes at £7 each.

Closing times
Closed 25 December

Prices
Meals: a la carte £ 21/36

Typical Dishes
Yorkshire plate
Duo of spring lamb
Vanilla crème brûlée

3.5 mi southeast of Boroughbridge by B 6265. In the centre of the village. Parking.

Newton-on-Ouse

25   Dawnay Arms

**Newton-on-Ouse,
YO30 2BR**
Tel.: (01347)848345
Website: www.thedawnayatnewton.co.uk

**Black Sheep Best Bitter, Treboom Drum Beat and
Yorkshire Sparkle**

In the shadows of the somewhat impressive 18C Beningbrough Hall and Gardens, you'll find this handsome whitewashed pub – its own garden leading straight down to the River Ouse. Once inside you'll discover solid stone floors, low beams, open fires and walls filled with countryside art, not forgetting a delightful rear dining room with views across the terrace and garden to the river. The experienced chef – a native Yorkshireman – lets the seasons guide him, offering sandwiches and good old pub classics at lunch and more complex dishes in the evening, such as potted local rabbit, duck ravioli with pumpkin purée or pork '3 ways'. Game plays a huge part in the cooking and is locally shot. Portions are large, so two courses will probably suffice.

Closing times
Closed first week January,
Sunday dinner and Monday
except bank holidays
Prices
Meals: a la carte £ 25/43

Typical Dishes
Smoked salmon & crab
roulade
Fillet of beef
with horseradish
croquette
Ginger crème brûlée
with Yorkshire rhubarb

 8 mi northwest of York by A 19 and minor road west. Parking.

26   Black Swan

**Oldstead,
YO61 4BL**
Tel.: (01347)868387
Website: www.blackswanoldstead.co.uk

 VISA **MC**

🍺 **Black Sheep and Copper Dragon Best Bitter**

The Black Swan is a proper village pub and a real family affair. Its owners, the Banks, have lived and farmed in Oldstead for generations – and still do. The pub is stone-built and has a characterful beamed, flag-floored bar with welcoming open fires, where you'll find top-rate bar meals such as beef casserole. Head to the upstairs dining room for more ambitious but expertly crafted dishes like duck terrine with foie gras, followed by herb-crusted fillet of wild turbot. Cooking is modern and highly skilled but remains satisfyingly unpretentious, and they are particularly proud of the sourcing of their meats. Antique-furnished bedrooms boast modern fabrics, luxurious bathrooms and patios overlooking the surrounding farmland.

Closing times
Closed lunch Monday-Wednesday

Prices
Meals: £ 25 (weekdays) and a la carte £ 42/54

🛏 **4 rooms:** £ 160/230

Typical Dishes
Tuna tartare, wasabi, ginger & lime

Lamb, gnocchi & ratatouille

Lemon drizzle cake

 Signposted off A 170 7.5 mi southwest of Helmsley. Parking.

England • Yorkshire and The Humber • North Yorkshire

Osmotherley

27

Golden Lion

**6 West End,
Osmotherley, DL6 3AA**
Tel.: (01609)883526
Website: www.goldenlionosmotherley.co.uk

Hop Studio Blonde, York Brewery First Light, Wall's Brewers Gold and Mithril Flower Power

This 18C stone inn sits overlooking the market cross of a historic village in the North York Moors National Park. With its low beamed ceiling, dark wood bar, cushioned church pew seating and welcoming wood-burning stove, it's the kind of place that the locals know and love; make for the atmospheric bar, which offers over 65 different whiskies. The cooking is traditional and satisfying, featuring filling dishes such as steak and kidney pie with suet crust or homemade chicken Kiev. The main selection stays largely the same but there's also a more ambitious weekly changing specials board to consider and be sure to save room for one of the tasty puddings with homemade ice cream. Modern bedrooms have heavy oak furnishings and good facilities.

Closing times
Closed 25 December, lunch Monday and Tuesday except bank holidays

Prices
Meals: a la carte £ 22/36

5 rooms: £ 65/100

Typical Dishes
Grilled aubergine with ratatouille & parmesan
Rump of lamb with spinach couscous
Ginger sponge with stewed plums

 6 mi northeast of Northallerton by A 684. Parking in the village.

28   **Nags Head Country Inn**

Pickhill,
YO7 4JG
Tel.: (01845)567391
Website: www.nagsheadpickhill.co.uk

VISA · MC · AE

Theakston Best Bitter, Black Sheep Best Bitter and Rudgate Brewery Viking

This rustic pub is set close to the A1 and has been run by the same quick-witted owner for over 40 years. It has a large garden, a small front terrace and a quirky interior. Over 700 framed ties hang on the walls of the open-fired bar – have a beer here with the locals before heading through to the dining area, with its booths and framed hunting prints; there's also a large, Georgian-style dining room used at busier times. The blackboard menu features all the classics, accompanied by seasonal vegetables and a jug of gravy – the owner is an avid shooter, so game season is the best time to visit. The wine list offers a good choice of half bottles but if you'd rather have a whole one, book one of the cosy bedrooms in the pub or the annexe.

Closing times
Closed 25 December

Prices
Meals: a la carte £ 16/32

🛏 **12 rooms:** £ 50/97

Typical Dishes
Twice-baked blue cheese soufflé

Roast haunch of venison with mini shortcrust pie

Baked vanilla cheesecake

7.5 mi northwest of Thirsk by A 61 and B 6267. Parking.

Roecliffe

29 **Crown Inn**

Roecliffe,
YO51 9LY
Tel.: (01423)322300
Website: www.crowninnroecliffe.com

 Black Sheep Ale, Timothy Taylor Landlord, Ilkley Brewery Gold and Theakston Best Bitter

England • Yorkshire and The Humber • North Yorkshire

Delightfully set by the village green, this smart 14C inn displays a stylish country interior with stone floors, exposed beams and open fireplaces. Out the front there's a small terrace and inside, the choice of three different rooms – one decorated in red, one in green, and the last, housing the bar counter. The good-sized menus are chalked up the board, as well as being printed out, and display a nice balance of meat and fish. Dishes like crab soup, tempura prawns, fish pie and belly pork are mainstays and the dedicated 'meat free' menu ensures that vegetarians are well-catered for. A carefully chosen wine list provides the perfect accompaniment. Smart bedrooms boast antique-style furnishings, feature beds and free-standing baths.

Closing times
Open daily
Prices
Meals: £ 17 and a la carte £ 26/41

4 rooms: £ 80/120

Typical Dishes
Scallops with pork belly & black pudding
Lamb tasting plate
Lemon soufflé with honeycomb

 1.5 mi west of Boroughbridge by minor road. Parking.

30 **Anvil Inn**

**Main St,
Sawdon, YO13 9DY**
Tel.: (01723)859896
Website: www.theanvilinnsawdon.co.uk

 Wold Top Brewery Headland Red, Daleside Bitter and guest ales

As its name suggests, this charming inn was formerly a smithy, and much of the associated paraphernalia remains, including bellows, an open forge and the original anvil. In marked contrast, but blending in seamlessly, is the boldly coloured, contemporary sitting room. Cooking is classical in essence, with the odd international influence, so expect crispy duck and pancakes alongside Shetland mussels or slow-roasted daube of beef. Local chef Mark prides himself on the use of locally sourced produce; eggs come from the pub's own hens and the local Stillington pork is a firm favourite. There are only seven tables in the intimate restaurant, so be sure to book ahead; particularly for Sunday lunch, which has become something of an institution.

Closing times
Closed 25-26 December, 1 January, Monday and Tuesday
Prices
Meals: a la carte £ 24/38

Typical Dishes
Trio of Yorkshire game

Conchiglie grande filled with smoked Whitby cod

Liquorice crème caramel

10.5 mi southwest of Scarborough by A 170 to Brompton and minor road north. Parking.

Sinnington

31

Fox and Hounds

**Main St,
Sinnington, YO62 6SQ**
Tel.: (01751)431577
Website: www.thefoxandhoundsinn.co.uk

Copper Dragon Best Bitter and Wold Top Anglers Reward

It's always a good sign if a pub has regulars: diners so au fait with what's on offer that they don't even need to look at the menu – and this pretty 18C inn has plenty. What keeps them coming back are the big portions of proper, hearty, Yorkshire cooking: pub classics like beer-battered haddock and chips or calves' liver; maybe some traditional slow braises or some brisket, and plenty of game in season. Customers not only return to eat but also to stay – in one of the spacious, homely, individually decorated bedrooms – with second generations of families now returning to experience the pub's excellent hospitality. Keeping all the balls in the air is Helen – who worked her way up from chambermaid to manager – backed up by a charming team.

Closing times
Closed 25-27 December
Prices
Meals: a la carte £ 22/43
🛏 **10 rooms:** £ 59/170

Typical Dishes
Twice-baked blue cheese soufflé
Slow-cooked shin of beef with horseradish croquettes
Duo of chocolate

🚗 *Just off A 170 between Pickering and Kirkbymoorside.
Parking.*

32

Coachman Inn

**Pickering Rd West,
Snainton, YO13 9PL**
Tel.: (01723)859231
Website: www.coachmaninn.co.uk

🛏 🏠 *VISA* **MC** **AE**

🍺 **Wold Top Ales and Treboom Ales**

This Grade II listed inn dates back to 1776 and was the last staging post before Scarborough for the coaches taking the York mail. It boasts a well-tended garden to the rear and a charming interior: there's a rustic bar displaying quarry tiles and chunky wood furniture and a spacious linen-clad dining room which runs the length of the building, finishing in a small garden room at the end. The place is run with some formality – menus are presented in smart folders and cooking is very much in the classical vein, although with a modern, refined style of presentation. Produce is seasonal and of good quality but prices remain fair. Lunch offers simpler pub favourites and the concise wine list is well-thought-out. Bedrooms are smart and spacious.

Closing times
Closed dinner 25 December
Prices
Meals: a la carte £ 20/31
🛏 **6 rooms:** £ 80/110

Typical Dishes
Pan-fried lamb's kidneys
Steak & chips
Chocolate truffle torte

West of the village on B 1258. Parking.

Sutton-on-the-Forest

33 Rose & Crown

**Main St,
Sutton-on-the-Forest, YO61 1DP**
Tel.: (01347)811333
Website: www.theroseandcrownyork.co.uk

Timothy Taylor Landlord and Black Sheep Golden Sheep

This welcoming pub is found in a beautiful village, in amongst some delightful Georgian country houses. There's always a local or two to be found beside the log burning stove in the cosy bar, tucking into a pub favourite like steak and Black Sheep ale pie, while the elegant restaurant and airy conservatory are a hit with those after just a little more occasion. The atmosphere is relaxed, courtesy of the smiling owner and her friendly young team, and the hidden garden and super terrace are a must on sunny days. Menus offer plenty of choice, from tempting afternoon teas through to hearty classics like local asparagus with a free range poached egg and hollandaise, followed by halibut with wild rice and tomato and coriander salsa.

Closing times
Closed first 3 weeks January, Sunday dinner and Monday
booking essential

Prices
Meals: £ 19 (lunch and early dinner) and a la carte £ 25/38

Typical Dishes
Scallops with belly pork
Lamb 'Henry' with redcurrant reduction
Raspberry crème brûlée

 On B 1363 north of York. Parking.

34 Milestone

84 Green Ln,
Sheffield, S3 8SE
Tel.: (0114)2728327
Website: www.the-milestone.co.uk

 Wentworth Ales and Wells Bombardier

The owners of The Milestone are passionate about organic, locally sourced produce; they consider the quality of their ingredients to be the key to their success and don't believe in buying in things like bread, pasta and puddings, since they can make them in-house. Some of the hearty dishes on the menu like the lamb burger and the beef Bourguignon have become classics but the emphasis is on evolution and seasonality, so what's on offer changes frequently. Things never stand still here – they serve weekend brunch and takeaway sandwiches, and they even hold cookery demonstrations. Downstairs is spacious with understated décor, simple wood tables and banquettes, while the beamed first floor room provides a more formal dining space.

Closing times
Closed 25-26 December and 1 January

Prices
Meals: £ 15 (weekday lunch) and a la carte £ 23/30

Typical Dishes
Pan-roasted belly of pork

Coley with cauliflower purée

Dark chocolate tart with orange curd

Yorkshire and The Humber • South Yorkshire

 Between A 61 and River Don. Parking in Green Ln and Ball St.

Sheffield

35   Wig & Pen

**44 Campo Ln,
Sheffield, S1 2EG**
Tel.: (0114)2722150
Website: www.the-wigandpen.co.uk

Kelham Island and Sheffield Brewery Ales

The team behind the Milestone have moved closer into the heart of the city with this, its sister pub, which overlooks Paradise Square. The name comes from the legal offices which surround it, and the busy bar, with its high stools and sofas, is a magnet for office workers on their journey home. Those here to dine should head for the smarter area towards the rear, with its stylish feature wallpaper and wooden floors. Lunch offers sandwiches and a good value menu of light dishes like fishcakes or risotto, while dinner sees the ambition of the kitchen translated into elaborate dishes presented in a modern fashion; perhaps roast scallops with oxtail and crispy ox tongue, or loin of venison with celeriac purée, mulled pear and cocoa jelly.

Closing times
Closed 25-26 December and 1 January

Prices
Meals: £ 18 (early dinner) and a la carte £ 19/30

Typical Dishes
Beetroot salad with goat's cheese panna cotta
Pork chop with a black pudding fritter
Yorkshire parkin

 Just behind Sheffield Cathedral. On-street parking meters.

36 **Cricket Inn**

**Penny Ln,
Totley, S17 3AZ**
Tel.: (0114)2365256
Website: www.cricketinn.co.uk

 Thornbridge Ales

Hidden away in a delightful spot in the valley, next to the cricket ground, this is a proper pub in every sense of the word. Three rooms boast open fires and rustic wood floors: the walls are filled with cricketing paraphernalia, while the scrubbed tables are home to bottles of Sheffield's spicy Henderson's sauce. Food comes in big, hearty portions, not for the faint-hearted, and there's something for everyone, from sandwiches and snacks like home-roasted pork scratchings, to things like cheese on toast or homemade fishcakes, as well as dishes such as steak and ale pie or slow-braised shoulder shank of lamb. 'Cricket Inn boards' come in ploughman's and fisherman's varieties, there's a little person's menu and some nice nursery style puddings.

Closing times
Open daily

Prices
Meals: £ 15 (weekdays)
and a la carte £ 17/35

Typical Dishes
Belly pork & apple koftas

Braised ox cheek with mashed potato

Sticky toffee Yorkshire parkin

 6 mi southwest of Sheffield by A 61, A 621 and Hillfoot Rd. Parking.

Halifax

England • Yorkshire and The Humber • West Yorkshire

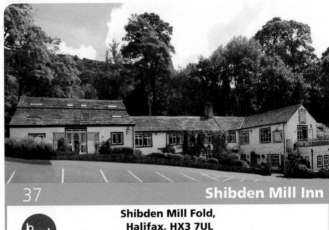

37 — Shibden Mill Inn

**Shibden Mill Fold,
Halifax, HX3 7UL**
Tel.: (01422)365840
Website: www.shibdenmillinn.com

VISA MC AE

Moorhouse's Shibden Bitter, Little Valley Withens, Small Beer IPA and Black Sheep Bitter

This is a pub of paradox: you're in the middle of a deep-sided valley in the quiet, unspoilt countryside, yet only a few minutes' drive from the centre of Halifax; it's popular with locals, yet people travel for miles to visit; and the menu promises 'Comforts and Favourites', like sausage and mash, as well as a 'Gourmet Dining Menu' with dishes like poached and sautéed wood pigeon. In a previous life this was a corn mill and the stream which used to turn the wheel runs alongside, adding to the tranquil feel if you're dining alfresco. Character is not in short supply either, with beamed ceilings, welcoming fires and lots of cosy corners. Staff are well-drilled and bedrooms, individually furnished; choose No. 14 if it's luxury you're after.

Closing times
Closed dinner 25-26 December and 1 January

Prices
Meals: £ 15 (lunch and early dinner) and a la carte £ 22/42

11 rooms: £ 90/182

Typical Dishes
Shibden pork & black pudding pie
Saddle of rabbit with pearl barley risotto
Rhubarb soufflé

Signposted off A 58, 2.25 mi northeast of Halifax. Parking.

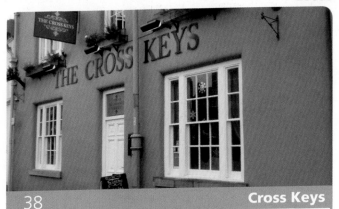

38   **Cross Keys**

**107 Water Ln,
The Round Foundry, Leeds, LS11 5WD**
Tel.: (0113)2433711
Website: www.the-crosskeys.com

🛜   *VISA*   **MC**   **AE**

🍺 Acorn Old Moor Porter, Kirkstall Prototype and Red Willow Feckless

This traditional, brick-built pub stands in a regenerated area of the city and was once the watering hole for workers of the 19C Round Foundry; the first floor dining room is named after James Watt, the inventor of the steam engine (although it's been said he stole many ideas from his inebriated workers!) It's a cosy, friendly place featuring flagged floors, old beams and exposed brick, along with welcoming wood-burning stoves in winter – and it's always busy, so be sure to book. The cooking is hearty, tasty and British through-and-through: lunch sees a simple menu of sandwiches and pub classics such as cottage pie or chicken with pearl barley broth; dinner is more substantial, featuring the likes of chicken liver pâté and braised lamb shank.

Closing times
Closed 25-26 December and 1 January
booking essential
Prices
Meals: a la carte £ 22/32

Typical Dishes
Roast wood pigeon & beetroot

Haunch & cottage pie of venison

Chocolate & hazelnut tart

🚗 Just south of the River Aire in the Holbeck area. Metered parking adjacent.

Marsden

39

Olive Branch

**Marsden,
HD7 6LU**
Tel.: (01484)844487
Website: www.olivebranch.uk.com

🏠   *VISA*   **MC**

🍺 **Regularly changing Greenfield Ales**

This roadside pub's rather bland exterior gives little indication as to what's inside: a central bar, four cosy rooms, plenty of character in the form of stone walls and exposed beams, and a chatty, bustling atmosphere. The menu offers plenty of choice, with dishes like salad of Bury black pudding, crisp belly pork or Yorkshire Blue soufflé; cooking is straightforward and generous, and lets the ingredients speak for themselves. The pub is particularly popular for its well-sourced steaks and holds steak nights on a Tuesday; seafood isn't neglected, either, with a daily blackboard menu and fish supper nights on Fridays. There's a secluded garden and terrace as well as comfy, modern bedrooms: take your pick from 'Duck', 'Topiary' and 'Serengeti'.

Closing times
Closed first 2 weeks January
dinner only
Prices
Meals: £ 20 (weekdays)
and a la carte £ 23/42

🛏 **3 rooms:** £ 60/110

Typical Dishes
Smoked haddock fishcakes

Roast wood pigeon with a red wine sauce

Caramelised lemon tart

 1 mi northeast on A 62. Parking.

Scotland may be small, but its variety is immense. The vivacity of Glasgow can seem a thousand miles from the vast peatland wilderness of Caithness and Sutherland's Flow Country; the arty vibe of Georgian Edinburgh a world away from the remote and tranquil Ardnamurchan peninsula. And how many people link Scotland to its beaches? But wide golden sands trim the Atlantic at South Harris, and the coastline of the Highlands boasts empty islands and turquoise waters. Meantime, Fife's coast draws golf fans to St Andrews and the more secretive delights of the East Neuk, an area of fishing villages and stone harbours. Wherever you travel, the scent of a dramatic history prevails in the shape of castles, cathedrals and rugged lochside monuments to the heroes of old. Food and drink embraces the traditional, too, typified by Aberdeen's famous Malt Whisky Trail. And what better than Highland game, fresh fish from the Tweed or haggis, neeps and tatties to complement a grand Scottish hike…

17 Pubs without bedrooms
19 Pubs with bedrooms

1   Cock and Bull

**Ellon Rd,
Blairton, Balmedie, AB23 8XY**
Tel.: (01358)743249
Website: www.thecockandbull.co.uk

VISA   MC   AE   ◎

Burnside 3 Bullz

The Cock and Bull is a quirky, atmospheric pub with a sense of fun befitting of its name; check out the mural on the men's toilet door and the profusion of knick-knacks throughout. There's a choice of three rooms in which to dine: a cosy lounge with an open fire and low leather sofas, a more formal dining room and an airy conservatory. Wherever you sit, the menu's the same, and there's plenty of choice. You'll find classics like Arbroath smokie kedgeree or Cullen skink, alongside some more restaurant-style dishes such as confit pork belly or mushroom, watercress and ricotta tart; dishes are satisfying and everything arrives neatly presented. Some of the contemporary bedrooms are in a nearby annexe – a complimentary shuttle service is provided.

Closing times
Open daily
Prices
Meals: a la carte £ 20/41

🛏 **8 rooms:** £ 85/120

Typical Dishes
Pigeon breast
with Serrano ham &
apricot purée

Gressingham duck with
caramelised red onion

Toffee apple &
frangipane torte

 On A 90 6 mi north of Aberdeen. Parking.

Memus

2

Drovers Inn

**Memus,
DD8 3TY**
Tel.: (01307)860322
Website: www.the-drovers.com

Inveralmond Ales and Sinclair Ales

Good cooking relies on good ingredients, so if the owner of a pub also has estates nearby that supply much of the produce, it's little wonder that the chef seems so contented. This remote Highland inn with its immaculate lawns was once a crofter's cottage. The bar with its open fires is a lovely spot but there's also a more formal dining room – to which the freshly baked breads add their wonderful aroma – and to the side, a lovely beamed room with a map of the area covering one entire wall. The well-priced menu makes particularly good use of the abundant local produce, such as game and venison from the shoots. Further value for money is provided by a wine list that eschews the usual 'mark-ups' and instead makes a uniform corkage charge.

Closing times
Closed 25-26 December
Prices
Meals: £ 10 (weekdays) and a la carte £ 23/39

Typical Dishes
Sea trout with smoked mussels
Venison steak with spinach & glazed carrots
Gooseberry & custard tart

 4 mi north of Kirriemuir by B 955 and minor road east. Parking.

3 Tayvallich Inn

**Tayvallich,
PA31 8PL**
Tel.: (01546)870282
Website: www.tayvallichinn.com

  VISA **MC**

Loch Ness Brewery Light Ness and Wilder Ness, Orkney
Brewery Dark Island and Red MacGregor

The Tayvallich Inn's sign shows the silhouette of a lobster, which gives a clue as to what this pub is all about. The chef knows a thing or two about seafood and you can expect to see plenty of locally caught fish and shellfish including langoustines, mussels, lobster and lemon sole – as well as scallops by the bucket load; but the menu also offers classic pub dishes like steak and chips and a popular curry of the day. The owners worked on local fish farms before taking over the reins here and make the most of their extensive local connections to source the best produce possible. Dine in the bar, in the more formal dining area or out on the decked terrace, with its rustic style bench seating and picturesque views out over the bay.

Closing times
Closed Monday November-March

Prices
Meals: a la carte £ 18/44

Typical Dishes
Moules marinière
Scallops with chorizo
Orkney fudge cheesecake

12 mi west of Lochgilphead by A 816, B 841 and B 8025; on west shore of Loch Sween. Parking.

Swinton

4

Wheatsheaf

**Main St,
Swinton, TD11 3JJ**
Tel.: (01890)860257
Website: www.wheatsheaf-swinton.co.uk

VISA

**Stewart Brewing Edinburgh Gold and Scottish Borders
Foxy Blonde and Game Bird**

Set in the heart of the village overlooking the green, this substantial stone inn is far from your typical pub. Inside there are numerous sofa-filled rooms and two small dining areas – one linen-laid, the other with an attractive pine ceiling and furniture to match. The hands-on owners are extremely passionate when it comes to food and only serve lunch at weekends so they can give dinner their full attention. The extensive evening menu offers ambitious dishes such as wood pigeon tartlet or white crabmeat beignet, followed by Scottish venison saddle or ballotine of partridge. Specials feature seafood from Eyemouth and meat comes from the surrounding border farms and is then smoked on-site. Bedrooms are spacious, cosy and well-equipped.

Closing times
Closed 2-3 January
dinner only and lunch Saturday and Sunday
booking advisable
Prices
Meals: a la carte £ 22/43
🛏 **14 rooms:** £ 89/159

Typical Dishes
Chicken liver parfait
Roasted monkfish
Wheatsheaf sundae

 In the centre of the village. Plenty of parking on the road.

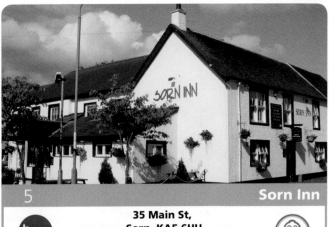

5   **Sorn Inn**

**35 Main St,
Sorn, KA5 6HU**
Tel.: (01290)551305
Website: www.sorninn.com

 Houston Brewery Ales

It's a real family affair here, with the father checking you in to one of the bedrooms and his son cooking your meals. The first clues as to the quality of food are the framed menus and the copy of the chefs' bible, 'Larousse' – and the cooking doesn't disappoint. The chef adopts an international approach, a result of his time spent on the QE2, so along with prime Scottish beef are dishes like wood pigeon with polenta and chicken with banana rice. There's plenty of flexibility here too: some dishes come in a choice of sizes and you can choose to have them either sitting in a high-backed leather chair in the restaurant or with your dog beside your feet in the pub. The blackboard specials are always worth a look and the lunch menu is a steal.

Closing times
Closed 6-16 January and Monday

Prices
Meals: £ 14 (weekdays) and a la carte £ 20/28

4 rooms: £ 40/90

Typical Dishes
Curried onion tart with yoghurt & mint dressing

Chump of lamb with fennel & tomato

Raspberry parfait with caramel meringue

 In centre of village. Parking.

Edinburgh

6 · **N The Scran & Scallie**

**1 Comely Bank Rd,
Stockbridge, Edinburgh, EH4 1DT**
Tel.: (0131)3326281
Website: www.scranandscallie.com

VISA **MC** **AE**

William Brothers Ceildh 90, Stewart Edinburgh Gold and Highland Dark Munro

Found in the smart, village-like suburb of Stockbridge, this pub is the more casual venture of well-known chefs Tom Kitchin and Dominic Jack. It might seem an unusual name but 'Scran' means food and 'Scallie' means children, which reflects their desire for good food to be shared with the whole family. Pass through the heavy wood furnished bar to the dining room with its mix of rustic and contemporary décor; some walls are brick, others are stone, and some are boldly wallpapered and hung with old framed recipes. Extensive menus follow a 'Nature to Plate' philosophy, focusing on the classical and the local – and a map in the bar locates their suppliers. Where else can you start with sheep's heid broth and finish with jelly and ice cream?

Closing times
Closed 25-26 December
booking advisable
Prices
Meals: a la carte £ 24/35

Typical Dishes
Roasted bone marrow, shallots & parsley
Scran & Scallie fish pie
Clementine jelly & ice cream

 On the northwest side of the city. On-street meter parking.

7 — Ship on the Shore

**24-26 The Shore,
Leith, EH6 6QN**
Tel.: (0131)5550409
Website: www.theshipontheshore.co.uk

 Belhaven Best

With its neat blue façade inset with ship's navigation lights and modelled on the Royal Yacht Britannia, this period building on the quayside looks ready to set sail. Inside, the walls are papered with European maritime charts, scrubbed wooden floors mimic a ship's deck and it's filled with nautical bric à brac. The kitchen follows a philosophy of 'sustainable Scottish seafood served simply with style', and 99% of the menu is just that. Classic dishes such as fishcakes and Cullen skink are mainstays and there are some more unusual offerings such as crispy curried squid with lime and mint yoghurt. What draws people from far and wide though, is their 'Fruit de Mer' platters. Champagne is the recommended drink; available by the bottle or glass.

Closing times
Closed 24-26 December
Prices
Meals: a la carte £ 27/41

Typical Dishes
Scallops with parmesan sabayon
Shetland salmon with Stornoway black pudding
Ship's cheesecake

 On east side of river. On-street parking.

Glasgow

8 **The Finnieston**

**1125 Argyle St,
Glasgow, G3 8ND**
Tel.: (0141)2222884
Website: www.thefinniestonbar.com

 No real ales offered

This was once a conventional old boozer but an enthusiastic young team with a real passion for food and drink have resurrected it, and it now specialises in seafood dishes and gin-based cocktails. It's small and cosy, with an intriguing ceiling, a welcoming fire and lots of booths. The anchor motif on the glass reminds you where their strengths lie and the Popeye and Olive Oyl pictures on the toilet doors continue the theme. All of the seafood is from Scottish waters, with mackerel from Peterhead, langoustines from Troon and oysters from Cumbrae. Dishes are light, tasty and neatly presented, relying on just a handful of ingredients so that flavours are clear; if you have the fish and chips, 50p will be donated to the local Fishermen's Mission.

Closing times
Closed 24-26 December
Prices
Meals: a la carte £ 22/55

Typical Dishes
Scallops, apple purée & pancetta
Hake with dill & parsley pesto
Peanut butter & chocolate délice

 On the west side close to Kelvingrove. On-street parking.

Achiltibuie

9 · **Summer Isles (Bar)**

**Achiltibuie,
IV26 2YG**
Tel.: (01854)622282
Website: www.summerisleshotel.com

VISA MC

An Teallach Ales

Set to the side of the Summer Isles Hotel, this tiny pub was originally an old crofters' bar and dates back to the mid-19C. Still popular with the locals today, it boasts two snug rooms filled with black ash tables, a large lawned area with bench seating and a small two-table terrace affording glorious views over the Summer Isles. Concise, daily changing menus have a strong seafood base, offering baguettes, salads and platters at lunchtime, supplemented by more substantial blackboard specials in the evening; although the star of the show has to be the plump, tasty langoustines, which are locally caught and best enjoyed with a chilled glass of Sauvignon Blanc. Comfortable bedrooms are available in the adjoining hotel.

Closing times
Closed November-March
bookings not accepted
Prices
Meals: a la carte £ 18/45
13 rooms: £ 115/310

Typical Dishes
Langoustines
Seafood platter
Sticky toffee pudding

15 mi northwest of Ullapool by A 835 and minor road west from Drumrunie. Parking.

Applecross

10   Applecross Inn

**Shore St,
Applecross, IV54 8LR**
Tel.: (01520)744262
Website: www.applecross.uk.com

VISA **MC**

An Teallach Crofters Pale Ale and Isle of Skye Hebridean Gold

Arrival at Applecross can involve a drive over the hair-raising, single-track Bealach na Ba, with its stunning views and hairpin bends; learner drivers and vertigo sufferers should travel the less scenic route along the coast road instead. This is an unpretentious sort of place, with a wood burning stove and an abundance of pine panelling. Service is friendly and the atmosphere, bustling; on sunny days, the terrace is unsurprisingly the most popular spot. Food-wise, the highlight is the freshest of seafood, often straight out of the sea and sometimes from within sight of the door; expect prawns, crabs and lobster from Applecross and oysters and mussels from Skye. Simple bedrooms in the next-door fishermen's cottages have marvellous sea views.

Closing times
Closed 25 December and 1 January
booking essential
Prices
Meals: a la carte £ 19/42
7 rooms: £ 75/140

Typical Dishes
Haggis with Drambuie & oatcakes
Scallops in garlic with crispy bacon
Whisky & honey ice cream

 From Kishorn via Belach nam Bo (Alpine Pass) or round by Shieldaig and along the coast. Parking.

11 **Kylesku (Bar)**

Kylesku,
IV27 4HW
Tel.: (01971)502231
Website: www.kyleskuhotel.co.uk

 VISA **MC**

 An Teallach Beinn Dearg, Isle of Skye Brewery Blaven and Red Cuillin

Breathtaking views of Loch Glendhu and the spectacular surrounding scenery make this inn an essential stop-off point if you're ever in the area. Friendly staff welcome guests and there's a cosy, homely atmosphere in the spacious, fire-lit bar. Sup on local ale while you trade tales with walkers and cyclists, before settling down to eat seafood so local it practically swam in the door. Langoustines and fish come from the jetty in front of the bar and mussels are rope grown 200 yards away. Classic dishes might include salmon fishcakes or a fish pie, a satisfying bowl of soup or a platter of mature local cheeses; if you're after something a little more meaty, try a mature local steak. Eight comfortable bedrooms are upstairs in the hotel.

Closing times
Closed November-February
Prices
Meals: a la carte £ 16/43
8 rooms: £ 65/120

Typical Dishes
Summer Isles scallops with Thai dressing
Kylesku local seafood platter
Blueberry & almond tart

32 mi north of Ullapool by A 835, A 837 and A 894. On street parking.

Lewiston

12
Loch Ness Inn

**Lewiston,
IV63 6UW**
Tel.: (01456)450991
Website: www.staylochness.co.uk

VISA **M©**

Loch Ness Brewery Ales and Belhaven Best

Considering its location, it would have been all too easy to make this inn a paean to all things 'Nessie' but thankfully, the only sign of the famous monster is in the pub's logo. Inside, it's refreshingly contemporary, with a small locals bar serving pub classics like fish and chips, and a two-roomed restaurant with exposed stone walls, bright timbered beams and a wood burning stove. The one place where the pub's location is justly celebrated is on the menu, so expect hearty, robust, flavoursome dishes which champion Scottish produce; perhaps Cullen skink, loin of venison or whisky-flambéed haggis. Service is sweet and well-meaning – and if you're after somewhere to lay your head, you'll find the bedrooms spacious and comfortable.

Closing times
Open daily
Prices
Meals: a la carte £ 19/36

12 rooms: £ 65/112

Typical Dishes
Applecross Bay prawns
Pan-fried pork
with blue cheese sauce
Sticky toffee pudding

14 mi southwest of Inverness by A 82. Parking.

13 **Plockton Hotel**

**41 Harbour St,
Plockton, IV52 8TN**
Tel.: (01599)544274
Website: www.plocktonhotel.co.uk

h̄ṯ̄ṯ *VISA* MC AE

🍺 **Plockton Brewery, Orkney Brewery and Houston Brewery**

With its distinctive black exterior, this one-time ships' chandlery is easy to spot. Owned and run by the Pearson family for over 20 years, it offers a warm welcome as well as stunning views over Loch Carron to the mountains beyond. Most of the action takes place in the wood-panelled bar, with its red leather banquettes, tartan carpets and wood burning stove; though if the weather's good, the front terrace fills up the fastest. Cooking is honest, fresh and hearty, with a strong Scottish influence, so expect Talisker whisky pâté, Plockton smokies, haggis and whisky or herring in oatmeal – and don't miss the Plockton prawns. Simple, comfortable bedrooms are split between the pub and an annexe; those to the front have wonderful views.

Closing times
Open daily
Prices
Meals: a la carte £ 17/37
🛏 **15 rooms:** £ 55

Typical Dishes
Plockton smokies
Seared hand-dived local scallops
Cranachan & raspberries soaked in whisky

🚗 *5 mi north of Kyle of Lochalsh. Parking 50 yards away in village car park.*

Torridon

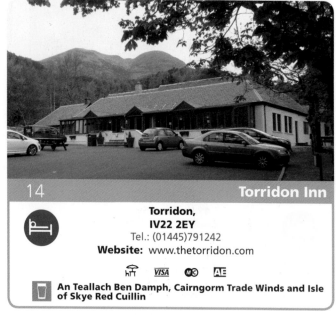

14 — Torridon Inn

**Torridon,
IV22 2EY**
Tel.: (01445)791242
Website: www.thetorridon.com

VISA MC AE

An Teallach Ben Damph, Cairngorm Trade Winds and Isle of Skye Red Cuillin

This is an easy place to miss, as from the outside it looks more like a Tourist Information Office than a pub, but it's well worth a visit, whether for a drink, a bite to eat or to take part in one of their many activities, from glen walks and kayaking to rock climbing and gorge scrambling. If these sound more like spectator sports to you, then simply sit back and enjoy the tranquil surroundings and glorious loch views from either the restaurant or the spacious, part-panelled bar decorated with stags' antlers and Ordnance Survey maps. The interesting menu and daily specials feature satisfying walkers' favourites and a few more elaborate dishes such as cheese soufflé or seared scallops. Simple, modern bedrooms are in the old stables.

Closing times
Closed mid-December-January and Monday-Thursday November, February and March

Prices
Meals: a la carte £ 19/36

12 rooms: £ 104

Typical Dishes
Chicken liver parfait
Seafood platter of local shellfish
Chocolate cup

1.5 mi south of Torridon on A 896. Parking.

15   **Stein Inn**

**MacLeod Terr,
Stein, Waternish, IV55 8GA**
Tel.: (01470)592362
Website: www.stein-inn.co.uk

VISA   **MC**

Caledonian Deuchars IPA, Isle of Skye Red Cuillin and Cairngorm Trade Winds

With 'INN' emblazoned in bold letters on either end, there's no missing the oldest inn on Skye; a family-run establishment in an idyllic spot, with views to the Outer Hebrides. Sit on the grassy terrace or by the wood-burning stove in the cosy bar, with its exposed stone walls and nautical artefacts. The fishing boats bobbing along on the loch might well be bringing in the latest catch; local seafood dominates the menu and is what you should go for – perhaps some sweet fresh shrimps, half a lobster or some rollmop herrings for lunch, and Isle of Skye mussels or lemon sole for dinner. Bedrooms are simple and comfortable; they may not have TVs, but with such a superb view – and over 90 whiskies on offer in the bar – who needs one?

Closing times
Closed 1 January and 25 December

Prices
Meals: a la carte £ 16/34

5 rooms: £ 43/110

Typical Dishes
Scallop salad

Venison casserole with chocolate

Apple & blueberry oatmeal crumble

22 mi northwest of Portree by A 87, A 850 and B 886; on the shore of Loch Bay. Parking.

Dalkeith

16   **Sun Inn**

**Lothian Bridge,
Dalkeith, EH22 4TR**
Tel.: (0131)6632456
Website: www.thesuninnedinburgh.co.uk

🛖   *VISA*   **MC**   **D**

Stewart Brewing Pentland IPA

This smartly refurbished pub, set on the main road from Edinburgh to Galashiels, started life in the 17C as a blacksmith's and only later becoming a coaching inn. It's a large place, consisting of two open-fired rooms with part wood and stone-faced walls hung with contemporary black and white photos of the area. Menus are extensive and feature good quality local produce, with suppliers listed on a blackboard. Lunch keeps things simple – you might find ham hock potato cakes, kipper pâté or liver and bacon – while dinner is more ambitious, with the likes of monkfish wrapped in ham, pig's cheek and black pudding or sea bass with saffron risotto. Completing the picture are smart, modern bedrooms boasting handmade furniture and Egyptian cotton linen.

Closing times
Closed 26 December and 1 January
Prices
Meals: £ 15/18 and a la carte £ 19/42

🛏 **5 rooms:** £ 55/150

Typical Dishes
Seafood baked in pastry
Spiced monkfish with king prawn skewers
Dark chocolate & salted caramel tart

 2 mi southwest of Dalkeith on A 7. Parking.

17   **N Dalmore Inn**

Perth Rd,
Blairgowrie, PH10 6QB
Tel.: (01250)871088
Website: www.dalmoreinn.com

🍴   **VISA**   **MC**   **AE**

🥛 **No real ales offered**

With its whisky kegs out the front, it may look like a traditional pub, but cross the threshold and the Dalmore reveals a surprisingly stylish modern interior. Brightly coloured walls hung with photos of Scottish scenes are juxtaposed with old stonework; giant potted plants occupy the centre of the room; and a life-sized picture of a Highland cow greets you at the door. The cooking is good value, unfussy and full of flavour – everything is freshly prepared to order and they like to use Scottish produce wherever possible; you might find ham hock terrine or Arbroath smokie risotto, followed by venison and black pudding meatballs or a homemade burger topped with haggis. Service is warm, welcoming and well-executed.

Closing times
Closed 25 December and 1-2 January

Prices
Meals: a la carte £ 20/38

Typical Dishes
Rabbit & wild mushroom terrine

Loin of venison with bramble & beetroot

Banana tarte Tatin

🚗 *1.5 mi southwest of Blairgowrie on A 93. Parking.*

Glendevon

18 Tormaukin Inn

**Glendevon,
FK14 7JY**
Tel.: (01259)781252
Website: www.tormaukinhotel.co.uk

VISA

Harviestoun Bitter and Twisted

After a breathtaking drive along the A823, stop at the door of this characterful inn, where the owner and manageress will welcome you as if you're old friends. Cross over the threshold and a huge granite fireplace greets you; pass by it and you'll come to a dark beamed bar and a spacious, classically decorated dining room. The well-priced, carefully executed dishes are largely traditional – you might find home-smoked salmon or pressed terrine of game for starters, followed by steak and Guinness casserole or chicken stuffed with haggis; while tasty homemade breads and ice creams are offered at either end of your meal. Smart, tartan-floored bedrooms are spread between the inn, a stable block and a chalet; the former are the most comfortable.

Closing times
Closed 25 December
Prices
Meals: a la carte £ 20/39
11 rooms: £ 60/80

Typical Dishes
Home-smoked duck, chicken & guinea fowl

Venison with potato rösti & parsnip

White chocolate & vanilla panna cotta

In centre of village on A 823. Parking.

19   **Inn on the Tay**

**Grandtully,
PH9 0PL**
Tel.: (01877)840760
Website: www.theinnonthetay.co.uk

h╥   **VISA**   **MC**   **AE**   **⬤**

No real ales offered

As its name suggests, this smart, modern inn is located on the banks of the River Tay; head to the large dining room for superb views over the water, where you'll often see people rafting or canoeing. The bar menu offers the likes of scampi and chips or a burger with mozzarella and red onion jam, while the all-day menu is a little more ambitious, featuring dishes such as confit spring rolls or hot smoked salmon with beetroot and crème fraiche. If you're planning to stay the night, you'll find the bedrooms comfy and cosy; if you've not long to stop, pop in for coffee and a slice of homemade cake in the bar – try to bag one of the squashy sofas beside the log burning stove. The owners are cheery and welcoming, and the atmosphere is laid-back.

Closing times
Open daily
Prices
Meals: a la carte £ 18/32
🛏 **6 rooms:** £ 70/110

Typical Dishes
Game terrine &
date chutney

Salmon with sun-dried
tomato & dill risotto

Blackberry
frangipane tart

🚗 *5 mi northeast of Aberfeldy on A 827. Parking.*

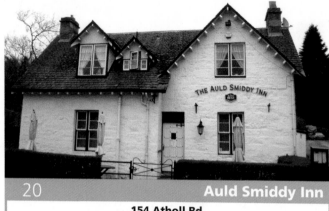

20 **Auld Smiddy Inn**

**154 Atholl Rd,
Pitlochry, PH16 5AG**
Tel.: (01796)472356
Website: www.auldsmiddyinn.co.uk

 **Inveralmond Brewery Ales and Orkney Brewery Ales**

As its name suggests, this building started life as a blacksmith's forge, before spending a short spell as a tea room and later finding its calling as a pub. A small but colourful garden stands out against smartly whitewashed walls and there's a large terrace and courtyard round the back. Inside it has a likeable simplicity, with polished slate floors and wood burning stoves; sit at the front beside the counter or in the rear room where the blacksmith would once have worked. In the summer, salads and fish dishes fill the menu; in colder months, the choice may be smaller but the portions certainly aren't, with hearty classics such as haggis, neeps and tatties or local steak, sausage and ale pie. They also hold a seafood festival twice a year.

Closing times
Closed last week
January-first week February
and 25-26 December
Prices
Meals: a la carte £ 18/40

Typical Dishes
Game terrine
Sirloin of Aberdeen Angus
Crème brûlée

 At northern end of the main street. Pay and display parking nearby.

It's nearly six hundred years since Owen Glyndawr escaped the clutches of the English to become a national hero, and in all that time the Welsh passion for unity has bound the country together like a scarlet-shirted scrum. It may be only 170 miles from north to south, but Wales contains great swathes of beauty, such as the dark and craggy heights of Snowdonia's ninety mountain peaks, the rolling sandstone bluffs of the Brecon Beacons, and Pembrokeshire's tantalising golden beaches. Bottle-nosed dolphins love it here too, arriving each summer at New Quay in Cardigan Bay. Highlights abound: formidable Harlech Castle dominates its coast, and Bala Lake has a railway that steams along its gentle shores. Hay-on-Wye's four pubs and eighteen bookshops turn perceptions on their head, and Welsh cuisine is causing a surprise or two as well: the country teems with great raw ingredients now employed to their utmost potential, from the humblest cockle to the slenderest slice of succulent lamb.

Wales

Rhoscolyn

1   **White Eagle**

Rhoscolyn, LL65 2NJ
Tel.: (01407)860267
Website: www.white-eagle.co.uk

Weetwood Eastgate Ale, Conwy Celebration Ale and Great Orme Ales

Set in a small coastal hamlet on the peninsula, this pub boasts stunning sea views from its spacious decked terrace. From the outside it may look more like a restaurant but swing a right through the door and you'll find regulars nursing their pints in the cosy open-fired bar. It's rightly popular, so you might have to wait for a table; fill your time by glancing over the display of the owners' business history – they also own Timpson Shoe Repairs. The monthly menu offers something for everyone and dishes arrive well-presented, in a contemporary style; whether it's the huge battered haddock and chips or pan-fried salmon with prawn and chorizo butter. Daily fish specials and regular themed weeks – maybe pie, sausage, Indian or Italian – feature.

Closing times
Open daily
Prices
Meals: a la carte £ 21/39

Typical Dishes
Confit of duck leg with celeriac purée
Menai moules marinière
Pear & honeycomb cheesecake with lemon sorbet

5 mi south of Holyhead by B 4545 and minor road south. Parking.

2 **The Conway**

**53 Conway Rd,
Cardiff, CF11 9NW**
Tel.: (029)20224373
Website: www.knifeandforkfood.co.uk/conway

VISA MC

Otley Oxymoron, Tiny Rebel Cwtch and Wickwar
Cotswold Way

Located in a residential area just north of the city, The Conway offers everything from a pint and a bowl of chips while you watch the rugby to a full three course meal accompanied by a well-priced bottle of wine. A makeover has given the pub a fresh, light feel, with comfy sofas by the fire and shelves crammed with books and board games. Although prone to the odd over-elaboration, the Swedish chef's approach to food is, in the main, pleasingly simple, showcasing fresh, seasonal produce from the local allotments and foraging trips in tasty pub classics like steak and chips, toad in the hole or apple and raisin crumble. Choose from the daily changing blackboard menu, then place your order at the bar. Service is friendly and efficient.

Closing times
Open daily
Prices
Meals: a la carte £ 20/30

Typical Dishes
Quail, rabbit loin &
pancetta
Lamb rump with goat's
cheese mousse
Olive oil panna cotta
with maple jelly

On the northwest side of the city off the A 4119. Parking in neighbouring roads.

Nantgaredig

3   **Y Polyn**

**Nantgaredig,
SA32 7LH**
Tel.: (01267)290000
Website: www.ypolynrestaurant.co.uk

Otley 01 and 03 Boss

The food is the focus at this small, rustic and pleasantly unfussy pub, which sits on a busy country road close to a stream and affords pleasant views. Mark, the owner, was previously an inspector with the AA, hence all the restaurant menus on display, which make quite a talking point. Pleasingly, he's just as welcoming to those on their first visit as to his trusty band of regulars. His wife Sue looks after the kitchen and her cooking is stout, filling and British at heart; the slow-cooked meats, fresh salads, satisfying soups and classic puds all hit the spot, both with the lunchtime couples and the more youthful crowd that gathers in the evening. Prices are kept realistic and the complimentary filtered mineral water is a nice touch.

Closing times
Closed Sunday dinner and Monday
booking advisable
Prices
Meals: £ 40 (dinner) and a la carte £ 21/30

Typical Dishes
Fish soup
Roast rump of lamb, onion & garlic purée
Toffee apple crumble

 6 mi east of Carmarthen by A 4300 on B 4310. Parking.

4   Harbourmaster

**Quay Par,
Aberaeron, SA46 0BA**
Tel.: (01545)570755
Website: www.harbour-master.com

VISA   MC

 Purple Moose Glaslyn and Harbourmaster Best Bitter

With its vibrant blue exterior, you'll spot this place a mile off; not that the owners need worry about being noticed, as their reputation for good food and hospitality goes before them. As the name suggests, it once belonged to the harbourmaster and it offers lovely views out across the water. There's a bar-lounge with slate walls, a nautical New England style and an oval pewter-topped counter, as well as a modern dining room – make a play for 'cwtch', a table offering excellent harbour views. Choose between the bar menu or a more substantial evening à la carte supplemented by daily specials. Smart bedrooms, split between the house and a nearby cottage, are brightly decorated and well-equipped; some boast oversized windows or terraces.

Closing times
Closed 25 December

Prices
Meals: £ 30 (dinner)
and a la carte £ 30/44

🛏 **13 rooms:** £ 65/250

Typical Dishes
Potted Cardigan Bay
crab with sourdough

Rib of Welsh
beef, béarnaise
& greens

Chocolate fondant
with salted caramel

🚗 *In town centre overlooking the harbour. Parking on street and around the harbour wall.*

Llanfihangel-y-Creuddyn

5   **Y Ffarmers**

**Llanfihangel-y-Creuddyn,
SY23 4LA**
Tel.: (01974)261275
Website: www.yffarmers.co.uk

VISA

Evan Evans Cwrw Cayo and Wye Valley Butty Bach

More than just the village pub, the passionately run Y Ffarmers is also the village hub. It's a characterful whitewashed building in a remote, picturesque valley, and was originally a farm and later a tax collector's office. With no village hall, life here really revolves around the place, which hosts everything from yoga classes and quiz nights to meetings of the local choir and bee keeping group. Turn right for the locals bar or left for the homely, open-fired restaurant, which opens out onto the garden. The concise, monthly à la carte offers a good range of satisfying, original dishes that are big on flavour. Most produce is from the valley, including locally grown organic veg, game from nearby shoots, and lobster and crab from Cardigan Bay.

Closing times
Closed first week January, Monday except bank holidays, and Sunday dinner

Prices
Meals: a la carte £ 20/32

Typical Dishes
Cockle fritters with lemon mayonnaise
Ceredigion beef & oxtail pie
Bara brith Welsh whisky pudding

7.75 mi southeast of Aberystwyth by A 487 and A 4120, turning right after Pant-y-crug. Parking in the village square.

6 **Pen-y-Bryn**

Pen-y-Bryn Rd,
Upper Colwyn Bay, Colwyn Bay, LL29 6DD
Tel.: (01492)533360
Website: www.penybryn-colwynbay.co.uk

🍴 *VISA* 💳 🆎 ⓪

🍺 **Great Orme Red Dragon and Purple Moose Snowdonia Ale**

You might need your sat nav, as even when you've located the right residential street, you could easily pass Pen-y-Bryn by. Looking more like a medical centre than a place to dine, it boasts impressive panoramic views over Colwyn Bay, especially from the garden and terrace. The spacious, open-plan interior is crammed full of pictures, bookcases and pottery, yet despite these and the oak floors, old furniture and open fires, it has a modern, laid-back feel. The extensive all-day menu offers plenty of choice, ranging from a classical ploughman's to more adventurous pheasant-based dishes; while during 'Beer and Bangers' weeks 12 varieties of sausage and over 20 beers are also offered. Large tables make it ideal for families or groups of friends.

Closing times
Closed dinner 26 December and 1 January

Prices
Meals: a la carte £ 22/37

Typical Dishes
Home-smoked loin of lamb
Slow-roasted belly pork with apple purée
Poached pear with dark chocolate mousse

1 mi southwest of Colwyn Bay by B 5113. Parking.

Conwy

7

Groes Inn

Conwy,
LL32 8TN
Tel.: (01492)650545
Website: www.groesinn.com

VISA MC AE DC

Great Orme Ales

Located in the foothills of Snowdonia, with the estuary in front and the mountains behind, the setting couldn't be more beautiful. Flowers greet you at the door and the characterful beamed interior is filled with pictures, copperware and china, all bathed in flickering firelight. If you're after nooks and crannies, there are several small rooms encircling the comfy bar, as well as an airy conservatory and an intimate dining room. The menu features British favourites in neatly presented, generous portions and everything is homemade. Specials are often a little more adventurous and feature fish from the nearby waters, lamb reared on the salt marshes or game from local estates. Bedrooms have lovely views; some boast balconies or terraces.

Closing times
Open daily
Prices
Meals: a la carte £ 19/36

14 rooms: £ 100/230

Typical Dishes
Devilled kidneys on toast
Lamb's liver & bacon
Spotted dick with custard

3 mi south of Conwy on B 5106. Parking.

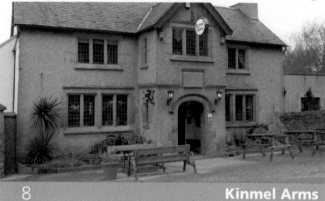

8

Kinmel Arms

**The Village,
St George, LL22 9BP**
Tel.: (01745)832207
Website: www.thekinmelarms.co.uk

$\underset{\text{hTT}}{\frown}$ ~~VISA~~ ⓂⒸ

🥤 **Thwaites Original and Facer's Flintshire Bitter**

This early 17C stone inn is hidden away in a hamlet by the entrance to Kinmel Hall. It's the type of pub that's not entirely sure if it wants to be a pub or a restaurant: true, there's a delightful open-fired bar with a slate-topped counter and low-level seating which hosts regular events for the locals; but there are also two spacious dining areas – one with chunky wood furniture and the other, with a more conservatory-like feel. Lunch sees classic pub-style dishes, while dinner steps things up a gear. They keep their own cows in the field over the road and even grow fruit and herbs in a small polytunnel. Stylish, contemporary bedrooms boast smart bathrooms and large kitchenettes – so you can enjoy your continental breakfast in your PJs.

Closing times
Closed Sunday and Monday
Prices
Meals: a la carte £ 24/40
🛏 **4 rooms:** £ 115/175

Typical Dishes
Citrus-cured salmon
with avocado
Hake fillet with
tomato confit
Dark chocolate mousse
with blackcurrant jelly

 In the centre of village. Parking.

Hawarden

9 **Glynne Arms**

**3 Glynne Way,
Hawarden, CH3 3NS**
Tel.: (01244)569988
Website: www.theglynnearms.co.uk

Stonehouse Station Bitter, Off The Rails and Purple Moose Ales

This 200 year old coaching inn sits just across from the gates of Hawarden Castle and was once home to the Glynne family, hence its name. They're not the only family involved here though, as the descendants of PM William Gladstone (who own most of the village, including several farms and an interior design company), now have the Glynne Arms back under their wing. Their experience with interiors means that the pub's been smartly refurbished and has a slightly funky feel. Cooking follows in a similarly modern vein and presents some original, ambitious flavour combinations, but traditionalists aren't forgotten – there's a 'Family Classics' section, as well as steaks from the estate farms; and be sure to save room for one of the tasty desserts.

Closing times
Open daily
Prices
Meals: a la carte £ 20/40

Typical Dishes
Smoked mackerel with roasted beetroot
Crispy pork belly & sticky pork cheek
White chocolate & raspberry crème brûlée

In centre of the village. Parking

10 **Glasfryn**

**Raikes Ln,
Sychdyn, Mold, CH7 6LR**
Tel.: (01352)750500
Website: www.glasfryn-mold.co.uk

Purple Moose Snowdonia, Phoenix Wobbly Bob and Great Orme Celtica

An early example of Arts and Crafts architecture, this glazed red-brick building was intended to be a judges' residence for the nearby courts but, never used, was turned into a farmhouse, before later falling into disrepair. It's a sizeable place, able to cater for a few hundred at every sitting, with some tables seating up to 20 at a time. Order at the large central bar and watch your order whizz past in the vacuum tube system on its way to the kitchen. Menus offer plenty of choice, from pub classics such as fish and chips to culinary classics such as plaice Véronique, with some lighter dishes alongside. Portions are generous, prices are sensible and service is surprisingly swift. The garden and terrace boast nice views over the town below.

Closing times
Closed 25 December
Prices
Meals: a la carte £ 19/31

Typical Dishes
Pigeon breast, chicken and wild mushroom sausage
Sea bass with crab croquette and gazpacho dressing
Chocolate ganache & raspberries

 1 mi north by A 5119 on Civic Centre rd. Parking.

Mold

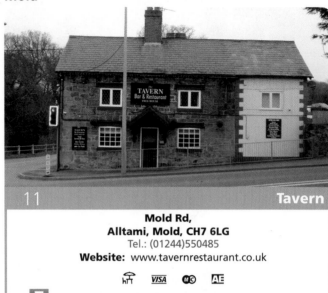

11   **Tavern**

**Mold Rd,
Alltami, Mold, CH7 6LG**
Tel.: (01244)550485
Website: www.tavernrestaurant.co.uk

🛖   **VISA**   **MC**   **AE**

🍺 **Hafod Brewery Ales**

Having worked in various locations around the country, chef Peter Wright jumped at the chance to buy a pub close to his heart – a pub in which his parents used to drink – when it came on the market. He has given the place a modern makeover and although the heavy tables and black and cream leather chairs may make it appear fairly formal, the menu is still very much in a hearty, comforting pub vein, offering the likes of half a pint of prawns and Welsh Black steaks. The daily specials – particularly the grilled market fish dishes – prove popular, while the set 'Chef's Choice' and 4 course tasting menus feature slightly more refined dishes such as assiette of seafood or Gressingham duck with parsnip purée, followed by peanut butter parfait.

Closing times
Open daily
Prices
Meals: a la carte £ 21/31

Typical Dishes
Cod with slow-poached egg
Pork, apple, sage & onion
Floating islands with rhubarb & custard

 2.5 mi northeast of Mold, on A 494. Parking.

12 **Riverside**

Pennal,
SY20 9DW
Tel.: (01654)791285
Website: www.riversidehotel-pennal.co.uk

 VISA **MC**

Blue Monkey Infinity, Purple Moose Madog's Ale and Glaslyn

If you fancy brushing up on your Welsh, head for this part-16C coaching inn with the name 'Glan Yr Afron' (Riverside) above the door, then make for the 'Cwtch' (cosy corner) with its welcoming wood-burning stove. The pub stands on the main road in the small village of Pennal, backing on to a tributary of the River Dovey, and despite various additions and its Grade II listing, has a fresh, modern feel inside – with one half of the room laid for dining and the other taken up by the bar. The friendly local team bring over tasty bread to nibble on while you study the menu, which features all the usual pub favourites along with some sharing boards. Cooking is no-nonsense, full of flavour and keenly priced, and the portions are suitably hearty.

Closing times
Open daily
Prices
Meals: £ 10 and a la carte
£ 17/34

Typical Dishes

Fish stew with king prawns & chorizo

Crispy duck with sautéed potatoes & plum sauce

Spiced apple & almond tart with custard

 On A 493 between Aberdovey and Machynlleth. Parking.

Llandenny

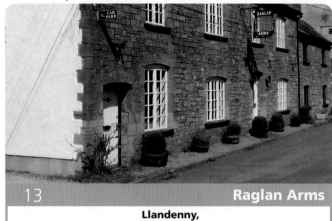

13　　Raglan Arms

Llandenny,
NP15 1DL
Tel.: (01291)690800
Website: www.theraglanarms.co.uk

 Wye Valley Ales

With fireside leather sofas, simply laid scrubbed pine tables and vases filled with fresh flowers, the Raglan Arms offers a wholesome cosiness; dining happens mostly in the front of the room, although the conservatory at the back is popular with families at weekends. Menus change slightly at each service and are short and to the point. The kitchen is clearly serious about food, using local produce wherever possible and employing a range of cooking styles. Dishes are unfussy and flavourful and might include warm local ox tongue, imam bayildi or Tamworth sausages and mash, while dessert could be a toffee and whisky parfait or a rhubarb and custard slice. The lunch menu offers good value, service is cheery and the wine list is a labour of love.

Closing times
Closed 25-26 December,
Sunday dinner and Monday

Prices
Meals: a la carte £ 21/34

Typical Dishes
Foie gras & ham hock terrine
Thai green chicken curry with fragrant rice
Chocolate nut sundae

 In centre of the village. Parking.

14 **White Hart**

Llangybi,
NP15 1NP
Tel.: (01633)450258
Website: www.thewhitehartvillageinn.com

 Wye Valley Butty Bach and Brains The Reverend James

The 16C White Hart became the property of Henry VIII as part of Jane Seymour's dowry and, a century later, during the civil war, Oliver Cromwell used it as his Monmouthshire headquarters. The characterful interior proudly shows off ornate Tudor plasterwork, a priest's hole and 11 fireplaces dating from the 1600s; if that's not enough, it's even referred to by TS Eliot in the poem 'Usk'. When it comes to dining, there's an adventurous à la carte of well-prepared, precisely presented dishes, along with a slightly simpler set menu; many dishes arrive on slates and most ingredients come from within a 10 mile radius. If you fancy staying the night, you may have to fight off the competition for the only room – a double with an adjoining single.

Closing times
Closed Monday except bank holidays and Sunday dinner

Prices
Meals: £ 19 (weekday dinner)/45 and a la carte £ 25/40

1 room: £ 65/110

Typical Dishes
Scallops with lettuce & peas
Pork belly with truffle potato
Coconut, white chocolate & lime

2 mi south of Usk turning left after bridge over River Usk onto road signed to Llangybi. Parking.

Wales • Monmouthshire

Penallt

15   **The Inn at Penallt**

**Penallt,
NP25 4SE**
Tel.: (01600)772765
Website: www.theinnatpenallt.co.uk

Wye Valley Bitter and Butty Bach, Keystone Classic and Challenger

As enthusiastic owners go, Andrew and Jackie are up with the best of them. They bought the run down 'Bush Inn' back in 2009, spent 5 months refurbishing it and now it's their pride and joy. There's a choice of two rooms, both similarly styled in neutral hues and furnished with heavy wood; you'll find the locals gathered in the pubbier of the two, around the wood-burning stove, but for the best views, make for the comfy conservatory. Menus offer good-sized dishes with their roots firmly in the classics. Bread is freshly baked, the ice creams are homemade, and the majority of produce comes from within 40 miles. The beers are equally local and the Welsh whisky is also a big seller. Bedrooms are cosy, neat and tidy with modern facilities.

Closing times
Closed 1-20 January,
Sunday dinner and Monday
except bank holidays

Prices
Meals: £ 16 (lunch)
and a la carte £ 27/38

🛏 **4 rooms:** £ 45

Typical Dishes
Home-cured
Madgett's Farm duck
ham
Duo of Brecon venison
Dark chocolate &
almond tart

 5 mi south of Monmouth, off the B 4293 in village centre. Parking.

16 — **Bell at Skenfrith**

Skenfrith,
NP7 8UH
Tel.: (01600)750235
Website: www.skenfrith.co.uk

Wye Valley Ales HPA, Bitter and Butty Bach

The Bell offers uncomplicated warmth: a seat in a comfy sofa by the inglenook, candles and meadow flowers on the tables and friendly, unobtrusive service. The weekly changing menu features hearty, classical dishes with the occasional ambitious twist; these might include rolled fishcakes or sirloin of Brecon beef with mini steak and kidney pudding. Ingredients are allowed to speak for themselves, with local suppliers credited on the menu and much of the produce coming from their organic kitchen garden. Fruits of the vine are also taken seriously, with a large selection of half bottles and an impressive choice of champagnes and cognacs. Bedrooms are understated in their elegance, with super-comfy beds, fluffy towels and personalised toiletries.

Closing times
Closed Tuesday November-Easter

booking essential

Prices
Meals: £ 18 (weekday lunch)/26 and a la carte £ 29/42

11 rooms: £ 75/220

Typical Dishes
Scallops with pea purée & pancetta
Rump of Welsh lamb with champ
Crème brûlée with rhubarb compote

 12.5 mi. east of Abergavenny on B 4521. Parking.

Brecon

17   Felin Fach Griffin

**Felin Fach,
Brecon, LD3 0UB**
Tel.: (01874)620111
Website: www.felinfachgriffin.co.uk

Wye Valley Butty Bach, Brecon Six Beacons and Tomos Watkin OSB

This terracotta-coloured former farmhouse in picturesque countryside is rather unique in that you'll find visitors aged from 1-100 and from all walks of life – which creates an almost bohemian atmosphere. Bright paintwork, colourful art and a scattering of magazines about the place provide a very 'lived in' feel and the atmosphere is extremely laid-back. The young staff interact well but just as importantly, have a good knowledge of what they're serving. Starters like local goat's curd with black olive purée or brawn with apricot chutney are followed by braised shin of Welsh beef or red mullet with salt cod brandade – and they're a cut above your usual pub grub. If you've eaten yourself to a standstill, pleasant bedrooms with comfy beds await.

Closing times
Closed 24-25 December and early January

Prices
Meals: £ 21/28
and a la carte £ 26/34

🛏 **7 rooms:** £ 75/160

Typical Dishes

Pork belly with black pudding & grain mustard sauce

Saddle of lamb with smoked aubergine

Pineapple with passion fruit sorbet

 4.75 mi northeast of Brecon by B 4602 off A 470. Parking.

18

Bear

**High St,
Crickhowell, NP8 1BW**
Tel.: (01873)810408
Website: www.bearhotel.co.uk

VISA MC AE

Wye Valley Butty Bach, Gower Brewery Gower Gold and Theakston Old Peculier

The well-maintained Bear stands proudly on the main street of this small town, its hanging baskets creating a riot of colour. Step through the front door into the hugely characterful lounge-bar, with its shiny brass and open fireplaces, and you can well believe that it has been here since 1432. Diners can sit here or in the more formal restaurant; the latter may be more romantic but the former is undoubtedly the more appealing. The menu offers honest pub dishes like prawn cocktail, homemade faggots or braised Welsh lamb shank. The 'specials' add interest and a young cheery team provide swift, assured service, even when it's busy. Bedrooms are available in the hotel: the most characterful feature beams, four-posters and fireplaces.

Closing times
Closed 25 December
bookings not accepted
Prices
Meals: a la carte £ 20/37
36 rooms: £ 77/167

Typical Dishes
Salmon fishcake, mustard hollandaise
Pork belly with black pudding & cider cream
Bread & butter pudding

In the town centre. Parking.

Old Radnor

19   **Harp Inn**

Old Radnor,
LD8 2RH
Tel.: (01544)350655
Website: www.harpinnradnor.co.uk

Wye Valley HPA, Hobsons Town Crier and Three Tuns XXX

Built to house workers constructing the medieval church, this 15C stone inn welcomes drinkers and diners alike. On a warm summer's day take a seat outside and make the most of the glorious view; in colder weather, head through to the charming flag-floored room with its warming open fire and beams hung with hop bines. 'Seasonality' and 'sustainability' are keywords here; breads, ice creams and crackers are homemade and everything else is locally sourced. Menus may be concise but dishes are original; you might find leek and ale rarebit, scrambled egg and home-spiced chorizo, or mackerel fillet with fennel spelt risotto – while the Welsh Black beef with triple-cooked chips has become a mainstay. Simple bedrooms come with wonderful views.

Closing times
Closed Monday except bank holidays and lunch Tuesday-Friday - Restricted opening in winter

Prices
Meals: a la carte £ 20/32

🛏 **5 rooms:** £ 55

Typical Dishes
Home-cured gravadlax with potato salad
Welsh Black rump steak with triple-cooked chips
Border tart

🚗 Signposted south off A 44 east of Llandrindod Wells just before crossing the border into England. Parking.

20   **The Pilot**

67 Queens Rd,
Penarth, CF64 1DJ
Tel.: (029)20710615
Website: www.knifeandforkfood.co.uk/pilot

Brains SA, Otley 03 Boss and Raw Hop Pole

You might assume it has something to do with planes but 'The Pilot' is actually a reference to the Cardiff docks. Sister to The Conway, this once rundown neighbourhood boozer has been given a splash of paint and transformed into a neat dining pub. It has really become part of the local community: regulars gather in the front room to watch the latest sporting events, while diners head to the rear, with its wood-burning stove and partial bay views. Ingredients are laudably local, with produce from the kitchen garden, nearby suppliers and even some of the locals' allotments. A good-sized blackboard menu mixes classic pub dishes with more adventurous offerings such as huntsman chicken or venison carpaccio, and dishes are hearty and honest.

Closing times
Open daily
Prices
Meals: a la carte £ 18/29

Typical Dishes
Smoked mackerel with apple salad & ham hash

Gurnard with Puy lentils, chorizo & fennel slaw

Baked Alaska

5 mi. south of Cardiff in residential area of the town. Unrestricted on-street parking.

Gresford

21   **Pant-yr-Ochain**

**Old Wrexham Rd,
Gresford, LL12 8TY**
Tel.: (01978)853525
Website: www.pantyrochain-gresford.co.uk

**Purple Moose Snowdonia Ale, Brunning and Price
Phoenix Ale and Weetwood Eastgate Ale**

This is neither a typical rustic inn nor a 21C dining pub – but a classical country manor house in disguise. With Tudor wattle and daub walls backing a 16C inglenook fireplace, the place is steeped in history. Outside, mature gardens and well-manicured lawns stretch down to a small lake; and on a warm summer's day, lunch on the terrace or lawn is hard to beat. In rainier weather, follow the polished quarry tiled floors to the large central bar and choose from one of the numerous rooms surrounding it; some with ancient beams and exposed brick walls, all with nooks and crannies aplenty. The daily changing menu offers hearty, wholesome, all-day dishes, ranging from pies and casseroles to more interesting offerings like hake with crab butter.

Closing times
Open daily
Prices
Meals: a la carte £ 20/32

Typical Dishes
Crab, samphire & saffron tart

Calves' liver with mash & roast shallots

Bread & butter pudding

 4.5 mi northeast of Wrexham by A 483 and B 5445. Parking.

Llanarmon Dyffryn Ceiriog

22 **Hand at Llanarmon**

**Llanarmon Dyffryn Ceiriog,
LL20 7LD**
Tel.: (01691)600666
Website: www.thehandhotel.co.uk

 Wye Valley Butty Bach, Weetwood Eastgate Ale and Cheshire Cat

Set at the crossroads of two old drovers' roads, the Hand has been providing hospitality for several centuries and its current owners are continuing the tradition with flair, providing a warm welcome and hearty meals to travellers through this lush valley. There's a cosy bar, a spacious dining room and a pool room; and rustic charm abounds in the form of stone walls, open fires, ancient beams and quite a collection of taxidermy. The daily changing menu offers loads of choice, with plenty of wholesome pub classics like sausage and mash, steak and kidney pie or slow-braised lamb shank. Portions are generous, the produce is local and the cooking, fresh and flavoursome. Cosy bedrooms offer hill views and modern bathrooms; most have a roll-top bath.

Closing times
Closed 25 December

Prices
Meals: £ 19 (lunch)
and a la carte £ 21/36

13 rooms: £ 50/128

Typical Dishes
Beetroot & horseradish brûlée, parmesan crust
Shoulder of Welsh lamb with redcurrant sauce
Dark chocolate fondant

At the head of Ceiriog Valley northwest of Oswestry. Parking.

Wales • Wrexham

The presiding image of Northern Ireland for outsiders is buzzing Belfast, lying defiantly between mountain and coast. Its City Hall and Queen's University retain the power to impress, and it was within its mighty shipyards that the Titanic first saw the light of day. But the rest of the Six Counties demands attention, too. The forty thousand stone columns of the Giant's Causeway step out into the Irish Sea, part of a grand coastline, though Antrim can also boast nine scenic inland glens. County Down's rolling hills culminate in the alluring slopes of Slieve Donard in the magical Mourne Mountains, while Armagh's Orchard County is a riot of pink in springtime. Fermanagh's glassy, silent lakelands are a tranquil attraction, rivalled for their serenity by the heather-clad Sperrin Mountains, towering over Tyrone and Derry. On top of all this is the cultural lure of boisterous oyster festivals and authentic horse fairs, while farmers' markets are now prominent all across the province.

1 Pheasant

**410 Upper Ballynahinch Rd,
Annahilt, BT26 6NR**
Tel.: (028)92638056
Website: www.thepheasantrestaurant.co.uk

 No real ales offered

Set in the heart of County Lisburn, this sizeable creamwashed inn has a typically Irish feel, from the Guinness-themed artwork to the warm welcome and laid-back atmosphere. With its stained glass and dark wood, it has a somewhat Gothic style; the traditional open-fired bar is the place to sit when it's cold and the patio provides the ideal spot in warmer months. Internationally influenced menus showcase seasonal produce, with local seafood the speciality in summer and game from the nearby estate in winter. Children are well catered for too, with a dedicated selection of freshly prepared dishes, as well as toys and climbing frames. It's a popular place, so if you're in a group it could be worth booking the snug or the 'Gamekeepers Loft'.

Closing times
Closed 12 July and
25-26 December

Prices
Meals: £ 10/24 and a la carte
£ 20/36

Typical Dishes
Bang bang chicken
with peanut dressing

Duck breast
with curried sweet
potato mash

Chocolate nemesis

 1 mi north of Annahilt on Lisburn rd. Parking.

Bangor

2 **Coyle's**

**44 High St,
Bangor, BT20 5AZ**
Tel.: (028)91270362
Website: www.coylesbistro.co.uk

 No real ales offered

If you're after a quiet drink and a good meal then this is the place to come: there are no rowdy groups or noisy sports fans, just families and friends catching up and couples out for dinners à deux. There's the choice of a laid-back bistro with a small, modern bar area or a smarter first floor restaurant – each with a different menu, but both highlighting a selection of low fat dishes. Downstairs you'll find the likes of macaroni cheese, fishcakes or steak, as well as more international flavours such as chilli and ginger chicken; while the more ambitious upstairs menu steps things up a gear with offerings such as smoked salmon and blini gâteau, followed by scallops with spinach risotto or red pepper crusted pork with gnocchi Romana.

Closing times
Closed 25 December
Prices
Meals: £ 25 (early dinner) and a la carte £ 26/32

Typical Dishes
Mussels with Bloody Mary sauce
Slow-braised pork belly with BBQ vinaigrette
Chocolate fondant

 In the town centre. Pay and display parking 2 min walk.

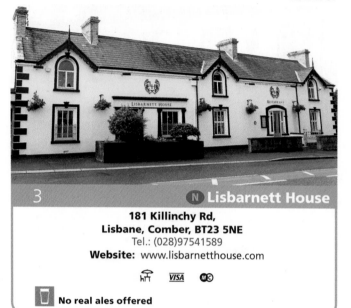

3 **Lisbarnett House**

**181 Killinchy Rd,
Lisbane, Comber, BT23 5NE**
Tel.: (028)97541589
Website: www.lisbarnetthouse.com

VISA MC

No real ales offered

This neat, modern building is Danny Millar's second pub venture and follows in the footsteps of its older sister, the Parson's Nose. Set in the centre of a small village, its ethos is satisfyingly, 'local is best', so you'll find Irish Dexter beef alongside prawns and mussels from Portavogie or Strangford Lough. They are gaining a good reputation for their beef dishes, be it one of their hearty burgers which come in styles ranging from 'Classic' to 'Texan', or one of their grills, which usually include sirloin, rump, rib-eye and flat iron steak. Cooking is robust and satisfying, and only those with the largest of appetites will make it to dessert. If you fancy a bottle of wine or whiskey to take home, pop into their adjoining off licence.

Closing times
Open daily
Prices
Meals: £ 13 (weekdays)/20
and a la carte £ 17/34

Typical Dishes
Prawn cocktail & crab cake
Gloucester Old Spot BBQ pork sandwich
Apple & rhubarb crumble

3.5 mi southeast of Comber on the main road to Killinchy.
Parking.

Donaghadee

4 **Grace Neill's**

**33 High St,
Donaghadee, BT21 0AH**
Tel.: (02891)884595
Website: www.graceneills.com

 No real ales offered

Having first opened as the King's Arms in 1611, this is reputedly the oldest pub in Ireland and is still going strong. Renamed in the 1900s after a former landlady who would greet every visitor with a kiss, it consists of a small, snug original room – the place where smugglers once gathered to plot and scheme – and two large extensions; one beamed and one more contemporary in style. The large menu is satisfyingly classical and might feature Portavogie prawn cocktail or Strangford Lough mussels, followed by homemade burgers or local beef and Guinness pie; for those tight on time or money, lunch also provides a good value 'express' menu. Live music is a feature at the weekends and a guitar and tin whistle can always be found behind the bar.

Closing times
Closed 25 December

Prices
Meals: £ 11 and a la carte
£ 16/34

Typical Dishes
Goat's cheese tart,
candied walnuts

Steak & Guinness pie
with mash

Apple crumble
with vanilla ice cream

 In town centre. Parking.

5

Pier 36

**36 The Parade,
Donaghadee, BT21 0HE**
Tel.: (028)91884466
Website: www.pier36.co.uk

VISA MC AE

No real ales offered

You couldn't pick a better spot for this family-run pub: it sits on the quayside overlooking the picturesque harbour and the lighthouse. But it's not just its location that marks it out; the hospitality here is pretty good too and the owners continually work to give their customers what they want – which explains why so many keep coming back. When it comes to the food, the menus are traditionally based and offer something for everyone. They purchase only the freshest seafood – so you can't go wrong with local sole or mussels – and they also sell an impressive number of steaks, which is due, no doubt, to the fact that they hang and mature the meat themselves. Bedrooms are bright and modern, and some have great harbour and sea views.

Closing times
Closed 25 December

Prices
Meals: £ 16
(weekday dinner)
and a la carte £ 20/47

6 rooms: £ 50/100

Typical Dishes
Clonakilty black pudding
with mustard sauce
John Dory
with tarragon & lemon
risotto
Bread & butter
pudding with crème
anglaise

 On the harbourfront. Parking in the street and at the rear.

Hillsborough

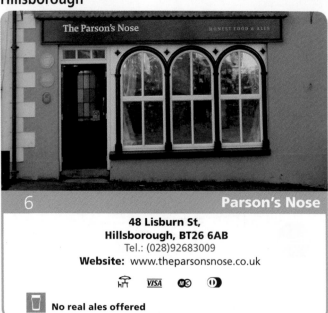

6   Parson's Nose

**48 Lisburn St,
Hillsborough, BT26 6AB**
Tel.: (028)92683009
Website: www.theparsonsnose.co.uk

No real ales offered

The second venture for Danny Millar and Ronan Sweeney is this characterful Georgian inn, which started life as a private house built by the first Marquis of Downshire and dates back to the 18C. The rustic, open-fired bar displays a collection of brewing and distilling paraphernalia, while the dining room above overlooks the Queen's Lake in the grounds of the castle. Food is important here and those in the know will immediately get the culinary reference in the pub's name. Menus are unashamedly traditional and portions are generous; Dundrum oysters and mussels play a big part and the daily fish specials are always a hit – as is the slow-cooked Dexter shin pie. Puddings are classical and comforting, and the service, quick and efficient.

Closing times
Closed 25 December
booking advisable
Prices
Meals: £ 18/22
and a la carte £ 15/32

Typical Dishes
Twice-baked Leggygowan goat's cheese soufflé

Dexter beef & kidney pie with champ

Apple & rhubarb pie with custard

In centre of the town. On-street parking.

7

Plough Inn

**3 The Square,
Hillsborough, BT26 6AG**
Tel.: (028)92682985
Website: www.theploughhillsbrough.co.uk

Hilden Ales

From its lush forest and glistening 40 acre lake to its impressive 17C castle and steep streets lined with antique shops, picturesque Hillsborough has plenty to offer, including the locally acclaimed Plough Inn. Having been trading since 1752, it's extremely well-established in the local community but it's not your usual kind of pub, as inside it's almost three establishments in one. The regulars can be found dining on pub classics in the dark wood bar or, from Thursday-Saturday, in the seafood restaurant, where the daily blackboard specials are a hit. The younger crowds tend to gather in the ground floor café-cum-cocktail-bar or in the trendy bistro above which offers an international menu. There are numerous multi-levelled terraces too.

Closing times
Closed 25 December

Prices
Meals: £ 10/22
and a la carte £ 21/29

Typical Dishes
Salt chilli squid,
langoustine & crab

Rib-eye steak with
lobster thermidor

Trio of brûlées

 At the top of the hill in the square. Parking.

It's reckoned that Ireland offers forty luminous shades of green, and of course an even more famous shade of black liquid refreshment. But it's not all wondrous hills and down-home pubs. The country does other visitor-friendly phenomena just as idyllically: witness the limestone-layered Burren, cut-through by meandering streams, lakes and labyrinthine caves; or the fabulous Cliffs of Moher, unchanged for millennia, looming for mile after mile over the wild Atlantic waves. The cities burst with life: Dublin is now one of Europe's coolest capitals, and free-spirited Cork enjoys a rich cultural heritage. Kilkenny mixes a renowned medieval flavour with a taste for excellent pubs; Galway, one of Ireland's prettiest cities, is enhanced by an easy, boho vibe. Best of all, perhaps, is to sit along the quayside of a fishing village in the esteemed company of a bowl of steaming fresh mussels or gleaming oysters and the taste of a distinctive micro-brewery beer (well, makes a change from stout…).

10 Pubs without bedrooms
15 Pubs with bedrooms

1 **Morrissey's**

Doonbeg

Tel.: (065)9055304
Website: www.morrisseysdoonbeg.com

VISA MC

No real ales offered

As a boy Hugh McNally helped out at his mother's fish and chip shop; when he was older he worked at his grandparents' pub just across the road; and today that pub in the small coastal village of Doonbeg is his. It's been smartly refurbished, with banquettes along the walls, scrubbed wooden tables and walls filled with local artwork and books. There's also a decked terrace which overlooks the river and the castle ruins and is great for sunny days. The menu may be a simple affair but cooking is carefully done and shows respect for ingredients. Locally caught fish and shellfish feature heavily and the crabs in particular are worth a try. Bedrooms are smart and modern – two overlook the river – and they have bikes and even a kayak for hire.

Closing times
Closed January, February, 2 weeks November and Monday
dinner only and Sunday lunch

Prices
Meals: a la carte € 26/36

6 rooms: € 45/100

Typical Dishes
Doonbeg crab claws
Salmon with lime & chilli
Profiteroles with chocolate sauce

In centre of village by the bridge. On-street parking.

Liscannor

2   Vaughan's Anchor Inn

**Main St,
Liscannor**
Tel.: (065)7081548
Website: www.vaughans.ie

🍽 *VISA* Ⓜ©

No real ales offered

If you need to pick up some groceries in the picturesque fishing village of Liscannor, why not stop off at this family-run pub? Its cosy, pleasantly cluttered bar comes complete with a small shop selling everything from sea salt to birthday candles. The self-taught chef has travelled widely and has visited some of the world's best restaurants, so although lunch might feature traditional scampi and chips, the scampi will made from langoustines and come in panko breadcrumbs and the chips will be homemade. Seafood plays an important role and will be on your plate just a few hours after it's landed; the seafood platter is a real hit – and how many pubs do you know that serve caviar? Smart bedrooms feature bright local art and colourful throws.

Closing times
Closed 25 December
Prices
Meals: a la carte € 30/48
🛏 **7 rooms:** € 70/80

Typical Dishes
Liscannor Bay crab crumble
Monkfish with seaweed and langoustines
Passion fruit soufflé

🚗 *2 km from Lahinch by coast road, on main route to Cliffs of Moher. Parking.*

3   Wild Honey Inn

Lisdoonvarna

Tel.: (065)7074300
Website: www.wildhoneyinn.com

VISA **MC**

🍺 **Galway Hooker**

With the Cliffs of Moher and the limestone landscape of The Burren on the doorstep, this roadside inn makes a great base for exploring County Clare; but it's also a great place to discover some good cuisine. From the outside, the three-storey building looks nothing like a pub – in fact, it started life as a hotel, and the garden was once the dance hall. It's a welcoming place, with a turf fire in the cosy bar and a peaceful guest lounge for those staying in one of the simply furnished bedrooms. When it comes to the food, they offer well-priced classic dishes presented in a modern way. They champion local produce, particularly seafood, and the kitchen shows respect for the natural ingredients, allowing their flavours to shine through.

Closing times
Closed first week January-12 February, 24-26 December and restricted opening November-December and February-April
bookings not accepted
Prices
Meals: a la carte € 29/45

🛏 **14 rooms:** € 50/100

Typical Dishes
Duck carpaccio, celery & cress salad
John Dory with Jerusalem artichoke Lyonnaise
Pineapple tarte Tatin

 Just south of the village, on the Ennistimon rd. On-street parking.

New Quay

4   **Linnane's Lobster Bar**

**New Quay Pier,
New Quay**
Tel.: (065)7078120
Website: www.linnanesbar.com

🍹   *VISA*   ⬤⬤

🥛 **No real ales offered**

If you've not been before, leave plenty of time, as this tiny hamlet can be something of a challenge to find. Linnane's started life over 300 years ago as a traditional thatched cottage and is a simple but likeable place; roaring peat fires welcome you in the winter and the full-length windows are opened onto the terrace in summer. From the front it overlooks The Burren and to the rear you can watch the local boats unloading their catch on the small pier – some of which is brought straight into the kitchen. Unsurprisingly, they specialise in fresh fish and shellfish, with the lobster being a particular favourite. Some dishes are cooked simply, others, with a little more imagination, but all are tasty, well-prepared and sensibly priced.

Closing times
Closed Good Friday,
25 December and Monday-Thursday October-Easter

Prices
Meals: a la carte € 21/38

Typical Dishes
St Tola goat's cheese salad
Scallops with bacon & white wine
Chocolate torte

🚗 *11 km northeast of Ballyvaughan following signs for Finavarra from N 67.*

5 Poacher's Inn

**Clonakilty Rd,
Bandon**
Tel.: (023)8841159
Website: www.poachersinnbandon.com

 VISA **MC**

 No real ales offered

It's not big, brash or colourful, but that doesn't mean the Poacher's Inn is lacking in a good old Irish pub atmosphere; in fact, if you're looking for the locals, this is probably where you'll find them. If you're in a rush, there are pre-prepared meals to takeaway; if you've time to stop, there's a whole array of menus to choose from. Lunch offers light snacks (the steak sandwich on homemade bread is particularly popular), supplemented by a good range of gutsy blackboard specials – the seafood dishes are the ones to choose. Dinner steps things up a gear and proudly showcases West Cork produce; maybe crab from Kinsale or fish from Skibbereen. Sit among framed maps and local prints in the wood-panelled front room or on stools in the cosy snug.

Closing times
Open daily

Prices
Meals: € 24 (weekday dinner)/35 and a la carte € 25/44

Typical Dishes
Roast monkfish with spiced lentils
John Dory with butternut squash
Lemon posset with blackberry granita

1.5 km southwest on N 71. Parking.

Castletownshend

6

Mary Ann's

**Main St,
Castletownshend**
Tel.: (028)36146
Website: www.westcorkweek.com/maryanns

  VISA

 No real ales offered

You've little chance of missing this boldly painted pub or, for that matter, its larger than life owner. It's set in the heart of a sleepy village, up a steep, narrow street and the walk is sure to help you work up an appetite; if not, then while away some time in The Warren, the pub's art gallery, where the owner proudly displays his collection of modern Irish art. After this, head for the rustic bar, the linen-laid restaurant or, if the weather's right, the garden, where an enclosed dining area with gingham tablecloths and a mature fruiting vine provides the perfect suntrap. Menus are all-encompassing and offer plenty of choice; seafood is often a feature and there are usually several authentic Asian dishes courtesy of the Malaysian chefs.

Closing times
Closed 9 January-
1 February, 24-26 December
and Monday-Tuesday
October-March
dinner only
Prices
Meals: a la carte € 25/50

Typical Dishes
Deep-fried goat's
cheese with chilli jam

Scallops with beetroot
purée & beurre blanc

Rhubarb & orange
sponge with custard

 Between Rosscarbery and Skibbereen south of N 71. On-street parking.

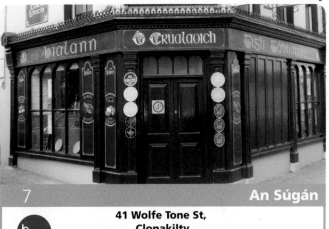

7 An Súgán

**41 Wolfe Tone St,
Clonakilty**
Tel.: (023)8833719
Website: www.ansugan.com

 VISA MC

No real ales offered

Offering charm aplenty and a real sense of history, this salmon-pink pub with its traditional shop front and memorabilia-filled interior is everything you could ask for. Run by a capable family team, it has established itself as something of a local institution so, along with the regulars, you'll find plenty of visitors too. Menus are traditional and largely based around the daily arrival of fresh, local seafood: lunch offers the likes of salmon and potato cakes or steamed Bantry Bay mussels, while dinner includes a selection of tasting plates and dishes such as Castletownbere scallops, flamed lobster or Ballyburden sirloin steak. Bedrooms are spacious and have bold feature walls; they are located in the old harbourmaster's house next door.

Closing times
Closed 25-26 December and Good Friday

Prices
Meals: € 30 (dinner)/38 and a la carte € 21/52

7 rooms: € 45/100

Typical Dishes
Scallops with ginger, chilli & basil butter

Hake with tomato & fennel broth

Dark chocolate délice

 On the eastern side of town. Parking in the street.

Clonakilty

8   **Deasy's**

**Ring,
Clonakilty**
Tel.: (023)8835741

VISA   MC

🍺 **No real ales offered**

Hidden away in a picturesque hamlet, this appealing pub and its small decked terrace offer lovely views out across the bay. It's well run by a confident team but they aren't open regularly all year, so be sure to check the opening times before you go. The open-fired, stone-floored interior is gloriously dated, with mismatched wood furniture and a maritime feel courtesy of framed fish prints and old boat propellers hung on the walls. Dishes – chalked on the board daily – are dictated by the seasons and the latest catch brought in by the local boats; you might find roast monkfish or surf clams with braised pork belly and the Thai coconut fish soup is well worth a try. Puddings are, in the main, traditional, but they do a tasty panna cotta too.

Closing times
Closed 24-26 December, Good Friday, Sunday dinner, Monday and Tuesday dinner

Prices
Meals: € 32 and a la carte € 31/47

Typical Dishes
Duck rillettes with pickled raisins
Brill with beetroot risotto
Milk chocolate with salted caramel

3 km southeast, signposted off N 71 following signs for Ring. Limited parking.

634

9   **Cronin's**

Crosshaven

Tel.: (021)4831829
Website: www.croninspub.com

 VISA **MC** **AE**

 Fuller's London Pride and Eight Degrees Brewing ales

Having been in the family since 1970, this good old Irish pub is now being run by the third generation of Cronins; you're still likely to find Mr Cronin Snr about the place, only this time on the other side of the bar. The keen team welcome one and all and being just a stone's throw from the harbour, that usually includes a yachtsman or two. The long bar is adorned with interesting artefacts, while the back room is filled with boxing memorabilia. During the week, they serve straightforward seafood dishes, while at weekends and midweek in summer, the restaurant is open for dinner, offering maybe scallops with leeks, fresh salmon tartare or their renowned shellfish platter. Produce is from nearby Oysterhaven and Ballycotton.

Closing times
Closed 25 December and Good Friday
lunch only and dinner Thursday-Saturday

Prices
Meals: a la carte € 28/40

Typical Dishes
Salt & pepper squid
Grilled Oysterhaven mussels with chips
Chocolate brownie

In the centre of town with free parking adjacent.

Kinsale

10   **Toddies at The Bulman**

**Summercove,
Kinsale**
Tel.: (021)4772131
Website: www.thebulman.ie

VISA

No real ales offered

This pub is set in a great location, affording excellent views over Kinsale and the bay. Its décor is fittingly maritime themed, with an interesting mural of Moby Dick, and a carving of the famed Bulman Buoy it's named after hung on the ceiling. Scrubbed tables and open fires give it a rustic feel and pictures from yesteryear fill the walls. The cosy bar offers simple pub classics at lunch but it's also the venue for the regular live music nights, when locals and visitors alike can be found enjoying the craic; while upstairs, the well-travelled owner – formerly of Toddies restaurant – can be seen cooking carefully prepared, globally influenced dishes in the more formal dining room. Unsurprisingly, fresh, local seafood is the star of the show.

Closing times
Closed 25 December, Good Friday and Monday dinner

Prices
Meals: a la carte € 27/49

Typical Dishes
Lobster risotto
Scallops with black pudding, calvados & truffle
Chocolate terrine with pistachio ice cream

East 2 km towards Summercove signposted to Charles Fort. Small free car park opposite.

11 Chop House

**2 Shelbourne Rd,
Ballsbridge**
Tel.: (01)6602390
Website: www.thechophouse.ie

 Carlow Brewing Company O'Hara's Irish Pale Ale

In a prominent position on the main interchange, just a drop goal from the Aviva Stadium, you'll find this imposing pub. Once a rather spit 'n' sawdust affair, it's been given a new lease of life by a local restaurateur – so much so, that dinner bookings are now advisable. For warmer days there's a small terrace; in colder weather head up the steps, through the bar and into the bright conservatory area. Lunchtimes see a relaxed menu of maybe beer-battered cod, wild mushroom tagliatelli or Landes chicken but to truly experience the kitchen's full talent come for dinner, where you'll discover the likes of North African spiced lamb breast with orange confit, raw tuna with teriyaki glaze or their speciality, 35 day dry-aged prime Irish steaks.

Closing times
Open daily
Prices
Meals: a la carte € 28/48

Typical Dishes
Scallops with duck confit
Pork shoulder with herb & brioche crumb
Chocolate fondant

5 min walk from Lansdowne Rd DART station. On-street pay and display parking.

Kilcolgan

| 12 | **Moran's Oyster Cottage** |

**The Weir,
Kilcolgan**
Tel.: (091)796113
Website: www.moransoystercottage.com

VISA MC AE D

Galway Hooker

The name says it all: it's been run by seven generations of Morans; its speciality is oysters; and with whitewashed walls and lovely thatch, it's every bit a country cottage. Set in a tiny hamlet down winding country lanes, you'd never find it unless you knew it was there, and on a summer's day it'll soon become apparent that plenty of people do. The latest Moran to take the helm, Catherine, continues the family's philosophy of straightforward cooking and good hospitality. The menu barely changes – but then why change something that works so well? Throughout the year you'll find tasty prawns, mussels, crab, smoked salmon and lobster, along with daily baked brown bread; September – being native oyster season – is the best time to visit.

Closing times
Closed Good Friday and 24-26 December
Prices
Meals: a la carte € 27/48

Typical Dishes
Native oysters
Mussel & clam linguine
Baileys cheesecake

5 min from the village of Clarinbridge. Parking in road.

13 O'Dowds

Roundstone

Tel.: (095)35809
Website: www.odowdsseafoodbar.com

VISA **MC** **AE**

No real ales offered

The O'Dowd family have been dispensing gastronomic delights at this eye-catching blue-hued pub for over one hundred years. Sit in either the cosy fire-lit bar or the more spacious wood-panelled dining room to enjoy fresh, simply cooked seafood. Tender, sweet crab arrives straight from the shore, teamed with a glorious garlic butter to make the perfect meal; while the likes of brill, turbot and plaice are given the respect they deserve – simply lightly dusted with flour and then shallow fried. If you're coming for dinner, be sure to book ahead, and if lunch is your thing, then arrive early, otherwise you may find yourself watching enviously from the quayside as others tuck into home-baked soda rolls and steaming bowls of seafood chowder.

Closing times
Closed 25 December
booking advisable
Prices
Meals: € 20 and a la carte
€ 17/48

Typical Dishes
Crab claws with garlic butter
Rack of lamb with dauphinoise potatoes
Blackberry & apple crumble

On R 341 13 km from Clifden. Parking outside and on the quayside.

Cahersiveen

14   **O'Neill's (The Point) Seafood Bar**

**Renard Point,
Cahersiveen**
Tel.: (066)9472165

No real ales offered

This smart pub has been run by the O'Neill family for over 150 years and, amazingly, several different generations are still involved. It stands in a great spot beside the Valentia Island car ferry terminal, with views of the sea and island, and has a pleasantly traditional feel, with family photographs, all manner of bric-a-brac and plenty of seafaring memorabilia. The menu offers generous portions of simply prepared, deliciously fresh, locally landed seafood. Lobster and crab are perennial favourites, salmon comes from the adjacent smokehouse and local fishermen bring their day's catch – which might include squid, monkfish or lobster – to the door. Unusually, they don't take credit cards and don't serve chips or puddings.

Closing times
Closed January-February
bookings not accepted
Prices
Meals: a la carte € 29/40

Typical Dishes
Crab salad
Pan-fried hake in garlic & olive oil
Irish coffee

4.5 km west of Cahersiveen: follow the signs for the ferry. Parking.

15 QC's

🛏️ **3 Main St,
Cahersiveen**
Tel.: (066)9472244
Website: www.qcbar.com

📶 *VISA* 💳

🍺 **No real ales offered**

Named after the owners, Quinlan and Cooke, this cosy little pub really delivers when it comes to character. Flagged floors, exposed stone walls and wood burning stoves feature, and there's a strong nautical theme running throughout, with oars, portholes and charts scattered about the place. Diners can eat either in the bar or in the pre-laid raised area towards the back. The menu is seafood-orientated, which comes as no surprise once you learn that the family also owns a local fish wholesalers. Cooking is fresh, unfussy and relies on classic combinations, with some more unusual choices appearing on the specials board; you'll find everything from fish and chips to sautéed squid with pesto. Spacious, modern bedrooms are just around the corner.

Closing times
Closed 2 weeks November,
Monday-Wednesday in winter
booking advisable

Prices
Meals: € 20 (dinner)/45
and a la carte € 26/56

🛏️ **5 rooms:** € 65/99

Typical Dishes
Lobster, prawn & crab bisque

Turbot with garlic & chilli salsa

Chocolate ganache with raspberries

🚗 *In the centre of town. Parking.*

Ballymore Eustace

16 — **Ballymore Inn**

Ballymore Eustace

Tel.: (045)864585
Website: www.ballymoreinn.com

Trouble Brewing Sabotage India Pale Ale and Ruddles Ales

Set in a small village close to the Aga Khan's stud, this pub's claim to fame is that Clint Eastwood and Larry Hagman have popped in on their way to the races. To the rear, a large bar screens sporting events and hosts live music, while to the front there's a spacious dining area with red leather banquettes, mosaic flooring and a Parisian brasserie feel. Lunchtime sees salads, homemade pizzas, stir fries and risottos, with some more substantial dishes appearing at dinner. The owner is keen to promote small artisan producers, so you'll find organic veg, meat from quality assured farms and farmhouse cheeses. Portions are generous but you won't want to miss the tasty bread or homemade tarts and pastries. Pleasant staff always go the extra mile.

Closing times
Open daily

Prices
Meals: € 21/34
and a la carte € 28/45

Typical Dishes
Ardsallagh goat's cheese with fennel salad

Hake with garden greens

Fruit tart with ice cream

 South of Naas on R 411. Parking.

17 **Fallon's**

**Main St,
Kilcullen**
Tel.: (045)481260
Website: www.fallonb.ie

 No real ales offered

Once half of the successful Fallon & Byrne food emporium in Dublin, Tom Fallon has taken his knowledge to the heart of Kildare, to share with the appreciative locals of Kilcullen. Satisfyingly, this is a proper bar, with a long wooden counter and a flagged floor – albeit one that's undergone a slight modernisation, courtesy of a boutique colour scheme and purple sofas – and at lunch the place is crammed with local office staff and ladies who lunch. Explore further, and you'll find a conservatory-style room at the back, while a linen-clad dining room provides a bit more formality in the evening. The menu offers plenty of choice, from a 'pie of the day' to grilled salmon with local black pudding, followed by tasty homemade puddings.

Closing times
Open daily
Prices
Meals: £ 28 (dinner)
and a la carte £ 21/40

Typical Dishes
Duck liver pâté with date chutney
Fallon's `pie of the day'
Chocolate brownie with vanilla ice cream

At the Nass end of the main street. Parking.

Carrick-on-Shannon

18   **Oarsman**

**Bridge St,
Carrick-on-Shannon**
Tel.: (071)9621733
Website: www.theoarsman.com

 Galway Hooker and Eight Degrees Ales

With the River Shannon just 50m away and always a boatman or two inside, this pub's name is perfectly apt. Its double-fronted windows are filled with pottery, county flags and old artefacts, while a plethora of objects adorn the walls and an array of fishing tackle is displayed above the bar. This is a traditional pub through and through; family-owned, with rough wooden floors, old beams and stone-faced walls – and, unsurprisingly, frequented by the locals, especially at lunch. Snacks are available in the afternoon and there's a fairly substantial bar menu in the evening, while later in the week the comfy upstairs area offers dishes such as confit of Thornhill Farm duck or trio of Kettyle lamb. Cooking is simple and produce, laudably local.

Closing times
Closed 25-26 December, Good Friday, Sunday and Monday

Prices
Meals: € 26/40
and a la carte € 27/46

Typical Dishes
Scallops with chorizo & cep cream
Thornhill duck with star anise sauce
Chocolate & pistachio torte

 In the town centre. On-street parking meters.

19   Fitzpatricks

**Rockmarshall,
Jenkinstown**
Tel.: (042)9376193
Website: www.fitzpatricks-restaurant.com

 No real ales offered

On the coast road to the peninsula, at the foot of the Cooley Mountains, you'll find this classical whitewashed pub overlooking Dundalk Bay. To call it characterful would be an understatement: this is a place where you can take in the whole of the Irish experience in one go. The car park and gardens are filled with colourful flowers planted in old bicycles, boots and even a bed; while inside there's a beautiful bar with brass rails, chock-full of memorabilia, including a fascinating collection of chamber pots and Victorian toiletries. The extensive menu features hearty, flavoursome portions of traditional dishes, with local steaks and seafood something of a speciality; come on a Tuesday evening for specials which are centred around lobster.

Closing times
Closed 25 December, Good Friday and Monday November-March except bank holidays

Prices
Meals: € 28 (weekdays) and a la carte € 26/47

Typical Dishes
Seafood grill
Turbot with lemon butter sauce
Apple & pecan sandwich with custard

 9 km northeast of Dundalk following N 52 on R 173. Parking.

Ballina

20 — Crockets on the Quay

**The Quay,
Ballina**
Tel.: (096)75930
Website: www.crocketsonthequay.ie

No real ales offered

This pub's vibrant orange exterior is matched on the inside by a lively atmosphere where there's always something going on, be it a poker night, a traditional Irish music session or a trivia quiz. Sports fans aren't forgotten either, with a pool table, TVs in almost every corner and two plasma screens in the garden. The place itself is rather dimly lit, but the light fittings that are located above each worn table really put the spotlight where it matters – on the food. Menus offer something for everybody, at prices to suit; fish and salads are popular in summer and the meaty game dishes and stews are a hit in the winter. Cooking is hearty yet refined and flavours are well-balanced. Bedrooms are currently too modest for us to recommend.

Closing times
Closed 24-26 December and Good Friday
dinner only and lunch Saturday-Sunday
Prices
Meals: a la carte € 21/45

Typical Dishes
Duck spring roll with Ballymaloe relish
Fillets of sea bass with leek fondue
Mango panna cotta

 On the northeast edge of town by N 59 besides the River Moy. Parking.

21 **Tavern**

Murrisk

Tel.: (098)64060
Website: www.tavernmurrisk.com

VISA **MC**

No real ales offered

Most people come to the area to visit Croagh Patrick, the famous rock with a chapel perched on top, but this vibrantly painted pub has also put itself firmly on the map in recent years. With its designer colours, leather banquettes and quirky basket lampshades, it's the type of place that would fit right into a 'Country Living' magazine. In keeping with this style, staff are smart and attentive, and the kitchen produces an array of dishes with wide-ranging influences and a touch of refinement. Local seafood and meat arrive in classical combinations and the specials board lists the fruits of the latest catch. The chowder is award-winning, the chicken with chargrilled bacon is a perennial hit, and the daily cheesecake is an absolute must.

Closing times
Closed Good Friday
and 25 December
Prices
Meals: a la carte € 22/42

Typical Dishes
Scallops with garlic &
smoked bacon
Cod with Clew Bay
mussels, tomato &
coriander
Fruit crumble
with crème anglaise

Westport

22   **Sheebeen**

**Rosbeg,
Westport**
Tel.: (098)26528
Website: www.croninssheebeen.com

☂   *VISA*   **MC**   **AE**

No real ales offered

This pretty whitewashed thatched pub stands in a remote location in the shadow of the magnificent Croagh Patrick mountain and boasts lovely views out across the bay. On warmer days, grab a seat on one of the outside tables; when it's colder, head for the traditional snug, the rustic open-fired bar or the slightly more formal first floor dining room. The owner is passionate about keeping his pub honest and true, so along with the laid-back atmosphere and cheery groups of locals drinking Guinness, you'll find a selection of hearty, unfussy dishes on offer, including the likes of mussels, oysters and lobsters from the bay, and lamb and beef from the fields nearby. To top it all off, there are live music sessions every Friday and Saturday night.

Closing times
Closed Good Friday,
25 December and lunch
weekdays November-mid
March

Prices
Meals: a la carte € 23/40

Typical Dishes
Calamari with wasabi
mayonnaise
Shoulder of lamb
with apricot & walnut
stuffing
Warm banana & ginger
cake, maple syrup

 West of the town beyond Westport Quay. Parking.

Hargadons

23

**4-5 O'Connell St,
Sligo**
Tel.: (071)9153709
Website: www.hargadons.com

 No real ales offered

Built in 1864 by a local merchant-cum-MP, this building started life as a grocer's (the original comestible drawers are still on display), before being acquired by the Hargadon brothers in 1909. To say it's characterful would be an understatement. There's a narrow passageway with booths; anterooms with oak-topped tables; thick walls hung with Guinness and Jameson's memorabilia; and a sloping stone floor designed to prevent flooding – there's even a lovely little "Ladies' Room" complete with its own serving hatch. Cooking is warming and hearty, offering the likes of Irish stew or bacon and cabbage, followed by tasty nursery puddings. They also have a good wine list, which makes sense when you see the large wine shop that adjoins the pub.

Closing times
Closed Sunday
bookings not accepted
Prices
Meals: a la carte € 17/27

Typical Dishes
Goat's cheese salad
Traditional Irish stew
Chocolate brownie

 In the centre of town. Public parking nearby.

Garrykennedy

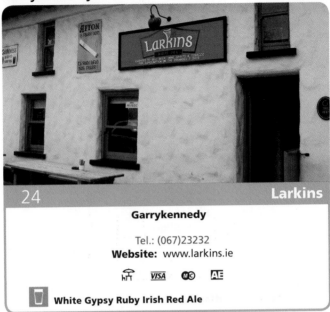

24

Larkins

Garrykennedy

Tel.: (067)23232
Website: www.larkins.ie

🛖 *VISA* MC AE

🍺 **White Gypsy Ruby Irish Red Ale**

Set in a charming location on the shores of Lough Derg, this thatched, whitewashed pub dates back around 300 years and is popular with the sailing set, particularly in the summer. As traditional inside as out, it boasts old flag and timber floors, a long wooden bar and original open fireplaces; and plays host to regular Irish folk music sessions and traditional Irish dancing groups. Throughout the day, the bar menu offers straightforward, unfussy dishes such as seafood chowder, homemade burgers or steak. In the evening, however, things step up a gear, with the likes of honey-roast duckling, herb-crusted fillet of cod or pan-fried lamb cutlets. Having come from farming backgrounds, the owners are passionate about sourcing local Irish produce.

Closing times
Closed 25 December, Good Friday and Monday-Tuesday November-April

Prices
Meals: € 18/30 and a la carte € 23/39

Typical Dishes
Mussels with white wine & garlic
Fish & chips with mushy peas
Belgian chocolate cake

🚗 *9 km west of Nenagh by R 494 and minor road north. Free public car park opposite.*

25 **Fatted Calf**

Glasson

Tel.: (090)6485208
Website: www.thefattedcalf.ie

No real ales offered

With the Farrell family having finally hung up their glass cloths, this pub has been left in the safe hands of Feargal O'Donnell, who used to work in the kitchen of nearby Wineport Lodge. Aside from the name, the pub's changed little since he took over, with original Guinness and Gilbey's signs still adorning the attractive wood panels of the bar, and locals gathering around the TV and pool table in the snug. Having spent years working in the area, Feargal knows all of the best local suppliers, and his experience has definitely stepped the cooking up a gear. Dishes range from handmade sausages to local rabbit terrine, while tasty specials and bar snacks, such as duck rillette or black pudding on treacle bread, appear later in the evening.

Closing times
Closed Good Friday,
25 December and Monday
except bank holidays

Prices
Meals: € 20 (weekdays)
and a la carte € 28/46

Typical Dishes

Scallops with confit pork shoulder

Sea bass, creamy crab & rock samphire

Limoncello & blueberry trifle

On the N 55 in the centre of the village. Parking.

Carne

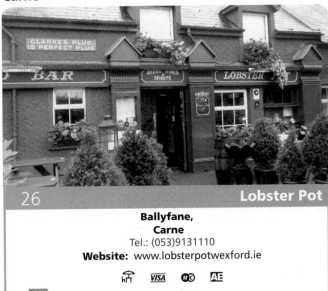

26

Lobster Pot

**Ballyfane,
Carne**
Tel.: (053)9131110
Website: www.lobsterpotwexford.ie

𝄟 *VISA* **MC** **AE**

No real ales offered

If you're on your way to the ferry crossing at Rosslare or returning from a stroll along the nearby beach, this bold green pub is definitely worth calling in at. The interior is spotless and as soon as you see the staff in their smart waistcoats, you know they take things seriously here. Make for a cosy, characterful nook amongst the huge array of memorabilia and study the extensive menu of tasty home-style cooking, which offers a simple selection of light bites at lunch and a dinner menu exclusively for adults – as children must leave by 6pm. There are a few grills, but, as the name suggests, it's mostly seafood, with oysters and lobster cooked to order the specialities. But be sure to arrive early, as this is Carne's not-so-well-kept secret.

Closing times
Closed 1 January-
10 February,
24-26 December,
Good Friday and Monday
except bank holidays

Prices
Meals: a la carte € 24/56

Typical Dishes
Garlic mussels
Grilled Dover sole with
lemon butter
Sticky toffee pudding

 Off N 25 follow signs for Our Lady's Island. Parking.

27   **Byrne & Woods**

**Main St,
Roundwood**
Tel.: (01)2817078
Website: www.byrneandwoods.com

 No real ales offered

A smartly restored Morris Traveller stands outside what is arguably the second highest pub in Ireland, set up in the Wicklow Mountains. Built from stone, it looks older than it really is and, as its name may suggest, it consists of two parts. 'Byrne' is a small, cosy bar with a stone fireplace and wood-burning stove – and is where you'll find the local drinkers and thrice-weekly live music sessions; while spacious, dimly lit 'Woods', is where the majority of diners head, characterised by dark wood furnishings, brown leather seating and a clubby feel. Cooking is fresh and straightforward, with lighter dishes on offer during the week, and the likes of pork belly with sage and apricot chutney or salmon with rocket pesto at the weekend.

Closing times
Closed 25-26 December
Prices
Meals: a la carte € 24/42

Typical Dishes
Dingle Bay crab with herbs

Sea bass, saffron potatoes & asparagus

Baileys & milk chocolate cheesecake

 On R 755 between Laragh and Killough. Parking.

Index of towns

L

M

N

Index of pubs & inns

The MICHELIN Guide
A collection to savour!

Belgïe · Belgique & Luxembourg
Deutschland
España & Portugal
France
Great Britain & Ireland
Italia
Nederland · Netherlands
Suisse · Schweiz · Svizzera
Main Cities of Europe

Also:

Chicago
Hokkaido
Hong Kong · Macau
Kyoto · Osaka · Kobe · Nara
Tokyo · Yokohama · Shonan
London
New York City
Paris
San Francisco

Notes

Notes

Notes

eating
out in
pubs

Michelin Travel Partner

Michelin Travel Partner
Hannay House,
39 Clarendon Rd
Watford WD17 1JA
Tel: (01923) 205247
Fax: (01923) 205241
www.ViaMichelin.com
eatingoutinpubs-gbirl@
uk.michelin.com

Michelin Travel Partner

Société par actions simplifiées au capital
de 11 629 590 EUR
27 Cours de L'Île Seguin - 92100
Boulogne Billancourt (France)
R.C.S. Nanterre 433 677 721
© Michelin et cie, Propriétaires-
éditeurs
Dépôt légal septembre 2013
Printed in Italy 09-13

Typesetting:

NORD COMPO, Villeneuve-d'Ascq (France)
Printing and binding:
L.E.G.O. SpA - LAVIS (TN) - Italy

Photography

Project manager: Alain Leprince
Agence ACSI – A Chacun Son Image
242, bd. Voltaire– 75011 Paris

Location Photographs:
Jérôme Berquez, Frédéric Chales,
Ludivine Boizard, Jean-Louis
Chauveau/ACSI

Thanks to:
Exchequer, Crookham.
Richard Onslow, Cranleigh
P12: Ariy/Fotolia.com
P20: Full moon/Fotolia.com
P22: C. Labonne/Michelin
P58: D. Hughes/Fotolia.com
P122: C. Eymenier/Michelin
P191: Jon Arnold/hemis.fr
P192: Robert/Fotolia.com
P207: Gail Johnson/Fotolia
P208: K. Eaves/Fotolia.com
P247: Jon Arnold/hemis.fr
P248: D. Hughes/Fotolia.com
P382: C. Jones/Fotolia.com
P490: D. Hughes/Fotolia.com
P519: D. Jones/Age Fotostock
P520: S. Smith/Fotolia.com
P563: M. Shannon/Fotolia.com
P564: O. Forir/Michelin
P587: D. Hughes/Fotolia.com
P588: L. Green/Fotolia.com
P614: O. Forir/Michelin
P624: O. Forir/Michelin
P654-655: C. Handl/imagebroker/
age fotostock

GREAT BRITAIN: Based on Ordnance Survey of Great Britain with the permission of the controller of Her Majesty's Stationery Office, © Crown Copyright 100000247